A History of the Poles in
America to 1908

A History of the Poles in America to 1908

PART I

by Wacław Kruszka

Edited, with an Introduction, by James S. Pula

Translated by Krystyna Jankowski

Associate Editors: M. B. Biskupski & Stanley Cuba

Assistant Editors: T. Lindsay Baker, Stanislaus A. Blejwas,
Daniel S. Buczek, Anne Cirocco, Anthony J. Kuzniewski,
Joseph J. Parot, Donald E. Pienkos, Thaddeus C. Radzilowski,
Frank A. Renkiewicz

The Catholic University of America Press
Washington, D.C.

This volume was translated and edited with the assistance of a
grant from the National Endowment for the Humanities and
generous support from Ms. Lucy E. Lisocki and the Reverend
Monsignor Alphonse S. Popek.

Copyright 1993

The Catholic University of America Press

The paper in this publication meets the minimum requirements of American National Standards for Information Science—Permanence of Paper for Printed Library materials,
ANSI Z39.48-1984.

Library of Congress Cataloging-in-Publication Data
Kruszka, Wacław, 1868-1937.
    [Historia Polska w Ameryce. English]
    A history of the Poles in America to 1908 / by Wacław
Kruszka ; edited, with an introduction by James S. Pula ;
translated by Krystyna Jankowski ; associate editors, M. B.
Biskupski, Stanley Cuba.
      p. cm.
    Includes bibliographical references and index.
    Contents: pt. 1. A general history of the Polish immi-
gration in America
    1. Polish Americans—History. I. Pula, James S.,
1946- .
II. Title.
    E184.P7K913 1993
    973'.049185—dc20
    92-24608
    ISBN 0-8132-0772-X (v. 1 : alk. paper)

Contents

Contents

Acknowledgments

A work of this magnitude would not have been possible without the professional, financial, and moral support of many organizations and individuals.

On the professional level, sincere appreciation is due Dr. Terrill May for his translation of German titles and passages, Rev. Joseph Trovato for various translations from Latin, and Mr. Joseph L. Ziarnik for translations of verse from Kashubian and Polish. Special thanks are also due to those who spent long hours typing the several drafts of this manuscript: Ms. Theresa Nickerson, Mrs. Winifred S. Pula, and Ms. Barbara Swigert.

Organizations providing financial assistance for the translating and editing of this work include: Holy Cross Roman Catholic Church (New Britain, Connecticut), the Institute for Polish Studies (St. John Fisher College), the Kościuszko Polish Arts Club, The Louis Skalny Foundation Trust, the Polish American Congress, the Polish American Congress Charitable Foundation, the Polish American Congress of Texas, the Polish American Priests Association, the Polish Heritage Club (Syracuse, New York), the Polish National Alliance, the Polish National Alliance of Brooklyn, the Polish National Union Spojnia, the Polish Studies Program at Central Connecticut State University, St. Casimir's Polish Arts Club (Elmira, New York), St. Casimir's Recreation Club (Elmira, New York), St. Stanislaus Church (Meridan, Connecticut), the Society of Jesus at the College of the Holy Cross, and the Union of Poles in America.

Individual financial contributions were provided by (in alphabetical order): Mr. Donald Bielak, Mr. M. Williams Blake, Dr. Stanislas A. Blejwas, Mr. Bernard Cebelak, Ms. Anne F. Cierpik, Ms. Irene M. Coulter, Dr. Casimir Czarnecki, Mr. Anthony J. Demski, Ms. Mary Loretta Dowling, Dr. Walter Drzewieniecki, Mr. T. Dudzinski, Rt. Rev. Alphonse

Fiedorczyk, Ms. Josephine Fronczak, Mr. Henry A. Gajda, Dr. Matthew A. Gajewski, Mr. Stanley M. Garstka, Mr. and Mrs. John Golla, Dr. Victor Greene, Dr. Henry J. Gwiazda II, Dr. Joseph T. Hapak, Mr. Thomas L. Hollowak, Mr. Anthony D. Iwuc, Lt. Col. Francis C. Kajencki, Mr. Al Kieltyka, Lt. Col. Anthony M. Klasinski, Rev. Msgr. John A. Kociela, Dr. Adam A. Komosa, Mr. Adam Komosa, Mr. Alexander Koproski, Mr. and Mrs. John E. Kostek, Mr. Jan Kowalik, Mr. Edward J. Kowrach, Mr. and Mrs. Frank J. Kozicki, Bishop Arthur Krawczyk, Mr. and Mrs. Norbert C. Kreseski, Rev. Chester M. Krysa, Dr. John J. Kulczycki, Mr. and Mrs. Charles Kulenski, Dr. Mark Kulikowski, Mr. Franciszek Lachowicz, Dr. Henry B. Leonard, Mr. Paul Libera, Dr. and Mrs. Richard Lukas, Dr. Jerzy Maciuszko, Rev. Philip S. Majka, Mr. Joseph T. Makarewicz, Mr. Thaddeus Maliszewski, Mr. William Manijak, Msgr. Joseph Marjanczyk, Mr. S. A. Milewski, Mr. Edward T. Mohylowski, Mr. Charles Morrissey, Ms. Helen M. Murawski, Mr. Matthew N. Obloza, Mr. and Mrs. John S. Oczytko, Dr. Gerald Ortell, Mr. Stanley A. Pachon, Mr. Francis F. Palma, Mr. Matthew L. Panczyk, Dr. Stanley F. Radzyminski, Mr. Chester S. Rog, Rev. Joseph C. Rutkowski, Ms. Florianne Rzeszewski, Mr. James H. Sebelski, Rev. Jerome Siwek, Mr. John F. Skibiski, Jr., Mr. Julius Sobolak, Mr. Frank Socha, Rev. Wojciech Sojka, Mrs. Helen Sokolowski, Ms. Irene Szewiola, Rev. Richard J. Talaska, Rev. John Terepka, Sr. Clarent Marie Urbanowicz, Mr. Arthur Waldo, Mr. Leonard Walentynowicz, Mr. Leon C. Walling, Mr. Edmund G. Wasiniak, Dr. and Mrs. Stefan P. Wilk, Mr. Raymond J. Winieski, Rev. Msgr. John P. Wodarski, Dr. Richard Woytak, Rev. John W. Yanta, Mr. Stanley W. Zamonski, Dr. Helen S. Zand, and Sr. M. Zygmunta.

Introduction

Background

The first Polish presence in North America lies shrouded in the mists of historical legend. There most certainly were Poles in the Jamestown colony as early as 1608; yet there exists only fragmentary and inconclusive evidence regarding either an earlier Polish presence or the purpose and activities of those who settled in colonial Virginia. We know, too, that there were Poles in New Amsterdam, in Pennsylvania, and scattered throughout the other North American colonies. It appears that most of these early settlers were tradesmen or professionals who were probably Protestant in their religious affiliation. Regardless of the lack of specific information, it is safe to conclude that these early Polish settlers represented individual migrations prompted by personal or religious reasons rather than general political or economic conditions.

During the long historical period before 1795, Poland was for the most part a nation tolerant of dissenting minorities. The Polish Crown was the oldest elected monarchy in Europe, and in 1652 the *liberum veto* provided that a single dissenting vote in the Polish *Sejm* [Parliament] was sufficient to block any legislation. Given these circumstances, and the agrarian nature of the Polish economy, there was little impetus to colonization or overseas expansion such as that which occurred in the countries of western Europe.

This situation began to change in the 1770s when Poland's powerful neighbors—Russia, Prussia, and Austria—began to conspire to divide Polish lands between them. Poland's struggle to maintain its independence, occurring simultaneously with the analogous American movement, led some Poles to an ideological bond with the New World. Tadeusz

Kościuszko, Kazimierz Pułaski, and several lesser-known Poles came to America to join the colonists in their quest for political freedom. They were followed by a number of Polish travelers, many of whom left important descriptions of the conditions in late eighteenth-century America. Yet these were also individual migrations, and many of these visitors, if not most, did not take up permanent residence in the United States.

The beginnings of a permanent Polish migration to the United States can be traced to the year 1795 when Russia, Prussia, and Austria succeeded in eliminating Poland from the map of Europe, dividing her lands among themselves. The dismemberment of Poland among the partitioning powers provided a political motivation for Poles to emigrate. Naturally, most of these early émigrés settled in neighboring European countries for what they hoped and expected would be a brief residence until their homeland regained its independence. With this purpose in mind, tens of thousands of Poles joined the legions of Napoleon I in the hope of reestablishing Polish independence through the force of French arms.

With the failure of Napoleon's armies, many Polish veterans migrated to North America to settle in the French-speaking areas around New Orleans, Mobile, and Charleston. These refugees were followed by small groups of political exiles who fled from Europe after the failure of Polish revolutions in 1830-31, 1846, 1848, and 1863. For the most part, with the exception of a group of Silesian farmers who settled in Texas in 1854, Polish immigration prior to 1870 was characterized by little groups of political exiles who resided individually or in small colonies within the environs of established urban areas. Despite their lack of numbers, these early émigrés established a framework of settlements, organizational structures, and communications which would soon expand manyfold.

Beginning in the 1870s the magnitude and composition of Polish immigration changed dramatically. The political exile gave way to the impoverished peasant as the typical immigrant. First hundreds, then thousands of agrarian laborers left the lands of partitioned Poland seeking jobs in industrial America. By 1890 their numbers reached into the tens of thousands annually and included mostly those from Russian and Austrian Poland, Silesia, Posnania, and Pomerania.

Between 1890 and 1910, nearly a million Poles arrived in the United States. Settling primarily in the eastern and midwestern industrial cities, they quickly established ethnic enclaves complete with businesses, newspapers, social organizations, and churches. As new immigrants arrived they settled in these burgeoning communities until the enclaves became Polish in culture as well as in language.

The Poles who came to America in this massive economic migration were by many standards a simple people, yet they were motivated by very clearly defined purposes. They came primarily for economic reasons, to make a better life for themselves and their families through employment in America's expanding mines and factories. They also sought freedom and respect in a national whose fundamental laws were touted in Poland as providing individual equality and freedom. Given Poland's sad history of oppression under the partitioning powers, her sons and daughters came to the New World in search of a land that would provide opportunity for a better life while at the same time guaranteeing them the right to maintain their own culture, to speak their own language, to worship as they saw fit, to own property, and to participate in a democratic society.

The America that the immigrants found met many of their hopes and expectations, but it presented them with an unexpected cultural shock as well. The crowded, hectic, often inhospitable surroundings of urban America were inconceivably different from those of the quiet, unharried lifestyle of rural Poland where most of the newcomers had previously lived. To survive in this urban environment, the Poles reacted much the same as other immigrant groups by forming ethnic communities within the various cities where they settled. The focal point of these communities was the local church. In Poland, a century of occupation by foreign powers had taught the people to turn to the church and the Roman Catholic clergy as their link to Polish culture and heritage. With proscriptions against the teaching of Polish, the study of Polish history and culture, and the printing of Polish books, the local churches became the center of a massive social system that preserved Polish culture and actively promoted the ideals of Polish nationalism. It is thus not surprising that the immigrant in America, alone and overwhelmed by the enormity of the cities and their attendant differences from the immigrants' native rural culture, turned to the Church for support. Indeed, huge amounts of money were spent on constructing and enlarging churches in every geographic area where Poles settled. The church was invariably one of the first "public" buildings to be erected. It provided a link of familiarity with the homeland, but more importantly it served as the focal point of the Polish community in America, providing cultural stability in a sea of instability, protection against outside influences, a source of education for both young and old, and a general group support system that allowed the immigrants to survive in their new surroundings. In partitioned Poland the influence of the Church as a transmitter of culture, values, and nationality was pervasive; in the United States its position was identical within the immigrant communities.

Yet, despite the essential services provided by the Roman Catholic Church to the immigrant in America, the Church was also the center of one of the earliest and most divisive controversies that led to the fragmentation of the Polish community. While the Church provided a link with the past and a source of stability in a foreign land, the Polish immigrant found that the Church in America was itself a foreign, non-Polish influence in the form of an American hierarchy dominated by Irish and German bishops. In Poland, religion and nationalism were inextricably interwoven; in America, the immigrant found that "Polish" parishes were all too often led by priests who did not speak the language of the parishioners or share their traditions. Simultaneously, the Irish and German bishops actively pursued a course of "Americanization" which reminded the Poles of the forced *kulturkampf* by which Bismarck's Germany attempted to denationalize the Poles in Europe. To the Polish immigrant of the 1880s, the predominant values were those of *polskość* [Polishness] and *równouprawnienie* [equality].[1] The immigrant came to America seeking equality of opportunity, a democratic participation in determining his own future, and the freedom to preserve his ethnic heritage. In America, the Church, as the single most important link with the Old Country and the focal point of the New World ethnic community, was also at once both the immigrant's succor and his antagonist.

In America, the Polish immigrant found the Church controlled by Irish and German bishops who opposed the use of the Polish vernacular in the Mass and the preservation of Polish heritage in the local parochial schools. Indeed, the Church, already nervous about the growth of the Cahenslyist movement, was often outspoken in its support for Americanization of the immigrant parishes. To many Poles, the Church which had been their best friend and benefactor in Poland appeared to be but an arm of oppression in America. It actively opposed *polskość* by objecting to the use of Polish, the teaching of Polish history and culture, and the immigrant's preoccupation with working for the eventual independence of the homeland. It ignored *równouprawnienie* by mandating at the Plenary Council in 1884 that the bishops hold title to all parish property, by refusing to allow democratic participation in parish management, and by passing over Polish priests for appointments as bishops.[2] Indeed, by 1900 there were nearly

900 Polish parishes in the United States, and Poles constituted about twelve percent of all Catholics in America. On a numerical basis, this should have dictated that there be eleven bishops and two archbishops of Polish background. There were none, and that fact, coupled with the obvious hostility of the Irish hierarchy to the appointment of Polish bishops, led to the issue of Polish bishops becoming the single most important symbolic issue in the struggle of the Polish immigrant with the Church.

Faced with a Church that they no longer considered sympathetic, many Poles became openly hostile toward the established religious order in America. In 1880, a group of Poles formed the Polish National Alliance (PNA), a fraternal organization that promoted self-help and support for the independence of the homeland. Though not specifically anti-Church in its conception, the early leaders of the PNA openly questioned the patriotism of Polish American priests, contending that they were not sufficiently interested in Poland and were too ready to submit to the authority of the Irish-German Church hierarchy. This emerging Nationalist element felt that faith and nationality were distinctly separable quantities and that religion was of secondary importance to the cause of Poland's liberation.

Responding to the perceived threat of the Nationalist element, the Religionists counterattacked with all of the ardor that faith alone can command. Using the Polish Roman Catholic Union (PRCU), founded in 1873, as a counterbalance to the PNA, the Religionists insisted that a true Pole could be only a Roman Catholic and promoted the restoration of the homeland, but only as a secondary objective to the preservation of the faith. Through their respective periodicals, the Religionists decried the Nationalists as "atheists" and "masons," while the Nationalists countered with the assertion that the priests of the PRCU were "autocrats" and "traitors." The Nationalists pointed to the undemocratic suppression of Poles by the Catholic hierarchy and demanded lay ownership of parish property and an accounting of all parish funds. The bishops countered with the threat of excommunication and denunciations of the Nationalists as "drunkards" and "unholy demons." At times open violence occurred.

Although the lines of battle were clearly drawn between the Nationalists and the Religionists, the latter did not constitute a monolithic entity. Given their own support for the ideals of *polskość* and *równouprawnienie*, many of the Polish American clergy found themselves in the difficult position of balancing their obligations to the bishop's authority with their own affinity for the wishes of their parishioners. In the extremes, the Polish priests acted with uncompromising ardor. On the one hand, the extreme dissidents followed the lead of Rev. Franciszek Hodur in breaking of the American hierarchy to form the independent Polish National Catholic Church (PNCC), the only successful schismatic movement in American Catholic history. On the other, the development of the PNCC served to polarize the attitudes of those who remained loyal to the established Catholic order. In the forefront of the latter group was the Rev. Wincenty Barzyński.

A Chicago Religionist and leader of the PRCU, Barzyński was a staunch supporter of episcopal authority who carried on a bitter and unremitting conflict against both the PNA and the infant PNCC. In many respects, Barzyński was typical of Polish leadership during the era between 1880 and 1910: unyielding and uncompromising. He considered the Nationalists to be "a clique of unbelieving saloon-keepers." He reserved a particular antipathy for the Hodurites, the followers of the independent PNCC movement under Rev. Hodur.

Between the extremes of Hodur and Barzyński lay a spectrum of individualized responses, but the most significant group, and the one which found itself in the greatest quandary, was composed of Polish priests who chose to remain within the authority of the American Church but refused to abandon their efforts to obtain equality for the Polish faithful and their clergy in the New World. Chief among these priests was Rev. Wacław Kruszka.

The Author

Wacław [Wenceslaus] Kruszka was born on March 2, 1868, in the village of Słabormierz, near Gniezno, in the Prussian sector of partitioned Poland. One of thirteen children of a peasant family, he attended elementary school in Gorzyce before being sent to the German school of Schwarzback in Ostrów in 1877. In 1881, his father enrolled him in the Polish public high school at Wągrowiec out of a growing fear that his education in the German school would lead to his denationalization. During these youthful years, Kruszka was exposed to the repressive Prussian *kulturkampf,* which sought to eradicate all save the German language and culture. Under the constant tutelage of his father Jan, an ardent Nationalist, and his brother Szymon, a priest who was imprisoned for his opposition to the kulturkampf, Kruszka developed an intense faith and nationalism which he retained throughout his adult life. Kruszka eventually left the school at Wągrowiec to enter the Society of Jesus at Stara Wieś, Galicia, in the Austrian sector of partitioned Poland. There, with the intercession of his brother Szymon, he was granted a probationary acceptance. After passing his aspirant's examination he was admitted to candidacy and received the habit as a Jesuit novice on August 23, 1883. After two years of novitiate he entered the scholasticate for classical studies. On October 7, 1886, he received his Minor Orders from Bishop Solecki and thereafter continued his studies. Completing his work at Stara Wieś in 1888, he was transferred to Tarnopol to study philosophy.

Soon after he arrived in Tarnopol, Kruszka contracted an eye inflammation which interfered with his academic endeavors. He spent two years in Tarnopol, but eventually had to leave for Lwów to seek medical treatment and was forced to postpone his final examination in philosophy. Assigned to teach at the Jesuit high school in Chyrów, he conducted classes in French, German, history, geography, mathematics, and religion, but his desire to continue his own studies made his stay in Chyrów less than happy. Perhaps because of his growing frustration, he eventually quarreled with another teacher, an act that resulted in his dismissal from the Jesuit Order.

Kruszka appealed for reinstatement, but met with a rebuff from both his provincial and the general of the order. Dispirited, he journeyed to Rome to seek the assistance of Cardinal Mieczysław Ledóchowski, who advised that he spend some time with the Resurrectionists. He did so, and while attending classes at the Gregorianum he met an American, Rev. Stabenau of Buffalo, who suggested that Kruszka consider moving to the United States. The idea apparently intrigued him, but he was determined to make a last appeal to the Jesuits before undertaking such a monumental decision.

Kruszka graduated from the Gregorianum in Rome in 1893 and reapplied for admission to the Society of Jesus. Surprisingly, in view of the earlier reluctance of the Jesuits to readmit him, he was offered admittance into the novitiate at Stara Wieś. After completing his preliminary training, he began theological studies in Kraków. He made rapid progress and soon he was scheduled to take his vows on October 24, 1893. At that point, Kruszka's pride and unbending principles intervened and he declined the new vows, insisting instead that his previous vows be recognized as valid. The Jesuits refused and Kruszka left the order because of this perceived injustice.

Once he abandoned his religious affiliation, Kruszka became subject to conscription into the German Army, a quandary he discussed at length with his brother. Together they determined that the only viable option was for Kruszka to leave Europe for America. He departed from Hamburg on November 17, 1893, arriving in New York on November 24. Once in New York, aided by funds provided by his half-brother Michał, he journeyed to Milwaukee where he arrived at his brother's home on December 1.

Once in Wisconsin, Kruszka entered St. Francis Seminary where he became president of the Literary Society and a professor of Polish. He also took an immediate interest in the Polish American press, contributing patriotic articles under a pseudonym to his brother's newspaper, *Kuryer Polski* [The Polish Courier]. His first effort, published on December 14, 1893, was entitled "Why Do Socialists Vote for Jesuits?" In it, he defended the Jesuits against criticism in the American press after the socialists in the German parliament voted to allow the order to return to Germany.

Kruszka was ordained at St. Francis Seminary on June 16, 1895, whereupon he was assigned to St. Josaphat Parish in Milwaukee. Eight months later, on February 25, 1896, he was appointed assistant rector of the Polish parish in Ripon, Wisconsin. There he exerted every effort in the organization of St. Wenceslaus parish, an assignment that he would hold until 1909. During his long stay in Ripon, a period that he later referred to as his exile, Kruszka had an opportunity to immerse himself in the political squabbles which were at that moment tearing the infant American Polonia asunder.

Given his early internalization of the ideals of Polish nationalism and the Catholic faith, Kruszka was incapable of abandoning either. The one was as much an ingrained portion of his character as the other. To Kruszka, the question was one of reconciling the two ideals so that the Polish clergy and their flock in America could express their nationalism within the framework of the Roman Catholic faith. In forming his own ideas he correctly observed that the controversy over "Americanization" within the Church was in actuality one of Polish opposition to "anglicization." Having clarified this point, he rapidly developed a concept of ethnic pluralism which was much in advance of his time. To Kruszka, the Church was indeed universal, but it did not follow that it therefore was monolithic. While it was unified in its faith and in spiritual matters, its existence throughout the world was proof that it need not be bound by a common language, a common culture, or a common nationality. The Church, he

X. Wacław Kruszka

argued with all the force of his still youthful exuberance, should foster an ethnic pluralism which recognized the dignity and worth of all people, granting them an equality of opportunity to attain Church offices and to express their own ethnic identity.

Frequent contributions published in his brother's *Kuryer Polski* further expounded upon Kruszka's concept of pluralism to the point of advocating the proportional representation of Poles in the American hierarchy and arguing that the Roman Catholic Church in the United States could not itself become truly American until it ceased being Irish. Michał Kruszka, an even more outspoken critic of the American Catholic hierarchy, rapidly earned the antipathy of clergy throughout the Midwest, who labeled *Kuryer Polski* as leftist and anti-clerical.

In early 1901, Kruszka submitted an article enunciating his concept of pluralism to the editor of the *American Ecclesiastical Review*. To his chagrin, the manuscript was pointedly rejected. Taking personal offense, the uncompromising priest refused to alter a single phrase of what he had written and launched into a fierce war of words with the offending editor, H. J. Heuser. The irate Kruszka finally succeeded in publishing the full, unaltered text in the *New York Freeman's Journal* on July 29, 1901. Titled "Polyglot Bishops for Polyglot Dioceses," the article stressed ethnic pluralism, the familiar unity-in-diversity theme that he had developed during his stay in Ripon. In the article, Kruszka maintained that diversity of language and customs actually served to strengthen the Church. A bishop who did not understand the language and culture of his flock, he argued, could not fulfill his religious obligations to them. Consequently, likening the situation to the gift of languages bestowed upon the Apostles, Kruszka reasoned that if at least 20% of the Catholics in a diocese spoke a particular language, the bishop of that diocese should be conversant in that language.

The wide circulation of *Kuryer Polski* provided an appropriate vehicle for the lucid, penetrating pen of Wacław Kruszka, propelling him into a position of prominence within the coterie of religious dissenters. In 1901, a Polish Catholic convention met in Buffalo to discuss a series of grievances, including the lack of a Polish bishop, the ownership of parish property, and the denationalization policies of the Church hierarchy in America. In the end, Kruszka and Rev. Jan Pitass of Buffalo were selected to carry a petition directly to the pope if the American bishops failed to address the Poles' concerns. Although Pitass did not make the trip,

Kruszka began his journey in 1903 in the company of Rowland Mahaney, a former Buffalo congressman. Kruszka stayed in Rome until 1904, presenting his memorandum to Pope Pius X, engaging in Vatican politics, and finally returning to the United States with what he thought was the Pope's assurance that something would be done to aid the plight of the Poles in America. However, when months passed and no papal action was forthcoming, the extreme dissidents held the first synod of the Polish National Catholic Church and elected Rev. Hodur as their own bishop. Schism, one of Kruszka's primary fears, became a reality.

Frustrated by the failure of the Vatican to act on his memorandum, by the failure of the American hierarchy to heed his warnings, and by his own continued stay in what he regarded as a less desirable assignment, Kruszka relieved his frustrations by lashing out against Bishop Sebastian Messmer in a series of pointed articles appearing in *Kuryer Polski* beginning on December 6, 1905. In them, Kruszka accused the American hierarchy of cooperating with the American Protective Association in its opposition to immigrants, repeated his support for Polish nationalism and ethnic pluralism within the Church, and faulted Messmer for purposely ignoring the seniority system in passing him over for appointment to one of the more desirable parishes in Milwaukee.

Messmer and his associates countered by founding the Milwaukee weekly *Nowiny Polskie* [The Polish News] to check the influence of the Kruszkas. Edited by Rev. Bolesław Góral, a professor of languages and an old Kruszka antagonist, the *Nowiny Polskie* enjoyed full ecclesiastical support to the point that Messmer managed to obtain an endorsement from Pope Pius X. With this support, Góral viciously attacked Kruszka's character and motives, intimating that his breach of faith and character were responsible for any events which might have befallen him.

Kruszka, seething at Góral's personal attacks, dubbed the new paper *"Nowiny Niemiecki"* [The German News] and filed a libel suit against its editor. Messmer countered by insisting that the priests within his diocese denounce the Kruszkas from their pulpits, forbidding Wacław Kruszka to write any more articles for *Kuryer Polski,* and announcing that the faithful should no longer read the offending newspaper.

Kruszka's feud with the Catholic hierarchy, set against the background of dissent prevalent at the turn of the century, was long and frequently acrimonious. The complexity of the issues included matters of faith, nationality, equality, democracy, and personal interest. Amid this plethora

of disagreements, one of the more significant issues which contributed to
the outbreak of the verbal war between Kruszka and the Messmer-Góral
faction was the publication of Kruszka's pioneering history of the Poles in
America—*Historya Polska w Ameryce* [Polish History in America].

Devoted as he was to the cause of Polish nationalism and to the ideal of
cultural pluralism, which would allow for nationalistic manifestation
within the Roman Catholic Church, it was no accident that Rev. Wacław
Kruszka became the first Pole to write a history of the Polish experience in
America. Indeed, the very idea provided him with an excellent opportunity to express his nationalism while at the same time arguing for the
validity of his concept of pluralism through use of the Polish experience to
demonstrate ethnic adherence to and promotion of the faith.

Kruszka's purpose in writing his *Historya* was to set forth the history of
the Polish communities in America in such a way that their contribution to
the development of the United States and the Roman Catholic Church
would become widely known. In the process he hoped to reinforce the
validity of his arguments for cultural pluralism while at the same time
advancing his own ethnic group. To obtain information for his project, he
issued repeated public appeals in various newspapers for information, sent
questionnaires to parish priests, visited archives and other repositories in
the United States and Rome, conducted oral interviews, corresponded with
the clergy and prominent lay people, and consulted published sources in
English, Polish, and German. Although he focused his informational
search on the parish and the parochial school, he also sought information
on agriculture, industry, literature, organizations, demographics, the press,
and other secular topics.

Beginning in November 1899, Kruszka devoted considerable time to
research before the first installment of his *Historya* appeared in print in
Kuryer Polski on September 1, 1901. The remaining portions of the *Historya* thereafter appeared serially in the daily *Kuryer Polski,* the weekly
Kuryer Tygodniowy [The Weekly Courier], and the farmer's weekly *Gazeta Wisconsińska* [The Wisconsin Gazette] until December 1904. During
this entire period, Kruszka continuously published appeals for corrections
and additional materials.

Upon completion of the newspaper serialization, Kruszka considered
each of the responses he had received to his request for reader input and
then prepared his revised text for publication in book form. This revised
version appeared in thirteen volumes encompassing over 2,300 pages pub-

lished between 1905 and 1908. This monumental work can be divided into two separate parts, with the first five volumes comprising a general overview of the American Polonia and the remaining eight volumes constituting histories of specific communities.

In Part I, Kruszka uses 710 pages to construct what he refers to as a "bird's-eye view" of Polonia. He deals specifically with such topics as the religious and educational life of the emerging Polish American communities, economic and political interests, the development of social organizations and the press, linguistics, and the statistics of immigration and settlement. One of the more significant questions he addresses at the outset of his opus is: "What is a Polish American?" He answers this by defining separate degrees of Polish nationality and then concluding that the American Pole, while legitimately "Polish," also constitutes a new form of Pole. Not surprisingly, this leads him to the conclusion that ethnic diversity is a vital component of a strong America.

Part II contains histories of individual parishes and settlements treated chronologically within separately defined geographic regions. Though he professed to be objective in his writing, Kruszka also noted that he at times attempted to prod people and to elicit responses. This side of his writing can be seen most clearly in Part II where he describes in considerable length the various parish scandals, personal animosities between priests themselves and between priests and their bishops or parishioners, and the beginnings of the Polish National Catholic movement under Hodur. Of particular interest are his rather serious charges leveled at the Resurrectionist Order in Chicago and Texas. In detailing its activities, Kruszka used information that he obtained from reports in the Resurrectionist archives in Rome, as well as confidential statements from various priests. These revelations, appearing in Volume IX of the *Historya*, placed the Resurrectionists' activities in a very unfavorable light. Furthermore, since each volume of the series carried the official imprimatur of Bishop Messmer, the publication of these statements placed him in a very embarrassing public position and further aggravated the relationship of the two principals.

Although Kruszka claimed innocence in the episode, the Resurrectionists were quick to charge him with misinterpretation, prejudice, and violation of confidence. *Wiarus* [The Old Guard], *Dziennik Chicagoski* [The Chicago Daily], and other Religionist newspapers were quick to condemn Kruszka for false conclusions based upon biased and inadequate scholarship. The *Dziennik Chicagoski* was particularly severe in its criticism, publishing on December 10, 1906, the Resurrectionists' complaints along with an explanation by Messmer, which was very critical of Kruszka. Indeed, the controversy engendered by Kruszka's treatment of the Resurrectionists was a contributing factor in the establishment of the *Nowiny Polskie* as a counterbalance to the Kruszkas and the *Kuryer Polski.*

As the controversy widened, several newspapers critical of the Catholic hierarchy were quick to take advantage of the opportunity to rise to Kruszka's defense. The most vocal supporters included the Polish National Alliance organ *Zgoda* [Harmony], Detroit's *Dziennik Polski* [The Polish Daily], *Rolnik* [The Farmer] from Stevens Point, Pittsburgh's *Wielkopolanin* [He From Great Poland], and the *Gazeta Buffaloska* [The Buffalo Gazette]. In his own defense, Kruszka argued that painting the Catholic Church as a totally divine entity was a disservice. Rather, he maintained, the portrait should also show the human side if it was to be balanced and believable.

Aside from the controversy with Messmer and the Resurrectionists, the publication of *Historya Polska w Ameryce* sparked other reactions of both praise and condemnation. *Dziennik Chicagoski* objected to Kruszka's definition of a Pole; *Dziennik Milwaucki* [The Milwaukee Daily] took exception to the description of St. Josaphat parish in Milwaukee; linguists chastised him for including Polish American slang and polonized English words; and threats of legal action were not uncommon. Yet there were those whose view reached beyond particular issues or inaccuracies to see the merit of Kruszka's attempt. Letters of praise consoled the author, while a flood of new materials arrived for his review. If it had accomplished nothing else, *Historya Polska w Ameryce* prodded Polish Americans to think of themselves as a group, as a culture, as a significant element in the development of their new nation. It challenged them to honor their nationality and to preserve their heritage within the framework of the Church and the new nation that they would call their own.

Kruszka's work, despite its importance as an early statement of ethnic identity and a source of valuable information, certainly suffers by comparison with modern standards of scholarship. Although he exerted great effort to be inclusive in his research, using a multitude of original sources and oral interviews, the lack of footnotes to define sources and the incomplete, often ambiguous references provided in the text greatly detract from the work's usefulness to modern scholars. This problem is heightened by the lack of a bibliography and an index.

Another significant methodological problem is Kruszka's tendency to include inconsequential and repetitious detail that destroys the work's continuity and often obscures its primary lines of development. Too much time is spent, particularly in Part I, on details of only local interest to the detriment of the points that each chapter endeavors to make. The impression this leaves—that of an author who has not fully organized or synthesized his material—is only compounded by the prolific detail accorded to some communities where much detail was readily available, if unnecessary.

Thirdly, a major problem with Kruszka's approach is his failure to place the history of the Polish communities into proper historical perspective, linking it to its place in the general development of American society. As such, Polonia appears to exist in a vacuum, divorced from the society in which it resides. This failure is particularly unfortunate in view of the author's wish to promote the idea of cultural pluralism.

Finally, in his zeal to present the Polish experience in America, Kruszka errs in two other important instances. Factually, his immigration figures and calculations of real wealth are without doubt inflated beyond reasonable proportions and are thus never taken seriously by scholars. This alone has led many historians to overlook the more positive aspects of his work. In the same light, his use of innuendo and inflammatory language when dealing with some individuals with whom he did not agree cost Kruszka the valuable objectivity that he so carefully espoused, thereby causing still further reservations on the part of later scholars.

Despite these deficiencies of style and content, *Historya Polska w Ameryce* remains a valuable source for the early Polish experience in the United States and the growth of segments in particular states and cities. It is a statement of purpose, of pride, and of community which bound the early Polish immigrants together despite their often severe disagreements. In this light, and as a source for further research, it is a valuable document whose translation opens new avenues for English-speaking scholars.

The Translation

The translation of works from one language to another involves innumerable problems, not the least of which is the form that the text itself will take. At the extremes of this spectrum there are literal translation and free translation. The former holds rigidly to the expressions of the author, often at the expense of clear understanding, while the latter stresses comprehension in the new language at the expense of the original "feel" of the work.

In translating Kruszka's work, the editors decided against a literal translation because the author, only moderately educated by today's standards, wrote in an old Polish style replete with analogies, allusions, repetitions, and lengthy, often cumbersome sentence structure. Consequently, although the translation attempts to retain the flavor of Kruszka's elaborate prose, its primary focus is to present a work that is readily intelligible to an English-speaking audience unfamiliar with Polish history, culture, or linguistic structures.

Similarly, in constructing the notes to the translation the editors attempted to identify significant individuals and events that might not be readily recognizable, to refer readers to other sources on specific issues, to place allusions and events into historical perspective, and to explain expressions and linguistic nuances important to the translation.

When it was originally published, *Historya Polska w Ameryce* was the first attempt to write a comprehensive history of the American Polonia. As such, it created controversy, generated ideas, and spawned new research on specific issues raised by its author. The editors hope that this English-language version of Kruszka's pioneering effort will similarly stimulate further thought and scholarly research.

James S. Pula
Editor-in-Chief

A History of the Poles in America

The Beginning, Growth, and Historical Development of Polish Settlements in the United States

comprehensively described by
Rev. Wacław Kruszka

Author of *Rzym* [Rome],
Hymny Wielkopstne [Lenten Hymns],
Neapol, Wezuwiusz i Pompeji [Naples, Vesuvius and
Pompeii], *O Piękności* [On Beauty],
The Unbeliever, Anarchism,
and others.

PART I

A General History of the Polish Immigration in America

To Henryk Sienkiewicz
the most famous novelist, as a token of deepest
respect and remembrance of pleasant memories from a
visit with Congressman Rowland B. Mahany at
Oblęgork [Sienkiewicz's estate] in the
kingdom of Poland on the 26th day of
September, 1903,[1] the present work is
dedicated by the author.

Preface

Original Preface to the Serialized Version

I am not a prophet, but I can foretell that the Poles will play a beautiful role in the Catholic Church in America. The immigration of other nationalities is diminishing. . . . The true era of Slavic immigration has arrived. . . . Since, however, the Poles here are a prevailing majority, a beautiful future awaits them . . . and I can assure you that here in America a second Polish history will begin.[1]

Bishop Spalding, Peoria, Illinois
August 14, 1892

Even in those countries possessing the best organization and the most freedom one can, and always will, find malcontents who feel stifled within the family environment and whom an insurmountable force drives out into the wide world. Human free will should always be respected. Such people should not be unconditionally condemned or left totally without protection if they require it. They are usually enterprising, courageous, and shrewd people who, when appropriately directed, influenced, and encouraged, often accomplish extraordinary things in a short time. Such malcontents were responsible for Rome and its colonies along the shores of the Mediterranean. Almost all of the Phoenician, Greek, and English settlements emerged as a result of such people. Colonies do not allow a nation to become idle, to lapse into one-sidedness or single-mindedness, to continually withdraw into itself, to waste away; they force a nation into a more active, versatile life, broadening its horizon of understanding and expanding its knowledge, wealth, and power. Colonies everywhere have always been evidence of a nation's vitality. A nation wastes away which does not expand, create, or possess the ability to found settlements. Without the power to grow, a state collapses.

The Polish nation became enslaved even before the emigration of its people began, and this enslavement occasioned their emigration.[2] There are still many other causes of an economic nature which continue to support this emigration.[3] We are familiar with them all, and we are strongly convinced that if today, through a Divine miracle, our dear Poland would become in one moment free, independent, and happy, even this miracle would not immediately stop the flow of emigration caused by many years of various adversities.

Even though our Polish emigration in North America met with almost no interest from either their fellow countrymen or from foreigners, the immigrants nevertheless instinctively sought out, counted, and organized themselves, and formed several hundred substantial settlements of their own.[4]

The Polish people—simple, agricultural, almost exclusively laborer—founded genuine and permanent Polish colonies in America. It is for that reason that the Poles here became free citizens and owners of both personal and real property. As a political entity they easily were able to participate in the representational process of the government of a free country and [by extension] to exert influence in the council of nations and in foreign policy.

When I published my descriptions of Rome (1895), and Naples, Vesuvius and Pompeii (1898), critics' voices from everywhere, both favorable and unfavorable, urged me to begin writing a description of our Polish settlements here, including their origins and historical development, since in this way I would render a great service to both American and European-Polish society. "When we old settlers die," I was told, "if nothing is left on paper, the memory of us will be totally lost; our history will accompany us to the grave, and there will remain only conjectures and legends about the beginnings of Polish immigration to America. To be sure, we have chroniclers' accounts of some individual settlements, but not about all of them, nor do we have an historical overview of the whole of the emigration. Undertake this work and write the history."

"Write the history"—these words were easy to say, but not so easy to accomplish. Difficulties arose that were as impenetrable as mountains. One cannot create history from nothing, nor can one inquire everywhere. Consequently, it is necessary to obtain information from others. Let those who have tried (in vain!) before me to write a history attest to the difficulty in obtaining such information. As we read in the old *Kalendarz* [Almanac],[5] published in 1876 in Chicago:

It would be a very good, and even a highly important and interesting thing, not only for us living here in America but also for our nation in the Old Country, if we could prepare an accurate record of Polish colonies that are already permanent and of all other places of residence, as well as the number of Poles residing in America. This idea was conceived at one point by *Orzeł Polski* [The Polish Eagle], a newspaper established in 1870 at the initiative of Rev. Matauszek, a Jesuit priest from St. Louis.[6] After retrieving from several places a census of our people, the newspaper published the figures in its columns. After these few contributions, the paper was discontinued and the majority of our people ignored this idea and did not send in information about themselves.

In 1888 the unforgettable Rev. Możejewski[7] attempted to write a history of the Polish settlements, but it went no further. We found his accounts of a few parishes (see the volumes of *Gazeta Katolicka* [The Catholic Gazette] and *Wiara i Ojczyzna* [Faith and Fatherland]).[8] According to Polonian newspaper annals, Szczęsny Zahajkiewicz[9] wanted to publish in 1890 a book entitled *Życie i czyny Polaków w Ameryce* [The Life and Achievements of the Poles in America]. Urging readers to submit information, he thusly explained the usefulness and need for such a history:

Each family fondly recalls what its father, grandfather, and great-grandfather accomplished, what kind of opportunities they had, what kind of dangers they encountered, how they lived, what they did, and how they acquired their property and status. Families create a nation, and so if members of families worked not only for themselves but also for the general well-being, for the public cause, then not only families, but the entire nation would honor and gratefully remember them. Fathers' lives are examples for the younger generation; for this reason do we record important events, the activities of more distinguished individuals, and the striving of the entire nation out of which is created history described by the ancients as the "mistress of life." The Poles have their own ancestral history, but what they have already accomplished and what they are doing today in America may sink into the gloom of oblivion. Future generations will not even know what hardships their fathers were subjected to, what dangers they had to overcome, how bloody sweat drenched their brows before they secured for themselves an independent position and fortune, before they established settlements, raised churches, and founded schools. The names of people who contributed to this cause should not become lost. On the contrary, they should be handed down to posterity and through their accomplishments shine like stars for the younger generation in the firmament of history.[10]

Despite such a beautiful poetic appeal, Mr. Zahajkiewicz did not publish the intended work. Another attempt subsequently was made by someone else. On August 1, 1891, Ignacy Wendziński[11] published an appeal in which he announced to countrymen that he would issue a book about Polish settlements, entitled *Kronika Polska w Ameryce* [The Polish Chronicle in America]. Every right-thinking Pole will agree that such a book will be an everlasting reminder of the existence of Polishness [*polskość*] on free American soil and, at the same time, a public protest of the defamation by those enemies who refused to acknowledge our merits and our existence. It will be an everlasting reminder, I repeat, because the notoriety of transitory publication is soon forgotten, while such a book will be inherited by children from their parents, from generation to generation for decades and be preserved for centuries in libraries, including the Library of Congress in Washington, D.C. Moreover, such a book will be the beginning and the cornerstone of further documentation of Polish history during the national diaspora following the Polish partitions.[12]

Despite such a grandiloquent announcement, Wendziński's *Kronika* never came to be. Once again, it ended with good intentions. In 1893, however, Rev. Łuczycki of Manitowoc, Wisconsin, actually began an account of the colonies, publishing the first (and last) volume of his *Album*.[13] Barely had he ascended above Milwaukee when his literary wings failed him. Later, in 1897, Mr. Zahajkiewicz published his *Złotą Księga* [Golden Book], but he met the same fate as Rev. Łuczycki.[14] So far no one has been successful in soaring like an eagle above the length and breadth of the [Polish] colonies throughout the entire United States. Let us try, in the name of God, and maybe we will succeed. God bless us, and we will succeed!

The history, or "happenings" relating what had occurred and what our immigrants had accomplished many years ago, is not only pleasant and interesting, but is also very useful because it develops a complete human being by cultivating and fostering all three powers of his soul: memory, intellect, and willpower. Firstly, history cultivates intellect, enlightening our mind with the truth of accomplished facts. Rev. Możejewski rightly observes in his *Prośbie do wszystkich parafian w Ameryce* [Request to All Parishioners in America] (wherein he requested parishioners to send historical information):

> It is true that other nationalities are also scattered here [in America], but they have already reflected upon themselves a long time ago . . . they have written down the entire content of their parishes: their origin, development, and present existence. In other words, everyone knows about each other. Although physically and geographically distant, they are bound through a moral force from which the physical grows.

Secondly, history stimulates our memory about people and their achievements; and thirdly, it stirs our will-power with either encouraging or discouraging examples. Therefore, as Cicero expressed it: "History is the torch of truth, the life of memory, and the mistress of life."[15] The purpose of history is to relate important facts and human achievements, whether good or bad, so long as they are true: the good, so that they may be enticing examples, the bad so that they may be frightening ones for future generations. History, as the torch of truth, avoids deceit but states the truth without any consideration as to whether it is unpleasant or pleasant. "Who does not know," as the ancient Cicero said, "that the first law of history is that it does not dare to record any falsehood or to hide any truth."[16] The truth, however painful it may be, has after all, the one great quality of healing and raising human beings from their lethargy, of curing and ennobling them.

These ideas guided me while working on the present history. It is clear that even with the best efforts, I could not personally check everything I wrote—for what mortal could do this?—but in many narratives I had to rely on the testimony of other people, always those who wanted and were able to tell the truth. This is not the work of an individual; rather, this history is a collective endeavor.

The following have collaborated with me, whom I gratefully mention here: Rev. Rem. Berendt, OFM; Rev. Franciszek Pruss, pastor of a Polish parish in Anderson, Texas; Revs. Świnarski, Wójcik, and others from Buffalo, New York; Rev. S. E. Niedbalski from Panna Maria in Texas; Rev. W. Przybylski from Eugene, Oregon; Rev. T. Kałamaja, OFM from Omaha, Nebraska; Rev. Benvenuto from Nanticoke, Pennsylvania; Rev. Zychowicz from Scranton, Pennsylvania; Rev. J. Kasprzycki, ex-provincial of the Resurrectionist Fathers; Rev. Dąbrowski from Detroit; Rev. Rainer and Rev. Góral from St. Francis; the Sisters of Notre Dame; Rev. Matauszek from St. Louis, Missouri; the Felician Sisters from Detroit; Rev. Dworzak, DD from Williamsbridge, New York; Rev. [Jan] Strzelecki from New York City; Rev. L. Bójnowski from New Britain, Connecticut; Rev. Stanowski from St. Louis; Rev. Jan Machnikowski from Oshkosh; Rev. Ignasiak from Erie, Pennsylvania; Rev. Rosiński from Cleveland; Rev. Józef Biela, DD; Rev. Stan. Przyborowski from Częstochowa, Texas; Rev. Korczyk from Pine Creek, Wisconsin; Mr. Jan Gawlik who arrived in Texas in 1855 and still lives there today (1902); and many, many others, both clergy and lay people.

I also drew upon the following sources: *Kalendarz* [Almanac] for 1877;

Rev. Z. Łuczycki, *Album*; S. Zahajkiewicz, *Złota Księga* [Golden Book]; Rev. Władysław Mścisz, *Kościół św. Jadwigi w Milwaukee* [Church of St. Hedwig in Milwaukee]; Henry Nagiel, *Dziennikarstwo Polskie w Ameryce* [Polish Journalism in America]; A. Małłek, *Dzieje parafii św. Trójcy* [History of Holy Trinity Parish]; *Związek Narodowy Polskie* [Polish National Alliance] its development and activities; Rev. J. Ciemiński, *Położenie i Potrzeby kościoła Katolickiego w Stanach Zjednoczonych* [The Position and Needs of the Catholic Church in the United States]; *Church History of Wisconsin*; letters of Revs. Kajsiewicz and Przewłocki, General of the Resurrectionist Fathers; *Kalendarz Jubileuszowy* [Jubilee Almanac] in Pittsburgh, Pennsylvania; Rev. Skulik, DD, *Historya Parafii św. Jacka* [History of St. Hyacinth's Parish] in La Salle, Illinois; Rev. Smolikowski, CR, *Historya Zgromadzenia Zmartwychwstania P.* [History of the Resurrection Order]; finally I abundantly drew upon the annals of newspapers in New York, Detroit, Buffalo, Chicago, and Milwaukee, and from various notes, local chronicles and parish records, such as *Początek i rozwój parafii św. Piotra w Stevens Point, Wisconsin* [Origin and Development of St. Peter's Parish in Stevens Point, Wisconsin], as well as the archives in Rome and others.[17]

My considerable, unremitting work was to gather and organize the accumulated historical material. In the process I conscientiously took into consideration, wherever possible, both chronology and geography. The ancients already called chronology and geography the eyes of history. I did not adhere solely either to a chronological or a geographical order, but to a combination of both of them. If these two auxiliary sciences are the "eyes" of history, then like eyes, they should be used together if a view of events is to be clear and lucid. In general, while organizing [my] historical material, I followed the advice of Cicero, contained in these words:

Historical facts require a time order (chronological sequence) and a description of countries (geography). Moreover, in important and memorable occurrences everyone wants to know about the purpose, about the deed, and finally about the results of the deed. Therefore, historical facts also require that an historian first emphasize his opinion that personal motives can be the mainspring of certain human deeds; then he should tell not only about the accomplished deed—what happened—but how it happened. Finally, he should state the result of this; when he speaks of results or consequences of historical facts he should make knows all their causes, be it by chance, on purpose, through wisdom or through human recklessness. He especially should write about the life and character of the people themselves, those who are of importance in history not only through their deeds but who stand out by reputation and fame.[18]

We divide the present history into two parts. In Part I we will present a general outline of the history of the immigration, and in Part II we will delineate the history of individual settlements. Therefore, before we begin a detailed account of each individual parish and settlement, we will describe, as if from a bird's-eye view, a general picture of the life of the entire immigration. We will present the development of immigrants in their vast proportions and manifestations, in religion, politics, education, art, and customs. Human society is like a multi-storied building. In Part I we will present in one picturesque account the entirety of the building of Polish-American society, in its length, breadth, and height, from its foundations to its summit. In Part II we then will pass through its chambers, alcoves, halls, and rooms. In Part I, we will quickly fly, as if by air balloon, over the settlements in America and will note anything of importance. By contrast, in Part II, as if sitting on a simple cart or in an automobile, we will slowly make our way through the entire United States. Often stopping en route, we will look into each Polish settlement and parish. We will talk to the pastor at his rectory, to the tradesman at his workshop, to the worker in a factory or mine, and we will gladly go out of our way to look for outlying places, to chat with the farmer behind his plow, to speak with the teacher in school, to embrace friends, to meet strangers, to chat, to talk.

Let us not allow those beautiful memories to die, which have come to us through oral tradition but which for the next generation are receding and already fading. Let us awaken enthusiasm in a generation that has hardened itself to many ideals, even to that of the homeland [Poland]. But let this enthusiasm for the homeland be rational and let it be enriched by the dearly-obtained storehouse of painful experiences, as well as conscious and unconscious mistakes.

It is true that one should not be a hurry with an historical judgement. History, especially when treating recent years, must touch many things and people about which one cannot easily make a judgement. In a number of cases, history has yet to say anything about many events and people from past ages. Nevertheless, historical judgement about recent events has made claims to infallibility. Historical judgement is not the final one, although Goethe has said that "Weltgeschichte ist Weltgericht."[19] It could be that in the next life a number of surprises await us in this regard.

I wrote [this book] in Ripon, Wisconsin, at the Church of St. Wenceslas. I began in 1899 and finished in June 1901.

Rev. Wacław Kruszka

Preface to the Book Publication in 1905

Before appearing in the present format, *Historya Polska w Ameryce* had already been serialized from September 1, 1901, to December, 1904, in *Kuryer Polski* [The Polish Courier], the oldest daily, as well as in two weeklies, *Gazeta Wisconsińska* [The Wisconsin Gazette], and *Kuryer Tygodniowy* [The Weekly Courier].[1] After each section printed in the newspaper, the following comment was added: *Attention*: Reverend fathers and editors are asked for a critique of each chapter of the *Historya*, and all readers are asked to send in corrections, if they notice any mistakes, to the Rev. W. Kruszka, Ripon, Wisconsin.

As the *Historya* appeared in the newspapers, so many critiques, protests, comments, and corrections poured in—whether to the newspapers themselves or whether in private letters to the author—that they could have composed a second such *Historya*. All of these critiques, observations, and corrections were reviewed on their merits and were taken into consideration for the present publication. Its appearance in book form, therefore, can be rightfully considered as the second, revised, and supplemented edition containing a complete, thorough, and to the extent humanly possible, a comprehensively-compiled history of Polish settlements in the United States and Canada. This book, however, is not a perfect work. Only God can create a perfect work.

Let this *Historya* also be considered a modest contribution to the preparations for an appropriate celebration of the golden jubilee of Polish immigration in America. Its silver jubilee, as attested to by Chicago [Polonian] newspapers, was observed by the Poles in Texas on August 15, 1880; so therefore, the golden jubilee will occur on August 15, 1905.[2] It is to be expected that the entire American Polonia, from coast to coast, will observe this half-century jubilee of its immigration in a very festive but also a practical manner. This means that from their past fifty years in exile they will draw strength for the future in order to continue the fight against elements adverse to Polish faith and nationality.

Ripon, Wisconsin, December 31, 1904
Rev. Wacław Kruszka
Pastor of the Parish of St. Wenceslas

Chapter 1

The Distinct Type of Pole in America

"The soil is the mother life-giver" [*alma mater terra*], the ancients said. The soil is the mother who feeds, nourishes, clothes and nurses us at her bosom. For us Poles, the American soil is a mother; for many of us she is an adopted one, for many a real one, but for all, nevertheless, a mother and not a stepmother. The American soil surrounds both her real and her adopted children with truly maternal care. She makes an even greater effort regarding her adopted ones than the European soil, their real mother. But this circumstance does not change our common origin and nationality; nor does it influence a change in surname. It does not interfere with our being or what we call ourselves; what we formerly were, that is, Poles! We changed our mother, but not our father; the land, but not our fatherland.

Frequently it is possible to encounter this opinion: "A Pole is one born on Polish soil." This is false. From this, one could deduce that the whole host of our young, fellow citizens born here on American soil would not be entitled to call themselves Poles. This is not so. A Pole, as long as he maintains his own characteristic disposition, does not cease to be a Pole just because he was born on American soil; just as the potato, whose homeland is America, does not cease to be a potato because it grows on European soil. The soil which gives it birth may influence a change in some of its external characteristics, but it will not succeed in transforming its internal nature.

Poland is not just land along the Vistula River, but a collection of people with a common origin and lineage. Wherever a Pole settles, there a piece of Poland is born. Origin forms a nation, not soil. Soil molds fellow citizens, not countrymen.[1] A German born on Polish soil can be the fellow citizen of a Pole, but he will never be a countryman. On the other hand, a

Pole born in America will not truly be a fellow citizen of a Pole from the Old Country, but he will remain his countryman not only physically, but also in spirit, inasmuch as he possesses an inborn consciousness of his district nationality. Every American is his fellow citizen [*ziomek*], but only a Pole is his countryman [*rodak*].

American society is like a forest composed of various types of trees. Just as in such a forest, pine, oak, beech, fir, and hornbeam grow amicably next to each other, linking together and intertwining both their branches and their roots—so a Pole, a German, a Frenchman, an Englishman, an Irishman, and a Swede live next to each other in American society in an amicable relationship. In such a forest, both the oak and pine, although they draw their lifeblood from the same soil and breathe the same atmosphere, still remain themselves.[2] "Pines are begotten from pines, oaks grow from oaks, and it is not humanly possible to make an oak into a pine." Similarly, in American society each nationality preserves its own distinct nature and according to the rules of its nature, grows, lives, and develops not only physically, but even morally—although ostensibly for those observing from afar, this difference in nationality does not stand out in relief. Similarly, one who views a forest from a distance does not perceive the differences in the varieties of trees; and even some looking closely cannot distinguish a hornbeam from a beech, or a beech from an oak. Yet, would this indicate that there is no difference among them? There is, and it is essential. In the same way, a substantial difference exists among nationalities in American society, although initially from a distance this difference is difficult to see clearly and oftentimes even someone looking closely cannot detect it. In reality, however, there exists not only a distinct type of Jew, but also a distinct type of Irishman, German, and Pole. This Pole, although he did not grow up on Polish soil among his own people but on foreign soil among other nationalities, grew up after all as what he by nature was and is—a Pole. No one and nothing will erase the fundamental trait distinguishing him from other nationalities. This trait is noticeable to each perceptive eye, but is probably invisible to one who is notable to distinguish an oak from a pine or rye from oats. Foreign soil and an alien environment can influence a change in some of one's external characteristics, such as language, but it cannot transform one's internal characteristics. An Irishman, for example, although he has lost his language has not lost his fundamental national character. An expert on nationality will recognize him immediately as an Irishman and will distin-

guish him from others, just as he would a Jew. An expert will also recognize the difference between a Swede and a Muscovite,[3] between a Scot
and an Italian, a Norwegian and a Frenchman, a Spaniard and a Dutch-
man, and so on, not to mention Chinese, Japanese, Eskimo, and Negro.
One does not need to be a great expert on nationalities to distinguish them.
Besides language, there is in everyone something that distinguishes him
from others; and that something is his essence, the nature specific to him
alone.

It would, therefore, be necessary to be clearly aware of what constitutes
the nature of a Pole. Of what does our nationality consist? Our profound
philosopher, Karol Libelt,[4] thinks that the communality of language constitutes a nation, since he says: "Without a national language there is no
nation. Draw blood from a human being and his life will expire with it—
remove language from a nation and its existence will also dissipate. A
nation lives as long as its language does. . . ." Certainly there is a lot of
truth to this, because above all one nationality distinguishes itself externally from another by means of language. By losing the Polish language,
we are undoubtedly losing one of the most outstanding characteristics of a
Pole.

Besides language, however, there is something else that unites us into
one vast family called the Polish nation; and that something is the Polish
cause—the national cause. It blossomed not only from the fragrance of
Polish forests, meadows, and fields, from the taste of Polish bread, in a
word, from the attachment to and nostalgia for native Polish soil; but the
national cause grew mainly from the memories of our ancient history,
from injustices suffered, from the glory and happiness we experienced,
and finally from the feeling of solidarity, that is, the feeling of need to protect the ties of national unity and national interests. It also springs from the
feeling of national pride, that noble feeling causing a Pole, in whatever
part of the world he finds himself, not to tarnish the collective national
reputation through any contemptible or despicable action. He does not
deny his nationality, but rather proudly admits to the fact that he is a Pole,
and wherever he finds himself, he brings credit through his demeanor to
the Polish name.[5]

It is precisely this feeling of national pride and unity—and not language—that is the essential and vital force of nationality, because such a
feeling takes precedence over a sensory and sentimental attachment to an
ancestral land. It is a superior and more noble feeling, the only kind capa-

ble of uniting into one nation Poles born anywhere in the world.[6] During one of the sessions of the Department of History and Philosophy of the Academy of Science, Professor Włodzimierz Czerkawski[7] observed in his paper entitled "Badania nad ilością Polaków i ich ugrupowaniem w krajach zagranicznych" [Research on the Number of Poles and their Grouping in Foreign Countries]:

Without getting into disputes revolving around the definition of nationality, it is only right to point out that in the final analysis individual subjectivism determines national affiliation, which means its will and consciousness. All criteria for defining nationalities, such as language, race, culture, and so on, have the significance of external characteristics, as well as elements that influence individual views, but in no way do they possess enough force to always and everywhere categorically determine the nation to which a person belongs.

Rev. Maryan Morawski, S.J.,[8] writes in his work *Podstawy etyki i prawa* [Foundations of Ethics and Law]:

The political existence of a nation, as a body dependent on external conditions, may succumb under pressure or due to a change in these conditions; nationality, as a spiritual matter, remains and continues to fulfill its task in the general development of humanity. Even in a foreign nation to which it may become attached, the original nationality will live as a healthy and useful member of the whole—as long as it finds conditions of national life, conditions which it needs as much as a plant needs light and air.

Language is like a bulwark protecting the fortress of nationality from external foes. In the American Polonia, thank God, this bulwark remains unbreached, although it is damaged in some spots.

From our young people already brought up in America, it is difficult to demand a nostalgia for Poland, "for those forested hills, those green meadows, those fields painted with various grains, gilded with wheat and silvered with rye." They have never known these forest scents, never tasted bread from Polish soil, never seen these Polish fields. How can they yearn for them? This is psychologically impossible because "what the eye sees also comes from the heart." *In amore oculi sunt duces* [In love, the eyes are the guides], and so in the love of country the heart follows the eyes. It is not unusual that our young people cling in body and heart to this [new] land which smiles before them, and that they forget the land of their forefathers which they do not even know "by sight." They know the lands along the Warta and Vistula Rivers probably "from hearsay," from description, and from the stories of their parents and teachers if they attend Polish schools. Hearing so many beautiful things about Poland, Polish Americans would be glad to go and see it; but not so much from nostalgia as from curiosity. Hearing so much about the injustices and oppression of the old homeland, Polish Americans would be glad to see it free, independent, and prosperous; but not so much from an attachment to this land, which to them is foreign and distant, as from an attachment to their countrymen who are always close to them in blood and spirit. They would like to assist in resurrecting Poland not only through words but also through action; but whether they would want to return with Mickiewicz "to the bosom of the homeland" is another question.[9] Generally speaking, a Pole born in America knows the Polish language, Polish history to some extent, and Polish literature in general. He reads, writes, sings, and recites in Polish, gives Polish theatrical performances, prays and goes to confession in Polish, gives speeches in Polish at national celebrations, and if he is a priest (we already have a large number of them born in America) gives sermons in correct and eloquent Polish. We see Poles born in America in the professions as doctors, priests, teachers, editors, lawyers, public servants, and so on, and they all unanimously declare that they do not wish to eliminate the language of their forefathers, that Polish culture is equally dear to them as American culture.

This is the main type of Pole in America, but other types are not lacking. There are Poles born in America who do not know the country along the Warta or Vistula Rivers "by sight" or "from hearsay." They probably only know its worst side because sometimes they hear terrible things about it from their fathers. "Some of our adolescents in America," a certain newspaper recently wrote, "do not even like to think about the 'stupid' Old Country."[10]

Lastly, there is the type of Pole who would lose not only [national] customs but also the mother-tongue. Until now he has been very rare in America. He exists only as an exceptional type. He emerges most often as a result of mixed marriages and occasionally from those purely Polish marriages in which the Polish family lives alone among Americans. In 1897 I once arrived in a town called Wautoma in Wisconsin. Only one Polish family lived there among the Americans. I heard the children of this family speaking Polish. At first I was surprised, but not for long. Around suppertime, prior to sitting down at the table, the children knelt and recited aloud the *"Anioł Pański"* [Angelus],[11] not only with their hands folded in concentration, but also using correct Polish. In such a

house where the children are thus taught and brought up, neither nationality nor the holy faith will perish, even if this house were to stand alone and
isolated like an island in a sea of Anglo-Americanism.

But also in those children or grandchildren of Polish immigrants, who
as a result of adverse circumstances lost both their [national] customs and
mother-tongue, there always remains an innate consciousness of ancestral
and national distinctness. This inborn consciousness sometimes becomes
weak and lethargic, as it did at one time among the Poles in Silesia.[12] Yet,
it cannot be uprooted. *Naturam expellas furca, tamen usque redibit* [try to
drive out nature even by means of pitchforks], but you will not succeed,
especially with a nature as tough as that of the Poles.

This last type of Pole, unable to speak Polish but still considering himself a Pole, can often be seen in Southern states such as Virginia, Georgia,
Mississippi, and so on. F. Banaszyński, born in Milwaukee, relates in his
"Listach z Podróży" [Letters from My Travels] printed in *Kuryer Polski*:[13]
"In a railway passenger car I met a travel agent, a handsome gentleman. I
started a conversation with him about this and that—[in English, of
course]—until finally we touched on the subject of the conflict between
the North and the South, the Civil War of 1861-65. "That war," said my
traveling companion,"ruined my father. If not for that war, I would not
need to travel and work so hard for a comfortable life. If not for that war, I
might still be living on the plantation with my father, the Blacks would
still be working for us, and I would be carefree. As it is, I cannot forget
my resentment towards the war and sometimes I feel as though I have neither a home nor a country." After this acknowledgment, a silence ensued.
I was the first to interrupt it. I told him that his words seemed strange to
me, and that it is rather I who should say that I have no homeland. "What
is the reason that you have no homeland?" he asked me.

"I am a Pole," I replied, "and as you undoubtedly know from history,
my homeland has been erased from the map of Europe."

Upon hearing these words, my companion rose from his seat and, laying
his hands on my shoulder, eyed me up and down with a gaze that was both
sad and happy; shaking my hand, he asked me again:

"You say that you are a Pole?"

"Yes, I am."

"Hm, my father was born in Kraków."

"And so you are also a Pole? Do you speak Polish?"

"Not a word," he replied. "My father was born in Kraków. At an early age he arrived in New Orleans, whence he went to Jackson, Mississippi, where he married an American. I did not have the opportunity to learn Polish."

We sat this way until dawn talking about the country of which we both had only our parents' memories. I, however, became convinced that my companion possessed a far greater knowledge about Polish history—more than I had expected.

I asked him whether there were more Poles like him in the South. He answered that there were very many. Many Southerners are of Polish origin, but now are purely Americanized. Even though they do not speak Polish, a spark of Polish feeling burns in their hearts. This can be especially felt during Mme. Modrzejewska's performances or at Paderewski's concerts.[14]

There are very few such non-Polish-speaking Poles in relation to the total number of immigrants. Generally speaking, Poles born in America speak Polish and maintain national traditions even though they are second or third generation. In places where they live together in large numbers, where they comprise entire settlements and Polish parishes, where they have a good Polish school, there is no fear that they will lose their external national characteristics even in subsequent generations. True, they are not the same as the Poles in the Old Country. Their likes and dislikes have altered, their customs have undergone a change, their Polish language has become transformed in everyday use, as we shall see later in this history [Chapter 13]. In a word, the Polish American is a new type of Pole. This type is still undeveloped and indistinct, and for this reason still eludes the eye of today's historian. It is certain that such a type is being formed and was so from the very beginning of the history of [Polish] immigration to this country. However, on this basis it would be going too far to conclude that "the Poles in America have changed, and therefore have become denationalized."

Only those who would like to see the Pole in America as not differing in any respect from the Pole in the Old Country can see that Polish young people in America are losing their nationality because they do not yearn for the Old Country, because they do not like to speak about it, because they do not care for old-world dress, amusements and dances, or because they intersperse Polish speech with English. Is it necessary to go that far to preserve nationality? If so, the Mazurian, Kujawian, Silesian, and Krakovian would cease to be sons of Poland, because such has his distinct cus-

toms and ways, dress and amusements, and even distinct speech and pronunciation.[15] Let us not demand too much from the young Pole in America; let us especially not demand that, as a child of America, raised and
fused with it, he renounce his love for this land in the name of Poland. Let
him love this American mother-earth which gave him birth or which shel-
tered him in need. Let him honor and admire this land which nourishes
and feeds him, let him sing the praises of this land whose bread he eats,
because it is proper and just. Let him become acclimated, let him adapt
himself to new forms of dress, amusements, and customs—in a word, let
him create a new and distinct type of American Pole! Being the countryman of an American, let him also be a true fellow-citizen of every Pole
and let him be aware of his responsibilities toward Poland. That the Pole
in America is aware of them can already be seen not only in words
(protests, memorials), but also in deeds. Besides contributions to the
National Treasury in Rapperswyl,[16] the American Pole has sent his money
to Poland on such occasions as the observance of the jubilee celebrations
of Polish writers like Chociszewski,[17] Sienkiewicz, and others, and when
he found out about the atrocious treatment by the Prussians of the children
of Września.[18] In his heart a spark of national consciousness burst into
flame with force equal to that which burns in the hearts of Poles in the
mother country. Polish immigrants' purses then opened up and the contributions poured in for those persecuted by the Prussian barbarians. For this
"orphan's bread" the Poles throughout America contributed $12,000.
Indeed, the Poles in America had not forgotten that Sarmatian blood
flowed in their veins;[19] that they were a small part of the vast Polish family
of martyrs, and they hastened with their donations to generously replenish
the national fund.[20] Nevertheless, the American Pole cannot and should
not be molded according to the Old World model. Striving to develop
independently, soundly, and naturally, he must, like a plant, adapt to local
conditions. He must learn to live a Polish life in conditions different from
those in Poland.

His ancestral family history can best teach him this. "History is life's
model." "History," states A. M. Fredro,[21] "is the mother of good judgment;
it is necessary to understand both one's own and foreign history." The history of our ancestors, of old Poland, and of her former kings, can be very
beautiful, absorbing, and useful for a young Pole raised in America; but it
would be more ideal than practical. A history of his fathers, who have
lived on the same soil as he and functioned in the same geographical, eco-

nomical, political, and religious conditions, will be of more concern to him and a hundred times more useful. Such a Polish American history will teach him a more practical lesson as to how he must live in this country in order not to lose his faith and nationality. It will point out to him tangibly and concretely how to unite into parishes, how to foster the development of Polish schools, how to establish national and church-related organizations, how to cultivate Polish literature and the fine arts, and how to promote the interests of the Poles in politics.

When a gardener transplants a plant from one garden to another, that plant at first lowers its leaves, grows haggard, wilts, and seems to dry up and deteriorate. However, after some time, when it puts roots into its new soil, it comes back to life, growing and developing in this new soil in a full and luxuriant manner. Such is the picture of our emigration. Separated from the maternal trunk—from Poland—transplanted onto American soil by the hand of Providence, for some time it seemed both to us and to our fellow citizens in the Old Country that we were deteriorating. Nevertheless, as soon as we put down roots in this new land, as soon as we became familiar with local social and political relations and blended with local institutions—as everyone will become convinced from this history we are writing—then like the transplanted tree we splendidly "took root." Like a tree transplanted onto foreign soil, we assimilated the lifeblood of this land and of those American customs that suited our Polish nature. We consequently live and prosper as Poles, we grow constantly and develop as a society, admittedly not European but Polish American. Breathing different air, we naturally had to grow up differently, but in this different environment our relations by nature have already arranged themselves in a rather normal fashion. We have formed organizations in every aspect of social life to counteract hostile attempts on our faith and nationality. A beautiful division of social work exists. Schools, churches, orphanages, hospitals, and so on, are the concern of parishes and church organizations. Politics, work for one's country, and education of the older generation, are the tasks of a national party, as represented by the powerful Polish National Alliance. This division of work should be adjusted only to bring these two parties to a tolerable understanding—we then would constitute an excellently organized society.[22] We do not have a distinct political life, but nor do our fellow citizens in the Old Country. Nevertheless, they rightly call themselves a society and a thoroughly Polish nation.[23]

There was a time in Poland when we were much thought about, a lot was expected of and anticipated from us; but precisely for this reason, and because we did not satisfy these great hopes and expectations, complete apathy ensued which is a natural psychological symptom. The "Fourth Province of Poland,"[24] as we came to be known, immediately ceased to exist for them. In place of the "Fourth Province" those in Galicia invented a "New Poland" in Brazil.[25] Some new "Commercial-Geographical" Society is responsible for it. To us it decidedly seems that involvement with this "New Poland" is also artificial and unnatural. The Poles in Brazil are as plants in a greenhouse covered by a glass roof of old-world protection. The Poles in the United States, however, grow naturally and freely under the bare sky, and develop luxuriantly without such care. In the opinion of the Messrs. Dunikowski,[26] accustomed to the sight of plants nursed artificially in a greenhouse, this natural growth and exuberant development of our emigration seems bizarre. Yet, not all natural development is wild. It is already inherent in the American's nature that he prefers to grow naturally rather than artificially in a greenhouse. This is also better for poor Galicia.

Even the *Kuryer Lwowski* [Lwów Courier] itself admits that the Poles from North America are saving Galicia from the worst kind of poverty.[27] In 1899 the immigrants in North America sent some 1,100,000 crowns in cash to the Jasło district alone to help their relatives in distress.[28] "Let now," adds this same *Kuryer*, "the gentlemen from 'The Polish Circle' and dignitaries of the parliaments [Sejm] such as Hupka and company, wrack their brains to try and find a source of income in our Galicia which would approximately equal the above result! Let them further think about what awful poverty would exist in Galicia if it were not for this succor from across the ocean!"[29]

Each reader of these pages on Polish American history must admit that in a comparatively short time, not quite half a century, we have grown here tremendously. We have "grown up," I say, but have we "measured up" and "matured" socially? This is another question which we will let the judgment of history answer.

Chapter 2

When Does Polish Immigration to America Really Begin?

The origin of the immigration—Jan z Kolno in America, 1476—a Polish professor, 1659—the Zborowskis, 1562—Kościuszko, Pułaski, Niemcewicz—Rev. (Count) Galliczin (1792) and the Jesuits from White Russia—The political emigrations of 1831, 1848, and 1863—Poles fight the Indians in Florida—The peasant emigration: voluntary from 1854, then sporadic, and from 1870 extensive.

The Census Office, a statistical agency in Washington, D.C., simultaneously gave with the results of the last census of the United States[1] a general view of immigration from the time the states freed themselves from British rule to the end of 1900. This historical sketch is very interesting. Immigration of Europeans to the New World began in 1790; it existed before this time, but it was small and to some extent obligatory. Persecuted Catholics fled from England and Ireland, and criminals were sent to Louisiana from France. Many mercenary soldiers of the British Hudson Bay Company settled in this country. Therefore, the great voluntary immigration did not begin until 1790. At that time only the Germans, Swiss, and British left their homelands. The general number of these immigrants during the first three decades, i.e., to 1820, amounted to 250,000 people, an average of 8,000 annually. For many reasons, the immigrant movement then began to grow; above all on account of the development of steam navigation, because of political reaction in Europe, growing tax burdens, a general draft, et cetera. The defeat of the native Indians [in America] greatly increased the safety of life and property and became one of the important reasons for the growth of immigration. From 1820 to the end of the nineteenth century, thirty million people permanently immigrated from Europe. This influx was not uniform, but was constantly rising, while at the same time the immigrants' nationality was changing. There were fewer Germans and Anglo-Saxons, while there were increasingly more Slavs and Italians. The following proportion existed among these nationalities: thirty years ago the Germans alone constituted 45% of the total number of immigrants, twenty years ago the Germans and British combined gave us 32% of all immigrants, and ten years ago only 14.5% of the total number of immigrants came from Germany, Britain, and Scandinavia. All the others came from Latin or Slavic countries; for every two immigrants of Latin descent there were three Slavs.[2] At the same time, with such a change in the immigrants' national origins, laws began to appear in the United States to impede the immigrant influx. The Census Office explained this as a fear that the general level of education and morality in this country might be lowered; we, however, think that the greater fear was that the country might lose its exclusively Anglo-German traits. We base this supposition on a reference by the Census Office in a chapter to social relations from a criminal standpoint. It is stated therein that "blue-collar districts in large cities (until recently centers of debauchery, drunkenness, and crime) do not differ greatly from other neighborhoods once the docile and religious Slavic people predominate in those blue-collar urban areas." A good reference to us!

For a long time we have called ourselves and were so referred to by others as a nation of pilgrims. Even poets acclaimed the "Polish pilgrimage as the soul of the Polish nation."[3] Together with the poets, many supposed that through this pilgrimage and emigration we, like Jews in the desert, would reach "the Holy Land, a free homeland." Whether and to what extent we, the immigrants in America, are this "soul of the nation," and whether we have this mission to save Poland is not being presently addressed, since we do not intend to expatiate upon the centuries-old plan or intentions God has for us American Poles, or Polish Americans. We do, however, ascertain the obvious fact that among all the Polish colonization efforts throughout the world, ours in America is the most substantial not only as to the number of settlers but also as to both material and moral resources. We know that the main reason driving our Polish immigrants to America is the desire to better their lot. An emigrant crossing the Atlantic does not intend to rebuild Poland; his purpose is to "improve his life." But this human intention does not at all exclude other higher ones which God unfailingly has for the Polish emigration. What are these higher designs? We still do not know.

Leaving the future to God, let us meanwhile examine the past—the beginning of our emigration.

When did Polish immigration to America begin in broader proportions? When, in fact, did the first Polish settlements appear here?

The beginning of a specific Polish immigration to America—numerous, massive, and peasant—can be seen in the arrival of three hundred Upper-Silesian farmers in Texas. By the end of 1854, under the leadership of Rev. Leopold Moczygęba, they had founded the first purely Polish settlement of "Panna Maria."

Prior to that time individual sporadic settlements had occurred [in America].

Let us not go into what some scholars/researchers wrote, both Polish (Maciejewski, *Piśmiennictwo Polskie* [Polish Literature],[4] Vol. II, p. 735; Gowiński and Czarkowski, *Wykład geografii powszechnej* [Lectures on general geography]; Oleszczyński, Supiński) and foreign (Miguel Gomara in a work published in 1553, *Historia de les Indies* [History of the Indies]; Cornelius Wytfist in 1599; George Horn in 1671; Humboldt in 1837). Namely, sixteen years before Columbus arrived in America, a Pole named Jan z Kolno—a Mazurian who was first a sailor in the service of Gdańsk and later of the Danes—arrived as commander of their ships in America (in "Labrador") in 1476, while Columbus arrived here only in 1492.[4] A Kashubian canto, after all, attests to this fact, singing the praises of this "Jasiu z Kielna" [Johnny from Kolno] as follows:

I Jaś z Kielna świętego tędzim beł wiarusem
Co w Ameryce bywoł jesz przed Koląbusem,
I tak liczne rozmnożeł w niej kaszubście plemnię,
Że tu druge ju mąmę obiecaną zemnię.

Johnnie from sacred Kolno was a sturdy guard's name
Who went to America before Columbus came
And so abundantly propagated the Kashubian band,
That we now have here our second promised land.[5]

Following the discovery of America, Poles were already dwelling there in the sixteenth and seventeenth centuries. That they were intelligent is mentioned time and time again in English letters. A Jesuit, Rev. J. Conway, stated in his debate on higher education in America that by 1659 Dutch colonists from Manhattan Island had brought over a Polish professor to educate their youth: "As early as 1659 the Dutch colonists of Manhattan Island hired a Polish schoolmaster for the education of the youth of the community."[6]

The earliest Polish family we know to have arrived in America are the Zabrieskis [Zabriskis] who live in New Jersey and New York.[7] Actually their original surname was Zborowski. The first Zborowskis arrived in America and settled near the city of Hackensack, New York [later New Jersey], in 1562 following the execution of Samuel Zborowski in Poland during the reign of Stefan Batory when the Great Crown Chancellor was [Jan] Zamojski [Zamoyski]. The first who resumed the original family name and the title of count was Marcin Zborowski, a lawyer and real estate speculator. Marcin Zborowski made a substantial fortune which his son, William Elliot Zborowski, inherited in 1878 and skillfully increased. Count Elliot Zborowski, born in New Jersey, was killed in 1903 at the age of fifty-two in a car race from Nice to La Turbie, France. The estate of the deceased was valued at ten million dollars. His annual income amounted to one-half million dollars. He owned two theaters in New York and a number of other buildings.

Countess Zborowski, Baroness de Steuers, was the daughter of Carey. Her mother was descended from the Astor family, and she had her own yearly income of eighty thousand dollars. Count Zborowski's sister, Anna, married Baron Fontenoy.

We will not go into the fact that even before the arrival of Kościuszko and Pułaski[8] (therefore, before 1777) a chronicle mentions the Poles settled in Virginia. This emigration, however, comprised only individuals who so disappeared into the mass of local nationalities that today it is difficult to find any trace of them.

We will, however, mention here the political emigration of individuals from the end of the eighteenth century, which gave us the heroic memory and contributions of Kościuszko, Pułaski, and Niemcewicz. Tadeusz Kościuszko, descendant of an ancient Lithuanian noble family bearing the Roch coat-of-arms, was born in 1746 in the village of Mereczowszczyzna, parish of Kosów. In 1769 he was sent abroad at government cost to improve himself in the art of war. He returned to Poland in 1774 as a captain of the artillery. After becoming acquainted with [Benjamin] Franklin in France in 1777, Kościuszko left for America where he enlisted as a volunteer, stating that he wanted to fight for American independence. "Of what use are you?" asked his commander. "Try me! See what I am capable of," Kościuszko laconically replied. During the American Revolution, he so distinguished himself by his bravery and talent, especially at Bemis Heights, Yorktown, and the siege of New York City, that, having acquired [George] Washington's respect, he was nominated adjutant and received the rank of colonel of engineers. Following the conclusion of the War of

Independence in 1783, having been awarded the rank of brigadier general, the Order of the Cincinnati, [American] citizenship, a substantial yearly income and landed estates, Kościuszko returned to Poland where his heroic deeds are known. After the fall of Poland and its final partition, Kościuszko and Niemcewicz once more sailed to America, in 1796. However, Kościuszko did not remain here, but returned to his native country and died in 1817 in Soleure, Switzerland. The Americans erected a monument in his honor and memory at West Point, while the Poles in America dedicated magnificent monuments to Kościuszko in 1904 in Chicago, Milwaukee, and Cleveland.

Kościuszko transferred his entire property in the United States to redeem the Blacks. The following is the pertinent last will of Kościuszko:

I, Thaddeus Kościuszko, being just in my departure from America, do hereby declare and direct that should I make no other testamentary disposition of my property in the United States, I hereby authorize my friend Thomas Jefferson to employ the whole thereof in purchasing Negroes from among his own or any others and giving them Liberty in my name, in giving them an education in trades or otherwise, and in having them instructed for their new condition in the duties of morality which may make them good neighbors, good fathers or mothers, husbands, or wives and in their duties as citizens teaching them to be defenders of their Liberty and their Country and of the good order of society and in whatsoever may make them happy and useful, and I make the said Thomas Jefferson my executor of this.   T. Kościuszko, May 5, 1798.[9]

Count Pułaski, Kościuszko's contemporary, born in 1747, arrived in Philadelphia in 1777 and enlisted as a volunteer. Congress nominated him brigadier general and commander of United States Army dragoons. Pułaski is, therefore, the first cavalry general in the history of the American military service. He took part in many skirmishes and battles, and on October 9, 1779, he fell at the siege of Savannah, pierced by a bullet. Thanks to Lafayette a monument later was erected to his memory in Savannah.

Julian Ursyn Niemcewicz,[10] a descendant of well-to-do Lithuanian nobility, was born in 1758 and came to America with Kościuszko in 1796. He struck up various friendships with [Thomas] Jefferson, later president of the United States, and with others. Niemcewicz visited various parts of the country and, following Kościuszko's departure to France, settled permanently in Elizabethtown [New Jersey], where he lived on meager funds.

In *Century Magazine* of February 1902, we find an interesting article, that also serves as an historical document of the Polish poet, Niemcewicz.

The article, entitled "A Visit to Mt. Vernon a Century Ago," refers to Niemcewicz's visit to Washington's Virginia home. The preface to the article was written by Washington C. Ford, and the historical material was furnished by Mr. W. M. Kozłowski. Also included is a portrait of Niemcewicz and a facsimile of his manuscript. It is worth citing a few details from this article. The reader learns, for example, that when Kościuszko left America for the second time to go to Europe where the famous Polish legions were then being formed,[11] Niemcewicz had to pretend that Kościuszko had not left. The purpose of this was so that Kościuszko would not be stopped in his travel on the ocean en route to France by that country's enemies. Niemcewicz hid the truth and wrote about this to Jefferson, who was Kościuszko's sincere friend. He wrote that publicly he must pretend that he was travelling after Kościuszko to the southern parts of the United States, although Kościuszko was already at sea. He could tell Jefferson the truth, although in his letter to him Niemcewicz was careful not to mention Kościuszko's name and only indicated the person [in question] using the initials G. K. [General Kościuszko]. A passage in a letter to Jefferson proves that Niemcewicz carried out his role very well. It states that some people supposed that Niemcewicz was travelling south after Kościuszko, while others supposed that he had quarreled with him, and still others thought that Jefferson had hidden Kościuszko at Monticello.

Niemcewicz actually went south and stayed in Georgetown at the home of Mr. Law. There, in May 1798, he met with Washington who was visiting relatives. Washington asked him about Kościuszko and Niemcewicz admitted that he had lied about his travels. Washington invited Niemcewicz to his home and the poet, together with Mr. Law and his family, arrived at Mount Vernon on June 2, 1798. Niemcewicz remained there until June 14, and the chronicle of his stay with Washington, which Mr. Kozłowski found in a library in Poland, is presently being carried in *Century Magazine*. It is interesting, but too lengthy to summarize here. It is enough to say that Niemcewicz was very pleased with the visit and that he received gifts from Mrs. Washington and her daughter.

Mr. Ford for his part verified that the visit had actually taken place and mentions that portion of Washington's diary in which he recorded daily notes about the weather and visits. Washington noted the following under the date of June 2, 1798: "Mr. Law and a Polish gentleman, an associate of General Kosciaski, arrived here for dinner."

And under the date of the fourteenth: "Mr. Law, Mrs. Law, and Mr. Niemcewitz (that Polish gentleman) left after breakfast."

In 1800, Niemcewicz married a wealthy widow, Mrs. Livingston Kean, and began life as an American squire. In addition, it seemed that reception of United States citizenship in 1804 would tie him forever to the New World. But it happened otherwise. After the formation of the Grand Duchy of Warsaw, Niemcewicz returned to his native country, parting for good with his American wife. He wrote much and died in 1841. These were the outsanding Polish political figures who immigrated to America at the end of the eighteenth century.

The first Polish-speaking priest in North America was Rev. Prince Demetrius [Dimitry] Augustine Galliczin,[12] around whom grouped the Polish Jesuits. These were the Byelorussian Fathers active in America from the beginning of the nineteenth century. As far as existing historical research shows, Rev. Galliczin was also the first Polish priest to be ordained not in Europe, but here on American soil (1795). His associate, Rev. Brozyusz, was a Czech.

In the *Pamiętnik* [Memoir] of Rev. Władisław Sebastyański, SJ,[13] a famous missionary working in America for twelve years from 1884 to 1896, we read that Prince Galliczin came to America in 1792 at the young age of twenty-two as a tourist, bringing from his father letters of introduction to Jefferson and Washington. An ardent Catholic, the young prince immediately became acquainted with Bishop Carroll in Baltimore and took up residence at his home. From there he wrote sincere letters to his mother, Countess Amalia of Schmettau, a saintly Catholic, in which he signed his name as John Smith. On March 16, 1795, Prince Galliczin was ordained a priest.

For the larger group of Poles, Czechs, and Slavs, Bishop Carroll established a parish, "Bohemia Manor," in Cecil County, Maryland, where a church was built under the name of St. Francis Xavier. As the *Pamiętnik* notes, Rev. Galliczin kept the Polish order and system in the church, since he despised the Anglican one, the so-called "pew system and trustee system."

The emigration at that time in Cecil County, Maryland, comprised the more notable circle of political (Pułaski's and Kościuszko's) friends and comrades-in-arms and the names of Poles from Kościuszko's time can be found in Rev. Galliczin's books and in the church ledgers. Some of these were heroes from Dąbrowski's Legions that Napoleon I sent to Santo

Domingo in 1801 and 1802 under the threat of the gun. Some reached the United States, but another part was decimated by fever. Władisław Jabłonowski, the leader of the expedition, himself fell victim to it and only a handful returned to Europe to join the old cavalry legions in the homeland.[14]

For Bishop Carroll, a great comfort was the handful of Poles, Kazimierz Pułaski's former comrades. Kościuszko and his comrades also belonged to the same circle of the Bishop of Baltimore's cordial friends. Rev. John Carroll (1736-1815), first bishop of the United States, was an ardent Jesuit and the superior of the Jesuit mission in North America prior to the order's dissolution.[15] Although he later became a bishop, he adhered to the rules of Saint Ignatius and loved the Jesuits as brothers until his death. The young Prince Galliczin would often cheer him up with tales of the Jesuits of White Russia. When Kościuszko returned from Poland to America in 1797, he was greeted by Bishop Carroll and Prince Galliczin, already a priest, as well as by Washington and Jefferson. A hero of two continents, Kościuszko was a friend of the Jesuits. His cousin, Rev. Kazimierz Kościuszko, born in 1727 and nineteen years his senior, was a Jesuit (College in Krasnysław) and a missionary in the Diocese of Chełm in Podlasie.

Having obtained certain information about the Jesuits from Rev. Galliczin, Bishop Carroll began to beg the superiors Rev. Lenkiewicz, Rev. Kareu, and the order's General, Gruber, for missionaries from White Russia. As a result, Revs. Korsak, Eppinette, Britt, Henry, Malave (around 1808), and later Revs. Grivel and Rantzau, were sent to America from Połock. From this group, Rev. Korsak (a Pole born on June 7, 1773, in Połock) entered the Jesuit novitiate in Pusza on August 28, 1788. He did not stay long in America because we see him in England in 1810 where he died in Stonyhurst on February 17, 1846. Later on, still other Jesuit Fathers left White Russia for America where Bishop Carroll greeted them with open arms.

Besides the above-mentioned, five more Byelorussian Fathers left for America from the Province of Galicia after the order's dissolution. Rev. William Feiner, born in Połock on December 27, 1792, entered the novitiate in 1808 and died in 1829 in Georgetown, near Washington, D.C., where in 1789 the Jesuits had established Georgetown University with its medical department. Rev. Bonifacy Krukowski, born August 4, 1777 in Dyneburg, entered the order in 1797, served as a missionary to Poles and Lithuanians in Riga, and worked in America from 1820 until his death on

October 11, 1837; he is buried in Philadelphia, Pennsylvania. Rev. Franciszek Dzierożyński, born in Orsza on January 3, 1779, entered the order in 1794, was a professor of dogmatic theology and consultant of the province in Połock, and from 1821 to 1848 was a missionary and the superior of the Jesuit mission in North America. He was chosen to be a bishop, but he excused himself pleading a monastic vow. He died in 1850 in Frederick, Maryland. Provincial and diocesan synods often mentioned his name. Rev. John Menet was born in 1793 and died in Quebec, Canada, in 1869. Rev. Philip Beatrix Sacki [Jacchi] was born in Moscow in 1791 and died in 1850 in Worcester, Massachusetts, where in the pre-dissolution Council of the Holy Cross, the Jesuits founded the famous boarding school which still exists.[16]

And so, at the beginning of the nineteenth century, the Polish Jesuit Fathers from White Russia had dewed the Eastern states with their sweat and blessed them with their graves. The work of these Jesuits in North America in the first half of that century is a part of church history. They have left us little memorabilia. From catalogues and diaries of old councils and residences it is possible to gather a few little mementos. Some stories have remained a part of tradition, for example, that Rev. Dzierożyński was to have been made bishop, but declined on the basis of his monastic calling and kept himself away from the center of things.

At the beginning of the nineteenth century, especially after 1831, we see Polish immigrants to America becoming somewhat more numerous. From what we had heard from older Polish immigrants, an entire group of Poles, refugees of the November Insurrection of 1830 were sent from England to America after 1831.[17] The people from this era, at least those remembered by the Polish emigration, were brave, respectable, and highly intelligent individuals. The venerable Dr. Kałussowski from Washington belonged to this era.[18] Likewise, there was the famous translator of Polish poets into English, Paweł Sobolewski;[19] Colonel Bielewski [Bielawski] from San Francisco;[20] and finally in Santiago, the capital of Chile, Ignacy Domejko [Domeyko],[21] an illustrious geologist and mineralogist, and Adam Mickiewicz's dear companion. Born in the District of Grodno in 1802, Domejko took an active part in the November Insurrection, later immigrating to France where he became a proficient chemist and mineralogist. Directors of a French college sent him to Chile where he established a chemical laboratory in Conquimbo and began lectures in chemistry and mineralogy which were considered irresistible. In Domejko's honor, one of the minerals he discovered was named "domeyt." He reported on his expeditions into the Cordilleras in the *Annales des Mineurs*. As a result of these expeditions, he was placed in charge of the physics, mineralogy, and chemistry department at the University of Santiago and finally was made rector of that university. He wrote in Spanish and French; while *Araukania* (1860) was in Polish. He died in Santiago in 1889. To this émigré era also belongs Rev. Antoni Rossadowski,[22] a Conventual Franciscan from Wilno, a former army chaplain in 1830, and prior to this a captain in the Polish army. "After the failure of the uprising," we read in Buffalo's *Polak w Ameryce* [The Pole in America], 1887, "very many insurgents entered Austrian territory where they were arrested and sent by that same government from Trieste to the United States of America. Among them were two Polish priests, Conventual Franciscans from Wilno: the previously-mentioned Rev. Antoni Rossadowski and one other. Many insurgents arriving at the port of New York were sent by the United States government to fight the Seminole Indians in Florida.[23] This bloody fight lasted a long time. The Seminoles were conquered and taken from Florida to Mexico to the banks of the Rio Grande River near the Texas border. Following these Indian wars many of the Polish insurgents began longing for their homeland and returned to the Old Country.[24] Some went to France, others to England. Rev. Antoni Rossadowski remained in London, and the other chaplain (whose name I cannot recall) went to Ireland where he died."

After 1848 a new wave of political exiles arrived in America. From this era we have Professor Boeck,[25] as well as Director Tyssowski,[26] who died in Washington.

The old Jesuits from White Russia were followed by their younger brothers from the province of Galicia. Rev. Gaspar Matoga,[27] born in Siepraw in Galicia on December 30, 1823, joined the order in Stara Wieś in 1839. In 1848 he left for America and here, after four years of higher education at St. John's College in New York from 1849 to 1852, was ordained a priest and worked apostolically only among Poles. A dear, respectable person, he quickly became a victim of his vocation. He died in Guelph in the Diocese of Hamilton, Ontario, Canada, on August 21, 1856. Guelph is a mission station where the Jesuits zealously work to this day.

Rev. Antoni Lenz,[28] my Greek professor, born in Rojaw, Bohemia, on August 4, 1823, joined the order in Stara Wieś in 1843. As a seminarian he left for America and from 1852, he was a professor at a Jesuit college in New Orleans, Louisiana. His Galician superiors forgot about him and many years passed before he was ordained a priest. He was quite short in stature, but he was a very learned professor, especially in Greek. A huge Greek dictionary was always open on his table, which he constantly and lovingly read and reread as if it were a novel, never getting bored with it. Rev. Lenz died in Chrów, Galicia, on December 22, 1888.

Rev. Ignacy Peukert[29] was born in 1821 in Prjedemost and died in 1878 in Florissant, Missouri. In May, 1855, Rev. Edward Martynowicz arrived in Indiana. He was called "Father Martin" and "The Father of the St. Vincent's Parochial School System." He built the first brick rectory in St. Vincent's, Indiana. From there he moved to Shelby County, but it is not known what later happened to him.[30]

Finally, the year 1863, like previous and subsequent ones, flung upon our American shores entire masses of political castaways.[31] This was an emigration of select intelligentsia, who came as individuals. There was still no mass peasant emigration on a large scale; however, the peasant emigration did already exist on a small scale. It began sporadically immediately following the second half of the nineteenth century. Around 1855 the first Polish colonies, with Polish names such as "Panna Marya" and "Częstochowa," appeared in Texas. To the north in the state of Michigan, Parisville (1857) appeared almost simultaneously near Detroit and in Wisconsin the nucleus of a settlement called "Polonia" was established in 1855. A Polish parish was founded in Milwaukee in eastern Wisconsin (1862) as well as in Northeim (1868); while in western Wisconsin, in Pine Creek near the Mississippi River, the Poles organized themselves into a parish in 1864. In that same year in Chicago, the Polish Society of St. Stanislaus Kostka was formed—the nucleus of what became the largest Polish parish in America. Active among this peasant emigration were Polish Franciscans (Rev. Moczygęba from 1854), Jesuits (Rev. Matauszek from 1864, Rev. Szulak from 1865), Resurrectionists (Revs. Bakanowski, Barzyński, Żwiardowski from 1866), and others about whose missionary activities we will speak of in greater detail in Part II.

Nevertheless, until 1870 all of these were sporadic settlements, not colonies in a true sense. Rather, they were nuclei of future Polish settlements, already composed of peasant folk but still made up of only a few individuals. These were infant settlements still in need of many years of historical development.

A mass peasant emigration on a large scale began only around 1870, and especially after the Franco-Prussian war that year. Substantial Polish settlements then were established and grew quickly, especially in Chicago, Milwaukee, Detroit, Buffalo, and a few places in Pennsylvania. In the interior of Wisconsin the town of Stevens Point was virtually surrounded by Polish farmers and became a Polish marketplace. In 1870, *Orzeł Biały* [The White Eagle] the first popular [Polonian] newspaper, began publication in the Polish colonies in Franklin County, near St. Louis. In New York and vicinity, the immigration, thus far composed of the intelligentsia, became supplemented after 1870 by uneducated but persevering, hard-working, and energetic people.

Chapter 3

The Gradual Growth and
Historical Development of Polish Settlements,
Sketched in Their General Outlines

The origin of colonization—The Pioneers—The number of settlements,
churches, and priests—Before 1870—The fight between Nebraska and
Arkansas for a "New Poland"—Statistics for 1876—How many of us are
there?

In exile the Polish people found their first succor and their first organizational ties in their churches.[1] The names of those pioneer priests, active
even before 1870, under whose leadership the Polish immigrants in America established their first parishes and built their churches are as follows:
Rev. Leopold Moczygęba, patriarch of the Polish American clergy, who
was first active in Texas beginning in 1854; Rev. Jan Polak in Polonia,
Wisconsin (1855); Rev. Piotr Kluk in Parisville, Michigan (1857); Rev.
Antoni Rossadowski in Texas (1857); Rev. Julian Przysiecki in Texas
(from 1860 to 1863, when he fell off a horse and died); Rev. Bonawentura
Buczyński in Milwaukee, Wisconsin (1863); Revs. Franciszek Breitkopf,
Jan Wołłowski and Szymon Wieczorek in Michigan; Revs. Adolph
Bakanowski, Wincenty Barzyński, Felix Żwiardowski (from 1866); Rev.
Adolph Śnigurski in Texas; Rev. Matauszek, a Jesuit, in St. Louis, Mis-
souri (from 1864); Rev. Szulak, a Jesuit, and Rev. Juszkiewicz in Chicago
(from 1866); Rev. T. Węglikowski and Rev. Jaster in Milwaukee (1867).
The following arrived in Texas with Rev. Wincenty Barzyński in 1866:
Revs. Józef Bitkowski, Klemens Kucharczyk, and Felix Orzechowski;
Revs. Teophil Bralewski and Frydrychowicz arrived in Texas in 1868.[2]
Such is the list—very likely incomplete—of the Polish clergy active
before 1870 at the very outlet of our immigration. There were approximately twenty-five of them. There were even fewer organized parishes.

Due to the massive immigration of peasant folk, Polish settlements in America grew rapidly in number and strength after 1870, and parishes multiplied everywhere like mushrooms after a rain storm. While in 1870 there were only about ten small Polish parishes and the number of Polish settlers throughout the entire United States amounted to no more than 50,000 souls. Five years later—in 1875—as attested to by the annual volumes of *Gazeta Polska* [The Polish Gazette] and *Gazeta Polska Katolicka* [The Polish Catholic Gazette], there were in Chicago alone over 20,000 Poles and in the entire United States there already were 200,000 of them. Furthermore, the above-mentioned volumes for 1875 list the total number of Polish settlements at 300, with close to fifty constructed churches and organized parishes.

But here are the detailed statistics of Polish colonies found in old clippings of the *Gazeta Polska Katolicka* (Chicago) covered with a quarter-century layer of dust. We read under the date of September 23, 1875, as follows:

We have stable and genuine colonies in Chicago, Chester, Lemont, and Radom (Illinois); Detroit, Grand Rapids, Bay City, Calumet, La Salle, Bronson, Cooper Harbor, Parisville, Wyandotte, Trenton, Manistee, and Hancock (Michigan); Milwaukee, Steven's Point, Polonia, Pine Creek, Arcadia, Northeim, Beaver Dam, Green Bay, Berlin, Manitowoc, and Two Rivers (Wisconsin); Pittsburgh, Shamokin, Philadelphia, Mt. Carmel, Nanticoke, Lykens, Gilberton, Shenandoah, Excelsior, Scranton, Blossburg, Antrium, Parson Station, and Mahoney City (Pennsylvania); Kraków, Clover Bottom, and St. Joseph (Missouri); South Bend (Indiana); Buffalo, Dunkirk, Williamsburgh, Haverstraw, Albany, Utica, and Syracuse (New York); San Francisco (California); Winona, St. Paul, Minneapolis, Perham, Delano, and Minnesota Lake (Minnesota); Toledo (Ohio); Newark, Jersey City, Trenton, Camden, Orange Valley, and Newton (New Jersey); Panna Maria, Martinez, St. Hedwig, San Antonio, Bandera, Yorktown, Colleto, and Meyersville (Texas); Louisville (Kentucky); New Orleans (Louisiana); Hartford and New London (Connecticut); and Renfrew and Hopefield in West Canada. In addition, there are in America 154 Polish colonies where only a few families reside, and they will soon grow and expand to such an extent that they will become a part of the first permanent local colonies. We have omitted from this listing many more—at least fifty Polish colonies that are worth mentioning—since we did not have the time or the occasion to acquaint ourselves with them. In the above-mentioned colonies (as the *Gazeta Polska Katolicka* further states in 1875) the Poles own their own land, houses, livestock, schools, churches or chapels, have their own clergy, and they support two Polish newspapers. They collectively number at least 200,000 people.

We read further in the *Gazeta Polska Katolicka* for 1875:

Let us now begin a count of established parishes and Polish churches built in the United States of North America: in Chicago, 3 churches; Milwaukee, 2; Radom, 1; San Antonio, 1; Panna Maria, 1; Martinez, 1; Yorktown, 1; Colleta, 1; Bandera, 1; Huntsville, 1; in Polish Settlement, Dakota, 1; St. Paul, 1; Winona, 1; Manitowoc, 1; Northeim, 1; Berlin, 1; Polonia, 1; North Creek and Elk Creek, 2; Arcadia, 1; Pine Creek, 1; Salem Crossing, 1; Cincinnati, 1; one being built in Pittsburgh; Blossburg, 1; Shamokin, 1; one being built in Nanticoke; one half-Polish and half-Irish in Mount Carmel; one mixed in Bronson; a chapel in Cleveland; Parisville, 1; Bay City, 1; Detroit, 1; Buffalo, 1; Dunkirk, 1; South Bend, 1; a chapel in St. Louis, and one to be built in Grand Rapids.

These are the statistics which were published in 1875 in *Gazeta Polska Katolicka* under the editorship of Jan Barzyński.

The serious proportions assumed by the immigration movement between 1870 and 1875 provoked alarm in the Old Country press, whereas here in America it resulted in a massive settlement on farms. In the big cities there was already a lack of work and wages, due to an excessive and rapid influx of immigrants, so they began to seek a livelihood in the farm-lands. Many dreamed at that time of gathering the Poles in one state and thereby establishing a "New Poland," while at the same time they immediately began quarreling about which state would be more appropriate: Arkansas or Nebraska. This quarrel over Nebraska and Arkansas even left an echo in the letters of the famous Sienkiewicz who, although he stubbornly kept silent about the existence of Poles in America, does in fact mention this quarrel in his *Listy z Ameryki* [Letters from America].[3]

Between 1870 and 1875 (writes Henryk Sienkiewicz) much was heard about the numerous, but serious peasant immigration to America from the regions of Galicia and Poznań. After its arrival, this peasant and, therefore, agricultural population often endured great poverty in the cities. Hence, the tendency arose to settle on farms. This tendency manifested itself with particular strength around 1875. That is the time when negotiations were conducted to buy from the railroads several thousand acres in Arkansas, between the Arkansas and Mississippi Rivers. This wooded land was suitable for raising various grains and cotton, and at that time was almost fifty percent uninhabited. However, another faction—and rather led by the clergy—wished to lead its flock to the steppe-like, unwooded pasture lands of Nebraska. Both of these factions waged an obstinate battle in which both sides were unscrupulous in their means, as well as in their statements.

Thus, according to Henryk Sienkiewicz, who stayed in America until 1876, Nebraska "beat" Arkansas.[4]

Polish immigration to America constantly grew and became more powerful. By 1877, as we are convinced by the old, moldy *Kalendarz* for that

year, in addition to the above-mentioned settlements we also find: Cottage
Hill, Mullberry, Bluff, Flatonia, and Plantersville in Texas; West Brim-
field, Lanesville, Jeffersonville in Indiana; Cedar Rapids, Michigan;
Faribault, Minnesota; Northport, Wisconsin; Fort Wayne and Teresa, Indi-
ana, Brooklyn, New York; and Locust Grove, Pennsylvania. To the
above-mentioned list of Polish clergy active in the Polish American vine-
yard of the Lord before 1877, the same *Kalendarz* includes the following:
Revs. Józef Barzyński, Adalbert Mielcuszny and Dominic Majer in
Chicago; Revs. Franciszek Xavier Kralczyński, Hyacinth Gulski, Hipolite
Górski and Jan Rodowicz in Milwaukee; Rev. Floryan Klonowski in
Shamokin, Pennsylvania; Rev. Antoni Klawiter in Pittsburgh; Rev. Jan
Pitass in Buffalo; Rev. Józef Musielewicz in Parisville, Michigan; Rev.
Józef Dąbrowski in Detroit; Rev. Zaręczny in Berea, Ohio; Rev.
Dąbrowski in Polonia, Wisconsin; Rev. J. Wałuń in Stevens Point, Wis-
consin; Rev. Teodor Gieryk in Berlin, Wisconsin; Rev. Wołłowski in
Radom, Illinois; Rev. Karol Lanc in Dunkirk, New York; Rev. Józef
Niedzielski in Brooklyn, New York; Rev. Klimecki in North Creek, Wis-
consin; Rev. Rademacher in Beaver Dam, Wisconsin; Rev. Rademacher
in Fort Wayne and Teresa, Indiana; Rev. A. Rosochowicz in Northport,
Wisconsin; Rev. J. Zawitowski in Oshkosh, Wisconsin; Rev. J. Czar-
nowski in Princeton, Wisconsin; Rev. Bratkiewicz in La Salle, Illinois;
Rev. Damazy Socha in Delano, Minnesota; Rev. Byzewski in Winona,
Minnesota; Rev. Strupiński in Shenandoah, Pennsylvania; Rev. Lenar-
kiewicz in Philadelphia; Rev. Wincenty Lewandowski in Toledo; Rev.
Kandyd Kozłowski in Cincinnati; Rev. F. Schmelar, a Czech, in Cedar
Rapids, Michigan; Rev. Szklorzyk in Bay City, Michigan; Rev. Machdz-
icki in Otis, Indiana; Rev. K. Winsierski in West Brimfield, Illinois; Rev.
F. Fudziński in Lanesville, Indiana; Rev. A. Cichocki in Panna Maria,
Texas; Rev. A. Heinke in San Antonio, Texas; Rev. Rogoziński in Mull-
berry, Texas; Rev. F. Dąbrowski in Bluff, Texas; and Rev. F. Orzechowski in Planterville, Texas.[5]

Adding these priests (from 1870 to 1876) to the above list from 1870,
we obtain an approximate figure of eighty Polish clergy whose activities
before 1877 have been chronicled.

In the following years the influx of the Polish population into America
did not by any means decrease, since twelve years later—in 1889—as the
chronicles reveal, the number of Polish priests had doubled, the number of
Polish churches tripled and the general number of Poles in America

quadrupled. This is what the German-Catholic newspaper *Der Califor-nische Volksfreud* [California People's Friend], which cannot be suspected of exaggeration in this matter, writes in issue number 28, dated June 8, 1889:

Concerning the Poles in North America, from what can be concluded from church books, we count 800,000 in the United States. They have 132 churches and 126 priests. The state of Wisconsin has the most Poles; however, the greatest local number is in Chicago. Polish churches in Chicago, Detroit, Buffalo, Cleveland, and Milwaukee are considered the most beautiful in the country. There are 122 Polish parish schools which are almost all under the administration of Polish nuns; namely, the Felician Sisters and the Sisters of Notre Dame. The Polish theological seminary is in Detroit, Michigan. Since the Poles are, for the most part, persistent workers, obliging and conscientious entrepreneurs ("businessmen"),[6] most of them have already accumulated for themselves a considerable fortune and enjoy a good reputation and popularity with their fellow citizens in America.

In the next twelve-year period (1889 to 1901) the number of Polish churches tripled and the number of Polish clergy also tripled, while the general number of Polish immigrants increased more than twofold.

The immigration movement has not ceased by any means. It peaked in 1904, when the number of immigrants reached one million. In none of the previous years was there such an increase!

The immigration statistics for 1900 show that in that year 304,148 men and 144,424 women permanently moved to the United States from Europe. This figure included 54,624 children under fourteen and 23,566 people older than forty-five. There were 32,797 Poles; 1,165 Russians; 12,515 Finns; 37,011 Polish Jews; 2,161 Lithuanians and Estonians; 7,987 Ruthenians, and 13,295 Germans.[7] We are omitting other nationalities because we have quoted the above figures only so that it would be easy for everyone to judge that the relatively large number of Polish, Finnish, and Jewish immigrants corresponds to the extremely difficult situation of these nationalities in Europe. The politics of oppression and denationalization forced many to leave their countries and take their national fortune with them. Here we must emphasize the direct impoverishment of the home-land caused by immigration. For a few years now there has existed in the United States a law whereby an immigrant must be a completely healthy person, who should at least know how to read and write in his own lan-guage, and should possess at least thirty dollars. Whoever does not meet these conditions must immediately return to the ship on which he arrived; however, if he does not have the thirty dollars, and still finds a permanent job while in port, he is allowed to stay. And so, in 1900, the 13,295 Germans brought with them $847,062; the immigrants from the three Scandinavian countries had $548,969 combined; Jews had $527,163; Italians $500,037; Poles $466,939; and Ruthenians $29,802. In 1900 all the immigrants combined brought $6,271,821 from Europe to the United States.

The statistics also divide immigrants according to their occupations. From this it can be seen that many intelligentsia immigrated from Western [European] countries, while almost all immigrants from Italy and the Slavic lands are farmers and workers. Thus, doctors, engineers, lawyers, teachers, artists, musicians, clergy, and so on, numbered 1,096 Germans, 450 French, 351 English, 826 Italians, 253 Jews, 23 Poles, 18 Spanish, 6 Slovaks, and 2 Ruthenians. Most tradesmen were Jews, namely 21,047; they all registered as tailors, haberdashers, and hairdressers. There were 13,862 Italian tradesmen (stone cutters, bricklayers, grinders). German tradesmen usually registered as factory handymen and they numbered 4,660. Poles, registering as carpenters, cabinet-makers, shoemakers, and bricklayers, numbered 1,865. Immediately after them were the Japanese (1,798), Croatians (993), Russians (147) and finally Ruthenians (33).[8]

Immigrants from Western European nations usually settled in the cities; the Slavs made their way to farms and after a while purchased them.

Statistical data finally shows that, as a rule, the second generation of immigrants accepted the local language and customs.

According to our calculations, at the beginning of the twentieth century (1901) within the boundaries of the United States of North America there were about 550 Polish clergy, 520 Polish churches, and 800 Polish settlements.

It is possible that these calculations are inaccurate and incorrect. But, after all, our whole point is to accurately know how many of us there are—the point is not our infallibility. We could have made a mistake. And we will be grateful to anyone who will show us how we have erred.[9] So, to give everyone a chance to find mistakes in our calculations, we will specify here how many Polish souls we counted for each settlement. Therefore, let the gracious reader carefully check the statistical list given below and if he notices that in this list we have omitted any Polish settlement, or have counted too many or too few Poles somewhere, let him immediately send a correction or a supplement, and we will take it into consideration in the book edition of our *Historya*.[10]

How many of us are there in America, or at least here in the United

States? Have we counted ourselves? No. We are content with generalities. As with almost everything, we say that we Poles number one million, one and one-half million, then two million. Some even allege that there are more, but no one actually knows how many. But, after all, an accurate knowledge of numerical strength is very important and necessary to form a certain and unshakable sense of one's own strength of numbers. Vague generalities regarding our number only lead to uncertainty and indecision in our public activities within [this] society, while an accurate knowledge of the number of our compatriots would give us assertiveness and determination. I say "accuracy" in a relative sense, which means that even if we have made a mistake of a few or even several thousand Poles, still this knowledge will be relatively accurate. But if we made a mistake of hundreds of thousands or a million or a half-million—that is no joke. Such a grave mistake would have disastrous consequences for us in a number of public matters. To count too few of us would be disastrous; but also to count too many of us would not be any less damaging. For in both cases we would be under delusion, on the one side a pessimistic and on the other side an optimistic illusion. And to succumb to any kind of illusion is an extremely dangerous thing, especially in public life. Only truth and reality, true and real figures, can give us certainty in activities, a sense of our power, and awareness of numerical strength. Figures are stubborn facts.

Chapter 4

Statistics on Polish Settlements in the United States at the Beginning of the Twentieth Century

To begin this chapter we will first present the official statistics on Poles compiled in the United States census of 1900, and then our own obtained through private sources. It should be especially noted that the official census counted as Poles only considers those born in the Old Country, and not those born in America. Moreover, even among those who arrived from the Old Country the census takers counted as Poles only those who, when asked "Where were you born?" answered very clearly "in Poland." Those who did not so answer were not registered as Poles. Due to these two considerations, it is safe to say that the official census of 1900 included only one-fifth of the general Polish population in the United States; in other words, to obtain an accurate estimate of the number of Poles in America, it is necessary to multiply the census figure by five.[1] There are important reasons for doing this. It can reasonably be supposed that at least two-fifths of the Poles, when asked "Where were you born?" answered [by giving the name of the partitioning country]: "in Germany" (Prussia), or "Austrian Galicia," or "in Russia." Those who did so were counted into the number of Germans, Austrians, or Russians and comprise at least two-fifths of the Poles in America. Another two-fifths, if not more, were born in America and counted by census officials as Americans rather than Poles.[2]

Consequently, there is reason to believe that to obtain a true estimate of all Poles living within the borders of the United States, the official census figures should be multiplied by at least five. The list of the Polish population in the United States acquired in this way is as follows:

	Official Census 1900	Estimated True Number of Poles		Official Census 1900	Estimated True Number of Poles
Arkansas	315	1,575	Alabama	133	665
Illinois	67,949	339,745	Connecticut	10,698	53,490
Indian Territory	199	995	Delaware	1,526	7,630
Iowa	751	3,755	District of		
Kansas	691	3,455	Columbia	132	660
Louisiana	168	840	Florida	22	110
Minnesota	11,361	56,805	Georgia	169	845
Missouri	3,680	18,400	Indiana	6,067	30,335
Nebraska	3,094	15,470	Kentucky	668	3,340
North Dakota	1,054	5,270	Maine	443	2,215
Oklahoma	156	780	Maryland	3,683	18,415
South Dakota	472	2,360	Massachusetts	21,503	107,515
Texas	3,348	16,740	Michigan	28,366	141,830
Wisconsin	31,789	158,945	Mississippi	90	450
Total in			New Hampshire	864	4,320
"West"	*125,027*	*625,135*	New Jersey	14,357	71,785
			New York	66,745	333,725
Alaska	13	65	North Carolina	35	175
Arizona	22	110	Ohio	16,822	84,110
California	1,320	6,600	Pennsylvania	76,358	381,790
Colorado	620	3,100	Rhode Island	1,862	9,310
Hawaii	72	360	South Carolina	103	515
Idaho	46	230	Tennessee	322	1,610
Montana	213	1,065	Vermont	359	1,795
Nevada	25	125	Virginia	148	740
New Mexico	55	275	West Virginia	633	3,165
Oregon	313	1,565	*Total in*		
Utah	65	325	*"East"*	*253,108*	*1,260,540*
Washington	496	2,480			
Wyoming	79	395			
Total in the					
"Wild West"	*3,333*	*16,695*			

From the above figures we see that the general number of Poles who arrived from the Old Country, according to the official census of 1900, totaled 383,595. Multiplying this number by five yields an approximate figure of 1,902,370 Poles living in the United States.[3] Approximately the same result can be arrived at through the use of private sources. Yet, before we begin to present detailed figures we must stipulate that our figures do not indicate "parishioners"; rather, they denote in every case the total number of Poles living "within the borders of a parish." Many Poles belong to parishes of other nationalities, either due to a lack of space in the Polish church or for other reasons, while many others do not belong to any parish at all.

Settlements marked with a cross (+) have their own Polish churches and, for the most part, Polish schools. Here are our detailed statistics:

POLISH SETTLEMENTS IN ILLINOIS

A. *In the Archdiocese of Chicago*

Blue Island	1,000	Downers Grove	500
Braidwood	500	Elmhurst+	300
Chicago+		Hegewish	1,000
Avondale+	1,500	Hyman	800
Bridgeport+	10,000	Joliet+	6,000
Cragin+	1,000	Kankakee+	600
Hawthorne+	1,000	Kensington+	1,500
Holy Trinity+	15,000	Lemont+	5,000
Independent+	10,000	Maywood	1,000
St. Adalbert+	15,000	North Chicago+	1,000
St. Ann+	5,000	Poznan+	300
St. Casimir+	4,000	Pullman+	1,000
St. Hedwig+	10,000	Sobieski (Hammond)+	1,500
St. John Kanty+	12,000	South Chicago+	
St. Josaphat+	7,500	Immaculate Conception+	15,000
St. Joseph+	7,500	St. Michael+	12,000
St. Mary+	4,000	Waukegan+	400
Sts. Peter and Paul+	1,000	Dispersed	40,000
St. Stanislaus+	45,000	*Total in Chicago and vicinity*	*238,900*
Chicago Heights+			

In 1903 the author of this *Historya* asked Mr. Carter H. Harrison, long-time mayor of Chicago, how many Poles there were in Chicago. Mr. Harrison testified in writing at that time that there were 250,000. The following is the relevant document, personally signed by the mayor and the city clerk and bearing the seal of the city of Chicago:

City of Chicago
John F. Smulski, City Attorney

I, Carter H. Harrison, Mayor of the City of Chicago, County of Cook and the State of Illinois, U.S.A., do hereby certify, that to the best of my knowledge, information and belief, there are now resident in said city if Chicago two hundred and fifty thousand (250,000) inhabitants of Polish nativity or origin.

Witness my hand and seal of said City of Chicago, this Fifteenth (15th) day of July, 1903.

Carter H. Harrison, Mayor
Attest: Fred. C. Bender, City Clerk

Since the church census of 1901 reports that the Archdiocese of Chicago includes 800,000 Catholics, one can conclude that nearly one in every three Chicago Catholics is a Pole. According to this same 1901 church census, which we will adhere to in presenting the following statistics, there are a total of 475 Catholic priests in the archdiocese of which 68 are Polish; thus, one out of every seven Catholic priests is Polish.[4]

B. In the Diocese of Peoria

Brimfield	500	Peru+	2,500
Calumet	300	Rutland+	1,000
Kewanee	300	Spring Valley+	1,200
La Salle+	5,000	Streator	400
Minonk+	1,250	Toluca+	1,000
Oglesby+	400	Wenona	500
Peoria	1,000	*Total*	*15,350*

There are 112,000 Catholics in the Diocese of Peoria, with one out of every seven being a Pole. There are a total of 170 Catholic priests in this diocese, of whom eight are Polish; thus, out of every twenty Catholic priests one is Polish.

C. In the Diocese of Alton

Granite City	600
Madison	
Quincy	500
Springfield	500
Venice	400
Total	*2,000*

There are no Polish churches [in the Diocese of Alton] and Polish priests are prohibited.

D. In the Diocese of Belleville

Ashley+		Mt. Vernon+	
Assumption+	100	Nashville+	
Bald Hill+		Pickneyville+	100
Centralia+	100	Poznan+	800
Chester+	500	Random+	4,000
Dubois+	2,000	Rice's+	100
DuQuoin+	100	Sheller+	600
Gostyn+	500	Tamaroa+	300
Kinmundy+		Todd's Mill+	100
Madison+		*Total*	*9,300*

According to the above statistics there are 56 Polish settlements in the state of Illinois, of which Chicago, known as the "American Warsaw," is home to as many Poles as the Polish cities of Lwów, Kraków, and Poznań combined. In Illinois there are 49 Polish churches, 84 Polish clergy, and a Polish population, counting those scattered among many settlements, of 300,000. There are 721 Catholic churches in Illinois; therefore, one out of every fifteen is Polish. Since there is a total of 904 Catholic priests in Illinois, one out of every eleven is Polish. Considering further that there is a total of 1,037,000 Catholics in Illinois, Poles number more than one in four of all Catholics. Moreover, considering that the general population of Illinois is 4,821,550, then one in every sixteen is a Pole. Finally, since Illinois includes 56,650 square miles, for every square mile in Illinois there is an average of almost six Poles.

POLISH SETTLEMENTS IN WISCONSIN

A. In the Archdiocese of Milwaukee

Beaver Dam+	1,500	Northeim+	700
Caledonia	100	Racine	500
Cudahy+	500	Ripon+	350
Fond du Lac	100	Sheboygan+[6]	500
Fox Lake	100	South Milwaukee+	1,000
Kenosha+[5]	450	Dispersed throughout	
Manitowac+	2,000	the settlements	7,000
Milwaukee+		*Total*	*75,800*
St. Casimir+	8,000		
St. Cyril+	6,000		
St. Hedwig+	7,000		
St. Hyacinth+	11,000		
St. Josaphat+	12,000		
St. Stanislaus+	10,000		
St. Vincent+	7,000		

Mr. David S. Rose, the long-time mayor of Milwaukee, gave evidence in writing in 1903 that according to his count there were 65,000 Poles living in Milwaukee. This document reads as follows:

David S. Rose, Mayor
Anthony Szczerbinski, Jr., Secretary
Milwaukee, June 1, 1903

I, David S. Rose, Mayor of the City of Milwaukee in the state of Wisconsin, United States of America do hereby certify that, to the best of my knowledge information and belief, there are now resident in said city Sixty-Five thousand inhabitants of Polish nativity or origin.

Witness my hand and seal of said city of Milwaukee this 1 day of June 1903.

David S. Rose, Mayor
Attest: Edwin Hinkel,
Deputy City Clerk

According to the church census of 1901 there are 245,000 Catholics in the Archdiocese of Milwaukee. Therefore, one out of every three Catholics is a Pole. There are 315 Catholic priests in the archdiocese, of whom 26 are Poles; thus, one in every twelve Catholic priests is Polish.[7]

B. In the Diocese of Green Bay

Alban+	500	Menasha+	1,800
Almond		Merrill	
Angelica		Neshkoro	
Antigo+	800	Oshkosh+	450
Bayley's Harbor+	300	Pelican Lake+	80
Belmont+	800	Pilot Knob+	200
Berlin		Pine Grove+	600
St. Michael+	1,550	Plainfield+	205
St. Stanislaus+	1,500	Plover+	500
Bevent (Pike Lake)+	800	Polonia+	6,000
Crivitz+	300	Portage	
Eaton (Poland)+	1,000	Pound+	750
Fancher+	800	Princeton+	1,700
Flintville+	300	Pulaski+	1,800
Friendship+	120	Rhinelander	300
Green Bay+	600	Shawano	
Hatley		Sobieski+	400
Hofa Park+	1,200	Spruce+	300
Hull (St. Casimir)+	1,200	Stevens Point+	5,000
Jennings (Kosciuszko)+	300	Three Lakes+	300
Kilbourn	100	Torun+	600
Krakow+	400	Two Rivers+	600
"Krok" (West Kewaunee)+	350	Wausau+	600
Laney		Wautoma	
Langlade and Price Co.+	400	Dispersed throughout	
Little Suamico+	200	other settlements	10,000
Marinette+	800	*Total*	*46,485*

In the Diocese of Green Bay there are 125,000 Catholics. Thus, one in every three Catholics is a Pole. Further, of 151 Catholic priests in this diocese, 35 are Polish;[8] therefore, one in every five is Polish.

C. In the Diocese of LaCrosse

Allouez	100	Mosinee	50
Ashland+	1,500	North Creek+	1,000
Athens	50	Phillips	200
Cassel+	500	Pine Creek+	1,400
Centralia (Grand Rapids)+	400	Poniatowski+	800
Chetek+	200	Poznan (Thorp)+	1,500
City Point	100	Rib Lake	100
Dorchester	75	Rudolph	80
Drummond		Shell Lake	100
Eau Claire	100	Sigel+	600
Edgar+	200	South Superior+	500
Fairchild+	300	Sparta	
Fall Creek		Strickland (Kopernik)+	400
Hurley+	600	Superior+	500
Independence+	2,000	Tomah	150
Junction+	800	Washburne	
LaCrosse+	1,000	West Superior+	1,500
Marathon City+	300	Weyerhauser+	
McMillan+	350	Dispersed throughout	
Medford	75	other settlements	8,000
Mill Creek+	800	*Total*	*26,330*

In the Diocese of LaCrosse there are 97,000 Catholics. One in every four Catholics is a Pole. Of 132 Catholic priests in this diocese, fifteen are Polish; thus, one in every nine priests is Polish.[9]

There are 101 Polish settlements in Wisconsin, 76 Polish churches, 76 Polish priests, and a Polish population of 150,000.[10] Considering that there are a total of 708 Catholic churches in Wisconsin,[11] then one out of every nine is Polish. Since there are 598 priests, one in eight is Polish.[12] Further, since there are 467,000 Catholics in Wisconsin, one out of every three Catholics is a Pole. Moreover, since the population of the state is 2,068,963, thus one in every thirteen inhabitants in a Pole.[13] Finally, since Wisconsin occupies 56,040 square miles, there are three Poles per square mile.

POLISH SETTLEMENTS IN MINNESOTA

A. In the Archdiocese of St. Paul

Delano+	1,500	Silver Lake+	2,000
Edison+	500	Taunton+	500
Fairibault+	1,000	Waverly+	300
Glencoe+	500	Wilno+	2,500
Hasting	300	[ ]	500
Minneapolis+	3,000	Dispersed throughout	
Mt. Rose	300	other settlements	5,000
St. Paul, Adalbert+	4,000	Total	24,900
St. Paul, Casimir+	3,000		

In the Archdiocese of St. Paul there are 220,000 Catholics with one out of every nine Catholics being a Pole. Of 228 Catholic priests in this diocese, six, or one out of every 38, are Polish.

B. In the Diocese of Winona

Claremont	400	Owatonna+	600
East Chain Lake	500	Wells+	1,000
Hayward+	500	Winona+	10,000
Jackson+	500	Total	14,100
Minnesota Lake+	600		

There are 45,000 Catholics in Diocese of Winona, of whom one in every three is a Pole. There are 79 Catholic priests, of whom five are Polish.[14]

C. In the Diocese of St. Cloud

Alberta+	1,500	Oak Park	200
Browerville+	1,500	Opole+	600
Duelm+	300	Perham+	600
Effington		Randall+	
Elmdale+	300	Rich Prairie+	600
Flensburg+	800	Royalton+	200
Foley	200	Sauk Rapids (Lutrzy)+	5,000
Lastrup+	300	St. Anna+	800
Ledoux (Swan River)+	1,500	St. Cloud+	600
Little Falls+	600	Dispersed throughout	
Millerville+	600	other settlements	5,000
Motley+		Total	22,200
North Prairie+	1,000		

Suum cuique [To each his own]. The Bishop of St. Cloud, the Most Reverend James Trobec, a Slovene, in a letter written in 1901, and again in a letter to Rome dated 1903, maintains that the above figure is exaggerated. He counts only 6,915 Polish Catholics in his diocese. However, he counts only those who are active parish members.[15] Here is what he wrote to the author in 1901:

Reverend and Dear Father:
Some time ago I saw an article in the *Freeman's Journal* (written by Your Reverence) in reference to the number of Polish Catholics in the United States. As far as my diocese is concerned, the statement is not correct. In the Diocese of St. Cloud there are 100 missions, viz: 74 with resident priests and 26 stations. Of these only the following are Polish, or mixed (Polish and German) congregations:

> Alberta, 228 families—Pastor: Rev. J. Kitowski
> Brownerville, 210 families—Pastor: Rev. J. Dudek
> Duelm, 40 families—Pastor: Rev. J. Guzdek
> Flensburg, 60 families—Pastor: Rev. S. Laciński
> Ledoux, 215 families—Pastor: Rev. H. Susczyński
> North Prairie, 165 families—Pastor: Rev. A Gospodar
> Perham, 88 families—Pastor: Rev. Ignacy Wippich
> Opole, 82 families—Pastor: Rev. C. Zielonka
> St. Anna, 85 families—Pastor: Rev. Dąbrowski
> Total: 1,173 families.

N.B. Duelm has 80 families, but only 40 are Polish families. Also in Alberta and North Prairie are at least 50 German families, still I will not deduct them. Besides these missions with resident polish priests, there are polish Catholics in the minority in following places:

> St. Cloud—about 55 families
> Royalton—about 20 families
> Elmdale—about 30 families
> Little Fall—about 60 families
> Lastrup—about 30 families
> Millerville—about 15 families
>   210
>   <u>1,173</u>
>   1,383 Polish families

According to the correct Reports of last year [1900], there are 1,383 Polish families in the Diocese of St. Cloud. Counting 5 for each family, you will have 6,915 souls. This figure is correct, but it is very far from the figure given in the Freeman's *Journal* viz: 23,500 or more than one half of the Diocese which counts 41,500 souls. If I take the number of baptisms and multiply it by 3½, I have the number of families; multiplying this by 5 I have the number of souls and the result is the same as the above statement. . . . I understand a little Polish, but my Vicar General, though a Bohemian, speaks it fluently and has labored in a Polish congregation for 16 years. The good Polish people are attended to as well as possible.

Dear Father, do not think that I criticize your article; no, by no means. I only wish to state the real facts as far as this diocese is concerned, the *Report* in regard to other diocese may be correct as far as I know. Wishing you God's blessing and success, I am

Yours Sincerely

James Trobec

The Most Reverend Bishop bases the above statistics on official figures submitted by the clergy under him, and it is an open secret that priests in America, for no apparent reason, usually submit the lowest number of families to the bishop. In America the amount of the *Cathedraticum* depends on the number of families reported.[16]

In the Diocese of St. Cloud there are 41,500 Catholics, with one out of every two being a Pole. There are, in addition, many Lutheran Poles. Of 100 Catholic priests in this diocese, sixteen, or one in every six, are Polish.[17]

D. In the Diocese of Duluth

Badger+		Moose Lake+	300
Banum+	300	Polonia	500
Biwabik	200	Rice Lake	500
Duluth (two churches)+	10,000	Stanislaus (Englund P.O.)+	800
Gniezno+	1,000	Sturgeon Lake+	1,000
Greenbush (Barto)+	600	Virginia+	300
Hermanstown	500	Willow River	
Kroze+	400	*Total*	*16,400*

In the Diocese of Duluth there are 27,000 Catholics with over one-half being Poles. But there are few Polish priests! Out of 43 Catholic priests only four, or one in ten, are Polish.

In Minnesota there are sixty Polish settlements, 47 Polish churches, 31 Polish priests, and a Polish population of 80,000. Since there are 481 Catholic churches in Minnesota, one in every ten is Polish. Of the 450 Catholic priests in Minnesota one in every fifteen is Polish.[18] Further, of the 333,000 Catholics in Minnesota, one out of every four is Polish and of the total population of 1,751,395, one in every twenty-two is Polish. Finally, since Minnesota encompasses 83,365 square miles, then there is hardly one Pole per square mile.

POLISH SETTLEMENTS IN BOTH DAKOTAS

A. In the Diocese of Fargo, North Dakota

Ardoch		Sterling	
Bismarck		Vancouver	
Fried		Vesleyville+	
Geneseo (Gniezno)+		Warsaw (Pulaski)+	10,000
Jamestown+	600	Throughout other	
Lidgerwood		settlements	6,000
Minto+		*Total*	*16,600*

The population of North Dakota is 349,040 of which 52,000 are Catholics, among whom there are 16,600 Poles. Thus, there is one Pole for every twenty inhabitants, one Catholic for every seven inhabitants, and one Pole for every four Catholics. There are 146 Catholic churches in the Diocese of Fargo, which includes the entire state of North Dakota, five of which are Polish. Of 75 Catholic priests, three are Polish. North Dakota occupies 70,795 square miles with one Pole for every five square miles.[19]

B. In the Diocese of Sioux Falls, South Dakota

Lesterville+	300	Waubay	200
Scotland		Wauley	200
Thorson albo Puck+	4,400	Yankton	
(Grenville P.O.)		Dispersed	4,000
Tyndall+	100	*Total*	*9,200*

C. In the Diocese of Lead, South Dakota

Lead	750

South Dakota includes 77,650 square miles with 421,559 inhabitants, 55,000 of whom are Catholics. There are 76 Catholic priests, three of whom are Polish, and 132 Catholic churches of which three are Polish.[20]

POLISH SETTLEMENTS IN NEBRASKA

A. *In the Diocese of Omaha*

Ashton+	2,500	Loup City+	
Boleszyn+	800	Tarnow+	1,200
Broken Bow+		Omaha+	2,000
Brule		Ord+	
Burwell		Platte Center	
Chojnice+	1,000	Poznan (Farwell)+	2,500
Columbus+	400	Silver Creek+	
Danewirke		South Omaha+	1,000
Duncan+	2,500	St. Paul, Howard County+	
Elba+	1,500	Warsaw+	600
Genoa		Dispersed throughout	
Illyria		other settlements	7,000
Krakow+	600	*Total*	*23,600*

There are 65,175 Catholics in the Diocese of Omaha. One out of every three Catholics is a Pole. There are 118 Catholic priests in this diocese, of whom ten are Polish; therefore, one in every eleven priests is Polish.

B. *In the Diocese of Lincoln*

Boelus		Tecumseh+	400
Pilzno+	800	Throughout various	
Plattsmouth		settlements	3,000
Shelby+	600	*Total*	*5,400*
Smartsville+	600		

In the Diocese of Lincoln there are 25,340 Catholics and 62 Catholic priests, of whom one or two are Polish.[21] In the entire state of Nebraska there are 29 Polish settlements, twenty Polish churches, twelve Polish priests, and a Polish population of 29,000. Considering that there are 258 Catholic churches in Nebraska, then one out of every twelve is Polish. Since there are 180 Catholic priests in Nebraska, one out of every fifteen is Polish. With 90,515 Catholics in Nebraska, one out of three is a Pole; moreover, since the population of Nebraska is 1,068,901, one out of every 36 inhabitants of the state is Polish. Finally, since Nebraska occupies 77,150 square miles, there is one Pole for every two to three square miles.[22]

In the neighboring state of Iowa there are three Polish settlements:

Brighton (Polishville, +) with 600 people, Council Bluffs in the Diocese of Davenport with 400, and Pleasant Plain (+) with 400—not counting a total of 4,000 of our countrymen scattered throughout the rest of the state.[23]

POLISH SETTLEMENTS IN MISSOURI

A. In the Archdiocese of St. Louis

Clover Bottom+	300	Union+	200
Krakow+	300	Washington+	600
Owensville+		Throughout various	
St. Louis		settlements	6,000
St. Stanislaus+	10,000	*Total*	*22,400*
St. Casimir+	5,000		
St. Hedwig+			

There are 220,000 Catholics in the Archdiocese of St. Louis, one out of fourteen of whom is a Pole. There are 429 Catholic priests in this archdiocese, of whom ten are Polish; therefore, one out of every 42 is Polish.

B. In the Diocese of St. Joseph

Clementine	200
St. Joseph+	1,500
Dispersed	3,000
Total	*4,700*

C. In the Diocese of Kansas City

Bricefield+	800
Kansas City+	800
Total	*1,600*

Thus, in the entire state of Missouri, there are twelve Polish settlements, eleven Polish churches, fourteen Polish priests and a Polish population of 28,700.[24] Considering that there are 375 Catholic churches in Missouri, one in every 35 is Polish. Moreover, since there are 565 Catholic priests in Missouri, one out of every forty is Polish. Of 285,000 Catholics in Missouri, one out of ten is Polish. The population of Missouri is 3,107,117, of whom one in every 108 is a Pole. Finally, since Missouri encompasses

69,415 square miles, there is about one Pole for every two to three square miles.

In the neighboring state of Kansas there are two Polish settlements: Leavenworth with 800 people and Iola with 300. In all of Kansas there are 8,000 Poles.[25] Further, in the state of Arkansas there are 1,000 Poles in Marche(+), 400 in Hot Springs and 150 in Argentina for a total of 5,000. In the state of Louisiana there are 500 in New Orleans and a total of 1,000 in the state. In Oklahoma there are 300 Poles in Cavet and a total of 1,000 in the state. Also, in the neighboring Indian Territory there are 1,000 Poles.

POLISH SETTLEMENTS IN TEXAS

A. In the Diocese of San Antonio

Bandera+	400	Panna Maria+	800
Bluff+	400	Pulaski+	700
Coleto	500	Runge+	300
Cottage Hill	600	San Antonio+	500
Częstochowa+	800	San Marcos+	200
Falls City+	400	Seguin+	300
Flatonia+	400	St. Hedwig+	1,700
Gaina+	150	St. John's+	500
Gazeta+	200	Stockdale+	200
Kosciuszko+	800	Yorktown+	1,000
Meyersville+	400	*Total*	*11,550*
Mulbery (Praha)+	300		

Rev. S. Niedbalski[26] from Panna Maria, Texas, revised the above figures as follows:

Panna Maria has 71 families—St. Hedwig has 200 families—Meyersville has 45 families—Yorktown has at least 140 families—Częstochowa, together with St. John's, Pułaski, and Falls has 120 families. Kościuszko has 70 families. Stockdale has 25 families as does "Gaina," San Marcos and "Gazeta"—Seguin has twelve families—I have not even heard of Coleto and Cottage Hill [the author, however, found these settlements listed as permanent Polish settlements in the *Kalendarz* from 1876]—Bluff, Mulbery (currently Praha), and Flatonia are Moravian settlements in which Polish priests such as Rev. Klemens Rogoziński, Rev. Dąbrowski, and others initially worked. In Runge there are a few Poles, St. John's has mainly Germans and Moravians; and San Antonio has 45 families, as does Bandera, in which, nevertheless, the Germans and Americans rule.[27]

In the Diocese of San Antonio there are 75,000 Catholics of whom one in seven is a Pole. There are 73 Catholic priests including ten who are Polish; therefore, one in every seven priests is Polish.

B. In the Diocese of Galveston

Anderson+	800	Huntsville+	500
Bremond+	2,000	Marlin+	400
Brenham+	700	New Waverly+	1,000
Bryan+	400	Plantersville+	400
Chapel Hill+	800	Wallis	300
Houston+	400	*Total*	*7,700*

In the Diocese of Galveston there are 40,000 Catholics, one out of every five of whom is Polish. There are 64 Catholic priests, of which six are Polish; therefore, one priest in every ten is Polish.[28] There are also 500 Poles scattered throughout the Diocese of Dallas including those in a Polish settlement named Thurber.[29] In all of Texas there are 34 Polish settlements, thirty Polish churches, sixteen Polish priests and a Polish population of 19,750. Considering that there are 264 Catholic churches in Texas, one out of every nine of them is Polish. There are 203 Catholic priests in Texas, one in thirteen of whom is Polish. With 202,000 Catholics in Texas, one out of every ten is Polish. Moreover, since the total population of Texas amounts to 3,048,828, there is one Pole for every 160 inhabitants. Finally, since the area of Texas encompasses 265,780 square miles, there is hardly one Pole for every fourteen square miles.[30]

We include the above-named states (Wisconsin, Minnesota, the Dakotas, Nebraska, Iowa, Illinois, Missouri, Kansas, Oklahoma, Louisiana, and Texas) under the heading "West." States and territories still further west (Montana, Wyoming, Colorado, New Mexico, Arizona, Utah, Idaho, Nevada, California, Oregon, Washington, and Alaska) we include under the "Far West" or "Wild West." All other states located east of Chicago will call the "East."

The "West," therefore contains 654,000 Poles. Let us see how many there are in the "Wild West."

POLISH SETTLEMENTS IN THE FAR WEST

A. In Montana

Anaconda	200
Butte	200
Great Falls	400
Havre	300
Dispersed	1,000
Total	*2,100*

B. In Wyoming

Sheridan	1,000

C. In Colorado

Denver	600
Globeville+	600
Sopris	500
Dispersed	1,300
Total	*3,000*

D. In Idaho

Nampa+	300

E. In Utah

Salt Lake City	300
Schofield	200

F. In Washington

Ballard	300	Roslyn	500
Carbonado	200	Seattle	400
Clealum	200	Spokane	200
Enumclaw+	400	Tacoma	500
Frances	200	Wilkeson	400
Franklin		*Total*	*3,900*
Pe Ell+	600		

G. In Oregon

Brooks	200	Portland	300
Bunker Hill		Roots	
Cornwallis	200	Siletz	300
Eugene	1	Siletz Reservation	200
La Grande	200	St. Joseph's Valley	200
McMinnville	100	Dispersed	1,000
Oswego	200	*Total*	*2,901*

H. In California

Eureka	300	Shasta	100
Los Angeles	300	Throughout other	
Sacramento	300	settlements	4,000
San Francisco	1,000	*Total*	*6,000*

I. In Nevada

Total	200

J. In the Arizona Territory

Total	175

K. In the New Mexico Territory

Total	500

L. In the Alaska Territory

About 50 Poles work in Juneau
and Douglas and as many in
Skagway in the gold mines.

M. On the islands of Hawaii

Total	500

In the entire "Wild West" there are about fifty Polish settlements, eight Polish churches, three Polish priests, and a Polish population of 20,000.[31] There are 4,032,436 inhabitants in this entire area, among whom there are 688,600 Catholics. Thus, in relation to the total population of the "Wild West," the proportion of the Poles is one to 200; in relation to Catholics, the Poles number one to forty. There are 1,093 Catholic churches in the "Wild West" and a total of 771 Catholic priests.[32] Since the "Wild West" contains an enormous 1,778,419 square miles—which is almost as large as Russia—there is an average of two inhabitants per square mile and one Pole per 100 square miles.

Let us now soar like an eagle through the "East," through the states located east of Chicago.

POLISH SETTLEMENT IN MICHIGAN

A. In the Diocese of Detroit

Bronson+	800	Kinde+	600
Carleton	52	Parisville+	1,200
Copper Harbor	300	Pigeon	120
Delray+	4,000	Port Austin+	1,200
Detroit+		Red Jacket	200
Sacred Heart of Mary+	10,000	St. Joseph+	800
St. Adalbert+	10,000	Trenton	500
St. Casimir+	7,000	Verone	120
St. Francis+	6,000	Vienna	180
St. Hedwig+	4,000	Wittaker	140
St. Joseph+	5,000	Wyandotte+	1,500
St. Stanislaus+	2,000	Dispersed throughout	
Dorr	300	other settlements	8,000
Hilliards+	600	*Total*	*65,012*
Jackson+	1,000		

In response to our query in 1903 as to how many Poles lived in his city, Mr. W. L. Maybury, Mayor of Detroit, attested in writing that there were 50,000. We quote his statement here verbatim:

Executive Office
Detroit, Mich.
William C. Maybury, Mayor
Clarence A. Cotton, Secretary

I, William C. Maybury, Mayor of the City of Detroit, Michigan, United States of America, do hereby certify that to the best of my knowledge, information, and belief, there are now resident in said city and the immediate suburbs upwards of fifty thousand (50,000) inhabitants of Polish nativity or origin.

William C. Maybury, Mayor
Witness my hand and seal
this third day of June,
A.D. 1903.
Attest: J. Milton,
Deputy City Clerk

In the Diocese of Detroit there are 185,510 Catholics. Therefore, one out of every three Catholics is a Pole. There are 207 Catholic priests in this diocese, of whom 25 are Polish; therefore, one out of every eight priests is Polish.

B. In the Diocese of Grand Rapids

Alpena+	2,500	Metz+	
Au Sable	500	Midland	800
Bay City+	10,000	Ministee+	6,000
Beaver+	800	Mullet Lake+	600
Beavertown+	600	Oak Hill	1,000
Cleveland Town+	300	Oscoda+	500
East Lake		Poznan+	2,500
East Tawas+	600	Saginaw+	2,000
Empire+	300	Sheboygan+[33]	1,000
Filer City		St. Isadore+	1,000
Fisherville		St.Helen+	500
Freesoil		Stronach	
Gaylord+	1,000	Traverse City	400
Grand Rapids+		Williamstown+	800
Sacred Heart of Jesus	2,000	Dispersed throughout	
St. Adalbert+	6,000	other settlements	7,000
St. Stanislaus	4,000	*Total*	*52,900*
Ludington+	800		

There are 112,020 Catholics in the Diocese of Grand Rapids; consequently almost every other Catholic is a Pole. There are 92 Catholic priests in this diocese, of whom eighteen are Poles; therefore, one out of every five priests is Polish.

C. In the Diocese of Marquette

Atlantic Mine	400	Norway	300
Bessemer+	400	Ontonagon	150
Calumet+	2,700	Opechee	500
Cedar River	300	Stambough	300
Detour+	400	Sand Beach	200
Hancock	500	Sault Ste. Marie+	600
Hermansville	100	Stephenson	400
Iron River+	400	Vulcan	300
Ironwood+	800	Wakefield+	300
Laurium	200	Walton	300
Marquette	400	Watersmith	100
Menominee+	2,000	Dispersed	4,000
Negaunee	100	*Total*	*16,750*
Niedolipie+ (Gatesville)	600		

There are 80,000 Catholics in this diocese and about one in every five is a Pole. There are 68 Catholic priests, of whom eight are Polish; thus, one in eight is Polish.[34] In all of Michigan there are 73 Polish settlements, 48 Polish churches, 51 Polish priests and a Polish population of 140,000. Considering that there are 416 Catholic churches in Michigan, one in every nine is Polish. There are 367 Catholic priests in Michigan, one in seven of whom is Polish. Since there are 367,530 Catholics in Michigan, one in every two to three is a Pole. Moreover, since the population of Michigan is 2,419,782, there is one Pole for every eighteen inhabitants. With 58,915 square miles, there are almost three Poles for every square mile in Michigan.[35]

POLISH SETTLEMENTS IN INDIANA

A. In the Diocese of Fort Wayne

Bremen+	300	Reynolds+	400
Chesterton	300	Rolling Prairie	400
East Chicago	1,000	San Pierre	300
Egge+	400	South Bend	
Fort Wayne	400	St. Casimir	6,000
Francesville+	300	St. Hedwig	10,000
Goshen+	300	St. Stanislaus	3,000
Hammond	1,500	Sweet Home	
Medaryville+	300	Teresa	300
Michigan City	2,000	Terre Couppee	600
New Carlisle		Warsaw	200
North Judson+	600	Whiting	800
Otis	2,500	*Total*	*32,200*
Pulaski	300		

There are 78,000 Catholics in the Diocese of Fort Wayne, almost every other one of whom is a Pole. There are 177 Catholic priests in this diocese, of whom fifteen are Poles; therefore, one in every twelve is Polish.

B. In the Diocese of Indianapolis

Evansville		Shelbyville	
Indianapolis	300	Shellburn	
Jeffersonville	500	Siberia (Sabaria)	
Lanesville	400	Sullivan	100
Prescott	300	*Total*	*1,600*

In the state of Indiana there are 39 Polish settlements, eighteen Polish churches, fifteen Polish priests and a Polish population of 33,800. Since there are 314 Catholic churches in the state, one in every eighteen is Polish. With 362 Catholic priests in Indiana, one in every 24 is a Pole. Further, since there are 179,143 Catholics in Indiana, one in six is a Pole. Of the total population of 2,516,463, one in every 75 inhabitants of the state is Polish. Finally, since Indiana encompasses 36,350 square miles, there is one Pole per square mile.[36]

In the state of Kentucky—in Louisville and other places—there are about 4,000 Poles.

POLISH SETTLEMENTS IN OHIO

A. In the Diocese of Cleveland

Berea+	3,000	Fremont	500
Cleveland		Grafton+	800
Sacred Heart+	3,500	Lorain+	1,200
St. Casimir+	6,000	Toledo	
St. John Cantius+	2,200	St. Anthony+	8,000
St. Stanislaus+	10,000	St. Hedwig+	7,000
Independent+	6,000	*Total*	*48,200*

The Catholic Universe, published by the Bishop of Cleveland, accuses the author of exaggerating the above figures. It stated on August 23, 1901, that there are only 2,971 Polish souls! What accuracy in counting Polish parishioners! It counted each and every one of them!? Nevertheless, while personally visiting Cleveland and neighboring Berea in January, 1902, the author found the following Polish settlements within the Diocese of Cleveland:

Akron	150	Rossford+	500
Ashtabula	1,000	Sandusky	400
Barberton	500	Swanton	80
Kent	250	Warren	300
Mansfield	300	Willrully	300
Massillon	150	Youngstown+	900
Maumee+	100	*Total*	*5,030*
Oak Harbor	100		

There are 275,000 Catholics in the Diocese of Cleveland, therefore one out of every five is a Pole. There are 275 Catholic priests in this diocese, of whom twelve are Polish; thus, one in every 23 is Polish.

That the Diocese of Cleveland must contain approximately 100,000 Poles, or one-third of the diocese, is proven by the fact that the Polish parishes pay one-third of the diocesan tax. Furthermore, the following two statements by the mayors of Cleveland and Toledo proves that our figure of 53,230 is not exaggerated!

Mayor's Office
Tom L. Johnson, Mayor.
W. B. Gongwer, Secretary.

I, Tom L. Johnson, Mayor of the City of Cleveland, Ohio, United States of America, do hereby certify that to the best of my knowledge, information and belief, there are now resident in said city and the immediate suburbs upwards of Thirty Thousand (30,000) inhabitants of Polish nativity or origin.

> Tom L. Johnson, Mayor
> Witness my hand and seal
> this Fifth day of June, A.D. 1903.
> Edward H. Miller

When I asked Mr. Samuel Jones, long-time mayor of Toledo, how many Poles lived in his city, he at first replied: "I do not know any Poles, any Germans, any French in my city—I know only Americans." I then answered: "Mr. Mayor, not only do I not know Poles, Germans, and French, I do not even know Americans—I know only human beings!" Mr. Jones did not answer that, but without further argument he issued the following written testament that there were over 14,000 Poles living in Toledo.

EXECUTIVE DEPARTMENT
Of The City of Toledo, O.
Samuel M. Jones, Mayor

I, Samuel M. Jones, Mayor of the city of Toledo, Ohio, United States of America, do hereby certify to the best of my knowledge, information, and belief, that there are now resident in said city and the immediate suburbs upwards of fourteen thousand (14,000) inhabitants of Polish nativity or origin.

Samuel M. Jones, Mayor
Witness my hand and seal
this fourth day of June,
A.D. 1903
S. J. Heningshaw,
Deputy City Clerk

B. In the Diocese of Columbus

Dillonvale+	600
Glouster	
Steubenville	800

C. In the Archdiocese of Cincinnati

Cincinnati+	1,000
Dayton+	1,000

In the whole state of Ohio there are thirty Polish settlements, fifteen Polish priests and a Polish population of 80,000. Considering that there are 602 Catholic churches in Ohio, one out of every forty is Polish. Since there are 582 Catholic priests in Ohio, one out of every forty is Polish. Of the 535,000 Catholics in Ohio, one in every six is a Pole. With a total population of 4,157,545, one in every fifty inhabitants of the Ohio is Polish. In conclusion, since the area of Ohio includes 41,060 square miles, there are two Poles per square mile.[37]

POLISH SETTLEMENTS IN PENNSYLVANIA

A. In the Archdiocese of Philadelphia

Allentown+	500	Phoenixville	
Chester	500	Pottsville	
Clifton	500	Reading+	3,000
Easton		Shenandoah	
Gilberton+	600	St. Casimir+	3,000
Mahanoy City		St. Stanislaus+	3,000
St. Casimir+	2,000	South Bethlehem	
St. Mary+	2,000	Dispersed	40,000
McAdoo+	1,200	*Total*	*86,300*
New Philadelphia+	1,000		
Philadelphia+			
St. John Cantius+	5,000		
St. Josaphat+	3,000		
St. Lawrence+	10,000		
St. Stanislaus+	6,000		
Independent+	5,000		

There are 460,000 Catholics in the Archdiocese of Philadelphia, one out of every six of whom is a Pole. There are 454 Catholic priests in this archdiocese, of whom twelve are Poles; thus, one in every 37 priests is Polish.

B. In the Diocese of Harrisburg

Danville	500	Shamokin (Incl. 700	
Excelsior+	1,000	Independents)+	6,000
Locust Gab+	600	Stelton	
Lykens+	600	West Shamokin+	2,000
Minersville		Dispersed	8,000
Mt. Carmel		*Total*	*22,700*
Our Lady of Solace+	2,000		
St. Joseph+	2,000		

There are 45,000 Catholics in the Diocese of Harrisburg, consequently every other Catholic is a Pole. There are 72 Catholic priests in this diocese, of whom five are Polish; therefore, one out of every thirteen priests is Polish.

C. In the Diocese of Scranton

Antrim+	500	Nuremberg	500
Arnot+	800	Olyphant+	600
Blossburg+	3,000	Parsons	500
Dickson	800	Pittston+	1,000
Duryea (Incl. 820		Plains+	1,500
Independents)+	3,500	Plymouth (Incl. 1,450	
East Plymouth+	800	Independents)+	2,500
Edwardsdale		Priceburg (Incl. 1,350	
Freeland	1,500	Independents)+	3,000
Glen Lyon+	3,000	Redburn	400
Hazleton+	2,500	Scranton+	5,000
Hills Grove	500	Independents+	2,400
Hopeville (Weston)+	1,000	Sugar Notch	
Hudson (Mill Creek)+	1,500	Troop	
Kingstown+	600	Wilkes Barre (Incl. 1,000	
Mansfield+	200	Independents)+	5,000
Mayfield	200	Dispersed	25,000
Morris+	500	Total	74,900
Morris Run+	1,000		
Nanticoke			
Holy Trinity+	3,000		
St. Hedwig+	2,000		
St. Stanislaus+	3,000		

There are 150,000 Catholics in the Diocese of Scranton with every other being a Pole. There are 170 Catholic priests in this diocese, of whom 21 are Polish; therefore, one out of every eight is Polish.

D. In the Diocese of Erie

De Lancey+	800
Dubois+	1,000
Erie+	6,000
Houtzdale+	800
Oil City+	600
Osceola+	500
Dispersed	10,000
Total	19,700

There are 65,000 Catholics in the Diocese of Erie, one in every four of whom is a Pole. There are 116 Catholic priests in this diocese, of whom eight are Polish; therefore, one out of every fourteen priests is Polish.

E. In the Diocese of Pittsburgh

Alden	300	Irwin	
Allegheny+	400	Jeanette	300
Ambridge+		Johnstown	300
Beaver Falls+	300	Kaylor	
Ben's Creek	300	Latrobe+	1,000
Bidle		Mammoth+	3,000
Braddock+	2,000	Manor	
Bradenville+		McKees Rock+	
Butler		McKeesport+	2,500
Carnegie+	1,000	Mt. Pleasant+	3,000
Clarendon		Natrona+	1,500
Claridge		New Castle+	1,000
Connelsville	300	New Kensington+	1,500
Crab Tree (Goff P.O.)+	300	Patton	300
Donora+		Penn	
Dunlo+	300	Pittsburgh+	
Duquesne+	600	Sacred Heart of Mary+	7,000
Essen		St. Adalbert+	10,000
Everson+	2,500	St. Stanislaus+	15,000
Export+		Sharpsburg+	400
Ford City+	1,000	Stumerville+	
Galitzin	300	Vandergrift	
Glassport+		Westmoreland City	
Glen+	1,000	Wilderming+	300
Glenn Campbell+	4,600	Williamsburg+	300
Hastings	300	Windber+	1,000
Homestead+	1,000	Dispersed	30,000
Hoytville+		*Total*	*102,200*

There are 280,000 Catholics in the Diocese of Pittsburgh, of whom every third one is a Pole. There are 362 Catholic priests in this diocese of whom 35 are Polish; therefore, one out of every ten priests is Polish.[38]

According to Mr. W. B. Hays, Mayor of Pittsburgh, this city alone has over 50,000 Poles. His certification is as follows:

MAYOR'S OFFICE
Pittsburgh, Pa.
W. B. Hays, Mayor

I, William B. Hays, Mayor of the City of Pittsburgh, Pennsylvania, United States of America, do certify to the best of my knowledge, information, and belief there are now residing in the City of Pittsburgh and immediate suburbs upwards of fifty thousand (50,000) inhabitants of Polish nativity or origin.

W. B. Hays, Mayor
Witness my hand and seal this Sixth day of June,
Nineteen hundred three
Attest: William Black, Secretary

F. Diocese of Altoona

Total	*10,000*

In all of Pennsylvania there are 112 Polish settlements, 85 polish churches, 90 Polish priests and a Polish population of around 350,000. Since there are 827 Catholic churches in Pennsylvania, then one in every ten is Polish. Since there are 1,174 Catholic priests in the state, one in every thirteen is Polish. With 1,000,000 Catholics in Pennsylvania, one in every three is a Pole. Moreover, since the total population of Pennsylvania is 6,301,360, one out of every twenty inhabitants of the state is a Pole. Finally, since the area of Pennsylvania encompasses 45,215 square miles, we can conclude that there are eight Poles per square mile.[39]

POLISH SETTLEMENTS IN NEW YORK

A. In the Archdiocese of New York

Fishkill		Newburg	
Florida+	1,000	Port Richmond+	500
Green Point	400	Poughkeepsie+	700
Haverstraw	500	Rondout+	800
Linoleumville		Sing Sing	
New York+		Staten Island+	3,500
Extravagantes+	25,000	Tomkins	
Morisania+	2,000	Dispersed throughout	
St. Adalbert+	4,000	other settlements	30,000
St. Stanislaus+	5,000	*Total*	*76,400*
Williamsbridge+	2,000		
Yonkers+	1,000		

In the Archdiocese of New York there are 1,200,000 Catholics. One out of every sixteen is a Pole. In this archdiocese there are 680 Catholic priests, of whom thirteen are Polish; thus, one out of every 50 Catholic priests is Polish.

B. In the Diocese of Brooklyn

Bay Shore and Islip		Newtown (Long Island)+	4,000
Brooklyn		Riverhead (Long Island)+	4,000
M. B. Częstochowa+	7,000	Dispersed	20,000
St. Casimir+	4,000	Total	48,000
St. Stanislaus Kostka+	8,000		

In the Diocese of Brooklyn there are 500,000 Catholics and 320 Catholic priests; of the latter, six are Polish.

C. In the Diocese of Albany

Albany+	2,000	Schenectady+	4,000
Amsterdam+	3,000	Troy	
Cohoes		Watervliet	400
Herkimer	500	Throughout other	
Middletown+	500	settlements	10,000
Salem Crossing	800	Total	21,200

In the Diocese of Albany there are 145,000 Catholics and 182 priests; of the latter, five are Polish.

D. In the Diocese of Syracuse

Syracuse+	2,500
Utica+	2,500
Dispersed	10,000
Total	15,000

In the Diocese of Syracuse there are 70,000 Catholics and 101 priests; of the latter, two are Polish.

E. In the Diocese of Rochester

Auburn	500	Waverly+	500
Elmira+	3,000	Dispersed	11,000
Oswego+		Total	19,000
Rochester+	4,000		

In the Diocese of Rochester there are 100,000 Catholics and 123 priests; of the latter, two are Polish.

F. In the Diocese of Buffalo

Albion+	2,000	Lockport	200
Batavia+	400	Medina+	500
Buffalo+		Niagara Falls+	880
Ascension+	2,000	Olean+	900
Body of Christ+	10,000	Salamanca+	1,000
St. Adalbert+	8,000	Springville	250
St. Casimir+	1,500	Stony Point	2,500
St. John Cantius+	4,000	Suspension Bridge+	480
St. Stanislaus+	35,000	Tonawanda+	500
Transfiguration+	5,000	Warsaw	300
Independents+	6,000	West Seneca+	
Depew+	800	Dispersed throughout	
Dunkirk+ (2 schools)	6,000	other settlements	10,000
Fredonia	200	*Total*	*98,530*
Leonia	120		

The "City of the Buffaloes" numbers some 70,000 Poles, as attested to by its mayor in the following statement.

City of Buffalo
Mayor's Office
Erastus C. Knight, Mayor
Frank W. Hinkley, Secretary

I, Erastus C. Knight, Mayor of the City of Buffalo, County of Erie, State of New York, United States of America, do hereby certify that, to the best of my knowledge, information, and belief, there are now resident in the City and the immediate suburbs about seventy thousand (70,000) persons of Polish nativity or origin.

Witness my hand and the seal of the said City of Buffalo this 8th day of June, 1903.

Erastus C. Knight, Mayor

In the Diocese of Buffalo there are 156,000 Catholics; thus, over one-half are Poles. There are 215 Catholic priests in this diocese, of whom thirty are Polish; therefore, one in every seven is Polish.

F. In the Diocese of Ogdensburg

Lyon Mountain+	600

In the whole state of New York, then, we count some 90 Polish settlements, 46 Polish churches, 58 Polish priests, and a Polish population of approximately 340,000. Considering that there are 1,030 Catholic churches in the entire state, one of every 22 is Polish. Since there are 1,729 priests in the state, then one of every thirty is Polish. Moreover, since there are 2,249,000 Catholics in the state, one out of seven is a Pole. Further, since the population of the state amounts to 7,268,009, there is one Pole for every 24 inhabitants. Finally, since New York occupies 49,170 square miles, there are seven Poles per square mile.[40]

POLISH SETTLEMENTS IN NEW JERSEY

A. In the Diocese of Newark

Alpha		Orange+	500
Bloomfield+	1,000	Palisades Park+	1,000
Bayonne+ (Including		Passaic+	2,000
1,300 Independents)	3,000	Independents+	1,230
Jersey City+	10,000	Peterson	600
Newark+	3,000	Dispersed	18,000
Newton+	500	*Total*	*41,600*

In the Diocese of Newark there are 290,060 Catholics. Therefore, one of every seven Catholics is a Pole. There are 265 Catholic priests in the diocese, of whom ten are Polish.

B. In the Diocese of Trenton

Bound Brook	600	South Amboy+	3,500
Camden+	2,000	Trenton	
East Trenton+	1,500	Holy Cross+	2,500
Helmetta		St. Stanislaus+	2,500
Perth Amboy+	3,000	Dispersed	12,000
Sayreville		*Total*	*27,600*

In the Diocese of Trenton there are 72,000 Catholics. Therefore, approximately one in every three Catholics is a Pole. There are 121 priests, of whom nine are Polish. In the entire state there are thirty Polish settlements, sixteen Polish churches, nineteen Polish priests, and a Polish population of about 70,000. There are 271 Catholic churches in New Jersey, in which a total population of 1,883,669 occupies an area of only 7,815 square miles.[41]

POLISH SETTLEMENTS IN MARYLAND, DELAWARE, WASHINGTON (D.C.), AND WEST VIRGINIA

A. In Maryland[42]

Baltimore		Curtis Bay+	1,000
Holy Rosary+	8,000	Wagnerspoint	1,000
St. Stanislaus+	12,000	*Total*	*25,700*
Independents+	1,700		

B. In Delaware

Wilmington+	8,000

C. In the District of Columbia

Washington	800

D. In West Virginia

Monongah+	1,000
Wheeling+	1,000
Dispersed	1,000
Total	*3,000*

POLES IN SOUTHERN STATES

In other southeastern states Poles have not established settlements in a strict sense, but live scattered among the rest of the population. The census of 1900 proved, however, that there was no lack of them even in the outlying states, because Poles are listed in every state. Although they are scattered, they have still not lost their sense of nationality since they listed themselves [in the 1900 census] as Poles. These are the statistics:

Alabama	700	South Carolina	600
Florida	200	Tennessee	2,000
Georgia	1,000	(in the county of	
(in the city of Savannah		Clearfield there are	
there are about 50 Poles)		200 Poles)	
Kentucky	4,000	Virginia	1,000
Mississippi	500	*Total*	*10,200*
North Carolina	200		

POLISH SETTLEMENTS IN NEW ENGLAND

A. In the Dioceses of Boston and Springfield, Massachusetts

Adams+	1,200	Salem+	1,000
Bondsville+		Webster (including	
Boston+	10,000	1,350 Independents)+	8,000
Chicoppee (Including		Westfield+	
1,350 Independents)+	8,000	Worcester+	2,000
Haverhill+	1,800	In other settlements	43,000
Holyoke+	2,000	*Total*	*80,000*
Lowell+	2,000		
Independents+	1,050		

In both of these dioceses there are 860,000 Catholics and 771 Catholic priests, of whom there are 80,000 Poles and 20 Polish priests.[43]

B. In the Diocese of Providence (encompassing Rhode Island and the southern tip of Massachusetts)[44]

Fall River (Including 1,400		Thorndike+	
Independents)+	4,000	Three Rivers+	
New Bedford+	1,500	Warren and Ware	1,500
Providence+	2,000	West Warren+	
Taunton+	500	*Total*	*9,500*

In the Diocese of Providence there are 275,000 Catholics and 189 Catholic priests; of the latter, five are Polish.[45]

C. In the Diocese of Hartford (entire state of Connecticut)[46]

Ansonia+	1,000	New London+	500
Berlin		Norwich+	1,000
Brandford	500	Portland+	500
Bridgeport+	2,000	Rockville+	800
Bristol+	500	Seymour	
Collinsville		Stamford	500
Glastonburg		Terryville	500
Gleenbrook	500	Thomaston	500
Glenville		Torrington	
Hartford+	1,800	Union City	500
Higginum	500	Vernon	
Jewetty City	500	Wangatuck	
Luthington		Waterbury+	500
Meriden+	3,000	Winsted	
Middletown+	500	Throughout other	
Moodus	500	settlements	40,000
New Britain+	5,300	*Total*	*60,100*
New Haven			

The Diocese of Hartford has a total population of 908,355 including 270,000 Catholics, 60,000 of whom are Polish, and 273 Catholic priests, fifteen of whom are Polish.[47]

In all of New England there are seventy Polish settlements, thirty Polish churches, forty Polish priests, and a Polish population of 160,000. In these three states (Massachusetts, Rhode Island, and Connecticut) there are 630 Catholic churches, one out of every 21 of which is Polish. Since there are 1,233 Catholic priests in these three states, one out of every thirty is Polish. Of the 1,405,000 Catholics, one out of every nine is a Pole. Since the entire population of these three states numbers 4,142,257, one out of every 21 inhabitants is a Pole. Finally, the area of these three states comprises only 14,555 square miles, thus there are approximately a dozen Poles per square mile.[48]

POLES IN NORTHERN STATES

New Hampshire, Settlement in Manchester	5,000
Vermont, Settlements	
in West Rutland and Readsboro	2,000
Maine	3,000

To summarize, in the entire United States of America there are 1,903,000 Poles, 810 Polish settlements, 517 Polish churches, and 546 Polish priests. The 1900 census notes, in general, 10,356,644 "newcomers," that is, people who were not born in the United States. Among them are numbered 150,232 born in "German Poland," 58,503 born in "Austrian Poland," 154,436 born in "Russian Poland," and 20,436 born in "unknown Poland." Therefore, according to this census there would have been a total of 383,595 people born "in Poland" living in the United States in 1900!? This figure should be tripled, since over half of the local Poles, when asked "where were you born?" answered that they were born in "Prussia," "Austria," or "Russia." When we add to this number the Poles born in America we arrive at a figure close to 2,000,000.[49]

The same result is obtained by newspapers when they write about the census of Poles in the United States. This is shown in the following: "we received an official census of the Polish population in the United States from Washington. This census contains only those who listed themselves as Poles born in Poland. . . ." This census must be very inaccurate since European statistics show that within the last twenty-five years over

800,000 Poles have emigrated to America. However, the statistics on Russian immigrants list 424,372 and it is known that there were no more than 4,000 of them. Therefore, at least 420,000 Poles from the Russian sector should be added to the official census, along with at least two percent of the "Germans" who are actually Poles, a figure which amounts to 500,000. In the section under "Austria" the greater part consisted of Poles, but counting only half still amounts to some 150,000. Therefore, in total there are about 1,453,000 people of Polish descent living in the United States. To this figure should be added children [of Poles] who were born in this country, which in twenty-five years have probably totaled approximately 500,000. Therefore, there are about 2,000,000 Poles in the United States.[50]

Let us present still one more general view of these numerical relationships. As one can see, we have divided the entire United States into the East, West, and the Far (Wild) West. There are 1,227,000 Poles, 451 Polish settlements, 267 Polish churches and 299 Polish priests in the "East." In the "West" there are 654,000 Poles, 330 Polish settlements, 246 Polish churches, and 244 Polish priests. Finally, there are 22,000 Poles, 29 Polish settlements, four Polish churches, and three Polish priests in the "Wild West." Therefore, we certainly find more Poles, Polish settlements, and Polish churches in the East than in the West. But, in comparison to the general population, and especially to the Catholic population, the relative number of Poles in the West is a little greater than in the East.

The East, as we have described it, comprises 769,035 square miles inhabited by 48,132,309 people, including 6,929,529 Catholics and 1,227,000 Poles; therefore, there are 63 inhabitants per square mile in the East, of whom nine are Catholics, and one is a Pole. The number of Poles compared to the Catholics constitutes a ratio of one to six, while the number of Catholics in comparison to the general population is one out of seven. The West, as we have described it, encompasses 1,067,955 square miles. In this area, almost half again as large as the "East," live about half as many people, only 23,792,074 inhabitants including 3,154,800 Catholics and 654,000 Poles. Therefore, there are only twenty-three inhabitants per square mile in the West, including three Catholics and one Pole for each one and one-half square miles. The number of Poles compared to Catholics constitutes a ratio of one to five, and Catholics compared to the general population is one out of seven. Finally, the Far West, as we have described it, comprises 1,778,416 square miles, a vast area containing an inconsequentially small number of 4,032,436 inhabitants.

There are 688,600 Catholics here, including 120,000 Poles. Thus, for every two to three square miles there is one Catholic, and for almost every 100 miles there is one Pole.

The entire United States—not counting the islands of Cuba, Puerto Rico, Hawaii, and the Philippines—occupies an area of 3,615,409 square miles inhabited by 75,956,819 people, including 12,000,000 Catholics and about 2,000,000 Poles. Therefore, placing all the inhabitants of the United States into one long column, every seventh would be a Catholic and every fortieth would be a Pole. Every sixth Catholic would be a Pole!

Now, from the heights of this general overview of numerical relationships let us descend a bit and examine the Poles in America from a bird's-eye view in their other relationships in the Church, schools, organizations, the press, politics, commerce, industry, and so on.

Chapter 5

History of the Polish Church in America

The rapid growth of the Church—The lack of priests and teachers—The active faith of the people—The wealth and comforts of the clergy?—The know-how and organizational activities of Polish American priests—Parish disturbances—Outstanding organizers, preachers, missionaries—Polish deans and diocesan consultants—Congresses—Independent churches—Efforts to obtain a Polish bishop—Irremovable pastors and right to elect bishops.

The United States is the youngest of the great nations, yet it is in this country that the Catholic Church has made great progress over the last century, especially considering the obstacles it encountered.[1] In 1785 the first bishop in the United States, Dr. Carroll, stated in his report to Rome that there were 16,000 Catholics in Maryland, 7,000 in Pennsylvania, and 200 in New York and other states. There were some thirty priests in America, but no Catholic schools or colleges.

Now there are 86 dioceses in the United States abundantly provided with schools, colleges, and various charitable institutions. The Catholic population numbers over 11 million. In the hierarchy there are thirteen archbishops and eighty bishops distinguished for their erudition and piety, as well as 11,987 secular and monastic priests. There are 44 monastic orders with 5,500 members working in part as priests and as teachers. There are also 118 convents housing 50,000 nuns, and 3,395 students in higher education at eight universities and 76 seminaries. Over a million pupils are obtaining an education in 865 colleges and Catholic academies and in 3,812 parish schools. There are 35,000 orphans in 250 orphanages, besides which there are 287 other Catholic charitable institutions.

Most astonishing, however, was the progress of the Catholic Church in New York State. Initially no Catholic priest was allowed to reside in this state. A certain charitable Quaker died on the scaffold there because he was suspected of being a Catholic priest. At the beginning of the nineteenth century the state had only one Catholic priest, and he was tolerated only because he had been a chaplain on a French warship which rendered important service during the Revolutionary War. At that time there was only one small Catholic church and one school. In 1816 the entire state of New York had only four Catholic priests, but by 1818 its Catholic population already numbered about 16,000 with eight priests and seven churches. Today [1906], the Diocese of New York numbers 1.2 million Catholics and has over 1,000 priests and 68,000 school children.

As with the Catholic Church in general, the Polish church in the United States represents in particular an outstanding picture of progress and development. In reality this picture contains many blemishes and holes because it is a living and changing picture taken from nature, and it is not dead, stiff, or artificial. These blemishes and holes usually are noticed only by Polish travelers [in the United States] and by newspapers in Europe, since they want, or know how to assess the merits of the picture. We are not optimists by any means, silently overlooking the negative aspects of our Polish American society; but we will remind critics of our church relations in America of these appropriate words of [Adam] Mickiewicz: "Any fool will notice if there is a black spot or a hole in a picture; but only an expert will see the merits of a picture."[2]

The holes in the picture of our church relations are the "independent" churches, and the black spots are the parish disturbances; yet these do not detract from the brilliance of the white picture. Why, even the sun has spots and holes, or craters, but it still shines for us in all its brilliance. In the same way the Polish church in America, despite black spots and holes, is magnificent and dazzling in its progress and historical development. This is demonstratively presented in the following outline [of the founding of Polish parishes]:

1855—Panna Maria, Texas.
1856—Bandera, San Antonio, St. Hedwig, Meyersville, Yorktown, Texas.
1857—Parisville, Michigan.
1858—Polonia, Wisconsin.
1863—Milwaukee (first), Wisconsin.
1864—Pine Creek, Wisconsin.
1866—Washington, Kraków, Clover Bottom, Union, Missouri.
1868—Northeim, Wisconsin.
1869—Chicago (first), Illinois.
1870—New Waverly, Bluff, Texas; Manitowoc, Wisconsin; Shamokin, Pennsylvania.
1871—Plantersville, Cottage Hill, Texas; Bay City, Michigan; Milwaukee (second), Hull, Wisconsin; Otis, Indiana.
1872—Marlin, Flatonia, Texas; Detroit (first), Michigan; Cincinnati, Ohio.
1873—Bremond, Huntsville, Texas; Grand Rapids (first), Michigan; Berlin (first),

Wisconsin; Chicago (second and third), Illinois; Shenandoah, Pennsylvania; Buffalo (first), Dunkirk, New York; Berea, Ohio; Winona, Delano, Faribault, Minnesota.

1874—La Salle, Illinois.

1875—Brenham, Texas; Manistee, Michigan; Beaver Dam, Princeton, Independence, North Creek, Wisconsin; St. Joseph, Missouri; Random, Illinois; Nanticoke, Excelsior, Blossburg, Pittsburgh, Pennsylvania; Jeffersonville, Lanesville, Indiana; Brooklyn, New York; Toledo (first), Cleveland (first), Ohio.

1876—Częstochowa, Anderson, Texas; Poznań, Michigan; Stevens Point, Poniatowski, Wisconsin; Brimfield, Illinois; South Bend (first), Indiana; Toledo (second), Ohio; Poznań, Nebraska.

1877—Mt. Carmel (first), Pennsylvania.

1878—Krok, Wisconsin; St. Louis (first), Missouri.

1880—Pine Grove, Wisconsin; St. Paul (first), St. Cloud, Alberta, Duluth, Minnesota; Elba, Nebraska; Puck, Warsaw, Dakota, Boston, Webster, Massachusetts.

1881—Poland, Wisconsin; Wilno, Minnesota.

1882—Detroit (second), Calumet, Michigan; Milwaukee (third), Wisconsin; Philadelphia (first), Pennsylvania; Minnesota Lake, Minnesota; Duncan, Tarnów, Nebraska.

1883—Bryan, Texas; Bronson, Michigan; Hofa Park, Mill Creek, North Prairie, Minnesota; Chojnice, Nebraska.

1884—Pilot Knob, Francher, Wisconsin; Chenango (fourth and fifth), Illinois; Plymouth, Pittsburgh (second), Pennsylvania; Terre Couppee, Indiana; Stanislaus, Minnesota; Boleszyn, Nebraska.

1885—Scranton, Wilkes Barre, Erie, Pennsylvania; Cleveland (second), Ohio; St. Paul (sec ond), Ledoux, Browerville, Minnesota; Shelby, Nebraska; Jersey City, New Jersey.

1886—Wausau, Flintville, Bevent, Junction, Sigel, Wisconsin; Chicago (sixth), Illinois; Oil City, Pennsylvania; Buffalo (second), New York; Minneapolis, St. Anna, Perham, Gniezno, Minnesota; Baltimore, Maryland.

1887—Pulaski, Sobieski, Kraków, Wisconsin; Mt. Pleasant, De Lancey, Dubois, Pennsylvania; Wilmington, Delaware.

1888—Detroit (third), Michigan; Milwaukee (fourth and fifth), Menasha, Wisconsin; Chicago (seventh), Illinois; Reading, Hazleton, Hudson, Glenlyon, Freeland, Pennsylvania; Baltimore (second) Maryland; Chicopee, Massachusetts.

1889—Chapel Hill, Texas; Detroit (fourth), Michigan; Two Rivers, Fairchild, Wisconsin; St. Louis (second), Kansas City, Missouri; Maywood, Braidwood, Illinois; Houtzdale, Everson, Pennsylvania; Brooklyn (second and third), Buffalo (third), Rochester, Amsterdam, New York; Opole, Minnesota; Omaha, Nebraska; Newark, New Jersey.

1890—Detroit (fifth), Sheboygan, Hilliards, Saginaw, Menominee, Michigan; Poznań, Wisconsin; Chicago (eighth), Joliet, Dubois, Illinois; Dickinson, Priceburg, Philadelphia (second), Pennsylvania; Hammond, Indiana; Williamsbridge, Buffalo (fourth), Syracuse, Schenectady, New York; Dillonville, Ohio; Smartville, Nebraska; Bloomfield, Trenton (first and second), Camden, New Jersey; Fall River, Massachusetts; Tacoma, Roslyn, Washington.

1891—Port Austin, Ironwood, Michigan; Elmhurst, Hegewisch, Downers Grove, Waukegan, Spring Valley, Illinois; New Kensington, Pennsylvania; Michigan City, Indiana; Buffalo (fifth), Albion, Elmira, New York; Elmdale, Minnesota; Palisades Park, New Jersey; Meriden, Connecticut.

1892—Bricefield, Missouri; South Chicago (second), Sobieski, Rutland, Peru, Gostyn, Illinois; Mahanoy City (first and second), Natrona, McKeesport, Carnegie, Pennsylvania; Rolling Prairie, Indiana; Greenbush, Minnesota; Pilzno, Nebraska; Passaic, Perth Amboy, New Jersey.

1893—Milwaukee (sixth), Marinette, Spruce, Wisconsin; Chicago (ninth and tenth), Illinois; Duryea, New Philadelphia, Pennsylvania; Buffalo (sixth), Salamanca, Albany, New York; Kraków, Nebraska; Pe Ell, Enunclaw, Washington.

1894—Milwaukee (seventh), Berlin (second), Wisconsin; Leavenworth, Kansas; Chicago (eleventh), Kensington, Illinois; Nanticoke (second), Mammoth, Duquesne, Pennsylvania; Kroze, Minnesota; South Amboy, Bayonne, New Jersey; New Britain, Connecticut.

1895—Antigo, La Crosse, Wisconsin; Chicago (twelfth and thirteenth), Illinois; South Bend (second), Indiana; Florida, Utica, New York; Duelm, Flensburg, Minnesota; Worcester, Holyoke, Massachusetts; Ansonia, Connecticut.

1896—"Gazeta," Texas; Ludington, Michigan; South Milwaukee, Ripon, Plover, Belmont, Weyerhauser, Wisconsin; Mt. Carmel (second), Morris, Pittsburgh (third), Braddock, Antrim, Pennsylvania; Depew, New York; Cleveland (third), Ohio.

1897—San Marcos, Pulaski, Falls City, Texas; Niedolipie, Michigan; Alban, Oshkosh, Green Bay, Wisconsin; Shenandoah (second), Pennsylvania; Morisania, New York.

1898—Kościuszko, St. John's, "Gaina," Texas; Grand Rapids (second), St. Marie, Michigan; Plainfield, Torun, Wisconsin; Plains, Philadelphia (third), Homestead, Pennsylvania; Buffalo (seventh), Yonkers, New York; Cleveland (fourth), Ohio; Ashton, South Omaha, Nebraska.

1899—Seguin, Texas; Detroit (sixth), Michigan; Ashland, Wisconsin; Chicago (fourteenth), Minonk, Sheller, Illinois; East Plymouth, Windber, Pennsylvania; Bridgeport, Norwich, Connecticut.

1900—Williamstown, Michigan; Cudahy, Superior, Wisconsin; Poznań, Blue Island, Kankakee, Oglesby, Illinois; Nanticoke (third), Ford City, Latrobe, Pennsylvania; South Bend (third), Whiting, East Chicago, Indiana; Little Falls, Rich Prairie, Minnesota; Providence, Rhode Island.

From the above overview of Polish parishes it is evident that sixteen Polish parishes existed prior to 1870. In 1880 there were 58 more for a total of 74. In 1890 there were 96 more, totaling 170. Finally, by 1900 there were 160 more, for a total of 330 not including the innumerable "missions"—that is, churches without permanent pastors. Counting the missions, in 1905 there were over 500 churches! What a "crescendo" in the number of Polish parishes! They are increasing at an accelerated rate.

Polish parishes, nevertheless, do not encompass all those Poles who have arrived from the homeland; they include at most two-thirds in either non-Polish Catholic churches or no church at all, which always happens when there is no Polish or no other Catholic church nearby. This much, at least, can be said about the Poles: wherever a group of families lived together within a radius of several miles, they immediately thought of founding a Polish church—an exception being where a Polish settlement was composed solely of the intelligentsia, as in San Francisco or New York. This can not be said of all Catholics arriving from Europe. For example, the Italians cannot get used to donating to the support of the Church in America. They prefer to live without it rather than to pay for a priest and a church. In this way the Church loses many members—rotten members—but what relation this American loss has to "religious tolerance" as discussed in the Lwów *Gazeta Kościelna* is quite difficult to detect.

According to calculations, the number of Catholics in the United States should amount to 26,000,000, considering immigration statistics and the population growth of various nationalities and religions during the nineteenth century, but in fact this number amounts to 11,000,000. Undoubtedly, due to the lack of organized Catholic life, schools, press and clergy in the first half of the 19th century, many Catholic immigrants or their children have been lost to the church. . . . Today such a danger does not exist. Catholics have a secure clergy, and their faith is upheld through well-organized parochial school education, together with parish associations.[3]

The reason why so many members left the church was the lack of clergy, especially at the beginning of the immigration. Catholics immigrated in large numbers, but the clergy, probably due to shortsightedness, did not follow them. Missionaries were sent from Europe to China, Africa, and God knows where else, but they were not sent in the wake of their own emigrant countrymen. Whose fault was it? Was it not known that a flock without a shepherd must scatter?[4]

Due to the lack of Poles to care for their own, the Germans looked after us. And so, on Christmas Day, 1867, at Bishop Henni's request, Rev. J. M. Gartner, VG (a Bohemian German), left his position as professor of philosophy at the seminary in St. Francis, Wisconsin, in order to take care of the abandoned Poles, Czechs, and other Slavs.[5] Rev. Gartner established the "Słowiański Zakład Missyjny pod opięka Boskiego Serca" [Slavic Missionary Institution under the care of the Sacred Heart], and collected contributions throughout America for the Slavic mission. With the help of Rev. A. Lang and Rev. F. Heller he collected $2,764.90 in New York and Boston during the summer of 1868. The following summer he collected $2,380.54 in Illinois and Missouri and later gathered $4,352.20 in Cinncinnati, Reading, Dayton, and Hamilton, Ohio. With this money he built the "mother missionary church" (the Czech St. John Nepomulen) in Milwaukee and organized the "Kongregacyę missyonarzy Boskiego Serca" [Congregation of Missionaries of the Sacred Heart] into provisional and apostolic divisions. But by December 1, 1872, he ended his missionary work, since he felt "both the Czechs and Poles are managing on their own." In his *Schluss-Bericht ueber die Slavische Mission*, Rev. Gartner gives the following testimony about the Poles:

Up to this point I have dwelt upon the Bohemian constituency of the country, rather than on the numerically greater Slavic population. Now I feel the need to direct attention to those immigrating in unsuspected numbers, the Poles, a noble, devout people, who willingly make sacrifices. They deserve our warmest and most enthusiastic sympathy and support, not solely out of compassion for the national and religious persecution in their unhappy homeland, but also in gratitude for the offspring of those heroes, who, under their brave king, John Sobieski, saved Germany from destruction and subjugation by the Turks. They rescued Germany, torn and bloodied by religious wars, barely 200 years ago. Now these sons and daughters of the redeemers of our faith come to America, so that here we may help them preserve the faith which some attempt to wrest from them in their homeland through cunning and force. Though they come to us helpless and poor, they come with indestructible loyalty and dedication to the Holy Church, for which they so sorely suffered and bore the yoke of servitude. Acquaint yourselves with them and you will soon grow to love them. Though I and every priest drank deeply of the bitter chalice of suffering among the Bohemians before we could achieve some success, the poor, good Poles, no matter where I met them or how poorly I spoke their language, always gave me but comfort and joy. Their child-like reverence and devotion to the priest, their generosity with respect to parish concerns, together with a deep, often naive piety, earn them the affection of their colleagues in faith, even those who speak other languages. Based upon my conversations, all priests speak of them with deep compassion and respect.

Today, in 1900, there is still a great lack of Polish priests and Polish teachers. While 11 million Catholics in the United States are served by a total of 12,000 Catholic priests (less than 1,000 souls for each priest), there are only 500 Polish priests for two million Polish Catholics, which means about 4,000 Polish souls per Polish priest! In America there are approximately 250,000 Polish children of school age, and of those 70,000 attend Polish parish schools. Despite this, our teachers—barely numbering 1,000—are burdened with too many children, because for each Polish teacher there is an average of seventy children.

Despite this, the Catholic Church, and especially the Polish church, grew and developed extremely quickly and surprisingly well in America—even without tender care from the Old Country. Let the Old Country say what it wants, but God clearly watched over the Catholic immigration, and especially over the Polish immigration to America. Our people here instinctively found one another. Although sometimes without a shepherd, they gathered together for collective prayers and rallied and organized themselves into parishes. Before long, God also gave them zealous and energetic pastors, and in less than half a century about 500 new Polish churches stood in the land Washington founded! Have so many churches ever been built within forty-five years in old Poland? Maybe during the reign of Mieczysław, but even then the kings and nobles built neither as many nor as impressive churches as those built here by the working people.[6] It is true that some pastors, in order to build a magnificent church, also incurred magnificent debts in keeping with the ancient Polish principle: *Zastaw się ale postaw się!* [Pledge your fortune to put your best foot forward]. Nevertheless, these are rare cases about which more will be said later in this *Historya*. We will not mention anything here about schools, religious orders, hospitals, and other charitable institutions. Today the Polish churches and rectories in America are valued at ten million dollars and the Polish population in America spends close to one million dollars per year for the support of its priests.

In the United States there are no Catholics who, by habit or for profit, are Catholics in name only, as sometimes happens in Europe. Those in America who have remained true to the faith are Catholics by conviction, ready to actively support the Church. Although there is a relatively small number of them here, by their activity they surpass their European counterparts in certain respects. In Europe everyone finds his churches already built, his parishes and bishoprics organized, schools set up; in other words, the church is already funded and established. The European only needs to perform some religious function from time to time so that he may pass as a Catholic despite his passive and indifferent behavior regarding the Church. In North America, Catholics had a far more difficult task. Like the first Christians, they had by their own labor to erect churches, build schools, import and support priests, and organize and subsidize Catholic newspapers. In other words, they had to organize and build everything from scratch. Catholic priests in the United States again have a more difficult task than in Europe, because in America, in the words of St. Paul, *"omnia omnibus"* [all things to all men]. Here it is not enough to hear confessions, teach and preach in church, administer the Sacraments, visit and care for the sick, and bury the dead as the priests do in Europe. Here they must also organize parishes, establish sodalities and associations, edit journals, administer schools, organize reading rooms and libraries, collect and look after funds, administer circles and committees, and remember a thousand other matters that in Europe are usually taken care of by lay people. That the situation of priests in this country is more difficult is best illustrated by the fact that the most practical and most well-educated European priest sometimes cannot manage in a small American parish, despite his education and often long-term experience in Europe.

Our countrymen in Poland have an over-exaggerated notion of the wealth and comforts of the Polish priests in America. They presume that every priest in this country is a millionaire who shovels up dollars from the street. Also our countrymen here in America who live in large cities and observe only the urban pators, who are in fact well-to-do, presume that the rest of the Polish clergy is similarly well off. However, this is not the case.

It is a strange thing that people constantly living in the same environment get so accustomed to it that they often judge the rest of the world accordingly. For example, urban dwellers often have very strange views regarding the inhabitants of small towns, settlements, and farms. When they see wealthy, urban clergy making use of the public and private wealth of this world, they presume that clergymen all over the world enjoy these same conditions. They forget, or do not know, that these people constitute the exception, and that the greater part of the clergy must content itself with much less. They presume that all clergy lead comfortable lives with their parishioners grouped in a small circle around their church. They forget about those who, having parishes composed of farmers, live under Siberian-like conditions and are subject to many inconveniences and hard work. If we live grouped together within a huge body of people and constantly are with others of our own ethnic origin on a collective basis, we do not understand that it is possible to lose our nationality in this country, we do not understand that the use of the Polish language in small Polish colonies would perish were it not for the Polish church.

And so this little Polish church in the forests, mountains, and on the prairies is not only a strong mainstay of the Catholic faith, but the only hope for preserving Polish nationality. We have many such anchors of faith and nationality in the sea of other nationalities in America—in all states from the northern borders of Dakota to the southern boundaries of Texas, from the Atlantic to the Pacific, and especially in the state of Wisconsin. In the small Polish settlements and colonies of Two Rivers, Antigo, Poniatowski, Kazimierz, Oshkosh, Poland, Northeim, Princeton, Pułaski, Friendship, Facher, Mill Creek, Ripon, and others, as well as similar settlements in Minnesota, Michigan, Pennsylvania, and in other states, the Polish ethnic group would soon perish were it not for the Polish church with its sermons, hymns, confessions, and prayers in the Polish language. And the life of a pastor in such areas is not a bed of roses by any means. A priest there is a genuine missionary. There is a lot of work and many conveniences, and his life is often very simple due to a meager income. In the beginning, when these settlements were first being established, the priest was subjected to many inconveniences and sometimes even dangers. He sometimes had to suffer in real poverty. In Texas, for example, a priest often had to travel twenty miles or more on horseback to visit the sick. Similarly, he had to ride tens of miles to get from one settlement to another, say Mass on a quickly prepared altar, preach, and hear confessions.

In Wisconsin and the northern states it was worse, especially during the winter, and today it still is not much better. Many priests had several missionary parishes scattered throughout forests and hills, dozens of miles from one another. A priest was often called at night to someone's distant sickbed. He had to travel by sled through snowstorms and biting frost on a journey that often took four to six hours through wilderness, and then as many hours to return. Today, city folk used to driving even a few blocks in an electrically heated car, do not have and cannot have any idea of what such travels entailed and how they taxed one's health. And income? A tale comes to mind of a certain old priest who, a few years ago, had a small parish deep in the heart of Wisconsin. Once a bishop paid him a surprise visit. The poor pastor was quite concerned because he did not have anything to offer his dignified guest. At home he had only a piece of *kiełbasa* [Polish sausage], some thick bread, and the remains of a cheap wine. There was nothing warm to eat and the closest cottage was half a mile away. But he apologized to the bishop and offered him *czem chata bogata* [that in which the home is rich]. If we added to this that this pastor's rectory was a dilapidated one-and-a-half room hut, and that the unmarried organist—who simultaneously was the sexton, groundskeeper, cook, and so on—lived in a corner room of the church attic, then we can somewhat imagine the financial condition of the priest and parish. Today it probably is not as bad, especially in small towns, but in many parishes among the forests and prairies great privation still exists. Despite this, these priests do not complain, but gladly go into such regions to preach the word of God and to save the population from lack of religion and denationalization. They should neither be envied nor criticized, but every Pole should show them appreciation, respect, and gratitude.

Since his parish contains people of various nationalities, views and personalities, a priest in America is forced to speak two, three, and even four languages. He must sometimes reconcile the most incompatible dispositions and surroundings, and restrain the wildest explosions of hate, anger and revenge. Especially in the East, where church relations are less established than in the West, a priest must deal with people who possess tempestuous and rowdy temperaments, with people who left Europe for various reasons and who, in America, learned to treat all dignity with contempt, to ignore all authority, and to laugh at all responsibility to God and society.

Among the Polish clergy in America we encounter the spirit of initiative, motivation, and enterprise common to all Americans. We admire the outright shrewdness and organizational activity, unheard of in Poland, without which they would never have established so many Polish parishes in America, built so many churches, or founded so many schools, public institutions, and associations. This fervor sometimes carries them truly too far, but . . . which one of us is without faults?

In Europe our countrymen have often pronounced very unfair judgment on the entire clergy and Polish church in America due to hasty generalizations based on incomplete information. Should some parish disturbance occur, newspapers in the Old Country write about it as if it were an occurrence characteristic of the entire American Polonia. The fact that hundreds of other Polish parishes in America live and develop quietly has been ignored. Unfortunately, one disturbance is enough to condemn the whole American Polonia. This is strange and inexplicable logic.

In order to counteract this, the Polish clergy united itself into organizations. Such organizations include the Priests Association under the leadership of Rev. Wincenty Barzyński, a Priests' Association in Minnesota, and one in the East composed of clergy who were alumni of the Polish seminary in Detroit, and so on. Since 1902 the Association of Secular Priests has existed under the leadership of Rev. Stanisław Nawrocki and Rev. J. F. Szukalski. This association has been actively involved in church politics, especially the current and pressing matter of equal rights for the Polish clergy.[7]

Monastic orders, such as the Jesuits, Resurrectionists, Conventual and Reformed Franciscans, and later the Holy Cross Fathers, provided the most zealous priests, especially at the outset of the emigration, and they have rendered great service to the growth of the Polish church in America. Rev. Kajsiewicz, the General of the Resurrectionists, who twice visited Canada and the United States in 1865 and 1871, calculated on the later occasion that "for 60,000 to 100,000 Poles scattered throughout all of North America there were all of twenty Polish priests, of which six were Resurrectionists, three Jesuits, three Franciscans, and the rest secular priests. American bishops brought over immigrant priests in 1831, 1848, and even later. But at present, without discussing the reasons here, the American bishops reluctantly accept secular priests and they absolutely demand monastic ones. The bishop of Detroit demands missionaries from us for the Poles settled in his diocese. During pastoral retreats conducted by Rev. Kajsiewicz in Montreal in August 1865, the bishop of Alton (in southern Illinois) requested the same for me. He stated that he had a few Polish and Czech secular priests, but they finally got bored and went out into the world.[8] Beginning in 1860 the Resurrectionists extended their missionary activities among the Poles in Canada. Thereafter, they expanded to Texas (1866), Michigan (1868), Illinois (1870), and also made trips to other states. The first Polish Resurrectionist to arrive in America in 1860 was Rev. Franciszek Breitkopf, CR (German Resurrectionists were already in Canada from 1857). He worked in America 44 years and died in 1904. A second Resurrectionist arrived with him, or immediately after him. He was Rev. Edward Głowacki, or Głowalcki, CR, who was ordained in 1860. He worked in Canada and the United States for 22 years, and then returned to Europe. I saw him in Rome in 1904 when he was still robust and rosy-cheeked, although his hair had turned white as snow. Rev. Głowacki, a Pole by birth but not in language, is a descendent of the famous Bartosz Głowacki.[9] He was born in 1830 in Breslau [Wrocław]; his father was a native in Warsaw and his mother was a German. So that the Germans would not mispronounce his name as "Glowacki," he changed the "c" to "l" and Rev. Kajsiewicz in his *Listy* [Letters] calls him "Głowalski."

The Resurrectionists did not have enough recruits for the Polish mission in America, since their best members were engaged in their Bulgarian mission. But Divine Providence itself seemed to indicate to the Resurrectionists their future sphere of activity. American bishops sounded the alarm, requesting Polish Resurrectionists. Nor was there lack of direction from heaven itself. The general himself mentions this in his *Listy*. "I am full of hope," wrote Rev. Kajsiewicz in 1865, "that our congregation will quickly develop here [in America]."[10]

Meanwhile, both he and his successor, Rev. General Semeneńko,[11] thought of the dissolution rather than the development of the congregation in America. Thanks only to Rev. Adolf Bakanowski and Rev. Żwiardowski, and especially to the super-human efforts of Rev. Wincenty Barzyński, the Resurrectionist Fathers did not prove totally unfaithful to their historical mission, which Divine Providence pointed out to them.

There were two exceptional men who, in the history of the American Polonia, became forever famous by organizing huge Polish parishes: Rev. Wincenty Barzyński, CR, who died in the West in 1899, and Rev. Jan

Pitass in the East. Both became outstanding by establishing two of the largest Polish immigrant parishes in America. Barzyński founded St. Stanislaus Kostka parish in Chicago which numbered about 50,000 members during his lifetime, and Pitass founded St. Stanislaus, Bishop and Martyr parish, in Buffalo, which had some 30,000 members. We will not dwell on the positive or negative aspects of colossal parishes. We are only establishing the fact that these men were able to huddle, gather, and unite into one organizational entity such huge masses of immigrants, and that for over a quarter of a century they were able to remain as pastors of such huge parishes—ten times larger than many dioceses in America. This fact proves the great and uncommon organizational and self-preserving strength of both of these priests. In this regard both of them permanently shine in the firmament of Polish American history as stars of the first magnitude. Other permanent stars, around which many planets and satellites revolved, are those who have served interruptedly as pastors of the same parish for over a quarter century. These include: Rev. Benvenuto Gramlewicz in Nanticoke, Pennsylvania; Rev. Jacek [Hyacinth] Gulski in Milwaukee, Wisconsin; Rev. Czyżewski[12] in South Bend, Indiana; Rev. Dominic Majer in St. Paul, Minnesota; Rev. Paweł Gutowski in Detroit, Michigan; Rev. Urban Raszkiewicz in Otis, Indiana; Rev. Lenarkiewicz who died in 1904 in Shenandoah, Pennsylvania; Rev. Władisław Miśkiewicz in Pittsburg, Pennsylvania; Rev. Ludwik Dąbrowski in San Antonio, Texas; and perhaps a few other such stars. Permanent stars of second and third rank are the many pastors who established smaller or larger parishes and constantly labored in them for ten or fifteen years. There were, however, other orbiting satellites and planets passing through various settlements; and finally long-tailed comets crossing the entire length and breadth of America, not only in the North but also in the South.

We have a large group of preachers who are famous for their eloquence, men such as the golden-tongued Rev. Gulski, the pioneering Rev. Możejewski, the honey-sweet Rev. J. Kosiński, CR, the tearfully moving Rev. Byżewski, OFM, the convincing Rev. Paweł Rhode, the entrancing Rev. Wincenty Lewandowski, the soothing Rev. Cezar Tomaszewski, CSSp, the thundering Rev. Raczyński, CSC., the enlightening Rev. Dworzak, DD, the eloquent Rev. Edward Kozłowski, the fiery Rev. Bójnowski, the popular Rev. L. Garus, the eloquent Rev. D. Majer, the reproving Rev. Gramlewicz, and the humorous Rev. Zaręczny. It is difficult to name them all, since there are as many as there are beads on a rosary. Of the travelling missionaries who, with the evangelical plow, furrowed through the length and breadth of the Lord's vineyard in America, we know Rev. Szulak, SJ, Rev. Matauszek, SJ, Rev. Sebastyański, SJ, Rev. Jeka, OFM, Rev. Remigiusz Berendt, OFM, Rev. Rothenburger, SJ, Rev. Beigert, SJ, Rev. Wnęk, SJ, Rev. Warol, SJ, Rev. Janowski, SJ, Rev. Bieda, SJ, Rev. Antoni Wiśniewski, OFM, and others.

So far two Poles have held the position of Vicar General: the late Rev. Feliks Żwiardowski, CR, in the Diocese of San Antonio, Texas, and Rev. Msgr. Karol Langner in the Diocese of Marquette, Michigan. This is the highest position achieved by Poles in the Church. There are no canons or cathedral chapters in America. However, consultants and a diocesan council do exist. Therefore, we have among the Polish clergy about a dozen diocesan consultants or advisors to the bishop with the title of "Very Reverend": Jacek Gulski in the Diocese of Milwaukee, Wisconsin; A. W. Gara in the Diocese of La Crosse, Wisconsin; F. Lange in Chicago, Illinois; Jacek [Hyacinth] Fudziński, OMC, in Buffalo, New York; P. Gutowski in Detroit, Michigan; J. Sroka in Duluth, Minnesota; Andrzej Ignasiak in Erie, Pennsylvania; Edward Kozłowski in the Diocese of Grand Rapids, Michigan; J. Czarnowski in the Diocese of Green Bay, Wisconsin; Benvenuto Gramlewicz in the Diocese of Scranton, Pennsylvania; and J. Pacholski in the Diocese of Winona, Minnesota. A diocesan consultant is a shadow of the Old Country canon. Such consultants have only an advisory function; they do not have a deciding vote in any matter. An American bishop must, at times, seek the consultants' advice, but he is not obligated to follow it. It would be different if we had canons; for then, in some cases, a bishop would have to heed their advice. Canons and cathedral chapters have already existed for a long time in other missionary countries such as England and Holland. Although they are on the same missionary footing as the United States, only we are here in America still do not have canons. Why? Does Rome not wish to give us canons? Of course they do. By 1883 Rome already had endeavored to establish canons and cathedral chapters here, but the American bishops opposed it (according to Rev. Smith in his *Elements of Ecclesiastical Law*, volume I, p. 466). Canons would curtail the bishops' power. Since there are no canons, there is no canon law—the bishop is the canon law in America. Nevertheless, diocesan consultants in America have the right to choose candidates for the office of bishop. Irremovable, inviolable pastors (*rectores inamovibiles*) have the same right according to the decrees of the Third Council of Baltimore, which state that "every tenth rector of a parish is to be irremovable" (see Tit. II, cap. V). We Poles in America should have at least forty of them, but we do not have four. Rev. Jan Pitass, Rev. Lange, and Rev. J. Sroka are the only Polish *rectores inamovibles*. We also have a few Polish titular deans (Rev. Jacek Gulski, Rev. Jan Pitass, and Rev. Maryan Matkowski). We have an official of the bishop's *curia* in San Antonio, Texas (Rev. Ludwik Dąbrowski). Rev. J. E. Wróbel is part of the diocesan school administration in Fort Wayne, Indiana. Rev. J. Dworzak, DD, is an examiner of the clergy in the Archdiocese of New York and these are all the "distinguished" Polish clergy in America![13]

Strictly speaking, neither pastors nor vicars exist in America, since there are no canonically-established parishes; there are only so-called rectors and assistants. To date, very few churches have been truly "consecrated" (*ecclesiae consecratae*); of all the Polish churches, only one in Chicago was consecrated due to the energetic efforts of Rev. Stanisław Nawrocki. All the others are only "blessed" (*ecclesiae benedictae*).

Since its establishment in 1873, the Polish Roman Catholic Union has ably contributed to the development of the Polish church in America. The following clergymen played an exceptional role in that organization: Rev. Teodor Gieryk; Mr. Jan Barzyński; and Mr. Piotr Kiołbassa, as its founders; Rev. Wincenty Barzyński, CR, as the ingenious organizer; as well as Rev. Szulak, SJ, Rev. Rodowicz, Rev. Musielewicz, Rev. Józef Dąbrowski, Rev. Kandyd Kozłowski, and Messrs. Piotrowski, Jan Nowak, Wróblewski, Głosowski, Sonnenberg, Niemczewski, Jędrzejek, Manna, Gniot, and others.[14] But in chapters 10 and 11 we shall discuss more extensively the activities of the Union and other organizations, as well as the beneficial influence of newspapers.

Since 1895, as a result of the establishment of independent churches, there has been a need for some form of unified reflection, some kind of concerted activity to strengthen the faith, counteract the schism and to improve schools and Catholic education in general. There was a need to take care of immigration and colonization, to enrich the Catholic press, to counteract the unhealthy social trends that were renouncing religion and demanding its elimination from our civic and national life. Therefore, the idea of congresses emerged of which there have thus far been three: the first two were held in Buffalo, New York, in 1896 and 1901, and the last one in Pittsburgh, Pennsylvania, in 1904. They were initiated by Rev. Jan Pitass. At this juncture it would be premature to write about the results of the third congress, but what were the results of the first two? Since this writer [Kruszka] personally took an active part in the congresses and does not want to appear to be biased, he gladly yields to someone else the description of the progress and results of the first two congresses. That individual should be someone who was never overly involved in these congresses, who kept in the background and could, therefore, judge them impartially. *Dziennik Chicagoski* [Chicago Daily], the organ of the Resurrectionists, writes about these congresses as follows:

Endeavoring to reflect on the history of the convening and the results of both of the first Polish Catholic congresses in America draw lessons from them, it suffices to carefully look through the official reports of both of these congresses, which we presently have before us. The first of these congresses occurred on September 22-25, in Buffalo, New York and the second almost exactly five years later, that is, on September 24, 25, and 26, 1901.

After carefully reading both of these reports, we are struck by a singular and very important fact. . . . It is this: while preparations for the first congress undoubtedly were more conscientious and extensive, interest in it was much more widespread, and that interest was awakened not only in America but much more intensely in Europe—and the pre-congress work was more diligent, more abundant, and more energetic. Even the progress of the congress itself was more enthusiastic, and the development of activities and resolutions adopted were more extensive than those of the second one. But the results and consequences of the second congress were surely more successful and, if we may say so, more perceptible than anything the first congress could boast of. The results of the second congress were more positive, not because it was less carefully prepared and conducted than the first one, but, in spite of it; the factors responsible for this were different and we shall discuss them at a later time.

We will first justify our statement asserting that the preparations for the first congress were better and more comprehensive. When the need for convening a Polish Catholic congress was appropriately discussed in the newspapers, the first pre-congress conference was called on March 19, 1896, in Detroit, Michigan. It was attended by twenty priests and fourteen secular priests from eight localities, representing Michigan, Illinois, New York, Ohio, and Pennsylvania. This conference decided which issues would be discussed at the congress and chose the main committee whose task was to convene it.

From the time of the conference [we read further in the report], held in Detroit, the main committee made great efforts and worked most energetically in order to unite the largest number of advocates in support of the Polish Catholic Congress. To this end, it issued many appeals which were carried, at the time, by the entire Polish Catholic press in the United States. Finally, the reverend priests from the West, who from the outset took a wait-and-see attitude toward the congress, convened a separate conference on June 2, 1896, in Milwaukee, Wisconsin.

As the minutes of this conference show, 27 priests (there were no secular ones present) gathered from twelve localities in the states of Minnesota, Wisconsin, Illinois, Missouri, and Indiana. Besides this, over twenty other priests sent letters endorsing most of the probable resolutions.

Certain new desires were expressed at this conference, and the program of the congress drafted beforehand in general terms was approved and supplemented.

There was still a third pre-congress conference held on June 11, 1896, again in Detroit, Michigan. It was attended by only ten priests and four secular priests from eight localities, representing the states of Michigan, Illinois, New York, Pennsylvania, Maryland, and Ohio. A resolution was approved to invite a long list of personages from all regions of Poland to participate in the congress. The motions of prior conferences were approved.

On June 23, 1896, the main committee issued a proclamation to convene the congress in Buffalo on September 22, 1896.

According to its minutes, the congress in Buffalo was attended by 248 lay people and 69 priests, including a guest from Poland, the Very Reverend Father Chamberlain Wawrzyniak. Those attending hailed from 49 localities representing thirteen states. In addition, 27 priests from the West gave their votes by proxy to the Very Reverend Wawrzyniak. A huge amount of mail extremely favorable to the congress arrived from Europe and America.

We all know very well that the enthusiasm for the second congress was not so equally widespread. Unfortunately, the pre-congress conferences were taken up with squabbles of the Catholic press and part of the clergy, and Catholic lay people were excluded from the congress. While the first congress was honored by the presence of at least the Most Reverend John Verin, Bishop of Marquette, Michigan (a Slovak), and many Polish bishops and other highly-placed clergy from the Old Country sent very cordial letters, there was no bishop represented at the second congress. There were, however, 134 lay people and 67 priests from 48 localities in eleven states. Although there were over one hundred fewer delegates, the number of localities represented was almost the same.

Let us again add here that we are only reporting strict facts, which no one will be able to deny. We shall leave aside comments that are seen as unnecessary and that have already been amply analyzed. For the good of the cause, we desire that they should be ignored in the future.

The program of deliberations of the first Polish Catholic Congress in 1896 included deliberations on very many crucial matters. According to the recommendations of the first pre-congress conference, deliberations were to be held on the following points: (1) independent churches, (2) Polish theological seminary, (3) Polish National Alliance, (4) Polish Immigration Home, (5) general organization of the Polish Catholic labor organizations, (6) Polish teachers' seminary, and (7) Polish American press. This plan was modified and supplemented in such a way that five commissions took over these matters during deliberations: the first commission was recommended to deliberate on the matter of independent churches and the matter of including Polish priests within the hierarchy of the Catholic Church in America; the second concentrated on the issue of the Polish National Alliance; the third on theological and teachers' seminaries, as well as that of the Polish Immigration Home; the fourth on the Polish American press; and the fifth on Polish Catholic organizations in general and labor organizations.

From the 36 persons charged with preparing papers on these various issues, not less than fifteen of them actually completed written reports, of which at least a few continue to have great value today. On the basis of these papers and other conclusions arising from the committee debates, resolutions were adopted that were very beautiful and useful. On the last day of the congress, permanent committees were chosen whose purpose was to realize these resolutions. These committees embraced: (1) general Polish Catholic organization and labor organizations, (2) the press, (3) education, teachers, colleges, and seminaries, and (4) the hierarchy of the Catholic Church in America.

And, strangely, this congress, which was so carefully prepared and so beautifully conducted, and which so clearly comprehended the needs of the immigration [in America] and endeavored to satisfy them, made a very serious mistake at the end that is very obvious today, but which was overlooked at the time. Namely, it did not choose any executive committee to further direct the entire matter, to watch over the work of the various committees and to encourage their activity, to collect and organize these tasks and have control over them, and to call a second congress at the time when it considered them to be completed.

There was indeed a committee chosen with the power to convene the next congress when it felt the appropriate time had come. Since it was resolved that the next congress would be held in Chicago, it was understood that there was a need for designating a committee to prepare local arrangements. This committee was even called "local" and it had absolutely no power or instructions other than to fix the time of the second congress and to convene it whenever it felt that the right time had arrived.

As a matter of fact, this poor committee, which later fruitlessly called together committees with certain duties (although it was not so authorized), was greatly criticized for the inactivity of the other committees and for the fact that it was not able to convene the second congress. Due to the inactivity of the committee, it did not know how to justify convening the congress or how to bring it about.

Therefore, without its cooperation, preparations were begun to convene the second congress. The work of the first one went to waste. In the second congress, decisions were made to begin work anew in matters that had not ceased to be important and from among which the most important issues were chosen and given first priority.

As is known, and as we have already pointed out, lamentable auspices preceded this congress due, above all, to the unnecessary quarrel with the Catholic press, the withdrawal from the congress of part of the clergy and Catholic representatives, and the hurried and feverish convocation of the congress without adequate preparation.

With all this, two important matters placed in the forefront distinguished the second congress and its progress; its manner of deliberation, resolutions, and decisions were very significant. The means of deliberation was similar to that of the first congress. However, the conclusion was different. Above all, a permanent executive department was chosen and entrusted with a broad mandate. And although the congress went to the other extreme—again a mistake—since separate committees were not appointed to take care of various matters which were discussed at the congress, the executive department was only instructed to appoint them (which later proved almost unfeasible). Of course, the end result proved that they acted more appropriately than had the first congress.

And so the results were more successful in that the second congress put forward as its first priority two important matters: consideration of the Polish clergy within the Catholic hierarchy in America and a general Catholic organization. It found two especially energetic men who were to assume direction of the matters, Rev. Wacław Kruszka and Rev. Kazimierz Sztuczko.[15]

If we mention the names of Rev. Kruszka and Rev. Sztuczko as men whose choice was especially appropriate and fortunate (and the congress itself surely did not suspect to what degree), we do so to prove that the results of this congress would have been insignificantly small had it not been for the energy of these two men and for the financial and moral aid of the Very Reverend [Jan] Pitass, who should never be forgotten while discussing this matter.

Regardless of the attempts to present this in a different light, the undisputable fact is that Rev. Wacław Kruszka, together with Rev. Pitass, having been entrusted with the task of trying to achieve recognition for the Polish clergy in America, constantly encountered difficulties and opposition not only from those who doubted the suitability of this action, but also from those who initiated the project themselves, the very delegates of the second congress and even the members of the executive department. This began at the very outset and continued almost up to his [Kruszka's] departure for Rome. Faced with such difficulties and opposition and an absolute lack of support and assistance—especially financial (except for the personal aid of Rev. Pitass)—Rev. Kruszka found himself so alone and lacking any kind of cooperation that a hundred others in his place would have become disillusioned and would have abandoned their intentions to carry out the plan. His great ambition, in the good sense of the word, kept him from disillusionment and his special shrewdness, again in a positive sense, insured him partial or even complete success. He left by himself, since no one wanted to go with him, but travelled by coincidence with a non-Pole, Mr. Mahany, which proved fortunate. He had only meager resources and did not know if they would last through a stay of several weeks in Rome. But he left with a good imagination, with a reserve of great energy and strong will, and with confidence that no one else had. He later obtained support, forced acknowledgement from the doubters, and achieved significant success in his mission.

In all this the second congress did not have any other part except choosing the appropriate person, because the congress itself did not know how to give directions for conducting this matter nor did it have the financial means to effectively take care of it.

Almost the same may be said about the second important issue which was the subject of deliberation at both congresses; that is, federating the Polish Catholics in the United States.

The second congress was only capable of assessing and recognizing the need for such a federation (just as the first congress had). It did not define the means to deal with this matter, nor present the methods to achieve this goal. It presented details that were complicated and unclear, and—as the results indicated—to some extent unachievable. The second congress appointed the executive department which was entrusted with this matter. Its members were Rev. K. Truszyński, president; Rev. Rev. Wojtalewicz, acting president for quite a while; Mr. Stefan Czaplewski, vice-president; Rev. K. Sztuczko, CSC., first secretary; Mr. L. Szopiński, second secretary; and Mr. Lipowicz, treasurer.[16]

So much for the first and second congresses. The third congress was held September 27-29, 1904, in Pittsburgh, Pennsylvania, with the participation of two American bishops, but we will have more to say about it later.

At this time mention should be made of the Polish sect of independents in America, whose rise was the reason for convening the above mentioned congresses. "For there must be factions, so that those who are approved may be made manifest among you," said St. Paul (I Corinthians 11, 19). There is a saying that "everything evil comes from the clergy." A fish begins to putrefy from the head, and without a criminal priest there would be no heresy within the church. However, on the other hand, it is also true that an evil priest could not alone produce a new sect without the permission of the people. An evil priest is the father of each new sect within the Church, and the people are its mother, whether through license, force, or deceit.

Some call Rev. Mielcuszny the "father" of the Independents in America and consider Holy Trinity Parish in Chicago, Illinois, of which he was pastor from 1877 until his death in 1881, the first independent parish.[17] This view is erroneous, unfair, and cannot be proven historically, as we shall see later in this *Historya*. The first "independent" Polish parish actually was established through the efforts of Rev. Frydrychowicz (1873-1878) in Polonia, the oldest settlement in Wisconsin, in the place called Poland Corner where, in memory of this sad schism, a chapel has stood since the independence movement began.[18] This first movement, however, passed without a wider echo and influence on other Polish settlements. This schism had a strictly local, provincial nature. The name "niezależni" [Independents], or as the simple folk call them *"żelaźni"* [from "iron-willed ones"],[19] was still not known at all; it was generally accepted only after 1894 to mean the new renegades or Polish schismatics in America who preached independence from the Roman Catholic Church. The seed of "independence" [*niezależność*] which yielded a harvest was planted in America in 1886 by the late Rev. Dominic Kolasiński of Detroit, Michigan.[20]

The evil was warded off, to be sure, and the Detroit renegades made peace with the Church, but both the bad example and the scandal remained and subsequently bore bitter fruit. In the footsteps of Rev.

Kolasiński, Rev. Franciszek Kołaszewski, alias Rademacher, first declared himself in Cleveland, Ohio, in the summer of 1894. Like Kolasiński in Detroit, Kołaszewski in Cleveland proclaimed that he lived in unity and peace with all the Catholic bishops and the Holy Father, but that only Bishop Horstman from Cleveland was his personal enemy. The following year, 1895, an independent church was established in Buffalo of which first Rev. Klawiter and then the ex-organist, Kamiński, became the leaders. In the same year, 1895, Rev. Antoni Kozłowski founded the independent movement in Chicago.[21] Finally, in 1897 Rev. Hodur did the same in Scranton, Pennsylvania. In the four years from 1894 to 1898, a genuine storm arose and, in passing over the Polish communities, it strongly shook the tree of the Polish [Roman Catholic] church in America.

The Polish Independents in America did not form a homogeneous sect, but broke up into a few small ones. Although it is quite difficult to sort them out, it nevertheless is possible to divide them into three major sects. The first was in Chicago, headed by Antoni Kozłowski, the schismatic priest who was consecrated bishop by the Old Catholic bishops in Switzerland.[22] This sect called itself the "Polish Catholic Church." At the "First Polish Catholic Synod," convened by the "Most Reverend Bishop A. Kozłowski" in Chicago in 1898, there were 62 delegates and thirteen priests. On that occasion it was resolved that "a diocese is administered by a bishop elected by the clergy and the people" (Constitution, Chapter I, article 3). It was resolved to "strongly adhere to the Catholic faith (Yes!), based on the precepts of the Apostles and Holy Scripture" (Chapter II, article 1); "to acknowledge and accept the tradition of the Fathers of the Church and the profession of faith of St. Athanasius" (article 2); "to acknowledge the decrees of the Council of Trent with the exception of those that would obstruct the development of the Polish Catholic Church and the primacy of the Pope in the Western Church," (article 3); "to acknowledge the dogma of the Immaculate Conception of the Virgin Mary" (article 4); that "a parish will organize itself autonomously with regard to everyday matters" (Chapter III, article 1); and that "in religion the bishop rules regarding matters of the clergy" (article 2). At the Second Synod in 1904, it was resolved that "priests must be celibate" (Chapter VI, article 7); and that the Parish of the Transfiguration of Our Lord in Chicago cannot belong to the Chicago Diocese as long as its rector is Rev. T. Jakimowicz," a married ex-priest.[23]

Stefan Kamiński from Buffalo led the second sect. He was ordained a "priest," and was even made "bishop" by the notorious Vilatte.[24] He has under his jurisdiction one parish in Buffalo, one in Chicopee, Massachusetts, and one in Baltimore, Maryland. He is in charge of some priests ordained by Vilatte and some ordained by himself.

The schismatic Rev. Franciszek Hodur from Scranton, Pennsylvania, heads the third sect. From a handwritten letter of the "bishop elect"[25] Hodur dated January 9, 1905, which he recently directed to us from Scranton, we cited the following:

The Polish National Church is composed of thirteen parishes: Scranton, Pennsylvania (founded in July, 1898) with 350 families and 250 single men; Priceburg, Pennsylvania (founded in 1897), 200 families and 150 single men; Plymouth, Pennsylvania (founded in July 1898), 200 families and 250 single men; a church in Philadelphia was founded in the fall of that same year, 1898, and was thereafter placed under the jurisdiction of Bishop Kozłowski and Bishop Kamiński and failed; Fall River, Massachusetts, founded in July, 1899, with 200 families and 200 single men; a church in Chicopee, Massachusetts, initially founded by Bishop Kamiński, which came under my jurisdiction in 1899, and has 150 families and 120 single men; Duryea, Pennsylvania, founded in the fall of 1899, with 120 families and 100 single men; Bayonne, New Jersey, founded in the fall of 1890, with 200 families and 100 single men; Wilkes-Barre, Pennsylvania, founded in June, 1900, with 150 families and 100 single men; Passaic, New Jersey, founded in 1900, with 180 families and 150 single men; Lowell, Massachusetts, founded in 1900, with 150 families and 150 single men; Webster, Massachusetts, with 200 families and 150 single men; the church in Baltimore, Maryland founded in 1897, but only coming under my jurisdiction in 1904, with 250 families and 200 single men; and Shamokin, Pennsylvania, founded in October, 1904, with 100 families and 100 single men. This makes a total of 2,450 families and 2,020 single men. Therefore, there are presently 4,470 paying members and about 15,000 souls in the Polish National Church. I am not counting those who sympathize with our movement, but still do not have a permanent organization. Currently, a church is being established in Nanticoke, Pennsylvania, and I hope that about 200 families will join it, mainly members of the Polish National Alliance.[26]

The following priests are helping me in my work: Rev. W. Szumowski, a participant in the 1863 January Insurrection and former civilian director of Płock, who was appointed on behalf of the national government and is currently the pastor in Wilkes-Barre; Rev. M. Tolpa, the ex-Reformed Franciscan from Duryea; Rev. J. Dawidowski, who completed his studies with the Salesians in Turin and in Detroit, is pastor in Plymouth; Rev. Franciszek Kowalski, a priest from the Płock diocese and pastor in Priceburg; Rev. Franciszek Mirek, an ex-Dominican from Baltimore; Rev. W. Gawrychowski who studied at the Warsaw seminary and is pastor in Bayonne; Rev. Franciszek Bończak who completed classical studies at the Polish Gymnasium in Cieszyn and theology in America, pastor in Passaic; Rev. A. Pluciński, priest from the Kraków diocese, pastor in Fall River; Rev. M. C. Witorff, priest from the Wilno diocese, pastor in Chicopee; Rev. J. Kruszyński who studied in Poznań and is pastor in Lowell; Rev. W. Łagan who studied in Lwów and Wrocław and is pastor in Webster.

From 1901 we began introducing the Polish language into the liturgy and every National priest was obliged to say Mass in the Polish language at least once a month. Two priests are currently preparing liturgical books for print and when they are ready, we will totally eliminate Latin from the Church. In September of last year [1904] the First Synod was held in Scranton with the participation of 147 delegates, both lay and clergy. At this time a program I had outlined was approved, and I was chosen bishop. The teachings of our church are based on the Holy Scripture and Councils of Nicaea, Ephesus, Constantinople, and Chalcedon. The synod occurs with the highest solemnity, while the highest authority rests with the bishop who has had the additional help of the Great Council made up of six priests and six lay people.

As if on the sidelines, independent from all the Independents, stands Kołaszewski, alias Rademacher, in Cleveland, Ohio. He does not acknowledge anyone's jurisdiction and does not demand subordination from anyone. He himself bears the title of "prelate," or "vicar general," a position given him by René J. Vilatte. A few times he "converted," but whenever his state of health improved he would return to *vomitum suum* [to his own ways; or literally, "to his own vomit"]. "Gladly would a soul go to paradise, but its sins do not permit this."

The conditions that brought about the independent movement among the Poles in America are the following: the animosity, baseness, and ambition of some priests, on the one hand, and a blind confidence of the people in these priests, on the other; as well as a bad press and pseudo-philosophers. There was also the influx of the so-called intelligentsia from the Old Country, but it was not always genuine and was in extremely limited supply. Without a doubt more people arrived here who were a half-learned bad lot without any real education, but with a great dose of conceit. And since they were born "do-nothings" without any desire to work, they therefore stooped to agitating the people, expecting not only to live easily in this manner but also to acquire a certain fortune. They began by inciting brawls and disturbances in the Polish parishes, telling this one or that one that he was being treated unfairly because the priests were oppressing him, the bishops were taking advantage of him, and the entire Catholic Church was tyrannizing him. They began to tell the Polish parishioners that no one except them [the parishioners] should rule a parish, because the church, school, and other parish buildings were built with their money, because they supported priests and teachers, and because they paid the bishop his *cathedraticum* and so on. They began persuading the people they have the right to hire and fire priests, because a priest serves his parishioners just as a servant serves his master.

According to the resolutions of the Baltimore Council, parish property was, and is, bequeathed to the committee whose members include the bishop (as president), vicar general, pastor (as vice-president), and two trustees chosen from among the parishioners (as secretary and treasurer). Since the bishop, according to American federal law, acts as caretaker and, to some extent, as owner of the parish property, these evil advisors began to convince the people that the church, school, and other properties built with the parishioners' money do not belong to them but to a foreign-national bishop who can bequeath the parish plant to his relatives, sell it, or give it away to whomever he likes. This was always the primary argument raised by the independent leaders against the Roman Catholic Church. Even Hodur uses it as one of his strongest arguments to pull the wool over the eyes of his naive flock.[27] One of the first resolutions adopted at the second synod of Independents in Chicago in December, 1904, states: "We, as Polish Catholics, children of the one indivisible homeland of Poland, do resolve that all church properties founded by us will remain the exclusive possession of the Polish people in America. These properties cannot be bequeathed by any means to any bishops. In case of need by the homeland, our ethnic property can render a great service for the good of the Polish nation."

These agitators touched upon an extremely sore spot that we, the Roman Catholic clergy, had sold Polish church property to Irish and German bishops. Therefore, in many places the parishioners immediately began to demand the parish property and they started to administer the parish, taking upon themselves the right to manage the income of the priest, to collect his *jura stolae*,[28] and even to hire and fire clergy themselves.

The church authorities, of course, could not accept this type of demand and this led to an open revolt, to a break with the bishop and, subsequently, to a breach with the Church and the formation of independent parishes. Those priests deserve to be seriously reproved who due either to their reckless squandering of funds or to their inconsideration of the people and withholding of financial reports, gave the instigators ammunition with which to accuse them of misappropriation. Through their irresponsible incuring of sometimes enormous debts, those priests greatly contributed to the exasperation and estrangement of the parishioners who were already excessively burdened with interest rates, and this contributed to some effect to the schism.

In addition, conflicts often arose between priests and their parishioners due to the above mentioned factors. These disagreements could have been easily alleviated if the bishops had accurately known the Polish people, their living conditions, customs and traditions, and especially their language. So, as these conflicts intensified throughout the Polish parishes, the "lack of a Polish bishop" in America was felt all the more severely. All the Poles here, especially after 1891, wished—as a mushroom wishes for rain—for a Polish bishop in America! However, for a very long time they did not get one! Why? Because the American bishops were opposed it![29] But why were the Bishops opposed? The fault lay in the proverbial Slavic submissiveness and its spirit of subservience and servility. Submissiveness and obedience are a virtue, but servility and subservience are no less sinful than recalcitrance and disobedience. A Pole usually did not know genuine obedience that was compatible with human dignity, but was either servile or recalcitrant, going from one extreme to the other. In demanding a bishop of their own nationality, the Poles had law and justice behind them (only a lackey abdicates his rights), while their opponents, although strong in authority, based their opposition on very fragile foundations. What purpose did those who oppose the appointment of Polish bishops in America have in mind? Was it for the glory of God? Was it for the salvation of souls? Was it for the exaltation of the church? No! What then was the purpose? It was expressed in these words: "From the numerous elements inhabiting our country [the United States], from the numerous nationalities, a homogeneous nation will someday emerge. The task of the clerical leaders of the Polish people is to choose the wisest road to this homogeneity. . . . I repeat, that to choose this indirect road is no small task, but to choose it is absolutely necessary. If you, the future leaders of the Poles, will be able to choose this road and follow it wisely, then we, the Church hierarchy in America, will gladly place the helm of administration in your hands." This is what Archbishop Ireland of St. Paul, Minnesota, said, among other things, to the alumni of the Polish Seminary in Detroit on November 28, 1899. Probably no other bishop in the United States has stated his "Americanizing" tendencies as clearly and empathetically as did the Archbishop of St. Paul during his unforgettable visit to the seminary. "Endeavor to sensibly denationalize yourselves, and then you can expect something from us"—such was the essence of his speech.

Are we first to Americanize ourselves? But, for God's sake, we Poles already became Americans a long time ago! The difference between us and them is only that they are Americans of English, Irish, German, and other backgrounds, while we are Americans of Polish descent. So what is

Yankees suck!

their point? Not Americanizing us, but Anglicizing us! Their point is that
we should renounce our Polish heritage and become not Americans, but
Yankees! And will we do this? God save us from such a fate! A "Yankee"
is an American of English descent, or someone else who already has
became Anglicized. We are Americans, but never ever Yankees! Why
should a Pole in America deny his Polish heritage? Did the Englishman do
that? No! Did the German? No! Did the Irishman? Also no! Even today an
Irishman would gladly speak the Irish language if he knew how to; the
Irish even established an Irish language department at the Catholic University in Washington, D.C., but for naught, because a dead man will not
rise from the grave! After diligently reading English Catholic newspapers
such as the Milwaukee *Catholic Citizen*, the New York *Freeman's Journal*, and so on, for the past ten years, I must truthfully say that I found
more Irish patriotism in these newspapers than I found in those of Polish
Catholic origin! And I will bet anyone a horse and team who will prove
the thesis that in the Irish Catholic press there is more American patriotism than Irish! Other Americans are allowed to practice Irish, English,
German, and other patriotism, while we are not allowed to practice our
own Polish patriotism? So what is the point of this? Indeed, it is not to
make good Americans out of us, but to unhitch us from the chariot of Polish nationality and to harness us like work oxen to the plough! And shall
we voluntarily bend our necks to the foreign yoke? If so, we would surely
strip ourselves of human dignity! ✓

Thoughts of a Polish bishopric or vicariate were developing in the ingenious mind of Rev. Wincenty Barzyński as far back as 1870. At that time
he wrote from Texas to Rome:

There is only one way out, which is based on the principle 'generosity does not
wear down nature, but exalts it.' Are we allowed to trample on what God creates—
nationality, language? Did not God mix the tongues in order to show the power of
the Holy Spirit in the language of Catholic love! But he especially did not mix up
any language, because he would have destroyed intellect and conscience! Thus the
need for an office for the Slavic mission, the Apostolic Vicariate. For example,
there should be one for North America and another for South America, who would
know how to speak Polish and write and listen and judge and would have the
power from God the Church—otherwise thousands of souls who may yet be saved
will be lost. The Germans have many bishops for themselves. Even the French
have learned and without exception have German spiritual functionaries, as well as
those of other nationalities. The Slavs do not have this anywhere. Only a missionary can mingle with the people and the people themselves can also judge him without consideration or the right of appeal, and so on. Oh! scandal of scandals!

Rev. Wincenty also wrote on April 19, 1875:

I constantly believe that Jesus Christ will not allow the wolves to devour this beautifully greening Polish mission in America. I think that if God permits me to once
explain by spoken means how I fulfilled my calling in America for eight and one-
half years, then the Order itself will admit that it was especially devoted to the
poor people searching here for a temporary homeland. We Polish priests here that
have given each other a moral helping hand already number, together with the
Bohemians, about 15 to 25; those who are on a very uncertain path number about
six, and there are six others in the shadows. Since one of the uncertain ones does
not have the type of mission he would like, he is even ready to engage in intrigue,
but the bishops already know these old cheats who would not have been in America this long were it not for some bishops (mainly German) who are in love with
bunglers, thinking that they more quickly will do in the Poles. Although the number of settlements surpasses 200, there are no more that fifteen of those of the first
rank. One Apostolic Vicar who would be a Pole and would oversee the Polish
clergy and people is a holy necessity. It is understood that he would be under the
jurisdiction of the bishops but *quasi Vicarius Gen. in rebus polonis in quantum
esset necessarium* [almost a Vicar General in Polish affairs as much as is neces-
sary] that here we think of many, if not all Polish priests . . . . [But we must] wait
patiently for a manifestation of the Lord's will, until extreme measures no longer
force the Holy See to defend the Poles [in America] from wolves both internally
and externally and to give them a visible Guardian Angel arrayed with the strength
of the Holy Church. *Omnia tempus habent* [Everything in its own time], and when
we see one of the Polish cardinals (Ledóchowski), our hearts are confident that
God, Christ, and Holy Father remember us. Yesterday we began to sign an address
to our cardinal who, though imprisoned, still inflicts strong blows on the colossus
of Pagan greatness. The Holy Father is with us; who is against us? No one who is
good, while evil smash itself on God's Passion . . . .[30]

Following this letter from Rev. Wincenty Barzyński, a letter of protest
unfortunately was sent to Rome on December 3, 1875 by Rev. Dominic
Majer, Rev. Eugeniusz Bratkiewicz and Rev. Józef Molitor, a Bohemian
priest known as the "Procurator of the Slavic Mission." In this letter they
condemned the Polish Apostolic Vicariate project as an "attempt to break
free from the bishops' authority . . . and we feel this to be a great insult to
our Most Reverend Bishops and the Procurator of the Slavic Mission to
whom we want to remain faithful and obedient. We do not plan to support
any plans contrived in Rev. Wincenty's thick head."[31]

In 1890 the efforts of Mr. Cahensly, president of the German *Raphaels
Verein*, to create national dioceses in America came to nothing.[32]

In July 1891 through the initiative of Rev. Jan Machnikowski, a petition
was sent from here to Rome bearing over 100,000 signatures in support of

a Polish bishop.[33] We read in the annals of the newspaper *Nord Amerika* [North America] the following justification for this petition:

> The delegates who were instructed to deliver this humble request are in the position to prove with documents that all misunderstandings between the American bishops and the Polish and Lithuanian parishioners were brought about because the American bishops could not understand the just demands of the Polish nation. If such a state of affairs lasts much longer, there is reason for great anxiety that the Polish and Lithuanian immigration will not only lose its national attributes, but also its religious faith.

At the time, the exiled Rev. Hryniewiecki was the choice for bishop. That there existed "reason for great anxiety" was proven in the years 1894-98, which were fraught with schism. It was only surprising to some, and those were old Polish priests who did not see this "reason for great anxiety" at all and for this reason (and maybe others) considered a Polish bishop in America to be unnecessary.

A bishop who knew the Polish language, and through this the nature of the Poles (since knowledge of a language is the key to understanding a nation), would have more easily reached the source of evil, ripped off the mask of deceit from the suspected individuals, the more quickly removed misunderstandings and instituted order within the Polish parishes. A bishop unable to understand the Polish language may be genuine and good, but not for the Polish people. Such a bishop can indeed bless our people; then they can draw their faith from such a bishop. These same American bishops feel good because they always begin their sermon in the Polish church with the stereotypical phrase: "I am sorry, I cannot speak Polish." St. Paul understood this well. That is why he said: "I will pray with the spirit, but I will pray with the understanding also; I will sing with the spirit, but I will sing with the understanding also. Else if thou givest praise with the spirit alone, how shall he who fills the place of the uninstructed say 'Amen' to thy thanksgiving? For he does not know what thou sayest. For thou indeed givest thanks well, but the other is not edified. I thank God that I speak will all your tongues" (I Corinthians: 14, 15-18). Thus all these long sermons in English or German which American bishops sometimes preach in Polish churches for two hours are for nothing. Following St. Paul's train of thought, if, instead of preaching in English for two hours, they had uttered only five words in Polish the people would indeed have become more edified in their faith. "Yet in the church, I had rather speak five words with understanding, that I may also instruct others, that ten thousand words in an incomprehensible tongue" (I Corinthians: 14, 19).

Because the bishop did not understand the language of our people and they did not understand him, it so happened that the bishops began to consider our people as some kind of foreigners and barbarians and our people became of like mind about the American bishops. Is this surprising? Hardly, as it is an old truth which St. Paul stated in these words: "There are, for example, so many kinds of languages in this world and none without a meaning. If, then, I do not know the meaning of the language, I shall be to the one to whom I speak, a foreigner; and he who speaks, a foreigner to me" (I Corinthians: 14, 10-11).

The people lost their confidence in these "barbarians" and wanted to have "their own" bishops. They desired this for a long time and, not able to wait any longer for genuine Polish bishops, they started to create false ones in the form of numbskulls. In this respect our immigrant people are similar to the Israelites in the desert, who, because of Moses' long absence at Mt. Sinai, desired false gods.

Such is the psychological genesis of independent "bishoprics" in America. This idolatrous inclination exists in corrupt human nature. Whoever is bald and does not have real hair on his head adorns himself with false hair; who cannot afford genuine diamonds, adorns with false ones; a woman, not having her own real live child, plays with a doll, a dog, or a cat.

And when will the Polish bishop we so desire finally manifest himself here in America? Beginning in 1870, Rev. Barzyński wrote a series of imploring letters to Rome regarding this matter; but in vain. In vain, too, did Rev. Machnikowski submit in 1891 to the Office of Propaganda tons of petitions and signatures.

It was equally in vain that Rev. P. Gutowski and Rev. Francis Mueller knocked on the Vatican gate on behalf of the Polish-Catholic Congress held in 1896. Cardinal Steinhuber was said to have told him: "Present us with detailed statistics on the Poles in America and then something will be done." This "omniscient" Rome had no idea of the number of Poles living in America. When it was mentioned that 40,000 Poles were living in Detroit alone, Cardinal Ledóchowski exclaimed: "What? I thought that there are not that many in all of America!"

The second congress, held in Buffalo in September 1901, chose Rev. Pitass and Rev. Kruszka to select, in turn, a third representative with whom to begin securing a Polish bishop. The executive department of the second congress first presented this matter to the American archbishops

who were gathered for an annual conference in Washington, D.C. But this
is what his Excellency John J. Keane, archbishop of Dubuque[34] and secretary of the conference, replied on behalf of the archbishops:

Dubuque, December 16, 1901

Reverend Father K. Sztuczko, CSC.
Secretary of the Executive Department of the Polish-Catholic Congress
  Dear Reverend Father: The memorial of the Executive Department of the Polish-Catholic Congress was appropriately reviewed at the last annual conference of
archbishops. The gravity of the matter raised in this memorial was universally recognized, as well as the wisdom of thought and the true Catholic spirit presented in
this case. However, since archbishops do not have any power in choosing assistant
bishops—this matter belongs exclusively to the appropriate diocese or province—
it was therefore not in their power to do anything about it.

Yours in Christ,
John J. Keane
Archbishop of Dubuque,
Secretary

  The executive department thereafter turned to individual bishops, but
they received from them either an evasive answer or none at all. Therefore, nothing was left but to go to Rome. The delegates encountered
numerous obstacles prior to their departure. Finally in the spring of 1903,
Rev. Kruszka, armed with mandates, documents, etc., left for Rome
accompanied by Mr. Rowland B. Mahany. Mr. Mahany was born of Irish
parents in 1865 in Buffalo, New York. He completed public grammar and
high school there and received the "Jesse Ketchum" gold medal in 1881.
The following summer he worked on a farm near Fredonia in Chautauqua
County, New York, later becoming a teacher of Latin and Greek in the
Buffalo Classical School. He used his entire income for further studies at
Hobart College and Harvard University. He was also a special correspondent for the Buffalo daily newspapers *Courier*, *News*, and others. In 1882
he enrolled at Hobart College where he studied for two years. In 1884 he
enrolled at Harvard University and in 1888 passed his examinations, with
the highest honors (*summa cum laude*), especially in history and Latin.
After graduation from college, he worked as co-editor at the *Buffalo
Express*, from which he later resigned to accept a position as a high school
teacher of history and literature. On May 10, 1890, his dear friend Mr.
[James G.] Blaine, the Secretary of State, appointed him secretary of the
American mission in Santiago, Chile; but since that position was more
honorary than lucrative, Mahany was forced to decline this great honor.
Two years later, in February 1892, President [Benjamin] Harrison

appointed him Envoy Extraordinay and Minister Plenipotentiary to the Republic of Ecuador, but he was then in ill health. He therefore returned to the United States where he was elected speaker of the Republican National Committee to "win over" Minnesota and Missouri. During the campaign in Minnisota, Mahany was informed by telegraph of his nomination for Congress. Although it was a Democratic year, Mr. Mahany, a Republican, almost beat his opponent. Returning to Ecuador at the beginning of 1893, he negotiated the Santos Treaty in nineteen days, even though unsuccessful negotiations had been going on for the previous ten years. His relations with the government of Ecuador were very good and when he had to leave after being called back by the Democratic administration, all of Quito (the capital of Ecuador) saw him off. In 1894 the Buffalo Republicans once more nominated Mahany as a candidate for Congress, and this time he was elected. He was reelected in 1896. By profession he was a lawyer, and from 1898 he held the position of Commissioner of the Buffalo port. He was a pleasant, polite, resourceful, inventive man, and totally committed to the cause he had undertaken.

What was the result of our expedition to Rome for the bishop's golden fleece? At the third congress in Pittsburgh on September 27, 1904, Rev. Kruszka read the following report on his mission to Rome:

Having secured a mandate from the Executive Department on June 1, 1903 I left Ripon. I procured statistics on the Poles which were signed and sealed by the mayors of Milwaukee, Chicago, Detroit, Cleveland, Pittsburgh, and Buffalo. Since the Reverend John Pitass did not go to Rome with me on account of important reasons, I therefore tried to get a seperate mandate from him authorizing me to speak in his name.

I arrived in Rome on June 24, with Mr. Rowland Mahany, who accompanied me as an advocate for our cause. The next day, June 25, I immediately presented a memorial, which I had compiled and which had been reviewd by the appropriate committee and other priests, to Mr. Giuseppe Antonucci and Rev. Lasocki, canon from Płock, for review and corrections.

This memorial, entitled *Supplices Preces Suae Sanctitati Leoni Papae XIII, Ad Episcopos Polonos In Rebuspublicis Foederatis Americae Septentrionalis Pro Gente Polona obtinendos* [A supplication to His Holiness Pope Leo XIII in order to obtain Polish bishops for the Polish people in the United States], together with detailed statistics of Polish communities, authentic documents from American mayors, and mandates from the Executive Department and Rev. Pitass, was printed in Rome and first addressed to Leo XIII. While the Pope was still alive, we submitted this memorial to His Eminence Cardinal Gotti, Prefect of Propaganda,[35] on July 13 at a private audience. Before the conclave itself—that is, the election of the new Pope—we visited the cardinals a second time, speaking to each of them extensively about the matter of equal rights for the Polish clergy in America. The cardinals treated us graciouly; they were greatly interested in our case and they acknowledged its importance and the need to resolve it, not sparing words of high praise for the memorial we presented.

After the election of the new Pope, Pius X, we had a private audience that same evening with His Eminence Cardinal Svampa, who soon informed the new Pope of our business; and at the next audience he declared that our case presented to Pius X in the printed memorial had made the best possible impression on His Holiness.

On September 11, 1903, we had our first audience with the Holy Father, Pius X, at which time he stated to me: *"Perlegi totum vestrum supplicem libellum et causam vestram optime cognovi. Nunc utique res est sub consideratione S. Congregationis de Prop. Fide—sed ego libenter aliquid po vobis faciam."*

After this audience we left Rome for Poland, going to all three of its partitioned sectors. I visited the Very Reverend Bishop Wałęga in Tarnów, his Eminence Archbishop Józef Bilczewski in Lwów, the Very Reverend Bishops Pelczar and Fiszer in Przemyśl, Bishop Nowak in Kraków, Cardinal Puzyna in Kraków, Bishop Kuliński in Kielce, Archbishop Popiel and Bishop Ruszkiewicz in Warsaw, Bishop Zdzitowiecki in Włocławek, Archbishop Stablewski in Poznań, Bishop Andrzejewicz in Gniezno and Bishop Likowski in Poznań. I also visited the provincial of the Jesuit Fathers, Rev. Ledóchowski in Poznań, Chamberlain Wawrzyniak in Mogilno, Prelate Meszczyński in Poznań, as well as laymen Messrs. Ignacy Paderewski, Erasmus Jerzmanowski, and Henryk Sienkiewicz in Oblęgork and other distinguished individuals in Poland. They all promised support. That these promises were not meant lightly was proven by Bishops Bilczewski, Pelczar, Wałęga, Weber, and Fiszer, who collectively sent a letter concerning our case to the Prefect of the Propaganda. When these bishops went to Rome on a pilgrimage in the spring of 1904 they again personally supported our case both at the Vatican and at Propaganda.

In general, there was great enthusiasm for our case all over Poland; so much that it seemed that our compatriots in the Old Country were more interested in our case than those here in America.

In the second half of October 1903, I had to quickly return from Poland to Rome, since opposition had begun to rear its head.[36] Due to this oppossition, resolution of the matter was postponed from month to month.

On November 14, 1903, His Eminence Cardinal Gotti, Prefect of the Propaganda, told me in a private audience that the time and method of resolving the matter was not solely dependent on him, but also on the other cardinals of the Propaganda.

They, on the other hand, kept telling me that it was not up to them, but that it depended mainly on the Prefect of the Propaganda. On another occasion, the Prefect of the Propaganda told me that the final decision depended on the Pope. When I questioned the Pope in February 1904, he again sent me back to the Propaganda.

It was impossible to conquer by storm either the Vatican or the Propaganda. It was, therefore, necessary to secure the strongholds through a long siege, through patient waiting. I continued to visit the cardinals for the third, fourth, fifth, and even the tenth time; namely, Cardinals Gotti, Merry del Val, Della Volpe, Oreglia, Serafino and Vincenzo Vannutelli, Rampolla, Sattoli, Crettoni, Cassetta, Mathieu,

Martinelli, Steinhuber, Segna, Pierotti, Vives y Tutto, Agliardi, Svampa, Cavagni, DiPietro, Ferrata, Respighi, and Puzyna. I paid these cardinals approximately 180 visits, not counting the visits to archbishops, bishops, abbots, generals of orders, monsignors, prelates, and even the Roman pastors. Each one of them received our *Supplices Preces*, which through the monsignors and Roman pastors sometimes reached the hands of Roman lay princes having influences in the Propaganda and the Vatican. *Supplices Preces* was mailed to the following cardinals: Moran in Australia, Gibbons in Baltimore, Richard in Paris, Grusch in Vienna, Koppin Wrocław, Fischer in Cologne, Logue in Ireland, to all the archbishops in Germany and Australia, to all bishops in Poland, Ireland, Great Britain, and the United States, as well as to the editors of influential newspapers in Poland, Great Britain, Ireland, and America. I also resorted to prayers and distributing mass intentions. I wrote to the duke of Norfolk in England, but without any results.[37]

It was necessary to move heaven and earth. Through letters to the bishops in Poland and America, I gained additional strong support for our case.

On Candlemas Day I personally delivered to the Holy Father a fifteen-pound decorative candle on which among the flowers was painted the Polish coat of arms, the American Flag, and the inscription: "*A Polonis Americae Sept.*" [From the Poles of North America]. In delivering it I said, "*Beatissime Pater, memento Polonorum in America*" [Holy Father, remember the Poles in America]. On February 25, 1904, I printed a second request in Latin and delivered it to the Holy Father and the cardinals. On March 16 I received a letter from the Secretary of State, reference number 4334, in which I was officially informed that the request "submitted on behalf of the Polish-Catholic Congress was given to the Holy Father and the Holy Father ordered it to be sent to the Propaganda."

I learned from a reliable source that the Holy Father was from the very beginning favorably disposed toward our case. He had questioned the Prefect of the Propaganda about why he was postponing the resolution of our case for so long. To this the Prefect was said to have answered: "*Difficultas est ex parte—Americanorum*" [The difficulty lies with the American]. This statement by the Prefect had effect of dumping cold water on the Pope, but Cardinal Svampa, an ardent advocate of our cause, presented the Pope with convincing arguements which, despite opposition, should have helped to favorably resolve our case. As Cardinal Svampa talked, the Pope took a pencil and made notes of these arguments so that he could then consider them comprehensively.

Meanwhile, on March 28, 1904, a third request to the Pope in polished Latin was printed. Through the intervention of Cardinal Svampa, I simultaneously requested a private audience with the Pope. It had been made clear to me in no uncertain terms by the Propaganda that it would be better if the Pope himself would speak and give me a firm answer in this important but delicate matter. My request for a papal audience was favorably received by Chamberlain Monsignor Bisleti, but he kept putting off the audience for a few more weeks. Asked why he did not allow me through to the Pope for so long, he replied: "*Pendente cause*, that is, as long as the matter is in abeyance, I cannot grant Rev. Kruszka a papal audience, since it would put the Pope in a difficult position because the Pope still has not formed an opinion, he would not be able to give Rev. Kruszka any definite response. I will, nevertheless, ask the Pope this evening; maybe he has already reached a decision in this matter."

Finally, after waiting several weeks, Monsignor Bisleti announced to me that I was to have the audience. On the ticket next to my name was the designated day of the audience, April 15, and the hour of 3:45 p.m. in the throne room. What would be the Pope's answer in this matter of interest to the entire American-Polish population? Would it be negative or favorable? This was the question which constantly arose in my soul as I waited in that throne room for the Pope to arrive! Pius X finally appeared with his secretary and Monsignor Bisleti and—to my and your immense happiness—the answers from the lips of the Vicar of Christ was favorable with regard to equal rights for the Polish clergy in America. The Pope, directly and without any reservations, decidedly and emphatically declared that a decision in this matter would take place as quickly as possible and it would be according to our wishes: *"Decisio erit quantocius, et quidem secundum vestra desideria"* [The decision shall be as soon as possible and according to your wishes].

"Roma locuta est, causa finita est" [Rome has spoken, the case is closed]. With this papal declaration my mission came to an end, and it concluded successfully. On May 11, 1904, I was back in Ripon. The entire expedition lasted three weeks short of a year. My task, as a delegate had been to knock at the gates of the Vatican and to seek a favorable response. I achieved this goal. After long deliberation, the Pope finally declared himself decidedly and clearly in favor of our case. And the papal word is not like the wind. Let the doubting Thomases say: "We will not believe until we see the Polish bishop ourselves." However, we believe the word of the Pope. We believe strongly and unshakably that, according to the Pope, his decision will take place as quickly as possible, that it will be according to our wishes, that it will soon become flesh, and that we will soon have genuine Polish bishops here in America, just as we desired. Amen.[38]

Chapter 6

History of the Polish Education System in America

The importance of schools—The numbers and quality of teachers and nuns—
The Sisters of Providence—The Immaculate Nuns or "Angels"—The Incarnation Nuns—The Sisters of Notre Dame—The Franciscans—The Felicians—The Sisters of Nazareth—The Sisters of the Resurrection—The Sisters
and Fathers of the Holy Cross—The Benedictines—The Sisters of St.
Joseph—The Dominicans—The Sisters of Charity—The Ursulines—The Polish seminaries—The academy of the Sisters of Nazareth—Academies and
colleges in Canada, Kentucky, Chicago, Milwaukee, Pulaski [Wisconsin],
Shamokin [Pennsylvania]—Numerous Poles at St. Francis, Wisconsin, and at
other American seminaries, colleges, and universities.

GENERAL HISTORICAL OUTLINE OF THE POLISH SCHOOL IN AMERICA.[1]

The Polish school stands right next to the church in importance in
America. In the full sense of the word, it is the foundation of the Polish
church abroad. Without a Polish school, the Polish church, if it is to
remain Catholic, will certainly become Irish, English, and "American."
The Polish churches, where the Poles so often hear the word of God in
their native language, are citadels of patriotism; arks and vessels that protect the Polish people in exile from the flood of the deluge of denationalization and foreignness. But the foundations of these citadels, the hulls of
these arks and vessels, are the Polish schools! Without them, the Polish
church would sink like a bottomless vessel is a sea of Anglo-Americanism. Polish schools are the best sources and propagators of Polish nationality and patriotism on the foreign American soil. Here, in these Polish
parochial schools not only do our children learn that which is offered in
"public" or government-supported schools—that is, to read, write, and

count—but they also learn faith in God and love for our homeland—Poland. In the other schools our Polish children would hear about Poland only as much as, or even less than, they might hear about the wild tribes of Australia or distant islands.

Our people in America grasped and understood the importance of a Polish school quite early. Organizing themselves into a parish, they would establish a school simultaneously with, and often even before, building a church.

Polish schools in America came into being through the efforts of the Polish clergy, and they still remain solely under its administration. They are therefore called "parochial," as opposed to the "public" or government-supported schools, which are non-denominational.

The first and oldest Polish school in all of America was built where the oldest Polish church was founded, in Panna Maria, Texas. It was established around 1866 through the efforts of Rev. Bakanowski, CR, who seems to have been the first Polish teacher in this hemisphere. He was succeeded by Mr. Karol Wareński, and Mr. Jan Barzyński taught there until 1873; after 1880, Mr. F. H. Jabłoński, Leon Machnikowski, and others followed; in Chicago, Mr. W. Wilandt, and from 1872 A. Małłek, K. Małłek, and Kwasigroch.[2]

The second oldest Polish school in America, as the chronicles report, was undoubtedly the one in the parish of St. Stanislaus Bishop and Martyr in Milwaukee, Wisconsin. It was established in 1867 through the efforts of Rev. Jaster and with the help of Mr. Wilczewski. The first teacher at this school was Sister Tyta. In 1875 the best Polish school in America, as we read in the annals of the Chicago newspapers, was St. Stanislaus' school in Buffalo.[3]

Later, with each successive year, the number of Polish schools increased in step with the growth of parishes. Admittedly, some poorer parishes throughout the rural areas have not been able to maintain separate schools, but in such parishes the pastor himself usually functions as the teacher of the Polish language and religion. Therefore, one can broadly say that we have as many Polish schools in America as parishes, that is, over five hundred; but we have about four hundred schools when considered in the stricter sense of organized schools having and supporting their own teachers.

In past years this same proportion was more or less maintained. In papers left by the late Rev. Wincenty Barzyński, and kindly delivered to me by Rev. Kasprzycki, the current provincial of the Resurrectionist

Fathers, we found an historical document written before 1887 in which we read:

The number of Polish schools will be somewhat smaller than the number of churches. If there are about 100 of the latter, then there surely will be about 75 schools [in 1887]. In agricultural settlements, clearly, the school buildings represent a lesser value; in cities, a greater value. In St. Stanislaus Kostka parish in Chicago, a school costs $95,000 and often one hears that in other places it costs $15,000 to $20,000. Therefore, the total value of school buildings can be appraised at approximately $500,000 to $600,000 . . . .

Polish schools with convents of teaching sisters today are valued at $6,000,000. Then we read in a document from 1887:

So far the number of children attending the Polish schools has not been determined. In Cleveland, there are 650 pupils in two schools; in the school of St. Stanislaus Kostka parish in Chicago there are 333 boys alone. Taking this as a yardstick, an average count could be conducted as follows: in cities such as Chicago, Milwaukee, Buffalo, Detroit, New York, Brooklyn, and Pittsburgh there exist 22 primary parishes; therefore there are 22 large schools and about 400 children attend each of them. So a total of 8,800 children are getting an education in these 22 larger schools. A total of 18 secondary parishes could be counted. A school exists in each of them. If we estimate 200 children in each, we have a total of 3,600. That would still leave 35 schools in which, due to the fact that they are found in tertiary parishes, it can be assumed that there are only 50 children each. Therefore, multiplying 50 by 35, we have 1,750. And so the total number of children attending Polish schools is 14,150.

So much for 1887. Today (1900) in Chicago alone, there are 15,120 children attending Polish schools![5] In Milwaukee there are close to 6,000; in Detroit 5, 617; and in Buffalo 5,500. According to our count, a total of 69,919 children were attending all the Polish schools in America at the beginning of 1901. The greatest number of Polish school children is found in Illinois, where there are 17,495; followed by Michigan with 10,107; Wisconsin with 8,979; Pennsylvania with 8,430; New York State with 7,610; Ohio with 3,920; Minnesota with 2,950; Indiana with 2,168; Missouri and Kansas with 1,730; Texas with 1,500; Nebraska and the Dakotas with 1,100; Maryland with 1,012; New Jersey with 1,900; New England with 1,710; and Delaware with 300.

This 1887 document further reports on the salaries and numbers of teachers as follows:

The salary of male and female teachers is not everywhere fixed and identical. In Chicago, Milwaukee, and other cities it comes to $40-$60 per month; in agricultural colonies the highest it reaches is $30 . . . . The support of all the teachers costs $7,070 monthly and throughout the school year—encompassing ten months—it comes to $70,700 . . . . There are approximately as many male teachers as there are schools, that is 75. Of this number only ten at most have a professional education; the rest are so-called "God's fools," who can hardly read, write, or play the organ. The female teachers are nuns, or "sisters" as they are commonly called here (pages 24-25). The number of all male and female teachers is given as 257.

That is the way it was in 1887. Since that time the quality, quantity, and salary of male teachers [and even] female teachers, has risen considerably. We presently have about 200 lay teachers (including organists), for the most part fairly well educated in local teachers' seminaries such as Pio Nono College in St. Francis, Wisconsin, as well as (according to our calculation) 804 nuns or religious teachers. Therefore, we have a total of about 1,000 people in the active teaching force in our Polish American schools. The support of all the lay teachers costs $140,00 annually, and the support of all the nuns $160,000; thus, a total of $300,000 in annual salaries is paid for education by the Polish Catholics in the United States.[6]

The children here betray a greater intelligence than do those of the Poles remaining in Poland; nevertheless they cannot read and write Polish faultlessly because their language has already become greatly weakened by studying English. The textbooks are: *Elementarz Polski* [Polish Primer] designed by the teacher Zubka and a second text published by Dyniewicz; a catechism and Bible; an arithmetic book by Dyniewicz; English textbooks.[7]

The first elementary Polish primer published and designed here in America was *The Study of Writing, Reading and Arithmetic for School and Home Instruction for Polish Catholic Children in America*, by Ignacy Wendziński, a former teacher in Golańcza in the Grand Duchy of Poznań. The Lwów *Ruch Literacki* [Literary Movement] of November 18, 1876, favorably reviewed this primer, writing, among other things: "It is an elementary primer published in Chicago on beautiful paper with attractive type, and is illustrated with pictures engraved in wood and set up skillfully and practically." The newest primers include *Obrazkowy Elementarz Polski* [Illustrated Polish Primer] published in Chicago in 1899 by J. Smulski, and the primer published by the Polish Printing Company in Chicago.[8] In 1901 an English geography textbook published by Butler and Sheldon Printing Company included a section on Poland compiled by Rev. Franciszek Wojtalewicz, with a beautiful map of Poland from the seventeenth century, a view of Kraków, the Gniezno cathedral and portraits of Pułaski and Kościuszko.[9]

The school year in America lasts almost ten months, from September to the end of June. During the school year lessons are held each day of the week except Saturday and Sunday and some religious and legal holidays. Each day's lesson plan follows this schedule: Mass for children at 8:00 a.m., followed by lessons which last until 11:30, with a fifteen minute break after 10:00 a.m. In the afternoon, lessons also last three hours, from 1:00 to 4:00 p.m., with a fifteen minute break at 2:30.

Throughout farms and smaller settlements, there are of course, fewer grades and classes. In larger communities such as Chicago, Milwaukee, Buffalo, Detroit, St. Louis, South Bend, New York, and Baltimore, Polish schools usually have eight grades and often even more classes. Sometimes there are a few equivalent classes at the same grade level. Both in size and the number of pupils, such larger schools do not constitute a majority of the schools, since there are only about fifty of them. However, they do hold an undeniable majority of the pupils (about 50,000 children attend schools throughout the larger communities). And so, in these larger schools, the generally accepted program of study is more or less as follows:[10]

Kindergarten. Religion: prayers and the small catechism; biblical history of the creation of the world, our first parents, and their downfall. Language: Polish and English; recognition and composition of letters; reading of words and sentences included in the primer; writing of letters, words, and short sentences from memory; dictation at the blackboard and deskboards; explanation of the most important words and pictures in Polish and English readers. Arithmetic: comprehension of quantity of given objects as well as oral counting from 1 to 100; easy memory addition, subtraction, multiplication, and division; writing numbers as well as short formulas within the four functions. Art: copying on desk boards of figures drawn by teachers on the blackboard or included in readers. Music: easy songs twice a week. Physical education: hand exercise.

First Grade. Religion: first half of the smaller catechism; from biblical history, the story about the Flood and about some of the patriarchs. Polish and English languages: reading of first Polish book and first reader with commentaries; spelling and dictation; memory lessons, including poems, moral lessons, and proverbs; subjects and predicates in a sentence, as well as composition of original sentences on a theme assigned by the teacher; most important punctuation marks: period, comma, question mark. Arithmetic: memory sums of the four functions; more difficult formulas of the four functions in the range of 1,000; defining more important arithmetic symbols. Calligraphy: Lovell and Company Exercise Book Number 1. Art: Drawing of straight lines on desk boards; some geometric figures; drawing according to easy models. Music: somewhat more difficult songs. Physical education: exercise of hands and legs.

Second Grade. Religion: Entire smaller catechism; abridged version of the entire holy history. Polish and English languages: differentiation of more important parts of speech, as well as all of phonetics; original short compositions; memorization of poems. Arithmetic: reading and writing of numbers to one million; writing of four functions with up to five-figure numbers; memory arithmetic. Geography: four parts of the world, poles, and so on; division of the world's surface into land, seas, and so on; general geography of the United States. Calligraphy: Lovell and Company Exercise Book Number 2; Krones' Exercise Book Number 1. Music: most popular Polish and English songs for one voice. Physical education: exercise of hands, legs, and easier exercises for the entire body.

Third Grade. Religion: Deharb's Larger Catechism, Year 1; Chociszewski's Bible History, Year 1. Polish language: Third Polish Book by Dyniewicz or Smulski, published by the Polish Printing Company; Małecki's Abridged Grammar, including nouns, adjectives, numerals, and pronouns. English language: Gilmour's *Third Reader*; spelling from the reader; Harvey's *Elementary Grammar*, the first half. Arithmetic: Robinson's Junior Class Arithmetic up to functions (numbers in general are taught in English in Polish American schools). Geography: The Rand McNally Primary School Geography, the first half. History: History of the Polish Nation; narration of the most important events; history of the United States; the first half of Yeariger's Primary History of the United States. Calligraphy: Lovell and Company Exercise Book Number 3. Art: Krones' Exercise Book Number 2. Music: easier lay and church songs for two voices.

Fourth Grade. Religion: Deharb's Larger Catechism, Year 2. Chociszewski's Bible History, Year 2. Polish language: Fourth Polish Book; Małecki's Abridged Grammar including all inflected parts of speech. English language: Gilmour's Fourth Reader; Sadlier's speller, from lesson 1 to 50; Harvey's Elementary Grammar, the second half. Arithmetic: Robinson's Junior Class Arithmetic, including simple and decimal fraction. Geography: The Rand McNally Primary School Geography, the second half. History: Chociszewski's History of the Polish Nation, period 1 and 2; history of the United States; Benziger's Primary History of the United States, the second half. Calligraphy: Lovell and

Company Exercise Book Number 4. Art: Krones' Exercise Book Number 3. Music: More difficult songs for two voices; beginnings of notes.

Fifth Grade. Religion: Deharb's Larger Catechism, Year 3. Chociszewski's Bible History, Period III. Polish Language: Friend of the Children, Part l; Małecki's *Grammar*, including all parts of speech. English Language: Gilmour's Fifth Reader; Sadlier's Spelling from lesson 50 to 100; Harvey's *Grammar* as far as the verb. Arithmetic: simple and decimal fractions, as well as percentage rules according to Robinson's Progressive Arithmetic. Geography: The Rand McNally Grammar School Geography up to Europe. History: Chociszewski's History of the Polish Nation, Period lV; History of the United States from the Revolutionary War through the Civil War, by the Benziger Brothers. Calligraphy: Lovell and Company Exercise Book Number 5. Art: Krones' Exercise Book Numbers 4 and 5. Music: Part I. Szkoły Śpiewu [School of Singing] by Professor A. Małłek or Śpiewnika dla użytku Polaków w Ameryce [Songbook for the Use of the Poles in America], compiled by A. J. Kwasigroch (music) and S. Zahajkiewicz (lyrics).

Sixth Grade. Religion: Deharb's Larger Catechism, complete; Chociszewski's Bible History, complete. Polish language: Friends of the Children, Part II. Małecki's Grammar, including syntax. English language: Gilmour's Fifth Reader, Second Part; Sadlier's Spelling from lesson 100 to 150; Harvey's Grammar as far as syntax. Arithmetic: from percents up to raising to a power according to Robinson's Progressive Arithmetic. History: Chociszewski to the end; history of the United States from the Civil War to the Present; overview of general and ancient history. Mathematics: Robinson's Progressive Arithmetic complete; bookkeeping: Bryant and Strattons, first part; Robinson's Algebra as far as equations. Physiology: Johounot's How We Live, first part. Geography: Physical Geography. Calligraphy: Lovell and Company Exercise Book Number VII. Art: Krones' Exercise Book Number VII. Music: songs for two voices from sheet music.

Seventh Grade. Religion: Explanation of the principles of the Roman Catholic faith; history of the first centuries of the church. Polish language: composition; major principles of Polish pronunciation; selections from Polish authors. English Language: Gilmour's Sixth Reader; Harvey's Grammar from syntax to prosody; Sadlier's Spelling from lesson 150 to the end. Swinton's Composition and Rhetoric. Mathematics: Bookkeeping, Bryant and Stratton's, second part; Robinson's Algebra from equations to the end. History: United States Constitution; overview of general and modern history. Physiology: Johounot's How We Live, second part. Stenography: Graham's complete. Typewriting: Remington's. Calligraphy: Free calligraphic exercises. Art: Krones' Exercise Book Number VIII.

Eighth Grade. Religion: explanation of the principles of the Roman Catholic faith; history of the Catholic Church. Polish language: study of composition and the major principles of Polish pronunciation. History: overview History of the Polish Nation from the beginning up to our time; history of the United States from the Revolution to the end of the Civil War. Geography: Rand McNally Grammar School Geography from Europe to the end. Calligraphy: Lovell and Company Exercise Book VI. Art: Krones' Exercise Book VI. Music: Part II, School of Singing (Prof. A. Małek).

As can be seen from the above program, Polish schools in America consist of two courses: the elementary one, including kindergarten through the fourth grade, and the higher course (grammar school) including the fifth grade through the eighth grade. In their program Polish parochial schools do not always and everywhere measure up regarding execution of the program. This is because the Poles do not give their children the opportunity to finish school as often as do the Yankees. It should also be noted that the courses in Polish schools are much more difficult than the public elementary and secondary or high schools, since, besides having all subjects accepted in public schools in their program, they also have Polish language and religion. Despite this, it often happens that Polish pupils leaving the parochial school and entering a public one are promoted to a higher grade or at least go into the equivalent grade.

The program of everyday lessons in all grades is more or less as follows. Before noon: Mass at 8:00 a.m.; from 8:45 to 9:15 a.m. (and so for half an hour!) religion, catechism, Bible or church history; from 9:15 to 10:15 a.m. sums, arithmetic, algebra, bookkeeping, and commercial law; break until 10:30 a.m.; from 10:30 to 11:30 a.m. Polish language, including reading, grammar, Polish history. In the afternoon: from 1:00 to 2:00 p.m. English language; from 2:00 to 2:30 p.m. calligraphy or art; break until 2:45 p.m.; from 2:45 to 3:30 p.m. in the lower grades visual lessons, both oral and written; in the higher grades geography, history of the United States, or English grammar. From 3:30 to 4:00 p.m. music, physical education or needlework for the girls.[11]

TEACHING NUNS[12]

Nothing is totally perfect on earth—except God. But considering the circumstances, our Polish parochial schools in America can be considered relatively perfect. In many parishes the teacher, being also an organist, usually receives a monthly salary of $50 (sometimes less)—you get what you pay for.

Polish schools in America were and are mainly in the hands of nuns. These nuns were often fiercely criticized as teachers, especially by the so-called progressive, ultra-liberal party. It is understood that like everywhere there are and will be certain shortcomings in our schools; the progressive, liberal camp were unjust and malicious. They accused the nuns of a lack of education. This is ridiculous. Our nuns, in general, had and have the appropriate education. If exceptions (uneducated nuns) were found, then the exceptions, as usual, "proved the rule." It is true that the nuns lack university degrees, but the knowledge they possess is certainly enough for elementary teaching.

Besides, there was often neither time nor material to prepare the nuns to be teachers. We know how quickly Polish parishes in America have grown; and wherever there was a parish, a school has soon begun. Priests asked for nuns to fill these schools and often waited two or three years for them, while year after year a reply would come from the mother superior that there were not enough nuns to send to fill the needs of this or that school. It was not possible to bring many from Poland either. Therefore, there was, and still is, a shortage of nuns for the Polish schools. This naturally results in the hasty education of the candidates. It certainly does not allow for the university education of nuns. This surely is natural. But still, we must think about what has been accomplished up to now, despite all kinds of difficulties. A tremendous amount has been accomplished. Where have these hundreds of Polish Felician nuns, Sisters of Nazareth, Sisters of Notre Dame, Franciscan, Incarnate, Benedictine, Dominican nuns, and Sisters of St. Joseph come from? They were educated through iron labor under the most difficult conditions in a very short period of time. If it were not for them, who would teach our Polish children religion, morality, and the Polish language?

Besides, our religious teachers have been molded mostly from very primitive material. Our immigration is mainly composed of peasants, and so candidates for the religious sisterhoods must come mainly from this sphere; therefore, much more work must be put into training them to become good teachers. However, since they come from peasant population, they know its needs best.

The condition of our existence and our society make the sisters' work more difficult. Polish parents for the most part take their children out of school when they have barely reached the age of twelve or thirteen. This is the age when a child's mind develops best. Therefore, children in our schools sometimes study only three or four years, and in such a short time it is difficult for the sisters to make these young ones into little Solomons.

One should also see how difficult it is to conduct lessons in two languages or to conduct classes appropriately when at times they are overloaded with 130 children! Very often one sister must do the work of three. . . . We also know that our Polish schools cannot compare financially with schools of other nationalities, and especially with the public schools; consequently, due to a lack of parish funds, the sisters must often wait more than a year for their meager but hard-earned salaries.

Let us now proceed with a view of the ranks of the teaching sisters. It seems that the earliest ones were the Sisters of Providence, who taught in the Polish schools in Texas beginning in 1872. Rev. Żwiardowski, CR,[12] wrote to Rome from Panna Maria, Texas, on February 2, 1873: "I brought over the sisters because if there are no Catholic schools, there will be only the free public schools . . . . Therefore, not wasting any time, I went to the superior of the Sisters of Providence, Madame St. Andre in Castroville, who, upon arriving here, looked over the house and sent three sisters. I gave up my house to them and I live over the sacristy even though it is in the attic. The sisters are German or Alsatians and they are learning Polish." Rome was unfavorably disposed toward these German sisters. But to no avail Rev. Wincenty Barzyński[13] wrote from San Antonio on May 31, 1873, to ask the general of the Resurrectionists, "if the Order could send two brothers to help the school with the a, b, c's." And in a letter dated September 27, 1873, he explains why he cannot have the German sisters removed: "To remove the sisters from Panna Maria is difficult since (a) the people have come to like them because they in fact administer the school excellently and with dedication, they are learning to speak and read in Polish. They play and sing Polish hymns in church and besides the Silesian population has excessive sympathy for the Germans; (b) the difficulty has increased due to the entry of five daughters from the Polish population into their Order; and (c) Rev. Felix [Żwiardowski] himself brought them over. . . ."

Two years later Rev. Żwiardowski, with the permission of the new bishop Pellier, detached these sisters from their mother house in Castroville and formed a separate Polish Order of the Sisters of the Immaculate Conception, called "Immaculatas" or "Angels." He reported to the reverend general on March 24, 1875: "I changed their habits and now I have seven sisters dressed in habits of a sky blue color: four in Panna Maria and three in St. Hedwig . . . . I established the Order of Sisters of the Immaculate Conception of the Holy Virgin Mary as missionary sisters in Texas, a branch of the house in Poland." This proved an insult to Mother Marcelina[15] from Jazłowiec in Galicia, the founder of the Immaculate Conception Order in Poland. And so Rev. Żwiardowski wrote in a letter to Rev. Bakanowski:

After all, Reverend Mother Marcelina was not sent directly from heaven with a command from God that she alone in the entire world found Immaculatas of second rank. . . . On a carnival Sunday here in Panna Maria, I performed the final ceremony of the taking of the veil and since then I count seven nuns: two Germans, Polonized Alsatians, as well as five Polish nuns, including Albina Musioł and Cecylia Feliks from San Antonio; and Paulina Urbańcyzk, Kunegunda Krawiec, and Barbara Krawiec from Panna Maria. Sister Marya Salomea is the superior of the convent in Panna Maria, and Sister Maria Felix de Valois is the superior of the one in St. Hedwig. . . . After frequent conversations with the bishop, we became quite good friends. He appointed me his advisor and a member of the *Concilium* [council]. He announced that I alone, as the superior of the mission and of the school sisters, am the pastor of all the missions, and that all the priests, lay as well as monastic, are my assistants; . . . that I am his *Vicarius foraneus* or vicar general of Polish affairs and his counsellor, who is responsible for all the Polish missions; and that I will have an office to dispense the various needs of the Poles. He wants the order [of Resurrectionists] to supply as many priests as required for all the major missions to be occupied by members of the order, and wants me to live in San Antonio near him and only visit the missions.[16]

On October 20, 1875, [Rev. Barzyński] wrote to the general of the order:

Upon examining the Immaculata Sisters' rule, the bishop greatly approved and directed that it be applied with a few small changes to our local sisters. The bishop is our leader and lord. I, however, am the superior acting in his name. I myself have the right to accept postulants, veil them, disperse them throughout the missions, and dismiss them from the order. Since they are all still very young, the oldest being twenty-three, there is no superior, and in each school convent at a mission there is only a director or convent superior appointed by me. There are presently four school convents: (1) in Panna Maria with three nuns and two postulants; (2) in the newly built Częstochowa with two nuns and one postulant; (3) in

St. Hedwig with three nuns and one postulant; and, (4) in San Antonio with three nuns. In three parishes we have four schools, and the people are very satisfied with them. Every day the sisters' progress can be seen, and for this reason the people have given them their nickname of "Angels." Each year they all meet at one convent where they hold retreats. The reason why I undertook their administration is so that there would be a Polish order.

Rev. Wincenty Barzyński, CR, scoffingly responded from Chicago on March 25, 1875, regarding these new "Angels."

In Texas there is an immediate need for two Polish Sisters of Charity strong in spirit, because in Texas the bishop with Rev. Feliks [Żwiardowski] or rather Rev. Feliks himself has about ten girls dressed in a new manner, removed from the authority of the old superior (because she was too German). But today? They are like children without a mother, and their father is not really one of them in these matters . . . .

On June 5, 1876, Rev. Bronisław Przewłocki, CR,[17] wrote, "On Rev. Dunajewski's recommendation, Rev. Feliks is bringing with him a candidate from Kraków," and on September 30, 1876, he noted, "The clergy in Texas is indignant that Rev. Feliks took a few Polish nuns from Castroville . . . ." Two years later, on October 30, 1878, he stated, "The local sisters live here as elsewhere; the rule for them is Father Feliks." On July 9, 1879, however, Rev. Wincenty Barzyński's father wrote: "The bishop has lost confidence in Father Feliks, all the priests hate him, and there is the highest degree of distrust in all of the parishes in Texas. The bishop decided to send the superior of the hospital from San Antonio to Panna Maria for two months' investigation. Some parents decided to remove their daughter from the convent, and even Józef Moczygęba wrote to his daughter that he wanted to bring her home. Stories and foolishness and nothing more . . . ." Also the provincial, Rev. Funcken, CR,[18] wrote from Canada on October 20, 1878, warning Rome with a humorous poem: *Qui servit "nonnis," incertis navigat undis; Initio Klingklang—Stinkstank in fine laboris* [Who serves no one navigates through unknown waters; at the start of your labor it is "Clink-Clank," at the end it is "Stink-Stank"].

We learn from Rev. Tyszkiewicz's letter[19] on December 2, 1879, that Bishop Pellier took away from Father Żwiardowski the superior's position over the nuns and removed the entire novitiate and postulate from his parish. At that time, there were thirty Immaculatas. The bishop was advised to attach these poor Immaculatas to another order. However, the bishop replied that he could not allow this order to fail, because this would be too great a triumph for the Castroville superior from whom they had been detached. Despite this, these Immaculatas or "Angels" declined and became extinct, so that now no trace of them remains.

In their place today, the Polish schools in Texas are administered by Incarnation Sisters, or Sisters of the Incarnate Word. There are seventeen of these Polish nuns, and they teach about 1,180 children in six schools (in Texas).

The earliest teachers in Polish schools in America were the Sisters of Notre Dame[20] who, beginning in 1873, taught in Polish schools in Chicago; Milwaukee; Radom, Illinois; Winona, Minnesota; Berlin, Wisconsin; Dubois, Illinois; Grand Rapids, Michigan; Michigan City, Indiana, and Green Bay, Wisconsin. The 168 Notre Dame Sisters taught 11,313 children in a total of seventeen Polish schools. They took over the first school in Chicago on February 2, 1873, when Rev. Bakanowski, CR, was the pastor and Rev. Jan Wołłowski, CR, his assistant. "Father Jan organized our school and administered it successfully," wrote Rev. Bakanowski on February 28, 1873. The following are the chronological statistics sent to me (at the beginning of 1901) from Milwaukee by Sister M. Ernesta, assistant to the Mother General of Sisters of Notre Dame.

The Sisters of Notre Dame took over the following Polish schools.

1. In Chicago, St. Stanislaus Kostka, February 2, 1873; at the time of assumption there were seven nuns, 700 children; today there are 43 nuns, 3,014 children.

2. In Milwaukee, St. Hedwig, September 15, 1878; at the time of assumption there were two nuns, 90 children; today there are seven nuns, 650 children.

3. In Radom, Illinois, on November 1, 1880; at the time of assumption there were two nuns, 130 children; today there are four nuns, 159 children.

4. In Milwaukee, St. Hyacinth, on April 19, 1884; at the time of assumption there were two nuns, 500 children; today there are 19 nuns, 1,056 children.

5. In Milwaukee, St. Stanislaus, on January 12, 1884; (although in 1867 Sister Tyta, a Notre Dame nun, was already teaching in the old school); at the time of assumption there were two nuns, 700 children; today there are twelve nuns, 877 children.

6. In Winona, Minnesota, on September 2, 1887; at the time of assumption there were two nuns, 230 children; today there are eleven nuns, 545 children.

7. In Milwaukee, St. Josaphat, on November 5, 1888; at the time of

assumption there were three nuns, 200 children; today there are nine nuns, 900 children.

8. In Milwaukee, St. Vincent, on December 31, 1888; at the time of assumption there were two nuns, 200 children; today there are nine nuns, 570 children.

9. In Berlin, Wisconsin, St. Stanislaus, on August 30, 1890; at the time of assumption there were two nuns, 90 children; today there are four nuns, 240 children.

10. In Dubois, Illinois, on September 29, 1891; at the time of assumption there were two nuns, 90 children; today there are four nuns, 119 children.

11. In Grand Rapids, Michigan, St. Adalbert on September 6, 1892; at the time of assumption there were five nuns, 300 children; today there are eleven nuns, 597 children.

12. In Chicago, Illinois, St. John Cantius on January 2, 1894; at the time of assumption there were three nuns, 500 children; today there are ten nuns, 1,035 children.

13. In Milwaukee, St. Casimir, on November 14, 1894; at the time of assumption there were three nuns, 270 children; today there are eight nuns, 638 children.

14. In Milwaukee, SS. Cyril and Methodius, on January 9, 1894; at the time of assumption there were four nuns, 280 children; today there are nine nuns, 470 children.

15. In Michigan City, Indiana, on September 1, 1898; at the time of assumption there were two nuns, 200 children; today there are three nuns, 263 children.

16. In Grand Rapids, Michigan, St. Stanislaus, on December 29, 1900; at the time of assumption there were three nuns, 84 children; today there are three nuns, 100 children.

In 1874 the purely Polish religious order of Felician Sister began its beneficial activity in Polonia, Wisconsin; and throughout the years it has spread among the Polish settlements in America to such an extent that today it administers the largest number of Polish schools, that is thirty-nine. And so 17,822 Polish children find themselves under the care of 261 Felician teachers!

The Franciscan Sisters, who administer the second largest number of Polish schools, are responsible for a wide variety of stamps and types. There is a total of 176 of these sisters teaching 14,030 children in 32 Polish schools. The Franciscan Sisters from St. Joseph's convent in Milwaukee, had nine Polish schools under their care [1904]: in Chicago there were three, including St. Casimir in Bridgeport and Immaculate Conception in South Chicago; in Detroit there were two, Immaculate Conception and St. Francis; and there was one each in the Wisconsin communities of Stevens Point, Manasha, Puławski, and Princeton. This information was given to me by Sister Alphonsa, OSF, from Milwaukee.

Mother Thecla, OMC, reports to me that the Franciscan Sisters residing in St. Francis, Wisconsin, have administered only two Polish schools in that state—in Pine Creek since 1891 and in North Creek since 1898. In Nebraska yet another branch of Franciscans administered Polish schools from a convent in Lafayette, Indiana.

Through Father Wincenty Barzyński's efforts a new, purely Polish order of Franciscans under the protection of St. Kunegunda was founded in 1893 by Mother Anna, a Pole. This order provided teachers for Polish schools in Cleveland, Spring Valley, Cragin, and St. Michael's Parish in Berlin, Wisconsin, after 1904. This new order has a total of 40 nuns; its mother house is located in Avondale, Chicago, where there are also an orphanage and a home for the elderly under their care.

Beginning in 1885, the Sisters of Nazareth undertook salutary work in American Polonia. This purely Polish religious order was established only recently (1874). The Polish founder, Mother General Siedlicka, died in 1903 in Rome, where the motherhouse is located. The Sisters of Nazareth, as Polish teachers in America, perform a splendid service for us. They are comparable in numbers to the Polish Sisters of Notre Dame: 112 Sisters of Nazareth teach 9,178 children in sixteen Polish schools in Chicago, Pittsburgh, Philadelphia, Brooklyn, Scranton, Camden (New Jersey), and in Everson (Pennsylvania).

Finally, eighteen Benedictine nuns administer five Polish schools with about 1,000 children in Marche, Arkansas, and in North Prairie, Browerville, Perham, and Duluth—all in Minnesota. Also, six Sisters of St. Joseph teach 460 children in two Polish schools in Rochester and Albion, New York. In Chicago at St. Mary's parish seven Sisters of the Resurrection function as Polish teachers. Three Dominican Sisters teach in Port Austin, Michigan, and one or two Polish Ursuline Sisters are found in San Antonio, Texas. Three Sisters of charity (the grays) are in DeLancey, Pennsylvania. We should also remember that beginning in 1885 eight Sisters of the Holy Cross taught in St. Jadwiga's School in South Bend, Indiana. Thus this is an account of all the religious sisters on whose shoulders rests Polish primary education in America.[22]

As far as the male teaching force is concerned, it is certainly smaller in number than the female, but it is no less competent. At the head of this list of Polish teachers stand courageous brothers from the Holy Cross Order. There are only five Poles. Brother Stanisław, CSC (Michał Kurowski), was born in Galicia in 1852. He arrived in America in 1877, entered the order in 1881, taught in South Bend from 1882 to 1900, and since 1900 has been at Holy Trinity in Chicago. Brother Piotr (Hosiński), born in South Bend in 1871, entered the order in 1885. He taught in a school in South Bend for two and one-half years, and has been in Chicago since 1893. Brother Władisław (Hosiński), born in 1879 in South Bend, entered the order in 1894. He has taught at Holy Trinity in Chicago since 1898. Brother Doroteusz (Piotr Wojtalewicz), born in 1875, has taught in South Bend since 1900. Brother Jakób has taught in South Bend since 1900. Let us have more of these in America! Let them proliferate for us!

HISTORY OF THE FELICIAN SISTERS IN AMERICA (SINCE 1874)[23]

Due to the persistent efforts of the Rev. J. Dąbrowski, current pastor of the Polish parish in Polonia, Wisconsin, five Felician Sisters arrived from Kraków in the fall of 1874 to help with the upbringing and education of the local Polish immigrants' children.

During their first years in America the order, together with its highly respectable founder, experienced various difficulties. A few months after their arrival, a fire totally destroyed the presbytery, school, and the sister's home, as well as the entire library they had brought over with them. However, due to the fervent work and endeavors of the Very Rev. J. Dąbrowski and the generosity of the Polish people, a new wooden convent was built in a very short time. But this new building, together with the parish church, was totally destroyed by fire a few months later. Only human lives could be saved. The sisters, therefore, were deprived of any means of support.

These and many other adversities that God chose to bestow on the order at the very outset did not by any means weaken the enthusiasm of the venerable founder, but only spurred him on to newer and more heroic actions and sacrifices. For this reason, too, despite great difficulties and constant poverty, a new convent was built from stones gathered from the fields.

After God, the Felician Sisters are indebted for their welfare and development to Rev. J. Dąbrowski, their founder and director, who shared all of their vicissitudes.

When the new convent was built in Polonia, Wisconsin, Rev. Kandyd Kozłowski, then pastor of the Polish parish of St. Hyacinth in LaSalle, Illinois, summoned three sisters to take over the parish school. At the same time, a small orphanage was built there with voluntary contributions. After a short while, the orphanage was moved to Polonia. This was, therefore, the first American branch of the convent of the Felician Sisters.

Through the efforts of the late Rev. Sklorzyk, the sisters soon took over a second school, at St. Stanislaus' Parish in Bay City, Michigan. The sisters then were summoned to St. Adalbert's Parish in Detroit, Michigan. At this time the Very Rev. J. Dąbrowski, due to an overload in connection with the parish, missions, and the convent, became seriously ill, and the doctors decided that the only way to save his life was to move him to a milder climate. It was mainly for this reason that the Felician Sisters relocated their motherhouse, together with the novitiate, to Detroit, Michigan, where the newly built convent was ceremoniously consecrated on October 4, 1882. From that time it was the Motherhouse of the Province of the Presentation of the Holy Virgin Mary.

Soon, however, this house, which initially seemed spacious enough, was not able to accommodate the numerous orphans, whom the sisters gathered under their care. A few years later, therefore, an additional institution was built and soon thereafter the convent was also enlarged. In 1900 another more spacious institution was built, which currently houses ninety orphan girls and eighty candidates preparing to become teaching sisters. The convent, together with the institution, remains under the paternal direction of the Very Rev. J. Dąbrowski. The first provincial superior of the Felician Sisters in America was Mother Maria Monica, who managed the order for seventeen years.

In 1887 the Sacred Hearts of Jesus and Mary Shelter for the elderly of both sexes, as well as male orphans, was built along with a hospital in Manitowoc, Wisconsin. This institution was founded by Rev. I. Łuczycki, who in 1902 returned to live in Europe. A similar shelter dedicated to the Immaculate Heart of Mary was built in Buffalo, New York, and was ceremoniously consecrated and opened on October 4, 1896.

In September 1897 the Felician Sisters took over St. Joseph Immigrant Houses for Polish and Lithuanian immigrants in New York. The sole mission of the sisters of this house is to provide immigrant girls with solicitous care. From the time the sisters took over this house until 1901, they had cared for 2,605 girls.

In 1901 the Order of the Felician Sisters staffed five charitable institutions and thirty-nine Polish parochial schools, as follows:

A. Institutions

1. St. Clara Institution for orphan boys in Polonia,Wisconsin; forty-eight boys, nine nuns.

2. St. Felix boarding-house and institution for orphan girls, under the motherhouse in Detroit, Michigan; eighty boarders with seven teachers; ninety orphans, with four teachers.

3. Sacred Heart of Jesus and Mary boarding-house and hospital in Manitowoc, Wisconsin. About fifty elderly people of both sexes, forty-five orphan boys, about twelve sick, and seventeen nuns.

4. Immaculate Heart of Mary Orphanage in Buffalo, New York; eight elderly men; twenty-two women; seventy-three orphan boys; seventy-nine girls; twenty nuns working in the institution.

5. St. Joseph Immigrant House in New York. From the time the Felician Sisters began running the house in September 9, 1897, to May 25, 1901, there were 13,639 travelers and 2,605 girls passing through separately.

B. Parochial Schools

1. Sacred Heart of Jesus in Polonia, Wisconsin; 230 children, three classes, three nuns.

2. St. Hyacinth in La Salle, Illinois; 620 children, eight classes, nine nuns.

3. St. Stanislaus Kostka in Bay City, Michigan; 769 children, nine classes, ten nuns.

4. St. Adalbert in Detroit, Michigan; 1,400 children, 17 classes, 18 nuns.

5. Blessed Virgin Mary in Otis, Indiana; 130 children, two classes, three nuns.

6. St. Stanislaus Bishop and Martyr in Buffalo, New York; 1,600 children, twenty-one classes, twenty-three nuns.

7. St. Stanislaus Bishop and Martyr in Shamokin, Pennsylvania; 431 children, five classes, six nuns.

8. St. Casimir in Detroit, Michigan; 620 children, nine classes, ten nuns.

9. St. Stanislaus in Baltimore, Maryland; 614 children, eight classes, nine nuns.

10. St. Anthony in Toledo, Ohio; 900 children, twelve classes, thirteen nuns.

11. St. Joseph in Manistee, Michigan; 700 children, seven classes, eight nuns.

12. SS. Cyril and Methodius in Lemont, Illinois; 250 children, three classes, nine nuns.

13. St. Joseph in Chicago, Illinois; 700 children, eight classes, nine nuns.

14. St. Adalbert in Buffalo, New York; 830 children, eleven classes, twelve nuns.

15. St. Hyacinth in Dunkirk, New York; 450 children, four classes, five nuns.

16. St. Adalbert in Pittsburgh, Pennsylvania; 707 children, eight classes, nine nuns.

17. Blessed Virgin Mary in Alpena, Michigan; 320 children, four classes, five nuns.

18. Blessed Virgin Mary in Parisville, Michigan; 180 children, two classes, three nuns.

19. St. Lawrence in Philadelphia, Pennsylvania; 317 children, four classes, five nuns.

20. St. Josaphat in Detroit, Michigan; 630 children, eight classes, nine nuns.

21. Mother of God of the Rosary in Baltimore, Maryland; 424 children, five classes, six nuns.

22. St. Adalbert in Berea, Ohio; 350 children, five classes, six nuns.

23. St. Joseph in Webster, Massachusetts; 310 children, five classes, six nuns.

24. St. Stanislaus Bishop and Martyr in Erie, Pennsylvania; 390 children, five classes, six nuns.

25. Sacred Heart of Jesus in Cleveland, Ohio; 234 children, two classes, three nuns.

26. Transfiguration in Buffalo, New York; 550 children, eight classes, nine nuns.

27. St. John Cantius in Buffalo, New York; 360 children, four classes, five nuns.

28. Mother of God of the Rosary in Saginaw, Michigan; 237 children, three classes, four nuns.

29. St. Joseph in Mt. Carmel, Pennsylvania; 276 children, three classes, four nuns.

30. St. Hedwig in Wilmington, Delaware; 226 children, three classes, four nuns.

31. St. Stanislaus in Chicopee, Massachusetts; 132 children, two classes, three nuns.

32. St. Anthony in Jersey City, New Jersey; 530 children, seven classes, eight nuns.

33. St. Stanislaus in Newark, New Jersey; 320 children, four classes, five nuns.

34. St. John Cantius in Philadelphia, Pennsylvania; 250 children, three classes, four nuns.

35. St. Casimir in Cleveland, Ohio; 188 children, two classes, three nuns.

36. St. Casimir in Posen, Michigan; 160 children, two classes, three nuns.

37. St. Stanislaus Bishop and Martyr in Detroit, Michigan; 180 children, two classes, three nuns.

38. Mother of God of the Rosary in Isadore, Michigan; 157 children, two classes, three nuns.

39. Mother of God of the Scapular in Wyandotte, Michigan; 130 children, two classes, three nuns.

In 1900, due to the distance between many convents, the Province of the Presentation of the Blessed Mary was divided, creating a second province called the Immaculate Heart of Mary, whose motherhouse was located in Buffalo, New York. All the branch houses in the East belonged to this province. The remaining houses in the West belonged to the Province of the Presentation of the Blessed Virgin Mary in Detroit, Michigan.[24]

HISTORY OF THE SISTERS OF NAZARETH IN AMERICA (FROM 1885)[25]

Besides the Felicians, another purely Polish religious order founded by a Pole (Sister Siedlicka) and administered by Poles is the Order of the Holy Family of Nazareth. Having secured the permission of Archbishop Freehan [of Chicago], Rev. Wincenty Barzyński and Rev. Jan Radziejewski, pastor of St. Adalbert Parish, arranged for an order of Polish nuns through Propaganda in Rome. In 1885 the Sisters of the Holy Family of Nazareth arrived in Chicago. Their purpose was to help the church spread the Kingdom of Christ on earth. With this purpose in mind, they began teaching in private schools and institutions, as well as devoting themselves to all types of charitable work. We have already noted the number of parochial schools under their care.

Upon arriving in America, the Sisters of Nazareth endeavored to learn the relationships and needs of the Poles living here. They were most touched by the sight of Poles abandoned in hospitals of other nationalities. Since, for the most part, these Poles did not know English, they could not communicate their sufferings, obtain help and relief for their illness, or receive the moral and religious consolation so vital to those who are ill.

Wishing to aid their unhappy, suffering countrymen as quickly as possible, and being confident in God's help, the Sisters obtained a loan of $20,000. They bought a house with three plots of beautiful gardens and organized a hospital with twenty-four beds. The hospital opened on May 6, 1894. It is easy to surmise how many hardships and financial difficulties these sisters endured in order to comfortably and appropriately furnish their hospital. From the day the hospital opened until January 1, 1900, there were 956 patients, of whom 527 paid in full, 199 were accepted for free, and 230 for half-price.

This charitable institution could not expand in such cramped premises. The sisters had to think of building another hospital. Another circumstance that prompted them to do so was that, shortly after they had purchased the above-mentioned property, the city built and opened a subway near the hospital, the noise of which disrupted the peace so needed by the sick. This great obstacle forced the sisters to look for another more appropriate place where a building could be built according to their needs and requirements. We know well the magnificent buildings of charitable institutions that other nationalities possess. And why should not the buildings of the Poles, of whom there are so many thousands in Chicago, be equal to the others?

God, who always helps good intentions and endeavors, blessed the sisters' actions. It so happened that an entire block was bought in a good location close to the existing hospital. It consisted of fifty lots on Leavitt Street and is located in the center of [the Chicago] Polonia. Transportation is convenient from even the outlying parishes, since four streetcar lines lead to the hospital, including division Street, Robey Avenue, Chicago Avenue, and Webster Avenue. Another positive aspect of this location is that the air in this part of the city is healthy and clean, since it is far from the factories and closer to Humboldt Park. The surrounding streets are clean and pleasantly built. We also see the care of Divine Providence in that the owners of the property, wishing to aid the charitable institution, substantially lowered the price. The entire parcel cost $25,000. In 1902 this new Polish hospital was ceremoniously consecrated by Bishop Muldoon. Through 1904 it had 1,157 patients (647 Catholics and 510 non-Catholics); of these 96 died, and 457 were non-paying. In addition, 2,534 received free medical help on an outpatient basis.

In October, 1897, a group of noble-minded ladies established a society to provide financial and moral support for the Polish hospital in Chicago, under the name of the Mother of God of Nazareth, through monthly collections, voluntary contributions, theatre performances, and so on. In 1897 the administration was composed of: Mrs. E. Smulska, chair; Mrs. L. Hoffman, secretary; and Mrs. J. Jendrzejek, treasurer. In 1898-99: Mrs. W. Chodzyńska, chair; Mrs. L. Hoffman, secretary; Mrs. J. Jendrzejek, treasurer. In 1900: Mrs. A. Klarkowska, chair; Mrs. G. Żółkowska, secretary; Mrs. J. Jendrzejek, treasurer.

There will be more in elsewhere this volume about the Academy of the Sisters of Nazareth.

SISTERS OF THE RESURRECTION[26]

Mother of Celine Borzęcka, Founder and Superior General of the Sisters of the Resurrection, kindly delivered the following memorandum to me in Rome in 1904:

The Order of the Sisters of the Resurrection, founded by Mrs. Celine Borzęcka, had its beginning in Rome under the direction of Rev. Semeneńko, Founder and Superior General of the Resurrectionist Fathers.

Following the loss of her husband, Mrs. Borzęcka decided in 1874 to dedicate herself to the service of God. However, she first had to complete her maternal responsibilities toward her two daughters. After providing for the older one, she arrived in Rome in 1882 with her younger daughter, Hedwig. Here God revealed to them His intentions for them. The mother and daughter founded the order, desiring to spread the Kingdom of God among people, within the boundaries that are permitted women within the Church.

Seeing that society's moral wounds most often occur on account of a careless or false direction in upbringing, they decided that with whatever strength they had, they could remedy this evil by organizing elementary and high schools, as well as sewing shops and nursery schools. In this manner they could implant principles which would yield good fruit in the hearts of children.

God most clearly blessed this undertaking. Cardinal Parrocchi, Vicar of Pope Leo XIII, became intensely interested, through a strange coincidence, in this new work of God. He designated St. John Cantius as the patron of the finishing school these ladies had established in Rome, not suspecting that in the future, Kęty, the Saint's birthplace, would become the vineyard of the young order.

Four years later Cardinal Parrocchi gave the religious habit to the first five members of the order and accepted the professions of both mother and daughter, who committed their perpetual vows into his hands.

That same year Mother Celine Borzęcka was summoned by His Eminence Cardinal Dunajewski to work in Kęty, and she went there to establish a novitiate. However, before the convent was built, the Sisters of the Resurrection had to live in the attic of a wretched hut. Yet they were still thankful to God that they had been allowed to work in their native land. They did not delay in rendering services to their countrymen and, despite the lack of space and inconveniences they encountered, they immediately opened sewing rooms for poor girls to whom they taught catechism and needlework. Soon thereafter they also opened a nursery, which was a true blessing for the parish because not only were the small children cared for by the sisters, but the poorer ones also received meals. God was constantly sending workers for the harvest, a clear sign of His blessing.

Encouraged by Cardinal Ledóchowski, Prefect of the Office of the Propaganda in Rome, Mother Founder [Borzęcka] went in 1896 together with three other sisters to the mission of Małko-Tyrnowy in European Turkey. The Bulgarians then persistently asked for a Catholic school, since their children studying in schismatic schools often lacked religious instruction and were susceptible to evil influences. Trying to win the Bulgarians' confidence, Mother Borzęcka and the missionaries adapted themselves to local customs. She also conformed entirely to the Eastern rite, which greatly won over the inhabitants of Małko-Tyrnowy.

When this new mission opened, the Sisters of the Resurrection were in an extremely difficult financial situation. They lacked any monetary aid, because the local Catholic population was extremely poor, and the schismatic rich were so fanatic in their faith that they persecuted and insulted the sisters. The poor hut occupied by Mother Borzęcka was quite neglected—wide gaps in the wall let in the cold and the wind. Rain would seep through the poorly constructed roof and the primitive chimney often hindered the sisters' preparation of the modest meal. Their furniture consisted of a few carpets which at night substituted for beds. Pious Bulgarian women had given them to the missionaries. In such cramped conditions the Sisters of the Resurrection began to study Bulgarian with total fervor, and after a few months of persistent work they opened a Catholic school. But again there were new difficulties and unpleasantness from the schismatics! Trying to weaken the influence of the missionary sisters, they built a splendid schismatic school, equipped it magnificently and supplied it with teachers, hoping to overshadow the poor school of the Sisters of the Resurrection. But the love of Christ, which the sisters saw in each child's soul, triumphed over the enemy. Bulgarian, Greek, Armenian, and even Turkish children began to attend the Catholic school. Parents valued the Sisters' solicitous care, and the children—very intelligent, talented, and clever—gathered around them with full confidence. Their numbers grew with each passing day; not only were the schismatic children becoming converted, but they were influencing their parents toward the Holy faith. The missionaries aided sick and dying women regardless of their religion. This generosity and love for their fellow man won them recognition by the schismatics. Bulgarian women, feeling the sisters' genuine devotion in their hearts, would come to them for help and advice in spiritual and personal matters. Here was a great opportunity for work— to uproot truly pagan superstitions and customs. For example, the local women were used to confessing grievous sins, not to a priest but to an elder standing over a grave, or in the middle of the night in a forest in front of a dead tree, or to a virgin. This confession was considered a substitute for the sacrament of penance. Therefore, sometimes they would come to the sisters, wishing to lay before them the secrets of their conscience. Enlightened and carefully prepared for the sacrament of penance by the sisters, they would then go to the Bulgarian Catholic church, where they would proceed with their confession. They would return home grateful to God for allowing them to belong to the true church, and being faithful to it, they would convert their families.

In January 1900, with the permission of Cardinal Ledóchowski and Archbishop Feehan of Chicago, the Sisters of the Resurrection were summoned to that city, where at Holy Mary of Angels Parish they were given administration of the Polish school. In 1901 they took over administration of a second school in the same city at St. Casimir's Parish.

On a visit to her order in America in 1902, Mother Borzęcka became convinced that the sisters needed their own convent in Chicago so that they would have a permanent base of support for their work for the church and for the Polish immigrants, who in exile so quickly forget their mother tongue and their national history. There is, therefore, hope that her countrymen's generosity will charitably allow construction of a convent for the Sisters of the Resurrection for the purpose of gathering together and watching over Polish children.

POLISH SCHOOL SISTERS OF ST. JOSEPH, ORGANIZED IN 1901[27]

Polish girls had been entering the German convent on 22nd Avenue in Milwaukee in order to become teachers at Polish parish schools in America. As time passed the German superiors unfortunately disregarded this primary goal by removing lectures on Polish language in 1899 (Polish grammar was taught here by Professor Jan Kuk from 1893 to 1899) and by emphasizing nursing the sick in hospitals. Formerly, and as recently as 1899, the sisters from the convent at 22nd Avenue were called "school" Sisters, as can clearly be seen from the title of their constitution: "Constitution of School Sisters of the Third Order of St. Francis of Assisi in the Motherhouse of Milwaukee, Wisconsin, 1899." However, in the 1901 edition the word "school" had already been omitted. The sisters, especially the Polish ones, were being used as domestic help instead of being educated as teachers. Rather than becoming teachers of Polish children, the Polish sisters were becoming "hospital sisters" or custodians of sick Jews, Protestants, and other hospital patients. They not only were not taught the Polish language, but they were even forbidden to speak it under penalty of sin, which the guilty party had to confess to her German chaplain.

In 1900 six Polish girls from Stevens Point, Wisconsin, entered the above-mentioned convent. They realized, however, that not only would they not be allowed to become teachers, but they could not even remain Poles. They soon left this convent and returned to their parents in Stevens Point. Because of this, one of the fathers of these girls engaged in a sharp correspondence with the convent superior, Sister Alphonsa, who because of an insulting letter from one parishioner decided to take revenge on the entire parish. On February 25, 1901, she informed Rev. Ł. Peściński, the pastor in Stevens Point, that beginning with the next school year she would recall all the Polish teaching sisters from Stevens Point. In addition, in a letter to one of the sisters she clearly stated that in the future she did not wish any more Polish candidates from Stevens Point to be sent to her. The Polish teaching sisters were to leave the parish schools—not only there but also other ones in other communities—in order to become custodians in hospitals.

Rev. Peściński then found himself in a very difficult position, because he knew that it was quite difficult to find Polish teaching sisters in America. On April 17, 1901, he presented the matter in writing to the vicar general in Green Bay [Wisconsin]. On April 23, Revs. Peściński, Małkowski from Menasha, Manel, OFM, from Pułaski, and Wiśniewski, OFM, verbally presented this matter to the bishop in Green Bay. From the outset Bishop Messmer was of the opinion that the Polish sisters should separate themselves and establish their own Polish order. For this reason he sent Revs. Peściński and A. Wiśniewski, OFM, with a letter to Archbishop Katzer [in Milwaukee] via Rev. J. Gulski.

Archbishop Katzer brought to their attention the previously unknown fact that the rule of the Franciscan Sisters had been approved by Rome a year before and that, therefore, neither he nor any other bishop could permit the Polish sisters to leave that religious order and found another one. Nevertheless, Rev. Peściński, in conjunction with Revs. Nawrocki, J. Gulski, and others, informed the mother superior in Milwaukee on June 20,1901, "We are ready to found a Polish order of School Sisters this July 1." Mother Superior Aleksya responded by saying, I command all our sisters under holy obedience to return to the mother house immediately." She sent the same directive to Rev. Małkowski in Menasha. However, Bishop Messmer answered the sisters as follows: "I think that under the present circumstances, you are justified in remaining where you are and not returning to the motherhouse while awaiting the establishment of the new Polish order of sisters."

On July 1, 1901, this new religious order was organized under the name of "Polish School Sisters of St. Joseph," with the motherhouse to be built in Stevens Point, Wisconsin. This occurred with Bishop Messmer's clear permission. Mother Felicya became the mother superior and Rev. Łukasz Peściński temporarily became the chaplain. About forty-two Polish sisters left the German order and immediately entered the Polish one. However, this took place without formal sanction from Rome.

Efforts were then made to get permission from Rome. Over fifty priests signed a petition to the apostolic delegate, Cardinal Martinelli. On July 22, 1901, while visiting Milwaukee, he declared that without permission from Rome not even he could allow the Franciscan Sisters to leave the order. However, since the Polish sisters had already left, they could for the time being remain in their parishes until the decision arrived from Rome. In September 1901 the separated sisters sent a memorandum to the Prefect of Propaganda, Cardinal Ledóchowski. At the same time Rev. Peściński sent an entire package of documents to the Monsignor Meszcyński in Rome. Bishop Messmer also sent a personal letter to the Propaganda in which he presented the necessity of having a Polish order to teach in Polish schools. This succinctly and sensibly composed memorandum to Rome was signed by Sister M. Felicya from Stevens Point in the name of five sisters from the Green Bay Diocese; Sisters M. Bolesława and M. Damian from Detroit, Michigan, in the name of eighteen sisters; Sister M. Kleta from Chicago in the name of fourteen sisters; Sister M. Efrema from Pułaski [Wisconsin] in the name of three sisters; and Sister M. Seweryna from Menasha in the name of four sisters. In response to the sisters' request, Bishop [Messmer] and Rev. Peściński, the Vatican authorized Cardinal Martinelli in a letter dated February 15, 1902, to handle the entire matter.

Meanwhile, on January 15, 1902, a corporation was formed for the purpose of erecting a convent and academy or scientific educational institution for educating the sisters as teachers, as well as instructing young lay girls. The administration comprised the following directors: Bishop Messmer, Monsignor Fox, Rev. Jacek Gulski, Rev. Łukasz Peściński, Rev. Stanisław Nawrocki and Rev. J. Folta. There were also three sisters: M. Felicya (née Jaskulska), M. Klara (then in Chicago) and M. Bolesława (then in Detroit). This administration resolved to build a convent and academy at a cost of $30,000 to $40,000.

On April 9, 1902, the apostolic delegate, Cardinal Martinelli, with separate permission from the Propaganda, finally issued a formal decree confirming this new religious order of "Polish School Sisters of St. Joseph," and placed them under the jurisdiction of the bishop of Green Bay. On the same day—through an act of Providence—as the apostolic delegate in Washington issued this decree, Rev. Peściński in Stevens Point, unaware of the coincidence, laid the first stone for the foundation of the future motherhouse. This motherhouse, or convent academy, was built right beyond the borders of the city of Stevens Point about fifteen minutes from the Polish church, and in a very healthy and idyllic location of pine woods. The convent owned thirty-four acres of land. Not far from the house, in the place designated as a cemetery, there is a stone tomb which contains a chapel where the Peściński family can say mass. The remains of Rev. Peściński's mother and sister already repose there.

On May 20, 1902, Bishop Messmer, surrounded by numerous clergy and a great crowd of the faithful, consecrated the cornerstone for the new building of the School Sisters of St. Joseph.

On August 13, 1902, the first eight candidates were accepted for the novitiate, and about forty sisters either took or renewed their religious vows. The bishop blessed the habits of the candidates who then left the church and soon returned dressed in them. The novices received their crosses and rosaries and were crowned with wreaths of red and white roses. Those who had completed the novitiate and took their vows had their white veils changed to black ones and were wreathed with crowns of thorns.

On October 1, 1902, the exterior [of the motherhouse] was completed and Rev. Stanisław Nawrocki from Chicago consecrated the cross which was hoisted to the dome of the new convent. On November 26, 1902, the sisters moved into the new motherhouse. The interior of the building was completed during the winter and spring.

Ceremoniously consecrated in 1903, this new building of the School Sisters of St. Joseph, when taken together with the many acres of land, was valued at $75,000.

At the beginning of 1903 the statistics for the Polish School Sisters of St. Joseph and the motherhouse in Stevens Point, Wisconsin, were as follows:

1. Stevens Point: five sisters taught 350 children.

2. Chicago ("Bridgeport"): sixteen sisters taught 1,229 children.

3. Detroit, Heart of Mary Parish: eleven sisters and one candidate taught 1,195 children.

4. Detroit, St. Francis Parish: six sisters and two candidates taught 835 children.

5. Menasha, Wisconsin: four sisters taught 215 children.

6. Pulaski, Wisconsin: three sisters and one candidate taught 206 children.
7. Green Bay, Wisconsin, two sisters and a candidate taught 100 children.
8. Independence, Wisconsin: two sisters and one candidate taught 150 children.

A total of 4,280 Polish children were therefore already being educated in 1903 by this new order of "Polish School Sisters of St. Joseph," which had eighty members including the candidates.

The main purpose of this newly built school or convent and academy in Stevens Point was to supply teaching sisters for the Polish parochial schools in America, in both large and small communities. Not tens but hundreds of Polish communities were still deprived of Polish schools simply due to lack of teaching forces. In addition, another goal of this new institution in Stevens Point was to be an academy where those young girls not wishing to enter the convent could receive a higher education.

POLISH HIGHER EDUCATION IN AMERICA[28]

The history of Polish immigration, as presented here, is not really a chronicle of wars and annexations, but it does not cease to be history in the best sense of the word. History can become what even the pagan historians wanted—the mistress of human life and of the lives of nations and the foundation of the noble progress of civilization. This will happen only if the main thrust is not placed on the history of wars and annexations; if history does not honor with the most beautiful wreath those who shed the greatest amount of human blood and who greatly wronged those whom they conquer; and if education will be drawn from history according to Cicero's motto: *"cedant arma togae, concedat laurea laudi"*—let weapons be replaced by togas and military laurels by peaceful garlands.[29]

In the history of Polish education in America the name of Rev. Józef Dąbrowski has been inscribed in gold letters for at least two reasons: he founded a Polish seminary and he established the first Polish motherhouse for school sisters (Felician) in America.

Rev. Józef Dąbrowski was born in Żołtance in the Congress Kingdom in 1842. Having completed high school in Lublin, he attended Warsaw University, where he studied natural science and mathematics. The national insurrection caught him there by surprise in 1863. Always ready to save his nation, Rev. Dąbrowski joined the ranks of the rebellion under [Gen. Ludwik] Mierosławski and actively took part in numerous clashes.

In 1864 he crossed the border one night and went on to Dresden in Sax-
ony. From there he set out for Switzerland, where he spent most of his
time in Lucerne and Bern pursuing mathematical-technical studies. After a
few years of wandering, often sustaining himself with the "bread and chalice of tears," he felt a religious calling and wished to reach the Eternal
City. He then left for the capital of the Christian world, and this was the
first safe port in his life. After completing theological studies at the Polish
College under the direction of Rev. Semeneńko, CR, Rev. Dąbrowski was
ordained on August 1, 1869.

Having barely arrived on American soil, this providential man immediately recognized what the Polish immigrants lacked—schools, especially
those for higher education. Once crystallized, this realization was Rev.
Dąbrowski's guiding principle throughout his life, just as if it were a pole
star. We have stated that as soon as he arrived in America he immediately
began to think of a Polish school and seminary. Proof of this is found in
the first letters he wrote from America. They bare his soul and reveal his
aspirations and his guiding thoughts. And where did Providence direct his
first steps in America? It was to the seminary in St. Francis, Wisconsin,
where he stayed for a few months, though not for the purpose of studying,
since he was already a priest. On January 22, 1870, after his arrival in
America, he wrote to Rev. Semeneńko, CR, in Rome:

I arrived on December 31, 1869. In Kraków I went to Rev. Dunajewski where I
met Strzelichowski, and he then brought over Drohojewski. He, in turn, invited my
mother, who was planning to visit, to stay with him. And so I spent a very pleasant
two weeks with my mother and brother. In the beginning, I was afraid to tell my
mother where I was going, but slowly I told her everything and surprisingly she
took the news much better than I had expected. She ended by saying: "God has
directed you until now; go where he directs you further. I give you my blessing."
When I heard this, I was very happy. Up until now everything has been happy and
successful, but there is nothing permanent in this world and everything changes.
And so, sadness came upon me because of the lamentable state of our settlement
[in America]. And everything is so much more painful because all could be well.
The means do exist, but there is either a lack of a talented person to use them, or
someone's malicious hand is wasting it all. There are enough of our settlements,
but none of them has a school. The children are growing physically, but their
brains are asleep . . . and their Polishness becomes blurred. When an entire series
of Polish priests passed through and not one of them could lead himself or anyone
else, the bishop of Milwaukee, not knowing what to do with the Poles, handed
over in desperation the administration of their parish to a German (Rev. Jaster),
who knew as much Polish as I do English. He was the first to establish a school for
Poles. But what a school! It would have been better to send the children directly to
a German school, since everyone would know from the start that they would

become Germans. Here we have a Polish school in which they teach in German. The priest does not know Polish and the teachers know very little—what can be expected here? I went to see this priest and explained that he was acting incorrectly . . . . I asked him to hire a Polish teacher and to cut in half the hours per week devoted to German lessons, but God knows what will happen. The German priest about whom I speak is a decent person, I cannot take anything away from him. There are up to 450 Polish families here, and this German priest is Germanizing them out of necessity, because whoever wants to communicate with him must speak German. If you priests [the Resurrectionists] take over Chicago and Milwaukee, this will be good for the congregation. If as priests you will have these two locations, it can be said that you will have all the Poles of the United States in your hands . . . . I live at the seminary in Milwaukee and I like it here very much. This seminary has a total of 240 alumni. I very much like the rector and professors, of whom there are twelve.

From the very beginning in America, Rev. Dąbrowski recognized the lack of schools and the lack of Polish teachers and priests. But, unlike many others, he did not stop after simply recognizing these shortcomings. He immediately thought of ways to remedy them. There was a need for institutions of higher education that could train priests and teachers! But who would assume such a responsibility? An individual? He himself? If this was necessary, then he was prepared! Initially, however, he did not countenance it, since the Congregation of Resurrection could and should undertake this endeavor. On March 16, 1870, he wrote a second letter from St. Francis to Rev. Semeneńko, CR:

Since I was able to observe more clearly the situation and relations within our [Polish] communities in America, I have become convinced that the state of affairs is most lamentable in every way. I have finally become convinced that no one will be able to do anything, except maybe the congregation itself. Poles, wherever they have gathered in greater numbers, already have their churches, but there are no priests or schools and there is no hope that they could some day have them, unless they finally become denationalized. Our Poles live without the mass, confession, sermons, or education . . . some have settled in large cities, but due to a lack of priests and education (as reported to me by Mr. Kiołbassa of Chicago), they do not attend church. Since they are affluent, but lacking religion, dissipation has crept in. What will happen next? Schools cannot be established because there is no one to teach in them. Priests cannot be educated, since there is no place for them and no candidates. There is, in truth, a seminary in Milwaukee, but it is an English-German one. Even if a Pole were sent there, after eight or ten years in the seminary he would forget any Polish he knew, and by the time he finally became a priest he would be working for the Germans or the English. How will the Poles benefit from this? Help has to come while there is still time. The Resurrectionists can best counteract evil, since they can at once impose their supervision and care over everything. And if they cannot develop their activities at once, and later on a larger scale, then they can at least progress slowly in this direction. It could be that God actually entrusted Resurrectionists with the care of our unfortunate brethren, and it could be that He desires to place the entire administration over the Poles [in America] in the hands of the congregation. With such a large number of Poles the congregation could establish a religious house and novitiate here. And if the congregation puts its mind to it, it can perform numerous good deeds. If the order would come here and settle in a central point (like Milwaukee), it will have all the Poles in its hands. Missionaries could be sent from here to smaller, outlying communities. A grammar school and even a high school could be opened here so that our people could somehow progress, since today hardly anyone knows how to read or do anything other than physical work. Having well-qualified brothers, the congregation could easily open grammar schools in less important communities. Candidates to the religious state could and should of necessity be educated in high schools to the extent that they would attend the seminary only for theology.

The candidates should be educated in Polish so that they would not forget it during their stay at the seminary. Besides this, a boarding house should be opened for religious aspirants, to which they could come from outlying areas to prepare for the seminary. They could then return whence they came to be ordained. In this way even most distant communities, such as New York (300 families), Pennsylvania (50), and so on, could have a supply of clergy. There are up to 15,000 Poles in the United States. A large immigration lately has come to Wisconsin, and especially to Chicago and Milwaukee. I do not know who will remain in the Poznań area. Polish communities will not survive; they will be forced out by the Germans to the English. Everything that arrives from Poland arrives for the annihilation of our nationality. In our history there is no indication that our people liked to move about the country, they even hated to move to a neighboring village. Today? Our people leave for countries beyond the ocean where the heart and language are foreign.

This is how Rev. Dąbrowski perceived the fact that the young generation in a foreign land was sentenced to denationalization, if its soul was not nourished in its native language.

Despite these encouragements, entreaties, and arguments, the Resurrectionists were in no hurry to begin establishing a Polish institution of higher education, a college, or a seminary. They had founded colleges for Germans in Canada and for the Irish in Kentucky, yet they could not or would not do it for the Poles. Therefore, Rev. Dąbrowski himself began and completed this undertaking. In 1874 he brought the Felician Sisters over from Poland and built a motherhouse for them in Polonia, Wisconsin. This was an act of great consequence, since these sisters' activities proved so all-encompassing that today they have two provinces. As we already have seen, they administer Polish schools throughout the United States. They also administer orphanages for boys in Polonia, Buffalo, Manitowoc, an orphanage for girls in Detroit, and a shelter for the elderly, as well as the

Immigration House in New York. Ten years later, in 1884, Rev. Dąbrowski undertook a far more significant cause, which has crowned him with a laurel wreath of undying glory and honor among generations of Poles. Seeing that the power of faith and nationality can only be upheld only when the word of God is preached in the native language, he founded a Polish institution of higher education and a seminary, the Polish seminary in Detroit.

We have obtained its history from the most authentic source, Rev. Józef Dąbrowski himself, who describes as follows the beginnings and historical development of this institution, in a letter dated June, 1901:[30]

THE IDEA OF ESTABLISHING A POLISH SEMINARY IN AMERICA

When the Poles began to immigrate to America in great numbers around 1870, American bishops often wrote to Cardinal Ledóchowski requesting Polish priests from him in Rome. Not being able to comply with the bishops' requests, he suggested establishing a Polish seminary in America. He shared his idea with Rev. Leopold Moczgęba, who at the time was a member of the Franciscan Order and held the position of a confessor at St. Peter's Basilica in Rome. Rev. Moczygęba decided to work on this matter and asked permission to collect funds for this purpose. As a monk, he had to have special dispensation from the Vatican. This project was presented to Pope Leo XIII, who praised and blessed the idea.

After arriving in America, Rev. Moczgęba collected about $8,000 for this purpose. Since he was already advanced in age, he did not feel strong enough for this work. He passed along his execution to Józef Dąbrowski, who completed it with the help of God and through the generosity of our countrymen.

LOCATION AND CONSTRUCTION

Dąbrowski was pastor in Polonia, Wisconsin, for close to thirteen years—from 1870 to September 1883. He had moved to Detroit, Michigan, where he became the chaplain of the Felician Sisters. Here he began his work for the seminary. Detroit, Michigan, was chosen as its location because that city is in the center of the main Polish communities, and today Detroit itself has about 40,000 Poles. The city is beautiful and the climate is very healthful. Two and a half acres of land were brought in the city at St. Aubin and Forest Avenues. Construction began in 1884. On July 24, 1885, the cornerstone was laid. Bishop Ryan from Buffalo, New York, presided over the ceremony in the presence of Rev. H. K. Borgess, bishop of Detroit, with the participation of numerous representatives of the Polish clergy from throughout the United States. Revs. Urban Raszkiewicz and Domagalski delivered speeches in Polish. Bishop Borgess and Rev. Reily, pastor of St. Patrick's in Detroit, spoke in English. After construction had begun, Rev. Antoni Jaworski offered his help in collecting funds for a year. In 1887 the seminary building was completed. It measured 140 feet long by 68 feet wide, with four floors and a basement.

The seminary was opened on December 15, 1887, by Bishop Borgess. In the beginning there were six students: Jan Miller, Ernst Helly, Maksymilian Kotecki, Józef Letownik, and Feliks Kieruj—and all but Helly became priests. By the end of the year, there were twenty-six students from various parts of the United States. The seminary has two courses, that is, the classical one—or high school—consisting of five grades, and a five-year course of philosophy and theology—two years of the former and three years of the latter.

DEVELOPMENT OF THE SEMINARY

It is hard to believe how many difficulties the institution had to overcome. God, however, was compassionate and removed them all and the institution developed as follows:

At the outset, in 1887 there were six students; at the end of the year there were twenty-six of them. In 1888-89 there were 35 students; 1889-90, 65; 1890-91, 66; 1891-92, 77; 1892-93, 80; 1893-94, 105; 1894-95, 125; 1895-96, 123; 1896-97, 133; 1897-98, 131; 1898-99, 153; 1899-1900, 154; 1900-1901, 156.

SEMINARY PROFESSORS

As the building neared completion, Rev. Dąbrowski went to Europe in 1885 to bring over professors. He went to Rome. Initially he did not accomplish anything there, but he made various acquaintances through which a few professors later arrived. In Kraków, Rev. Baran and Rev. Bronikowski volunteered; however, a short time after their arrival they left the seminary. At this time Rev. Witold Buchaczkowski arrived from Rome. He is still at the seminary (1901) today and for many years has held the position of vice-rector and rendered great contributions to the development of the institution. He was followed by Rev. Mieczysław Barabasz, DD, and Mr. Karol Laskowski, who arrived from Rome; they also worked commendably. When the seminary was growing, Rev. Ciemiński, Rev. Godrycz, Rev. Kisielewicz, and Rev. Ćwiąkała from Kraków were brought over and they worked fervently for close to four years. Considering, however, that the constant search for professors for the growing institution was burdensome, it was decided to send talented and trustworthy students to Rome, who, upon their return, would devote themselves to the seminary. Rev. Jan Miller was sent to the Gregorian University in Rome, where he completed his studies with dedication. Revs. Jarecki and Chylewski were also sent there and worked to the credit of the seminary. For the future we again have one philosophy student at the Propaganda. For secular subjects we have many lay professors, such as Dr. Siemiradzki (professor of Latin, Greek, and history), Romuald Piątkowski (professor of astronomy, Latin, Polish, German, and French), Kazimierz Sypniewski (professor of Polish, arithmetic, and physics) and a few English professors. A year ago Rev. Jan Moneta, as full of devotion as the others, joined the seminary staff. Hail to all of them for their work and devotion! The institution numbers six clerical professors, three Polish lay professors, and two English professors.

CLERGY FROM THE POLISH SEMINARY

Thirty alumni thus far have been ordained here. They are: Kazimierz Wałajtys (Parisville, Michigan), Jan Gulcz (Wilmington, Delaware), Franciszek Miller (Detroit), Piotr Basiński (Buffalo), Jan Moneta (Detroit), Bronisław Jankowski (Canada), Antoni Duszyński (Baltimore), Leon Bójnowski (New Britain, Connecticut), Józef Dulski (Baltimore), Adam Marcinkiewicz (Buffalo), Franciszek Dopka (Toledo), Feliks Kieruj (Detroit), Bolesław Radka (Ashton, Nebraska), Jan Grudziński (Leavenworth, Kansas), Stanisław Jaszczyński (Elba, Nebraska), Karl Godrycz, Józef Fołta (Detroit), Jan Walczak (Detroit), Aleksander Grudziński (Detroit), Józef Culkowski (Norwich, Connecticut), Frank Nona, (Chapel Hill, Texas), Józef Czepanonis, Antoni Kaupas (Scranton, Pennsylvania), Andrzej Janiszewski (Waterloo, Illinois), Michał Dymiński (Albion, New York), Józef Czubek (Boston, Massachusetts), Karol Ćwikliński (Smartville, Nebraska), Wojciech Nowak, and Michał Kłosowski.

In June [1901] two more alumni will be ordained: Józef Dawid and Emilion Musiał. Thus, up to the present we have thirty-two active priests who have completed the entire course and have been ordained here. In addition, about fifty of our students were transferred to other institutions and were later ordained at them. As of this summer, over eighty Polish priests have completed the Polish seminary. We also have many laymen, such as lawyers and doctors, in various offices who, not being called to the religious life, chose a different profession for themselves and, like the clergy, proudly work among our countrymen.

This is what the founder himself reports. We can only add that in founding a Polish seminary in America, Rev. Józef Dąbrowski erected for himself a monument more permanent than the statue of Kościuszko in Chicago. *Exegit monumentum aere perennius* [I raised a monument to myself more lasting than bronze].

In 1902, thought had to be given to expansion of the seminary building. On April 5, 1902, foundations for a new chapel were dug. The old chapel, dining hall, and bathrooms had become too cramped due to the influx of students. Active to the end of his life and not disappointed by any adversities, Rev. Dąbrowski collected funds for the construction of the newly begun wing of the Polish seminary. Meanwhile, something unpleasant occurred which apparently hastened Rev. Dąbrowski's death. "On January 23, 1903," as Rev. Dąbrowski himself wrote,

. . . a written "petition" was submitted to me, signed by twenty-nine students (of theology and philosophy) requesting Rev. J. Mueller's dismissal from his position of vice-rector and professor within three days. The undersigned would otherwise leave the institution, report the matter to the bishop, proceed to the Polish priests for protection, and appeal to public opinion through the newspapers. As anyone can deduce, this was not a "petitio" or request, but a threat. The basic mistake was that subordinates had attacked authority and emphatically demanded the vice-rector's dismissal within three days. It was clear that this type of matter could not be tolerated. Otherwise, total anarchy would rule the world! No educational institution, especially a religious one, can tolerate demands and threats of this kind.

I still gave them a last chance to apologize to the vice-rector or they would be dismissed from the institution. And since they did not want to apologize, they have themselves to blame that they were dismissed.

He wrote this on February 2, 1903. On February 9 he suffered a heart attack caused by worries and grief and died of a stroke on February 15, 1903. He lived for the Polish seminary, he devoted himself to it, and it was, to some extent, the cause of his death.

After Rev. Dąbrowski's death, Bishop Foley of Detroit stated in a letter dated February 21, 1903, "The good work started by Father Dąbrowski will be further continued and preserved. With God's blessing, SS. Cyril and Methodius Seminary will be maintained and the plans of the noble founder of the first Polish seminary will be honored."

The seminary grows and develops with each passing day under the knowledgeable administration of Rev. Buhaczkowski. As of 1903 there were 260 students.

REFORMATIONIST FATHERS IN PUŁASKI, WISCONSIN

Chronologically, the next Polish secondary school that was founded initially for clerical and later for secular young members was the monastery of the Reformationist Franciscan Fathers in Pułaski, Wisconsin. It was founded on April 27, 1887, by Brother Augustine and Rev. Erazm Sobociński, Rev. O. Jeka and Rev. H. Schneider, OFM. This was the second group of Polish Reformationists to arrive in America. The first group, which was far more numerous, arrived in Chicago twelve years earlier and experienced bitter disappointment which caused it to become secularized and to disperse throughout parishes in Milwaukee, Beaver Dam, Berlin [Wisconsin], Toledo, and elsewhere. This occurred at the beginning of 1875, when General Semeneńko decided to permanently withdraw his order from Chicago. He then sent a letter to Rev. Wincenty Barzyński, CR, on April 12, 1875, ordering him to provide a financial accounting and then leave Chicago for Rome.

The Polish Reformationists were to take the place of the Resurrectionists. Rev. Wincenty did not directly oppose his general's commamd. He most obediently replied saying that he would leave Chicago immediately upon paying all of his debts! But since he never paid these debts as long as he live, he therefore remained in Chicago until his death. "So having read the last letter, that is, dated April 12," Rev. Wincenty wrote to Rome on May 5, 1875,

and praying as best I could, I am replying immediately with my first reaction. Let the Very Reverend Fathers judge from it and from subsequent letters the state of my soul and of the mission and even the unusual situation in which the very name of the resurrectionists contracted new ones. . . . I built a large house (by Polish mission standards) for the parish school and for the Sisters' living quarters—if only they were ours! And so, His Eminence, the Bishop, will not let me leave until I complete payment on this house. Why? Because of the carelessness or error of Rev. Bakanowski, and Rev. J Wołłowski's deceit, a new church (Holy Trinity) was founded a few hundred steps away from the old church of St. Stanislaus and is the source of the most horrible outrage among the parishioners and even the Polish priests. Therefore, His Eminence, the Bishop has a grievance against the Order until this matter is corrected. He allowed me to build the school on the condition that I undertake both of these problems to resolve so that he would no longer have them. And now that I am beginning to heal this extremely delicate wound . . . the order could irritate it in a most dangerous manner, if it were to withdraw from Chicago. . . . To have already once dissolved the Texas mission, leaving the secular priests and Rev. Machdzicki there . . . and with the help of Rev. Felix (Żwiardowski) and possibly Rev. Henryk (Cichocki) I will be able to do only so much to pay off the debts and to heal the wounds, and during the second year or at the beginning of the third, God willing, we will leave America for Europe. What I am promising today is the only thing I can promise, because I am now obliged to begin taking care of matters in such a way as to have free hands and wings as quickly as possible. It is clear that having been born in Europe, I must die there, as long as it is happily. Amen.

Anyway, in order to prolong his stay in Chicago, Rev. Wincenty sank more deeply into debt and he attempted to make sure that this "wound" did not heal to quickly; but he should be given credit for explaining unconventionally and wittily why he could not leave Chicago immediately. And who could deny that, were it not for Rev. Wincenty, there would be no Resurrectionists in Chicago, or even in all of America? If not for Rev. Wincenty—and he was the only one—the Polish Reformationists would have occupied the leading position [among the Polish religious orders in the United States] and would they not have built there long ago a Polish novitiate, college, and seminary? Rev. Wincenty alone decided the fate of the Resurrectionists and the Reformationists in America. That is why we quote here Rev. Wincenty's letters so that the reader can understand to what extent this resistance with its far-reaching consequences for the American Polonia was sensible and justifiable. General Semeneńko followed his first command with a second, even more emphatic one that Rev. Wincenty leave Chicago.

Rev. Wincenty replied on May 21, 1875, after receiving the letter.

I went with the news to the Bishop, who, not having received any notice from the Provincial (Rev. Funcken), was very saddened to hear of the Order's decision to leave the Polish mission in Chicago. And he said: "Your departure will bring the Polish mission to final ruin [as far as I know, other clergy in the Diocese are of the same opinion] but give me the address of your superior. Since Rev. Ludwik Machdzicki is free, there is therefore no other priest more suitable for our purpose." I asked if I could call my priest brother [Rev. Józef Barzyński] for help, to which he readily agreed. Regarding my conscience, I am convinced that my premature departure would be comparable to a spiritual abortion and that I am ready to be obedient even during labor pains, and so I do not myself assume any responsibility. The debts are a different matter, which necessarily require time, and there are still my personal responsibilities, separate from those of a Resurrectionist, other than those of rector of a mission, who is responsible for what he initiated, vouched for or even only encouraged . . . . After the arrival of my priest-brother I could have given a detailed financial statement, but presently work is tortuous, there are seventy children preparing for First Holy Communion and Rev. Ludwik does not bother to help me. Rev. Anthony Vaghi [CR] already has left for St. Mary's. If Rev. Henryk [Cichocki] arrived here in Chicago with my brother, the mission would blossom splendidly and there would be a secure future for the Polish mission in America.

Not only Rev. Józef Barzyński, but also Rev. A. Szklorzyk, arrived and they advised Rev. Wincenty to return to Rome in compliance with General [Semeneńko's] command. "For ten days now," wrote Rev. Wincenty to Rome in August 1875,

my brother Rev. Józef has been here in Chicago and Rev. A. Szklorzyk has been here for the past two weeks. The former thinks about the order, while the latter regrets having left it. Only God knows what to make of this. I am very anxious that God, the Order, the bishop, and the people with love would allow me to visit the Eternal City in this Holy Year. Much good would result because firstly much evil and many disagreements would be ended. This is the year of Holy Jubilee; therefore, I request and beg for the great favor of full remission of all my faults, both known and unknown.

But neither to this nor to his previous letter did Rev. Wincenty receive any reply from Rome. Up to this point, he did not yet know that the Reformationist Fathers were to take his place in Chicago. When he found out about it, he persisted in his decision to remain in Chicago. On September 7, 1875, Rev. Wincenty wrote to the general [of the order]:

I would have liked to come to Rome at least for a few weeks and pour out my troubled soul at the Very Reverend Father's feet . . . and with this thought in mind I sent my request over half a month ago to the Very Reverend Father through Rev. Father Julian. However, matters have developed as follows: the Reformationist Fathers from the Chełmo Diocese [in Poland] are beginning to introduce themselves to the local Bishop as Polish missionaries. His Eminence, the Bishop, is receiving them under the following conditions: (1) if our order this time will finally give up the opportunity to establish a regular house in Chicago for the Polish mission and (2) if they [the Reformationists] will establish such a *Dom Zakonny* [Religious Home]. So, to avoid any commotion he has enjoined and clearly instructed me to write to the Very Reverend Father once more, adding that he would be glad to see our regular house here, even with only three priests currently belonging to the Order and living accordingly to our Rule, and that he is very pleased with the way I am administering the Polish mission in Chicago.

At this point Rev. Wincenty presents a report of his activities in Chicago up to the present, saying that the parish is growing, its societies are multiplying, and the school is developing. He writes:

Up to this time, the people of St. Stanislaus' parish, consisting of the Kashubs (the best Catholics), the Silesians (average) and people from Poznań, did not know how to become reconciled and allowed any charlatan to divide them. Presently they have achieved unity, order, and power . . . . Until now the so-called caretakers of the parish [trustees] were the worst ones in the parish; today, ashamed, they are silent, and whenever they open their mouths, everyone laughs at them; they do not exist either *de jure* or *de facto*. They would still like to exist, but they realize the impossibility . . . of doing, so talk gives you gray hair and the Polish people become plainly terrified, at the thought of being abandoned by us, and evil triumphs beforehand as did the righteous Philistines. . . .

He further notes, once again, that he purchased a lot for the new "Great Church" and that he must pay it off; thus, how can he leave Chicago? "After all," he writes, "any change is a terrible plague for the people, who suffer so much with each change of priests. The bishop senses this, but the Philistines want to diminish the danger in his eyes and I am silent because what am I to say?" Furthermore, he continued, the entire American Polonia "has accepted the principles of the Resurrectionists" and has chosen Rev. Wincenty as its chief leader—is he to leave this position? Would he, a Resurrectionist, give up this seat of honor to the Reformationists? He continued:

The Polish mission in the United States, so numerous today in Polish communities, churches and societies, has come to feel the need for unity. Three Catholic conventions or congresses have been held which have accepted the Resurrectionists' principle, despite a few priests' opposition who were repudiated at the last conference, while the priests and civilian advisors of the *Centralne Zjednoczenie* [Central Alliance] chose me as their president but without knowing quite how. They also chose our foremost friend, Rev. Leopold Moczygęba, as the president of the Alliance, and the Polish priests already are thinking of uniting in a brotherly union. But this finally alarmed the Philistines and they did everything to divide us. It is rumored that they often go to the bishop, but it is fortunate that our bishop is not a German. The newspaper—*Polsko-Katolicka* [Polish-Catholic] edited by Jan Barzyński—is doing well and we made an agreement with one Reverend Father [Moczygęba] that he will give 12,000 francs toward its improvement. But let at least one Polish-Catholic order manifest itself in America, because it is shameful for us and will be the downfall of the (Polish) nation if there is no one to defend religious matters on our behalf. The Reformationist Fathers have presented themselves in a very bad light. They are simple alms gatherers, they drink and are quarrelsome.

This is all we need! Jesus, Mary, and Joseph save us and our poor people! And the children and orphans! If the Very Reverend Father does not save me, than I must sit for a long time imprisoned by various debts without being able to leave the mission ahead of time without causing it and the people despair and hopelessness, because unbelievable debts and scandals occurred there before my time . . . . I think that the feet of our order are meant to tread on Russia, our heart is to be in Poland, our head in Rome, the left arm in America and the right in Bulgaria—If this is true, then we are a whole human being! Let us not destroy what we have not built, but what God Himself through Jesus Christ accomplishes through us. Anyway, let the will of God be done on earth as it is in heaven, and I am dust. I kiss your feet and commend myself to your prayers; your minor servant, Wincenty.

Rev. Wincenty defended himself excellently, arguing that the order could not honorably withdraw from Chicago—but he did not receive any response from Rome to this letter either. This lengthy, ominous silence from Rome worried and distressed him very much, all the more so because the "Philistines," as he called his enemies in America, now endeavored by all the means at their disposal to undermine his position and to oust him from Chicago without fail. Lengthy letters were also being sent one after another to Rome with complaints about Rev. Wincenty listing all his mortal and venial sins. Rev. Dominic Majer of Chicago wrote to General Semeneńko on October 11, 1875:

. . . Two Polish newspapers are published here, one edited to some extent in the Catholic fashion, the second—a Catholic one whose editor is Mr. Jan Barzyński, brother of Revs. Wincenty and Józef, who at present is in Chicago. This latter newspaper is supported for the most part by parish revenues in order to give Mr. Barzyński some means of financial support. In addition, certain shares have been established at ten dollars each for the benefit of the newspaper, of which Rev. Wincenty took one hundred, making him its owner. Since I have six shares, I, therefore submitted my comments as a shareholder to the *Gazeta Katolicka*. For this, however, I was smeared with mud by the Resurrectionists. As long as I was needed, I was stroked, but when I was financially swindled, I was spurned like a used kitchen utensil. There was a time when the Very Reverend General, considering the past and present of the Chicago mission, decided to pack it in, he informing the local bishop about this, whose responsibility it was to try to obtain new priests from Europe. However, Rev. Wincenty, seeing the seriousness of the matter, thought up a plan and went to the bishop in the company of the Reformationists and Rev. Molitor, the procurator of the Slavic missions in America. Rev. Barzyński stated the he did not know anything, that no one had informed him about this, that he could not leave the Mission and that, indeed, he has instructions from his Rev. General from Rome that two priests from the Order would soon arrive, and so for the time being he is staying put. Furthermore, he ask the bishop that, in case the general does not send the promised priests, he be allowed to become secular and be accepted together with his brother Józef as diocesan priests to administer the parish. It is understandable that the bishop, surprised by such a speech, denied the request, and Rev. Wincenty compromised himself and the order, proving that he is more concerned with his own interests than with those of the order. If in this respect I am not to be believed, please contact Rev. Molitor, procurator of the mission, on Decoven Street. This was not enough for Wincenty, who was angered and embarrassed in front of witnesses, for he wanted to win over priests and to make a general appeal to the bishop, asking them not to easily accept priests unless they were presented by the Resurrectionists in America. In spirit he promoted his own interests rather than the order's, and I am morally convinced that he cheated Your Reverence as he demonstrated to you—and he thought to himself: if it works, fine; and if it does not, then it will be attributed to the Resurrectionists . . . .

Rev. A. Szklorzyk wrote from Chicago to General Semeneńko on November 12, 1875:

Rev. Wincenty does not have any religious rule, nor does he worry about it. For him reciting the breviary is old fashioned. . . . In preaching the word of God, if he would think about what he is going to say for even two minutes, but he doesn't even do that. . . . I threatened to write to Rome about this. He told me that he is not afraid of Rome. . . . He speaks ill of the Archbishop of Milwaukee . . . . the Bishop of Chicago told me that in September when this issue was still dragging on as to whether the Franciscans or our Order would take over St. Stanislaus' parish, Rev. Wincenty told him as follows: if the Rev. General would not send him any priests and wanted to recall him to Rome, he would then secularize himself and administer the parish. To this the bishop replied that if this happened, there would be no way he would want him in his diocese. . . .

And Rev. Gieryk wrote from Radom, Illinois, to General Semeneńko on November 12, 1875:

Barzyński's entire approach appears to be in the American business spirit, that is, through intrigue to enlarge his share and to get rich without any regard for anyone and not be liable to anyone. Toward this end Barzyński knew that through intrigue he could snatch the *Gazeta Katolicka* from Detroit and move it to Chicago, not remembering about restitution. . . . After dishonestly having Rev. Wieczorek dismissed, he brought his second brother to Chicago, set up a store for his father and in this manner he will have his entire family at his place. Having a good amount of debts on the printing firm, he knew how to set up a bank, to borrow money from private individuals. The Alliance I established to found, through common efforts, a high school, hospital, etc., was disorganized and diffused by Rev. Barzyński's disgraceful behavior, because I did not want to give the Barzyńskis anything from the coffers of the Alliance. The parish in Chicago has a total of 20,000 people. . . . The people built a second church in which Mass has been celebrated for some time, and now Rev. Barzyński is closing this church. . . . So, are many, many people to suffer spiritually so that casual profit may not be lost? . . . So the sack work is dearer than souls? Father, I am warning you to make order by sending in other priests and removing the Barzyńskis, because the time will come when it will be too late and the people will forcibly rail against your Order.

Rev. Szymon Wieczorek wrote from Manitowoc to the General on November 14, 1875:

Rev. Wincenty only used his religious office for his personal interests and for his own family, with which he has already surrounded himself. He should not only be driven out of Chicago, but he should also be suspended. He embroiled our Polish Union [*Zjednoczjenie*], which was to have been purely religious, and made it both political and religious. Furthermore, he wanted to appoint himself the General Procurator for the Polish clergy in America and through your efforts to wheedle from The Propaganda independence for himself from the American bishops, and to this end he constantly convenes diets, throws money around, bribes the clergy, intoxicates people. . . . He talks nonsense from the pulpit because he is never prepared. . . . You believe him to be tactful, but no one anywhere ever found a shadow of tact in him. . . . From among us forty Polish priests, he has only three allies and those are uncertain. . . . Try to summon him to Rome and you will see his obedience. . . . Or, finally, how did he behave toward Rev. A. Szklorzyk? What caused the people to threaten to go and beat up this Texas ox. The Bishop of Chicago has already brought over the Franciscans and certainly has promised to take them to Chicago . . . they arrived four weeks ago, only Rev. Wincenty entreated, deceiving the bishop, that the Resurrectionists will send three new priests any day now. . . .

Also Rev. E. Bratkiewicz and Prince Józef Molitor wrote that this "Texas ox" be driven out of Chicago. And who would not be crushed by such far-reaching and numerous accusations? For sure, the power of evil fell over one Rev. Wincenty and if it is true that *nec Hercules contra plures*, even then, Rev. Wincenty was a greater spiritual giant than Hercules. The people were against him, the clergy was against him, the leadership of his order itself was against him—but despite so many adversities Rev. Wincenty managed to remain in Chicago. What is to hang, will not sink. Yet, Rev. Wincenty was not without his defenders. Rev. Leopold Moczygęba, founder of the first Polish parish in America, courageously defended him, although he himself was a Conventual Franciscan; but at the time he insisted on keeping the Resurrectionists in Chicago—perhaps because he was afraid that he would lose the $2500 he lent to the Barzyńskis if Rev. Wincenty left Chicago? So Rev. Moczygęba wrote a beautifully composed and eloquent letter to Rev. Semeneńko from Jeffersonville, Indiana, on December 6, 1875:

> Very Reverend Father! You are aware that during the past few years many people of Polish nationality from Silesia, Prussia, Poznań and other parts of Poland arrived and continue to arrive in America. . . . It would be a great crying shame if these thousands of our countrymen were lost to the Catholic faith and to our exhausted but not yet deceased homeland. In the United States there are millions of Irish and Germans and they are strong in these parts in their fortunes, education, authority, etc., but they have achieved this status because they had beforehand their national leaders and priests to guide them. Here in America, religious orders of Benedictines (250 monks), Franciscans, Capuchins, Ligourians, Passionists, etc., as well as many lay priests work among the Germans. And the religious orders of Jesuits, Lazarists, Paulists, Dominicans, etc., work among the Irish. So that our Polish nation may achieve the same status, it is necessary for a Polish religious order apart from priests to also stand at the helm. . . . In this great need only you, Very Reverend Father, can aid the Polish people in America, and that is why I am on my knees begging you *per viscera misericordiae Dei*, to dedicate your order and establish it in America for this fundamental need of the Polish people. Rev. Wincenty Barzyński, a fervent priest, moral, knowledgeable and sincerely attached to your order, thoroughly knows our position as Poles in America, he can give the Dear and Very Reverend Father very practical plans and should be thoroughly relied on. With a Polish religious order here to lead our people, we can then work with a greater desire *quia fractus laboris mostri manebit*. Through your act of kindness, our people will also be saved from the many Polish priests who came here to accumulate money *et ad erdicandam crucem sanctam*; they only bring shame to the Polish people and to its priests. I know full well that I did not perfectly describe our need to you, Very Reverend Father, but you, in your enlightened wisdom will understand it quite well. As a Silesian, I have more Polish feeling than I am capable of expressing. With great hope that you will assist us and will send capable and good-spirited helpers for our honorable and dear Rev. Wincenty Barzyński, I thank you in advance and remain from the bottom of my heart a good servant, Leopold Bonaventure Maria Moczygęba, Definitor P. Ord. Min. Conv. P. S. I repeat once again to the Very Reverend Father, that Rev. Wincenty is the pearl of our Order in America. Help us and him!!! His brothers Józef and Jan are good, hard-working souls.

These convincing arguments were not, in fact, heeded by the general of the order at that time, but they undoubtedly gave him a lot to think about. As Rev. Moczygęba wrote: The Resurrectionists fundamentally did not establish a Polish order in America. The foundation was a novitiate and scholasticate, and it immediately should have been started on this basis, as the Reformationist Fathers did in Pułaski [Wisconsin] and as they no doubt would have done here in Chicago had they been allowed to—since even common sense dictates that the foundation must be laid first. This foundation for a Polish Order in America was not laid either by the generals of the day or by succeeding ones; that is why the building of their order here always stood on an uncertain footing; and were it not for this pillar, Rev. Wincenty, it would have collapsed long ago. In defense of this pillar, which they wanted to remove, Mr. Piotr Kiołbassa from Chicago also wrote to Rome:

> The people are ignorant and simple. The intelligentsia is a band, street rabble, that only curses and corrupts the people, and to this group should be added such priests as Wieczorek, Szklorzyk and consorts; and so it is no surprise that it is difficult for a conscientious priest—the clergy in America is of a very low level, excluding a few, that is Rev. Wincenty, Rev. Józef [Barzyński], Rev. Dąbrowski from Polonia [Wisconsin], Rev. Moczygęba, Rev. Żwiardowski and Rev. A. Klawiter from Pittsburgh. . . . In Chicago there are 5,000 families—I ask that you intercede with your honorable superiors so that they do not abandon Chicago.

And what result did all these letters have? For the moment it seemed none. General Semeneńko was stubbornly silent. He twice gave commands (in April and May 1875) to Rev. Wincenty to leave Chicago, but he stopped at this. He did not reply to any of Rev. Wincenty's explanations, as if he wanted to let him know: I gave you a command, obey it and that is flint. Rev. Wincenty, of course, interpreted this silence (in this regard he had a ingenious head) to mean that the Rev. General was leaving him in peace in Chicago. But deep in his soul he felt a great uneasiness, cares and worries. This uncertainty of his lasted from the spring of 1875 to the middle of 1876, and even afterward. At that time he was living through a true purgatory, as he wrote. During this entire time, General Semeneńko also did not write anything to his bishop. Rev. Wincenty constantly felt unsteady and uncertain ground under his feet and saw Damocles' sword hanging over his head in the form of the Reformationists. Finally, in order to get out of "such an indecent uncertainty," as he called it, he again wrote a meek but firm letter to the general on December 15, 1875:

With the end of the old year, I apologize for all my sins, insults and negligence, most humbly kissing your feet . . . and hands . . . On September 7 of this year I wrote a letter to the Most Reverend Father [General]. . . . After three months of waiting, a deathly silence prevails. To me the waiting is a purgatory; but I am not important in this case, only the one (bishop) in whose name I wrote. . . . Why won't the Very Reverend Father [General] favor him with a reply and either end it categorically with the dignity that he deserves, or clearly present to him the conditions under which the Order can accept a permanent effort for a Polish Catholic mission in Chicago. Besides, the bishop is not concerned that we immediately establish a large house, but at least a small regular one for which our Rule allows. The entire matter could then fall through over one Polish priest, this darling of the Church, whom Europe would not envy America, who would sacrifice himself for the Polish Catholic mission. Therefore, there is one issue here regarding the word: "Yes, we are founding our first regular house in the world for the Polish mission, for our nation" . . . ! The Order (say the people) has priests for Bulgaria, Kentucky, Canada, but where does it have a regular house for the Poles?! Does the Polish Order always have to give up only the Polish mission? . . . So far, God has not given the Order even one place in the carved-up land of our fathers, but Mary is giving us a place in America where the sons of quarreling fathers are coming together as one! . . . The Polish mission in Texas was an aborted fetus from the outset, because we had not established a regular house. It is true that we could not, but it is even truer that we did not want to do so. . . . Dearest Father, we can not go on any longer and here in Chicago I should not be left in such an indecent uncertainty—to be or not to be! I beg for a few words in Latin to the bishop for clear instructions for me. Meanwhile . . . . I await the judgment of God. . . .

This letter must have touched the heart of General Semeneńko and, we believe, that even the Reformationist Fathers will not hold it against Rev. Wincenty that he defended by various means this "place" of the Polish mission in America, the only one in the world that the "Blessed Virgin Mary gave" to the Polish order! This is a characteristic trait of Rev. Wincenty; as a clever diplomat, he knew how to circumvent those instances—when he was not able to leap forward. With the directive to leave Chicago, the general obstructed, as if with a high wall, his further activity and that of the order in America. Rev. Wincenty did not jump over this wall, because he could not. He, therefore, tried to circumvent it and succeeded. So, after Rev. Wincenty's last letter—we will not say that as a result of it, although we could say so, since it did mention that the bishop of Chicago himself awaited a definite reply from the general—but after this letter, we say, that Rev. Semeneńko finally wrote. It was not to Rev. Wincenty or to his bishop, but to the provincial of the Resurrectionists, Rev. Eugene Funcken, CR, in Canada. Rev. Semeneńko instructed him to go to

Chicago, to visit the bishop and Polish lay priests, who had complained about Rev. Wincenty; in other words, to personally investigate the entire situtation. Rev. Funcken (a German) did so and on January 14, 1876, he submitted the following report to the general:

Rev. Wincenty Barzyński and his brother, Rev. Józef, received me very cordially. I did not find the bishop at home, and although I waited for him for two weeks, no one could tell me when he would return. I visited Rev. Majer and Rev. Molitor; since I did not find the former at home, I therefore left my card; however, he did not repay my visit, and so I did not return to see him. Rev. August Szklorzyk had already left, having been accepted into the diocese of Detroit. . . . The two (Barzyński) brothers seem to be kind-hearted and zealous priests. They have a lot of work. . . and they really need help, but those who were to help them proved more of a burden and a worry. August wanted to rule in his own fashion; Simon worked for his own benefit; they both stirred things up. Machdzicki preferred to be independent. This was augmented by agitation from without. Rev. Majer is, as known, an ex-Dominican; in the short time he has resided here he has already switched to a third location in another diocese, which does not speak in his favor. Gieryk had to leave Detroit, because he drinks; in Chicago he was running around the saloons. It is quite probable that both were gambling on this parish (St. Stanislaus in Chicago), as was Szymon. This accounts for the envy and agitation. Besides, zealous and popular priests are always a thorn in the side of those who are evil and selfish, and woe to those who bear some kind of wound. And now the facts. The parish consists of two churches located near one another. It is not possible to make two parishes out of them. In any case, it would be a lamentable shame to lose this great parish which may eventually contain a flourishing cloister. What a beautiful place this would be for us if sometime there suddenly would be a crisis in Bulgaria. . . . The question now is: will those two priests suffice and will they hold up? My opinion is that in case of necessity they can do so for some time. It is even better that they are alone than if they were burdened by such people who, instead of building, only destroy. However, as soon as possible, they should receive assistance. Józef Barzyński is always ready to go to Rome and enter the novitiate as soon as we can substitute other priests for him. But as long as we cannot, let us quietly allow the issue to run its course on the condition that the bishop to whom I wish to write about this will be satisfied. I only ask the Rev. General not to send Rev. Wincenty back to Texas for anything—the world—and thereby again create a new temporary arrangement in Chicago. Let Texas help itself! . . . Because of Texas, after all, the Rev. General will not lose Chicago! Rev. Wincenty's temporary relocation could produce a great commotion! Revenues in Chicago were $3,263 in 1875, . . . expenses came to $2,716. . . . I will now discuss Rev. Wincenty's relation to the Polish newspaper. Such a newspaper is necessary. It was to have been based on shares, and various priests bought some of them at the time of the Polish Congress and later on. I seem to recall that at the time I also permitted Rev. Wincenty to acquire a few shares for the good of the cause. As a matter of fact, he used the remaining revenues to do so. His brother, the editor, also has room and board with his priestly brothers. . . . The actual loan taken for the newspaper comes to $3,000; it was given by Rev. Moczygęba, and the three Barzyński brothers assumed responsibility for it. It is to be understood that Rev. Wincenty should not have done this; still (1) one hopes that the newspaper itself will be able to repay this loan in a short time; (2) Rev. Moczygęba obtained the money for a good cause, and considering this newspaper to be one, he promised to make a present of it (as we shall see, he later asked to be repaid); (3) In any case the value of the guaranteed sum is encompassed in the business itself. And since one brother is helping Rev. Wincenty, I do not see any reason why Rev. Wincenty could not help his other brother, if this is not hurting the order. There is no shade of nepotism in this. It is better for the younger brother to be with his clergy brothers. Rev. Wincenty only acted rashly in assuming so many unnecessary burdens. His relation to the lay priests varies depending on the individuals themselves. Generally, it seems to me that the good Polish lay priests sympathize with our own. Good priests, headed by Revs. Moczygęba and Wincenty, founded the [Polish Roman Catholic] Union, whose purpose is: (1) to encourage harmony among Polish priests; (2) to help the bishops, who until now have had a lot of difficulties with Polish priests; (3) to avoid scandals in front of the faithful, arising from discord and mutual enmity among the priests; (4) to warn the Polish people against evil influences. . . . The point Rev. Majer raises in his complaint—viz., to ask the bishops in a separate circular not to accept priests without the recommendation of our order—was a misunderstanding and was not initiated by Rev. Wincenty but by Bishop Dwenger from Fort Wayne. In his approbation he added: I believe it is a good thing for the Polish Roman Catholic Union also to have as one of its goals the accumulation of accurate information about all Polish priests arriving in America, so that the Union employees can warn bishops of unworthy priests and recommend good ones. . . ." Quite a number of priests fear this. Rev. Wincenty definitely denies that he asked the bishop to keep him in Chicago as a lay priest if the order does not send any priests—and I also do not believe it. It is true that Rev. Simon suggested such a thought to the bishop, but the bishop immediately gave him an *exeat*. But Rev. Wincenty, being cautious, would not have taken such a silly step, especially since he knew well the bishop's intentions . . . . Let the following information serve regarding the Polish Franciscans the bishop wanted to accept: When the superior (of the Franciscans) reported to the bishop, the latter told him in Rev. Wincenty's presence: "If the Resurrectionists want to establish a regular religious house, then they have priority. If, however, the Resurrectionists would not be able to do so, then in such a case would you, the Franciscan Fathers, obligate yourselves to establish a religious house?" The kind-hearted Franciscan replied that he could not give a definite answer. And he could not because individual members of the order are dispersed and apparently *quaerunt quae sua sunt*. My letter to the bishop will state that: (1) we want to (found a religious house) but for the time being cannot; (2) we will establish it as soon as we can; (3) we wish you, the bishop, and ourselves to be content with this temporary arrangement (Wincenty and Józef Barzyński) that exists; (4) if you, the bishop, think you can do better, then we are ready to leave Chicago.

With this letter, Rev. Funcken cleansed Rev. Wincenty, absolving him nicely in front of the general of all allegations and tilting the scale, although not yet decidedly a victory for Rev. Wincenty. Rev. Semeneńko, however, still kept silent about Rev. Wincenty, ignored him, did not favor him with any letter and did not directly or indirectly approve his stay in Chicago. This worried and tormented Rev. Wincenty, but now his conscience was eased and more at peace, because at least Rev. Funcken, his provincial, approved his stay and activities in Chicago. Therefore Canada, where Rev. Funcken lives, is actually closer to his heart than Europe, where the Rev. General resides. Rev. Wincenty wrote to Rome on February 22, 1876:

I do not receive any replies to my letters, so that I am even more isolated, although Satan rejoices tremendously in Chicago, specifically at the Polish mission; but who is like God? Let the raging storm reach its peak, until the poor one learns to pray perfectly. . . . I consciously feel more at peace when my superior [Rev. Funcken] is closer to my heart and can more easily understand me. . . . Canada is true and quite a good neighbor of the United States. . . . The division of America from Europe is a terrible one in every respect, and that is why it is difficult to seal with a dead letter hearts that are so far away. . . . The Order soon will be convinced that it was not with the wind that I battled and still battle for almost ten years in America, and then it will understand my wailing! You want details. Well, I do battle every day with liars, blasphemers, Judases, etc., with the spiritually demented—if I am not telling the truth, then in a freer moment I will send a photograph of one of them. So, I am asking for help, for confidence. . . .

In vain did he call for assistants. At best he was sent tertiaries, so-called allies of the order, but not living according to its rule; such help most often debilitated the order. Rev. Wincenty did not get from Rome the strength of true members of the order; therefore, there was no possibility of establishing a regular religious house in Chicago and even less of a novitiate, a scholasticate, a college, etc. The bishop was not happy with this, because he felt his hopes placed in the Resurrectionist Fathers had been disappointed. Rev. Funcken wrote to Rome on September 27, 1876: "I do not know what to do with Chicago. It would have been better to lose Texas than Chicago, for sure. But I do not know how we will satisfy the bishop now." And Rev. Wincenty wrote to the general on August 7, 1876:

Upon his return from Rome, Rev. Felix (Żwiardowski) did not completely reassure us. After two years of promises and procrastination, the bisiop definitely expected Rev. Felix to bring at least one priest of the order to Chicago. Seeing himself again disappointed, he received us coldly, pointing out how haggard I looked. He knows well that my last serious illness, which forced me into the hospital for a month just before Easter, was brought about by an enormous workload. He knows that no more had I left the hospital, than I had to sit in the confessional in order to spare Rev. Józef who was working day and night and did not look any better than I did. He [the bishop] knows that Rev. Felix, passing through Chicago enroute to Rome, had himself seen us as convalescents. . . . Therefore, we cannot be surprised that neither the bishop nor the faithful are able to understand our policy. In answer to excuses that the order received various letters from Chicago, he said: "Why doesn't the order (that is, the general) come to me (the bishop) in such cases?" Rev. Felix again promised [the bishop] that in October one of our priests would arrive in Chicago to help. "Oh, I'm waiting", he replied, and so ended our visit. . . . I am herewith requesting that either the promises given the bishop are finally kept. . . . or, failing that, I be given clear instructions, because it is difficult to continue for any length of time in this uncertain position. . . .

But just as in previous cases, the general did not reply to this or subsequent letters; he probably thought: "What do you want?" I gave you "clear instructions" to leave Chicago, but you did not listen. You are deathly ill? You did not want to obey my command to leave Chicago? Then you will submit to the untimate authority of death, after which all my difficulties in Chicago will be ended. But Providence guarded Rev. Wincenty's frail health. The long crisis and the uncertainty finally passed, because a letter and assistants arrive from Rome, although not from the general, because he did not write at all anymore, but from the general procurator. Rev. Wincenty wrote Rev. Julian on September 27, 1876:

The Very Reverend Father's letter made me happy to the extent that I felt a warmer wind flowing for the Polish mission in Chicago. I say wind, because such assistants are not a more permanent blessing for the Chicago Polish mission. They can bring it the greatest blessing if they represent a nonviolent, nonstormy wind. However, the bishop demands at least two priests currently belonging to the order, which Rev. Felix definitely promised him. After extraordinary efforts Jesus Christ and Mary frustrated the plans of the freemason-Jewish-saloon clique in our mission, but still did not eliminate them. At present we are seriously beginning work on the construction of the great parish church for $60,000. But what kind of help can I expect from the Order if they always send me foreigners? I write this letter with a heart torn by pain, but with the greatest confidence. . . .

Rev. Wincenty was not being sent any religious assistants from Rome; as he noted in his *Listy* [Letters], he was sent only "tertiary" priests "who simply would have been laughed at by our educated countrymen in Poland." The Polish emigration generally was considered "condemned to death," so why should good priests be sent to Chicago? Basically, why should a Polish order be established there? The bishop of Chicago was dissatisfied and surely was sorry that he had accepted the Reformationists into his diocese. But this sorrow was untimely because in the interim the Reformationists had disbanded, dispersed, and secularized themselves because of Rev. Wincenty's impediment. And even if the bishop had wanted to, he could no longer get them together and settle them as an order in Chicago. Therefore, he did not touch Barzyński. Although it seems very probable that the bishops, especially at that time, did not care much about good Polish priests, they counted on the fact that the Polish people, bereft of the care of Polish priests, would more easily become denationalized and would attend Irish churches. But they were disappointed in their calculations—the people instead preferred to form national and independent churches than go to the Irish, who were watching for the demise of our nationality.

Through his unbroken will power, his delay in leaving Chicago, and his "hope against hope," Rev. Wincenty undoubtedly gained much for himself and his order. If the Polish Order of Resurrectionists exists, grows, and develops to this day in Chicago, it has only Rev. Wincenty to thank. It is true that the order did not bear as much lasting fruit there as could have been expected, and any other religious tree planted in its place would have undoubtedly produced more and better fruit, because it would have put down roots there and laid the foundation. The root is education, the foundation of the Polish order is the Polish novitiate and scholasticate, and the foundation should be laid before anything else. Examples are provided by the German and Irish religious orders in America, as well as by the Polish Reformationists. The first group, of the latter brought over from Europe in 1875, fell apart because it did not find a permanent base of support in Chicago. But the second group, sent over in 1887, thoroughly and fundamentally built its religious order in America, because it immediately began with the establishment of a novitiate and scholasticate and crowned its efforts with a secular school of higher education collegium, although it did not have as favorable conditions as did the Resurrectionists in Chicago.

This is the way the Franciscan Reformationists began their work and what they accomplished—not in a big community and a rich Chicago parish to which they were initially assigned, but on the farms in the Wisconsin forest to which jealous fate relegated them.

We read in the January 15, 1887, issue of *Wiara i Ojczyzna* [Faith and Fatherland]:

Following the closing of monasteries in Poland, some Reformationists went to America. Brother Augustyn Zajc (otherwise Zeytz), a professed Reformationist, also followed his co-religionists, who, upon their arrival, received a parish. But even here, Brother Augustyn did not have anything to do. Therefore, he worked in factories as a common laborer for a few years; he learned the language and somehow was able to fend for himself. But he was constantly tormented by longing for the monastic life and often this did not let him sleep after work. He thought a great deal about how and where to establish a Polish monastery in America, at which he could spend the rest of his life. Then he met Hof, a rich land speculator in Wisconsin. Hearing about his project, Hof latched on to him as the surest means of encouraging Poles to settle on farms. He immediately invited Brother Augustyn to reside in Pułaski [Wisconsin], where there already was a chapel in his home, which he presented to the monk for a residence and a school. Hof also donated one hundred acres of wilderness for a future monastery.

However, Brother Augustyn himself describes all of this in a slightly different manner, as relates in the March 1888 issues of *Polak w Ameryce* [Pole in America; Buffalo]. We read that Mr. Hof wrote to Brother Augustyn while he still resided at the Kraków monastery, offering him for free one hundred twenty acres for the monastery. Other Polish citizens (such as Władisław Dyniewicz, Stanisław Peszczyński, K. Kolka, M. Bendarajtys, and others) subsequently offered part of their land for this purpose. Sent by Rev. Provincial Joachim, Brother Augustyn chose the Pułaski colony as the most suitable.

Brother Augustyn then moved into this house, in which he immediately established a school and taught children. On Sunday and holidays he said prayers with those who gathered, sang the Rosary, canonical hours, hymns and read the Gospel. Since he was an intelligent and well-read individual, he therefore interpreted portions of the Holy Gospel, condemning offenses and encouraging virtue, for which the people also loved him. With their help he cut down and cleared part of the forest offered for the monastery and prepared the construction materials. Upon Bishop Katzer's recommendation, the Vatican gave permission for the establishment of the first Polish monastery of the Minor Brothers of the Order of St. Francis of Assissi in the United States, dedicated to the Assumption of the Holy Virgin Mary. It received all indulgences and privileges enjoyed by the Order of the Seraphic Patriarch. The founding date of both the monastery and the parish occurred on the same day, April 27, 1887.

In the September 27, 1887 issue of *Polak w Ameryce*, we find Brother Augustyn's "Odezwę do przewiel. duchowieństwa polskiego, oraz wszystkich towarzystw, obywateli i stowarzyszeń Grosza Polskiego w Stanach

Zjedn" [Proclamation to the Very Reverend Polish Clergy, as well as to Societies, citizens, and association of Grosz Polski [Polish Fund] in the United States]. It concluded as follows:

Contributions (for the construction of the monastery) which anyone desires to make should kindly be sent in care of His Eminence, Bishop Francis X. Katzer, Green Bay, Wisconsin, and to me only a list of contributors for the purpose of placing their names into the donors' book of the monastery. Respectfully, Brother Augustyn Zeytz, Reformationist, 119 West Water Street, Milwaukee, Wisc.

Brother Augustyn wrote imploring letters to the Rev. Provincial in Galicia, requesting a monastic priest and brothers. However, his requests did not produce results. He then wrote directly to the general in Rome, who designated three priests and two brothers for the first Polish monastery being established in America. They were: Rev. Erazm Sobociński as its superior and general commissioner, Rev. Stanisław Jeka and Hieronim Schneider as representatives of the first foundation of the order.

Revs. Erazm Sobociński, OFM, and Stanisław Jeka, OFM, and one brother reached Pułaski in April 1888. Rev. Hieronim, OFM, arrived a few months later with a second brother. Since construction of the monastery already had begun but was not yet completed, it was necessary to accommodate them all in Brother Augustyn's small house. The attic served as living quarters, the small store under the house as the kitchen and refectory, and the middle portion as the chapel. In September 1888 a few cells and a small chapel were completed in the newly constructed monastery into which they moved.

The following year the novitiate was opened on April 8, 1889, and two candidates for the priesthood and two for the brotherhood were accepted. There was hope for rapid growth. But the decrees of God are unfathomable!

In 1889 Rev. Erazm Sobociński, the superior of the monastery and the master of novices, went to his eternal reward following a short illness and edifying death. From that point the newly established order had to endure difficult and sad vicissitudes.

Brother Augustyn wanted to place this Polish monastery under the administration of the German Franciscans. When he did not succeed, he left the monastery in Pułaski and entered one of the German Franciscan monasteries in America, taking with him a great number of brothers. One of the brothers made it to the top as an Independent "bishop" in Buffalo, New York.

Rev. Erazm Sobociński, OFM, was born in Kempe in 1841. In 1862 he entered the novitiate in Szczawiennice. After the order was eliminated in Poland, he went to Italy and was ordained in Agniano in 1869. Until 1880 he lived in France and in Istria; from there he went to Galicia where he was master of novices until 1888. From there, at the order of the general, he moved to Pułaski [Wisconsin]. But the climate among the yet undrained swamps did not prove favorable, and he died there on February 5, 1890.

After Rev. Erazm's death, Rev. Hieronim Schneider took over the administration of the monastery. Through voluntary contributions and collections he paid off the debts encumbering the construction of the church and monastery. He endeavored to safeguard its future welfare by sending students to study at other institutions, by proposing new buildings, etc. But he could not manage everything singlehandedly. Twelve brothers, together with the founder of this monastery, Brother Augustyn Zeytz, transferred to a German province, from which two returned. Disturbances broke out in the parish and for these reasons he was forced to resign in 1896.

Rev. Stanisław Jeka succeeded Rev. Hieronim as superior and he was able to reestablish peace in the parish. In June newly ordained Rev. Franciszek Manel, OFM, and Rev. Antoni Wiśniewski, OFM, came to Pułaski, Wisconsin. Rev. Franciszek was sent to the parish of Hofa Park; Rev. Antoni, on the other hand, became the assistant in Pułaski. They jointly decided to build a house for the teaching sisters at the parish school. This happened easily and immediately the following year the above-mentioned Franciscan Sisters began teaching in a very modest schoolhouse built from wood some time before.

In 1898 Rev. Antoni took over administration of the parish. Through his initiative it was resolved in 1900 to build a new brick parish school with four classes, a "basement," and hall, construction of which was completed above the foundations.

On July 20, 1899, Rev. Romuald Byzewski arrived at the monastery. Following the suppression of monasteries in Germany, Byzewski fulfilled his pastoral obligations for twenty-four years in America at parishes in Winona [Minnesota] and Detroit. Then, putting aside his cassock, he again put on a monastic habit, so that he could work with greater benefit and zeal for the glory of God to achieve his own salvation and that of others. He served as an example worthy of emulation by all ex-Franciscans.

On September 17 of that year, Rev. Romuald, OFM, assumed the pastorate at Hofa Park, Wisconsin, and Rev. Franciszek was appointed master of novices in Pulaski. That same day, two candidates for the priesthood and one brother accepted the monastic habit from the hands of Rev. Stanisław Jeka.

In October 1900, Rev. Stanisław resigned from his post of superior, and Rev. Franciszek was named in his place. Rev. Romuald became the vicar of the monastery; Rev. Stanisław became the pastor in Hofa Park, where he stayed one year; Rev. Antoni became the superior of the new monastery and church under construction in Green Bay, Wisconsin with Rev. Hieronim as his associate.

In July 1901 the newly ordained Rev. Stanisław Kostka Lepich, OFM, augmented the number of Franciscan Fathers.

On September 9, 1901, a seraphic school was opened for candidates to the religious order, which presently has eleven students. Its rector is Rev. Romuald Byzewski, and vice-rector is Rev. S. Kostka Lepich.

The parish, then, has 258 home-owning families, as well as the monastery and a beautiful school in which the sisters teach and which is attended by over 200 children. The new school of brick and stone was completed in the beginning of 1902. With three floors it looks as magnificent as a seminary, measuring eighty by forty-six feet. On the top floor there is a chapel, and during inclement weather the school children do not have to go out in the cold or attend mass at the parish church.

Rev. Stanisław Kostka serves the spiritual needs of the parish in Kraków, Wisconsin, to which he currently travels from Pułaski.

Rev. Franciszek Manel, OFM, superior of the monastery and pastor of the parish in Pułaski, was born in Poland in 1864 and arrived in America in 1887. In 1889 he entered the Franciscan Order in Pułaski. In 1890 he completed the novitiate there and in 1893 was ceremoniously ordained. He studied philosophy and theology with the Franciscan Fathers in Teutopolis, Quincy, and St. Louis. On June 12, 1898, he received holy orders from Archbishop Joseph Kain.

Rev. Romuald Byzewski, OFM, is distinguished for his superior education, composure, tact, amiability and sociability. He is also an excellent preacher—a golden-tongued Bernard among the Polish clergy in America. More will be said about him in the history of the Polish communities in Detroit and Winona.

The Polish collegium or scholasticate of the Franciscan Fathers in Pułaski, Wisconsin, has as its goal the education of youth called to the religious life. Although private in character, this institution has nevertheless achieved abundant results. It is extremely important and useful for the entire Polonia because its objective is to sufficiently educate youth so as to render them capable of entering other higher seminary schools to become spiritual fathers, priests, and later leaders of their people.

In this beautiful and spacious institution twenty students were getting an education in 1903 under the leadership of five professors, two secular and three religious. The fruits of this education were shown in three-day examinations through which everyone could be convinced that these young people had made excellent progress. The subjects were: Latin, Greek, German, French, arithmetic, algebra, geography and astronomy, Bible, and Polish history, etc. They were taught concisely and conscientiously and it was proven that the students at this institution did not loaf all year, but made a sincere effort not to disappoint their superiors. They made such excellent progress that all of us present observers were really surprised. And if those Americans who think of the Poles as stupid and who laugh at them had been present, they would become convinced how our Polish children study, what they can accomplish, what they can achieve through their diligence, so that none of them need to be ashamed. Consequently, those Americans would probably no longer insult the Polish nationality. The Poles only need good schools to educate their children and soon all meaningful offices in this country would be held in their hands. The Poles, therefore, are not as backward and half-savage as the Americans imagine them, but are gifted and talented by nature and need to develop their intellects and talents through a good education. The great lack of monastic Polish priests is especially felt in this adopted homeland. Monastic orders are urgently needed; we greatly need monks, since they are the best professors, missionaries, and teachers of people.

The Franciscans did not stop with one institution in Puɫaski. In Green Bay, Wisconsin, the episcopal capital, they erected a second one, and it was truly magnificent, with all the modern comforts. It seems that the Reformationists do not have a similar monastery in all of Poland. Thirteen lots were purchased and a spacious garden borders the monastery. The monastery is built entirely of stone, 148 feet long, 50 feet wide, 3 stories high; the adjoining church is also made of stone and its 133 feet long and 60 feet wide. The monastery, as well as the church, was consecrated on July 2, 1903, by the apostolic delegate himself, Monsignor Falconio, a Franciscan, with the assistance of Bishops Messmer and Eis, as well as numerous clergy. The splendid institution in Green Bay is designed as a scholasticate, while the one in Puɫaski will remain a novitate. Following Rev. Jeka's resignation, Revs. Antoni Wiśniewski and Hieronim Schneider arrived in Green Bay, and later Rev. Jeka was transferred there. The superior of the monastery is Rev. Antoni, the pastor is Rev. Stanisław, and the vicar is Rev. Hieronim. There are also two brothers there.

HOLY FAMILY OF NAZARETH ACADEMY IN CHICAGO

Following the Felicians' establishment of the seminary in Detroit, the Sisters of Nazareth opened the Holy Family of Nazareth Academy in Chicago in 1887. The purpose of this institution is to educate children and young women in the Christian spirit, to awaken them to a love of virtue and knowledge.

This new and costly building is organized in a manner appropriate to the requirements of proper comportment; it is also furnished with all necessities for order and comfort.

The course of study in both Polish and English at the Holy Family Academy offers religion, church history, liturgy, reading, stylistics, composition, rhetoric, literature, grammar, arithmetic, algebra, geometry, bookkeeping, national history, universal history, geography, astronomy; from the natural sciences: physiology, zoology, botany, mineralogy, hygiene, physics, chemistry; German, French, regular and artistic calligraphy, basic and advanced art, stenography and typing, oil and water color painting, pyrography, piano, organ, violin, mandolin and guitar, and needlework (darning, mending, sewing of underwear, embroidery with color and gold threads as well as various elegant feminine needlework). In 1904 this academy had 143 girls and 43 boys.

THE RESURRECTIONISTS' COLLEGE IN CHICAGO

In 1891 the Resurrectionist Fathers finally opened a Polish College in Chicago. In fairness it must be admitted that the Resurectionists in America established and kept up for quite some time two German-English colleges, one in Canada and the other in Kentucky, in which—it should also be admitted—Poles were always allowed to get an education. The monastic house which educated monastic youth was already established in 1857 in Berlin (Ontario province) Canada. Rev. Kajsiewicz wrote in his *Pamiętniki* [Memoirs]: "His Excellency Rev. Charbonnel, Bishop of Toronto, Canada, practically in tears, begged us to give him at least two missionaries for the Germans, Czechs and Poles living in his diocese. He obtained Rev. Eugene Funcken, a Westphalian by birth, and one other seminarian and in the beginning of 1857 the mission in Canada was founded" (see Chapter 5). We read in Rev. Kajsiewicz's *Listy* [pp. 166-67] [Letters] from 1865:

Since the time the seminarian was ordained a priest, three others have arrived, and the sixth is to arrive in the fall. In addition they have three brothers, making a total of eight, and soon there will be more. During the first few years three of them served three sizable parishes (St. Agatha, Berlin, and St. Boniface or "Klein Deutschland" [Little Germany]); they would only meet every fifteen days for a spiritual meeting and to hear each other's confessions. For the past year, two remained at two parishes, but at the third there are three brothers and three priests; and as was already mentioned, the fourth is expected so that they can now lead an orderly life together. What is more, their bishop (in Hamilton), Monsignor Farrell, an Irishman, rewarding their many years of hardships, merged two parishes with homesteads and the land belonging to them with our order in Canada. It is, therefore, better off financially than we are, although its members there live among colonists working to make a living. For these reasons, at our chapter meeting held a year ago our Canadian mission was considered as the second house of the order (after Rome), and because of the monastic rule, I am burdened with the responsibility of visiting it and making sure that all is in order. Even more today, because when a school has been opened—and probably those living there will have a calling to the order—the new arrivals should be educated there so they would not have to be sent to Rome at great expense.

This school, opened in 1865, was named The College of St. Jerome in honor of the general of the Resurrectionists, Rev. Hieronim [Jerome] Kajsiewicz. But both the college and this monastic home "second after Rome" were German. Rev. Szymon Wieczorek, CR, wrote to the General on June 21, 1869:

I heard from many priests and from Protestants that if the College (in Canada) was conducted in English, it would be full of students—twenty-five or thirty, but up to three hundred. The same was suggested by the bishop in Detroit. He promised help, but in order to teach in English it was necessary to give up offering German. . . . Here our priests are friendly as Poles, but not as members of the order. And this can be seen immediately: they think that we have German rules. I myself heard it said (at the College of St. Jerome) that as long as I live, the German language must rank first. This is not surprising, as everyone should love his mother tongue—and I love mine, but we also need to know English. This is why in our school only English is taught, because even Rev. Jan (Wołłowski, CR) does not want to bother with Polish. Much is said here against institutions of our order in Canada. . . .

It is not without reason that Rev. Kajsiewicz (*Listy*, p. 209) himself states: "Some of our ultrapatriots bear a grudge that we do not concentrate solely on the Poles." But one [school] was not enough for him. He shouldered the burden of "the first monastic order from the bosom of Poland," as well as the second German-English collegium when, as we saw above, Rev. Józef Dąbrowski was entreating the Resurrectionists in Rome to urgently take care of the abandoned Poles. Rev. Kajsiewicz wrote in 1871:

Up until now, our missions lacked a central American house, spacious and comfortable enough so that the young men entering the order in America could be educated locally. It is true that we opened a small scientific institution in Berlin, Canada; but since this province is still being settled and has a small and very poor population desiring only the technical education of youth, this institution can be nothing more than a private school. In such a situation, Monsignor McCloskey (brother of the archbishop of New York), the first rector of the North American seminary in Rome and currently bishop of Louisville, Kentucky, a few years ago offered our order college buildings for 150 students with adjoining gardens located in St. Mary: he did so on the condition that we again conduct high school classes, even if initially only the lower ones. (*Listy*, page 324).

And for this German-English collegium "during the past two months Rev. Edward Głowalski collected contributions of $2,000 in cash and cattle. . . . We will have the largest beginning class and it will be possible on horseback. . . the son of every farmer has his own horse and each one will arrive and return home on horseback. Such nonresident students pay $40 per year here . . . In September 1871 there were already sixty students to start" (*Listy*, page 363). At the same time—Oh, the irony of fate!—a German, Rev. Gartner, must take care of the neglected Poles, as we wrote in the preceding chapter. Rev. Kajsiewicz explains this is not due to a lack of Polish Fathers, but to a lack of money! He wrote in 1871:

Oh! if we were not forced to struggle with daily privations and if we had some resources, how much more we could do here for the close to 100,000 countrymen scattered throughout Northern America. Rev. Gartner, a German Czech and the vicar general in Milwaukee, collected contributions throughout the United States for the so-called Slavic seminary which he plans to entrust to some Czech order (*Listy*, page 348).

We, therefore, are confronted by two historical facts: a German collected contributions for a Slavic seminary, while a Polish order collected contributions for German colleges—who will understand this? The German well understood that the loss of nationality in America entails a loss of the Catholic faith; but a Pole, Rev. Kajsiewicz, understood totally opposite. At the time (in 1871) he wrote:

as long as there are separate churches, German-Catholic and Irish-Catholic, these two ethnic groups will not begin to unite through family ties among themselves and with those inhabitants who settled here a long time ago. As a result, the Catholic church will not put down deeper roots in this country, but it will always remain a European colony supported from the outside (*Listy*, page 343).

On account of this view, that the unity of faith is not a diversity of nationalities, but only the merging of them into one entity will strengthen Catholicism in America, it is not surprising that the Resurrectionists did not care about Polish schools of higher learning in America—the only surprise is their support of the German ones in Canada and Kentucky. Rev. Wincenty Barzyński, CR, during his first fifteen years in a huge Chicago parish, had too few priests to help him and he, in fact, was occupied with accounts of the conscience and the parish cash box. He was not able, therefore, to concern himself with a Polish school of higher learning. As we already have seen and will see in subsequent parts, he was tempted in vain to establish a Polish "regular monastic house," since the religious authorities in Rome at the time were thinking about discontinuing rather than developing their Polish mission in Chicago. Due to the rapid growth of their parish and the overcrowding in the parish school, the Chicago Fathers had already given some thought to a Polish school of higher learning. Rev. Henryk Cichocki, CR, wrote from Chicago to Rome on December 16, 1878: "We are thinking about opening a kind of high school after Christmas, for the time being with only two classes. . . ." And we even find clear mention in the *Illinois Staats Zeitung* (number 17) of January 20, 1879, that this Polish academy (*Polnische Hochschule*) was indeed opened on January 2, 1879. The *Illinois Staats Zeitung* first points out that Poles began to settle in Chicago in 1852, that today (1879) the city has 25,000 of them, that there is a total of sixty-five Polish parishes in America, that the Kashubian people are especially thrifty, that many of them have $20,000-30,000. The newspaper goes on to compare Rev. Wincenty Barzyński, CR, with Octavian Augustus Caesar and with Pope Gregory VII for his iron will power, entrepreneurship and fearless courage, and finally it writes:

Rev. Wincenty has thought about founding a Polish academy for a long time. His parish finally decided to found an institution of higher education with its own funds. It was opened on January 2, 1879. The professors are: A. Stein, thirty years old, who studied in Torun and Poznań and who teaches German, Polish and mathematics here; as well as Professor Wenslow, who completed the local Jesuit College. There are forty-three students. The evening school has seventy-two students.

This news of a Polish academy in Chicago seems to have alarmed

Rome, since before long Rev. Wincenty had to explain his action to the Resurrectionist authorities in Rome. He explained it in a letter dated November 18, 1879:

> As far as the "academy" was concerned, it was only the simplest elementary school, opened in order to remove the nuns from the classroom and the big boys, or rather troublemakers, from the children. But there were not enough of them who were both talented and willing, to be able to create a certain advanced class. And so after a half-year trial we let them go, or rather they themselves left—some to work, others to idleness, and still others returned to the nuns. The premature praise written by Rev. Henryk to Rome came to nothing. . . . The people have money, but they don't know what to do with it because they are afraid of banks, and so they lend it to us at 3%, many without interest.

It was also for naught that (on March 3, 1879) Father Kandyd Kozłowski from LaSalle, Illinois encouraged General Semeneńko to establish a seminary or novitiate in Chicago:

> I told the Fathers already in Rome about the novitiate in America, about studies in Chicago, etc. But to this day there is nothing and everything is collapsing. Fathers! A Resurrectionist novitiate is definitely needed in Chicago, as we have many young men with the finest calling. I have five in my own parish. Only good direction is needed. Currently there are many localities without a priest and the Polish people suffer a spiritual deficiency. The Polish parish in Chicago where Rev. Wincenty is stationed is one of the largest. There is enough room to establish a novitiate and even the revenues are considerable. I know for sure that the yearly revenue at the church is $12,000, the three priests have an annual income of $4,200. With such revenue is it not possible to support a novitiate? And what is happening presently? Rev. Wincenty B. has debt on the church, exceeding $40,000, about $3,000 in personal debts, including in this figure what is owed Rev. Moczygęba. The reasons for such financial ruin are living beyond one's means, domestic disorder, and unnecessary expenses on vagrants and loafers. If only Rev. Walerian Przewłocki could come as the superior and procurator, and one other father as master of the novices, everything then would go forward, and soon there would be new priests who would amplify the glory of God. Now, for example, Rev. Henryk Cichocki wants to leave Chicago . . . because what is the pleasure of living in such order and looking at the ruins that finally may bring disgrace to the entire Resurrectionist Order? Rev. Wincenty is unparalleled as a priest and a pastor, but never as an economist: he throws fists full of money where it is not needed, he cannot repay the interest on his debts and incurs even greater ones. If this situation is allowed to continue, then undoubtedly the same is going to happen to him as happened to Archbishop J. B. Purcell from Cincinnati, under whom I lived for five years. He was four million dollars in debt. Today there is shame and disgrace in Protestant eyes and the entire archdicese is ruined. . . . I respect Rev. Wincenty very much, but I fear lest in the end these debts that he is incurring should disgrace him and the entire order. There is one way out and that is to open a novitiate in

Chicago, to appoint a procurator and superior and to slowly pay off the debts through frugality. If my parish brings me a net revenue of $1500 and it is barely one-tenth the size of the Chicago parish, why then with such huge revenues are they falling apart in Chicago? . . . In America, Chicago or the Detroit diocese is the place to work, more so than in Rome or Bulgaria! . . . Our Bishop T. Foley died. . . . Would that Rome desired to appoint a Polish bishop in Chicago. As the first candidate, I suggest Rev. Leopold Moczygęba, who knows English better than Polish and is most worthy of this.

But even these words bounced off Rome like peas thrown against a wall. [An old Polish saying the equivalent of "water off a duck's back."] The German and Irish religious orders could have their colleges here in America, but the Resurrectionists sent their Polish candidates for the religious or spiritual life to the German college in Canada or Kentucky, or in the best cases to Rome, which naturally represented no little cost to the Polish parishioners in Chicago.

And even when not only Polish and German priests, such as Rev. Gartner, but also the American bishops themselves began to understand that the lack of a Polish institution of higher learning is not favorable but detrimental to Catholicism, even then Rev. Wincenty Barzyński, CR, did not begin to create such an institution, although as pastor in the very center of Polonia and therefore occupying a leading position in it, he more easily could have brought it about than a cleric like Rev. Józef Dąbrowski. "We could do more if there were more Polish priests . . . ," wrote Rev. Moczygęba from Chicago to Rome on July 15, 1880. "The plan or intention of a Polish college in America will succeed once we begin, because the sensible Poles and some bishops feel and desire the need for such an institution." Again it was a German, Rev. John Fehrenbach, CR, who seriously set to work and wanted to start an academy in Chicago, but Rev. Wincenty soon impeded him. On August 30, 1883, Rev. Wincenty wrote to Rome from Long Branch, New Jersey, a seaside resort:

As for Rev. Fehrenbach, I still cannot at all understand where he got his ideas for an academy in Chicago. Was it through correspondence with Rev. Leopold (Moczygęba) . . . or was it from my visit to Rome when we talked about such a school as *pium desiderium infuturo contingenti*? Please ask him, because this idea is totally foreign to me at this time! If the order wants to make practical use of him, let it send him as quickly as possible to St. Mary's, Kentucky; there is the place for such men who someday want to become directors of schools. . . .

In his next letter from Brooklyn, New York, on September 1, 1883, to Rev. Anthony Lechert, CR, in Rome, Rev. Barzyński wrote about sending Polish students to Rome, Canada, and Kentucky:

Regarding the matter of Rev. John Fehrenbach—although it has not been my concern, but his and the order's—nevertheless I want to add something here, since the dear Father has informed me of it. In my letter sent two days ago (from Long Branch, New Jersey) I forgot, or rather I postponed a very important matter which may have a very practical connection with Rev. Fehrenbach's plans or dreams. It is as follows. At Rev. Leopold Moczygęba's instigation (which heretofore I have considered as God's decree), I attempted very serious matters and I think they are for all that is good and holy. (1) Travelling to Rome I took with me the four poor students totally supported by the mission of the Chicago house—those students now with you—but that is not the end of it. (2) Because of a real need by the Chicago house, I accepted a few young men as candidates for brothers. But I did not stop there, and (3) I accepted a few poor youngsters or boys as candidates for the Order (*in spe*). Of those mentioned under #2 and #3, including the dear brother "Idzi" (Tarasiewicz), four supported by us either totally or in part, and some two support themselves in Canada (at St. Jerome's College, Berlin, Ontario). Also, there are two at St. Mary's, one totally and one partially supported by us. In addition, there are four candidates for brothers whom we must support. (4) Beyond this we also have a few boys as candidates with monastic vocations in the house. In this state of affairs our expenses for those in Canada and at St. Mary's come to a very nice round sum, a total of 8,000 francs. If within the next few years it were possible to establish in Chicago the start of a collegium, then the resident and non-resident students combined would slowly bring in enough to support our aspirants. We could bring up many young souls out of the excrement of the earth and get better, more talented aspirants. The beginning of these dreams is not just the Rev. Father's mention of Rev. Fehrenbach, but the following: the parish elementary school at St. Stanislaus church has a total of 1500 children (boys and girls), of which 1300 are under the nuns' supervision, and 200 of the oldest boys, that is from ten to thirteen years old, are under lay male teachers (because we do not have brothers) and under one of the priests. This school for boys is only a year old, a trial year as it were, whether it can exist or not. This next year, which opens this week, will probably provide the final answer to this question. So if this school were to develop and improve, then in a year one advanced class could be arranged. In this way, with the help of a well-organized evening school, students could be prepared for the future college. It is to be understood that Rev. Fehrenbach, having experience at St. Mary's—or better and surer in Canada—would be very suitable for such an initiative. However, God Himself knows what obstacles and circumstances can still occur in these few years. So we still have time to consider this matter from every possible side. However, I think that if this collegium academy were not exclusively for Poles, it would have to succeed. With sufficient and appropriate regard for the students and Polish subjects, it definitely meets the need we feel in America and which the Germans themselves in the neighboring archdiocese of Milwaukee have taken into their hands in their own way. This last point will be the great incentive serving to direct toward us the Irish bishops and priests, who do not sympathize with Germanization. Our archbishop is to be in Rome shortly, having been summoned by the Holy Father for consultation with the other archbishops. That famous German, Archbishop Heiss from Milwaukee, will also be there. Both could be received, but Heiss should rather be avoided and ours should be lavished with all kinds of services. It could be explained to Heiss from afar so that he would not think that we completely indisposed you and that the Poles still are one and two generations old and each is a new immigrant. They are incapable of resisting on their own the bad influences of demoralized Poles and false patriots without the aid of good Polish missionaries who are truly nationalistic, but still Catholic. Nor is it possible for these missionaries to protect children from the loss of their faith or to shield the half-Lutheranized youth from ruin under Bismarck if the Polish Catholic mission will not be strong and radiant (ie., have Polish bishops).

This is how, for many years, Rev. Wincenty looked "from every possible side" at the issue of a college. Only after General Semeneńko's death were the novitiate and collegium undertaken, when the new general, Rev. Przewłocki, augmented the Chicago mission with a new host of priests (Rev. Szymon Kobrzyński, Rev. Wincenty Moszyński, etc.). New teaching forces also came from Poland. "In November 1889 Mr. Zahajkiewicz arrived from Lwów. We brought him over with the help of Rev. Paweł to teach here at our school. He came with recommendations from Bishop Puzyna, and perhaps with God's help we will slowly reform our school. . . ." And in October of 1890 "Mr. Ignace Machnikowski arrived with his family to teach at our school. . . ." Rev. Moszyński, CR, wrote to Rome on September 27, 1887:

The orphanage, or rather the house of the Sisters of Nazareth, will be complete in three weeks, a huge building with four floors. However, the second building, which will be the school and is only half finished, will also be magnificent and much larger than the orphanage. Both buildings will cost over $150,000, so we again go into debt, although the old ones are not paid off; but through the grace of God, it is not so bad and everything will be paid off in no more than four years. We have been collecting for one week only, and already I myself have gathered $1,000 . . . . The archbishop takes good care of the Sisters of Nazareth. They have enough work here, but they are also experiencing much unpleasantness from the Polish priests. . . . For the time being, I must refrain from sending any students to the house in Rome, especially since we must pay over $1,000 for lots, which are bought for the novitiate house. Such a financial squeeze will continue for a few years until these lots are paid off. . . . I do not understand how there can be a novitiate house here. If the Most Reverend Father considers the Chicago house as the only means of support of the one in Rome, then how can this aid come from here if construction of the novitiate house is to begin within a year? After all, the parish will not build it at its own expense, so all personal revenues must be used for this purpose. . . .

Construction of the novitiate somehow never began, although time and again we find mentions of it. Rev. Szymon Kobrzyński, CR, wrote on

November 27, 1890, "Regarding the novices, a year passed yesterday since they took the habit and began the novitiate" and Father K. wrote on June 7, 1893, "Monsignor Satolli told me at the train station that we must have a novitiate in America."

The Polish collegium finally came to be in Chicago. On June 24, 1889, Rev. Joseph Halter, CR, even wrote to Rome: "My proposition would be as follows: that you send Rev. Kasprzucki and we together would start a Polish collegium here. . . ."Nevertheless, it was established in 1891 and as reported by Rev. Szymon, "Rev. Jan Piechowski works with Rev. Halter at the collegium. In two classes they have twenty-seven boys" (in 1891). On January 11, 1894, Rev. Szymon noted: "Rev. Piechowski administers the collegium and it is developing successfully. He started with a few boys and today the school has up to fifty [students]. There would be hope for the future if we also had a boarding school." And again Rev. Wilhelm, CR, from Berlin wrote on October 3, 1895: "The collegium belongs to the order, not to the parish, and it has between seventy and eighty students. . . . " The collegium of St. Stanisław Kostka has the right to issue report cards and diplomas, just like the American institutions of higher learning. The students pay $3.00 per month. A boarding house was set up for the convenience of students living outside Chicago and for those who cannot get appropriate care and supervision at home. Students living in the boarding house receive housing, meals, laundry, supervision and help in their studies, [everything they would at home] except for parental attention. Careful attention likewise is paid to social behavior. In addition to book fees, one pays $185 annually for such a boarding school. One also pays $15 per year for music lessons and instruments.

The following is a roster of professors (for 1900-1901) and the subjects taught by them: Rector, Rev. John Kruszyński, CR, church history and algebra; (from 1901) Brother Stanisław Swierczek, CR, catechism, and Polish; Mr. P. A. Schadler, M.A., algebra, geometry, physics, chemistry, Greek, and modern history; Mr. M. Hecker, M.A., English literature, United States history, and commerce; Mr. S. Zahajkiewicz, Polish literature and history; (from 1901) Rev. Władysław Zapala, CR, nature studies, singing, and physical education; Mr. B. Klarkowski, and (from 1901) Mr. Tomasz Larecki, B.A., arithmetic, geography, and United States history; Dr. S. C. Pietrowicz, physiology and anatomy; Mr. T. Zukotyński, art; Messrs. F. Nowicki and P. Kostka, music; Mr. L. Jankowski, piano. Dr. S. P. Pietrowicz is the school doctor.

The Resurrectionists do not derive any material gain from this institution. As Rev. Spetz, CR, told me, one year they even had to contribute $3,000 from their fund to support it. During the 1899-1900 academic year there were seventy-eight students, of whom five were from Wisconsin, six from Pennsylvania, one from Nebraska and the rest from Illinois. During the 1901-1902 academic year there were already 109 students, of whom six were from Wisconsin, four from Pennsylvania, four from Nebraska, and the rest from Illinois. In 1902, there were six "graduates" (1e., those who passed the school's certifying exam): Edward Szubert, Jan Czapliński, Jan Drzewiecki, Stefan Krajewski, Szczepan Kolanowski, and Władisław Muszyński.

THE POLISH ACADEMY IN MILWAUKEE

A year after the establishment of the collegium in Chicago, a Polish academy was organized in the neighboring city of Milwaukee, Wisconsin, through the energetic efforts of Rev. Wilhelm Grutza. He was the founder and pastor (from 1888 to 1901) of St. Josaphat's parish. He organized the largest parish in Wisconsin and built the biggest, most magnificent and most expensive church in that state in the basilica style. Rev. Grutza was similar to Rev. Wincenty Barznyński, CR, in his uncommon strength of spirit and steel-like perserverance, his unbending will power and brave initiative, which does not stand for petty bookkeeping. Once he undertook more things than he could manage, he had to see it through, even if it cost him his life. With funds collected in Milwaukee, Chicago, and elsewhere, Rev. Grutza erected in 1892 a two-story brick building for the academy, measuring 50 by 47 feet and costing $17,000, as well as a spacious home in the vicinity for professors of this school. He immediately founded the academy, the so-called Normal School, with a three-year course of study. This despite the lack of support from the local priests, many of whom even hindered him. Other priests even shrugged their shoulders and said: "Grutza, what are you doing? What are you trying to accomplish?" Not paying attention to what was happening, Rev. Grutza brought in the Polish Crucifixionist Brothers from Notre Dame, Indiana, as professors in this academy and he ordered them to teach the boys religion, English, German, Polish, mathematics, bookkeeping, stenography, typing, drawing and physics. He intended all this for the noble purpose of paving the way for Polish youth to work in industry, commerce, and public service or at the seminary. However, the Crucifixionist Brothers did not administer this school for very long. The following year (1893), it was taken over by a "salaried departmental teacher" from Galicia, Mr. Jan Kuk, who from that time on became its mainstay and remained with it to the end. He simultaneously gave Polish language lessons at the German teachers' seminary in St. Francis, Wisconsin, and at the German institution of the Franciscan Sisters on Greenfield and 22nd Avenues. In addition to the lay professors at Rev. Grutza's academy, the following also taught: Rev. Lauth, a German ex-Crucifixionist who knew Polish; Rev. P. Szulerecki in 1894-95; Rev. J. Horbaczewski; in 1895 Rev. Wacław Kruszka taught religion and Polish grammar in the first year, stylistics in the second, Polish literature in the third; also Rev. Miklaszewski, Rev. Skulik, D.D., and for the last three years Rev. Józef Kempa. There were about seventy students in attendance. Although sometimes there was a lack of teaching personnel, Rev. Grutza always displayed a good dose of courage and good intentions, which never failed thim. If one praises his courage in starting this venture, then his perserverance in supporting this academy deserve even more praise. He still persisted in this venture even though the school—due to the lack of support he had hoped for when it began—did not pay for itself and did not develop. He continued to push the wagon of learning uphill until he himself fell from exhaustion. The academy lived as long as Rev. Grutza did; it only gave out when he died in 1901. This perserverance (we are not considering here whether it was combined with caution, justice, and restraint) was a characteristic trait of both Rev. Grutza and Rev. Barzyński. We Poles should commit it well to memory—and follow it. We Poles are capable of beginning something, but not "continuing" an already-initiated venture. We do not have a specific expression in Polish, but use the foreign one "continue"—and so this attribute likewise is foreign to us!

HIGH SCHOOL IN SHAMOKIN, PENNSYLVANIA

Like the Reformationist Franciscans (abreviated OFM) in the West, the Polish Conventual Franciscans (OMC) are active in the East. To the latter belonged Rev. Moczygęba, already known to us as the founder of the first Polish parish in America. In September 1904 the Polish Conventual Franciscans, or rather Rev. Franciszek Pyznar, OMC, established St. Stanislaus Kostka "Catholic Polish-English High School" in Shamokin, Pennsylvania; it was intended for boys and girls at least twelve years old who had finished the parish school and made their First Holy Communion, and continued to the age of twenty. The monthly tuition charge was three dollars. The professors at this school are priests, nuns and secular English teachers. The purpose of this school is to give our Polish young people broader education and to prepare them for specialized professions, as well as to train them for occupations affording an easier and less strenuous way of life than the hard and dangerous work in the mines and factories.

The course of study lasts two years. During this time the following subjects are taughts: religion, dogmatics and church history, Latin, Polish grammar and literature, Polish history, English grammar, mathematics or numbers, history and geography, physics, bookkeeping, typing, stenography, and music, which is paid separately.

THE IMMIGRATION HOUSE IN NEW YORK CITY

The "House of St. Joseph" in New York, the Immigration house or academy for "greenhorns" has a certain unfailing right to be called a "high school." The deplorable situation of Polish and Lithuanian immigrants arriving at the port of New York aroused the pity of Polish National Alliance members to such an extent that they voted many times at national conventions on pertinent resolutions (as seen in minutes of those meetings). We read in papers of the late Wincenty Barzyński: "The Polish National Alliance stands much higher morally than does the Polish Roman Catholic Union, since besides selling insurance it adopted more lofty goals for itself. Among others, it considered the care of incoming immigrants to be a pressing issue." However, it did not do anything about it. Only in 1890 did a few Polish priests begin work and through the particular efforts of Rev. Wincenty Bronikowski, the Immigration House of St. Joseph on Adelphi Street in Brooklyn came in to being. Its first chaplain was Rev. Józef Złotorzyński, who was succeeded by Revs. Aust and Machnikowski. A few years later this house had ceased to function. Consideration thereafter was given to reviving the Polish Immigrantion House. Rev. B. Gramlewicz hosted the first meeting of Polish priests for this purpose in Nanticoke, Pennsylvania. However, the meeting of January 8, 1896, held in New York with thirty-five Polish priests with the intention in view of opening an immigration house took a big step forward. The meeting established the St. Joseph's Society for the Care of Immigrants, which any Polish-Catholic could join for a monthly fee of two dollars. A decision was also made to incorporate the said society according to the laws of the State of New York. This incorporation was effected on May 16, 1896.

The aforementioned society found a house (at 18 Greenwich Street) in New York in which the administration representing this society was located and where immigrants were received. In this house the St. Joseph Society, through its representatives, ie, members of the administration, conducted its activities, which mainly entailed representing our immigrants before the authorities at the "Barge Office." Otherwise, they would have been exposed to various annoyances or would have been sent back to Poland. After freeing them from the hands of functionaries, the society protected the immigrants from exploiters, especially girls from white slave traders. The society sought employment for the immigrants, gave them advice, and paid attention to the moral and religious dangers confronting them. It also served as an intermediary in buying steamship and train tickets, sending or exchanging money, etc.

With the exception of a few laymen, mostly Catholic Polish priests and a few Lithuanian ones belong to the St. Joseph Society and support this useful institution. The chaplain was initially Rev. J. Dworzak, D.D., and after 1900 was Rev. Z. Świder, who came from Hamburg. He was followed by Rev. Strzelecki, who bought the new house. In September 1897 the immigration house was taken over by the Felician Sisters, as previously mentioned (see *Dzieje Siostr Felicyanek* [History of the Felician Sisters]). In February 1905 the Executive Department of the Third Congress took over care of the Immigration House and through the efforts of Rev. Truszyński the number of directors was increased from four to ten. The directors of the Immigration House were: His Eminence, Archbishop Farley of New York, Rev. L. Kwaśniewski, J. Brzoziewski, Stanisław Nawrocki from Chicago, Dr. M. Barabasz from Baltimore, Stachniewicz from Newark, Dr. Misicki from Brooklyn, C. Tomaszewski from Pittsburgh, A. Górski from Amsterdan [New York] and B. Krauze from Philadelphia.

It should be added that already in 1885 a Mr. M. Ulman founded a kind of information bureau in New York, which he named the *Dom Emigracyjny Polsky* (sic) *pod opiekę urzędu amerykańskiego* [Polish Immigration House] under the auspices of the American government.

POLES AT NON-POLISH INSTITUTIONS

Since we have been talking about Polish high schools in America, let us also mention those non-Polish schools at which very many Poles complete their educations. It seems that foremost among them is the seminary in St. Francis, Wisconsin, whose rector for many years has been Monsignor J. Rainer, a non-ethnic German, because he speaks fluent Polish. According to a report sent us by Monsignor J. Rainer, the following Polish priests studied and were ordained at this seminary: (1) Rev. Jan Jaster (actually a German, but speaking Polish), ordained August 12, 1867, was the first permanent pastor of St. Stanisław parish in Milwaukee—he died November 18, 1881, (2) Rev. Piotr Koncz, ordained October 18, 1871—died February 8, 1886, (3) Rev. J. Tokarski, ordained December 27, 1881—died October 6, 1891, (4) Rev. Lukasz Peściński, ordained June 24, 1884—presently at Stevens Point, Wisconsin, (5) Rev. Szymon Ponganis, ordained in 1885—presently in Gaylord, Michigan, (6) Rev. Andrzej Gara, ordained June 24, 1886—presently in Independence, Wisconsin, (7) Rev. Wilhelm Grutza, ordained June 24, 1887—died August 20, 1901, (8) Rev. Wiktor Zaleski, ordained June 24, 1887—died May 19, 1896, (9) Rev. Edward Kozłowski, ordained in 1887—presently in Bay City, Mighican, (10) Rev. Jan Szukalski, ordained June 24, 1888—presently in Milwaukee, (11) Rev. Franciszek Lange, ordained in 1888—presently in Chicago, (12) Rev. Stanisław Nawrocki, ordained in 1888—presently in Chicago, (13) Rev. Józef Małecki, ordained on March 6, 1889—died in 1892, (14) Rev. Antoni Prądzyński, ordained on June 15, 1889—presently in Milwaukee, (15) Rev. Paweł Szulerecki, ordained in February 1890—presently in Milwaukee (16) Rev. Emanuel Wróbel, ordained on June 22, 1890—presently in Michigan City, Indiana, (17) Rev. Teodor Lugowski, ordained on December 20, 1890—presently in Mill Creek, Wisconsin, (18) Rev. Franciszek Wojtalewicz, ordained in 1890—presently in South Chicago, Illinois, (19) Rev. Teofil Malkowski, ordained on December 19, 1891—presently in Polonia, Wisconsin, (20) Rev. Władysław Bobkiewicz, ordained in December 1891—presently in Rutland, Illinois, (21) Rev. Apoloniusz Tyszka, ordained in 1891—presently in Brighton, Iowa, (22) Rev. Adolph Nowicki, ordained in 1891—presently in Nanticoke, Pennsylvania, (23) Rev. Franciszek Byrgier, ordained in 1892—died in December 1901, (24) Rev. Stefan Nowakowski, ordained on June 29, 1892—presently in Alpena, Michigan, (25) Rev. August Drążkowski, ordained in August 1893—died on November 22, 1894, (26) Rev. Stanisław Łączyński, ordained in April, 1894—died in 1903, (27) Rev. Paweł Rhode, ordained on June 24, 1894—presently in South Chicago, Illinois, (28) Rev. Jan Kubacki, ordained in 1894—presently in East Chicago, Indiana, (29) Rev. Wiktor Stepka, ordained in 1894, (30) Rev. Józef Dudek, ordained on June 16, 1895—presently in Browerville, Minnesota, (31) Rev. Wacław Kruszka, ordained on June 16, 1895—presently in Ripon, Wisconsin, (32) Rev. Bolesław Nowakowski, ordained on June 16, 1895—presently in Sobieski, Wisconsin, (33) Rev. Józef Lewandowski, ordained in 1896—presently in Poznań, Michigan, (34) Rev. Maksymilian Dorszyński, ordained on June 20, 1897—presently in Milwaukee, (35)

Rev. Wiktor Dukat, ordained on June 20, 1897—presently in Washington, D.C., (36) Rev. Kazimierz Gronkowski, ordained on June 20, 1897—presently in Chicago, (37) Rev. Piotr Kurzejka, ordained on June 20, 1897—presently in Menasha, Wisconsin, (38) Rev. Jacób Korczyk, ordained in July, 1897—presently in Grand Rapids, Michigan, (39) Rev. Jendrzej Bieniawski, ordained in December 27, 1897—presently in Isadore, Michigan, (40) Rev. Stanisław Sosnowski, ordained on December 27, 1897—presently in Sheboygan, Michigan, (41) Rev. Stanisław Przyborowski, ordained in December 1897—presently in Częstochowa, Texas, (42) Rev. Feliks Kieruj, ordained in December 1897—presently in Detroit, (43) Rev. Jacób Gara, ordained on January 6, 1898—presently in Junction, Wisconsin, (44) Rev. Kazimierz Ambrozajtys, ordained on June 19, 1898—presently in Westville, Illinois, (45) Rev. Bronisław Celichowski, ordained on June 19, 1898—presently in Milwaukee, (46) Rev. Józef Cerański, ordained on June 19, 1898—presently in Dubois, Illinois, (47) Rev. Franciszek Jagielski, ordained on June 19, 1898—presently in South Chicago, Illinois, (48) Rev. Józef Pietrasik, ordained on June 19, 1898—presently in Ludington, Michigan, (49) Rev. Jan Pociecha, ordained in July, 1898—presently in Two Rivers, Wisconsin, (50) Rev. Józef Kempa, ordained on January 22, 1899—presently in Milwaukee, (51) Rev. Józef Bolka, ordained on May 28, 1899—presently in North Judson, Indiana, (52) Rev. Jan Blechacz, ordained on June 18, 1899—presently in Chicago, (53) Rev. Paweł Góra, ordained on June 18, 1899—presently in Milwaukee, (54) Rev. Bolesław Góral, ordained on June 18, 1899—presently in St. Francis, Wisconsin, (55) Rev. Jan Zwierzchowski, ordained on April 1, 1900—presently in Chicago, (56) Rev. Władysław Ślisz, ordained in 1901—presently in Wausau, Wisconsin, (57) Rev. Franciszek Kaczmarek, ordained in 1901—presently in Manistee, Michigan, (58) Rev. Władysław Krakowski, ordained in 1901—presently in Grand Rapids, Michigan, (59) Rev. Józef Lemka, ordained in 1901—presently in Detroit, (60) Rev. Michał Wenta, ordained on June 22, 1902—presently in Beaver Dam, Wisconsin, (61) Rev. Michał Domachowski, ordained on June 22, 1902—presently in Milwaukee, (62) Rev. Franciszek Cichocki, ordained on June 21, 1902, (63) Rev. Stanisław Cholewiński, ordained on June 21, 1902, (64) Rev. Franciszek Pattok, ordained on July 6, 1902.

The following should also be added to the foregoing list: Rev. F. Jachimiak, ordained in 1893; Rev. Władysław Przybylski, ordained in 1896; Rev. Franciszek X. Pruss, ordained in 1897; Rev. Aleksander Siwiec, ordained in 1894; Rev. Jan Andrezejewski, ordained in 1895; and many others, who also studied at St. Francis and who contributed to the development of an amicable spirit among the Polish students.

Many dozens of Polish priests graduated from the seminary at St. Francis, Wisconsin. No other seminary in all of America can boast such a group of Polish priests.

Rev. Rainer wrote to me in May 1901: "Presently, in the seminary can be found the following Polish students: Sixteen in theology, eleven in philosophy, twenty-one in the classics department—a total of forty-eight students (of a total of 240).

During the years 1883-85 Rev. Jan Rodowicz from time to time conducted Polish language classes for the Polish students at the Salesianum (the name of the seminary under the protection of St. Francis de Sales). From 1899, Rev. Bolesław Góral was its permanent Polish professor.

For the purpose of fostering Polish language and literature, the St. Stanislaus Kostka Literary Society was organized at the Salesianum on November 1, 1882; it continues to exist [1905] and prosper. The first members of this society were Polish students then enrolled at the school: Łukasz Peściński, Wilhelm Grutza, Jan Szukalski, August Baranowski, Jan Żylla, Antoni Prądzyński, Emmanuel Wróbel, Jan Kitowski, Ignacy Jagodziński, Władysław Bobkiewicz, Ignacy Moczygęba, Tomasz Kosmowski and F. H. Jabłoński. The following individuals held the office of president in this society: 1882, Rev. Jan Rodowicz (but he did not always attend meetings, so defacto the president was Ł. Peściński, the current vice president); 1883, Rev. Jan Rodowicz; 1884-1886, Rev. Wilhelm Grutza; 1887, Rev. Jan Szukalski; 1888, Rev. Antoni Pradzyński; 1889, Rev. Emanuel Wróbel; 1890, Rev. Władysław Bobkiewicz; 1891, Rev. Franciszek Byrgier; 1892, Rev. Franciszek Gzella; 1893, Rev. Jan Andrzejewski; 1894, Rev. Wacław Kruszka; 1895, Rev. Bolesław Nowakowski; 1895, Rev. Józef Lewandowski; 1896, Rev. Piotr Kurzejka; 1896, Rev. Maksymillian Dorszyński; 1897, Rev. Józef Kempa; 1898, Rev. Paweł Góra; 1899, Rev. Jan Zwierzchowski; 1899, and Rev. Bolesław E. Góral.

In 1901 the society had thirty-nine active and about seventy honorary members; it had a library which included the most prominent works of [Polish] literature, totaling about six hundred volumes. In general, the society is developing splendidly, especially since living and working conditions have improved.

Rev. Francis Mershman, OSB, informed me, that the seminary of St. John's Abbey of the Benedictine Fathers in Collegeville, Minnesota, graduated about twenty-five Polish priests, including: Baran Oswald, OSB, Paweł Giżmowski, August Gospodar, Jan Guzdek, Franciszek Jachimiak, Henryk Jażdżewski (or Jajeski), Menander Jaroszewicz, OFM, Piotr Kahelek, Jan Kitowski, Jan Kopera, Stanisław Kubiszewski, Władysław Kubiszewski, Władysław Polaczyk, Jan Sroka, Jan Studnicki, Edward Pachorski, Stefan Urbanke, Jacób Wójcik, Jacób Wojtowicz, and Piotr Wolnik. A few Polish students study there every year.

Also from the seminary in St. Paul, Minnesota, not one but several Polish "prophets" graduate every year, among them: Revs. Jan Andrezejewski, Hieronim Daszkowski, Antoni Szczukowski and others. The same is happening in every other religious seminary in America.

Not only religious seminaries, but also colleges, especially Jesuit ones, are filled with Polish students who graduate and become priests, lawyers, doctors, professors, or businessmen. A large number of Polish students annually attend Marquette College [University] in Milwaukee, Canisius College in Buffalo, or schools such as St. Ignatius College in Chicago, whose vice rector, Father F. Cassilly, SJ, among others writes me, "Our Polish students have done well."

In their college in Teutopolis, Illinois, the Franciscans are also educating every year a few Polish pupils to be monks. The Polish Franciscans working mainly in Nebraska have come from this college. At their own expense they are bringing over Polish youth, especially from Silesia.

Many very talented Polish teachers and organists have graduated from the "Pio Nono" teachers' seminary in St. Francis, Wisconsin, where Mr. Jan Kuk was professor of Polish from 1893 to 1901, followed by Rev. Bolesław Góral. The alumni included: Horris Uszler, Michał Klebański, Józef Bejma, Piotr Kamiński, S. Łukaszewicz, Józef Kamiński, Piotr Wąsowicz, Połczyński, J. Piechowski, Tadych and many others.

In 1902 Holy Spirit High School in Pittsburgh, Pennsylvania, had about thirty Polish students out of a total number of 250. Of the Poles, the following gentlemen received excellent grades in examinations: Fandraj, Dura, Dekowski, Jaworski, Sierakowski, Kollopiński, Burlaga, Polukajtys, Strawiński, Romanowski, Godelewski, Wielechowski and Pobleszek. Rev. Retka, a professor of Polish who worked untiringly for the good of the Polish pupils and especially to ensure they would not lose their native language, established the "St. John Cantius Debating Circle."

Let us end this historical review of Polish education in America by presenting a list of Polish doctors, lawyers, dentists, opticians, judges, artists, architects—just as we first presented a list of clergy. Many of our countrymen are studying at the university in Philadelphia, Pennsylvania. For example, in the law department, Piekarski, Butkiewicz, Leymel, Gronczewski, Kurzydlowski, Babin; Ratajski is studying medicine; Sosnowski, Błażejewski, Szpotański, etc., are being educated in other schools. In Chicago, the Polish capital of America, there are some thirty-two Polish physicians: Butkiewicz, I. M. Borucki, Bożynaz, Felix Borucki, Buzik, Czarkowski, Dowiatt, Drozdowicz, Grabowicz, Guzowski, Kolasiński, Kossakowski, Kuflewski, Karol and Jacób Klaszyński, Kaczorowski, Kacorowska, Lenard, Midowicz, Pietrowicz, Piszczek, Szwajkart, Strzyżewski, Sieminowicz, Stobiecka, Statkiewicz, Stupnicki, Train, Xelowski, Ziółkowski, Żurawski, Zaleski. There are close to twenty Polish lawyers in Chicago: Józef and Klemens Beliński, Chileski, Czarnecki, Drzymała, Dankowski, Danisch, Haremski, Koraleski, Kaczmarek, Muchowski, Najdowski, Piotrowski, Palt, Śmietanka, Smulski, Zaleski. Polish dentists in Chicago: Chrzanowski, Ekowski, Bizewski, Schiller, Zieliński. Optician: Pietrzykowski. Justice of the Peace: La Buy. Engineer: [Ralph] Modrzejewski [Modjescki]. Artists: Żukotyński, Markiewicz, Grabowski. Architects: Wierzbieniec and Wielkowski. Graphic artist: Olszewski. Anyone would be mistaken who would think that all of the above-named specialists were educated in Europe and not here in America! There are countless Polish pharmacists.

Chapter 7

Polish Industry and Commerce
in America

By the late nineteenth century, Poles in America had taken root in many areas of commerce and industry.[1] In 1871 Father Kajsiewicz,[2] CR, wrote, "Two young Polish counts have opened a bank in Chicago and are doing well; this is proof that a Pole can do anything as long as he wants to put in the effort. I had a letter and a special message for these gentlemen (their title is not used here); they received me at their house in the most pleasant manner."[3] Then in the old, musty, moth-eaten almanac from 1876 we find many advertisements from which it is clear that in those days the Polish business movement already encompassed wide circles: "Smitt and Betowski advertise their tailor shop in Waverly, N.Y.," . . . "A Kromolicki, 240 E. 30th Street, New York City, recommends his tailor shop." Next, in Chicago, "Maksymilian Kucera recommends to the Honorable Countrymen his 'Saloon,' on the corner of Pauline and 18th St." and "August Kunkel, a Polish undertaker, recommends his collection of coffins, 51 Sloan St." . . . "Peter Kiołbassa, a Notary Public, issues all legal papers and documents; issues records of landownership, bequests and legal testaments at 119 Cornell Street" . . . "J. Niemczewski Polish Saloon and Theater Pavilion is located at 515 Milwaukee Ave." . . . "A. Kamiński recommends his shoe and slipper shop at 491 Milwaukee Ave.," and "Józef Bilski Shop and workshop offers the best quality men's footwear at the only Polish shop of this kind in the great city, 90 East Randolph Street." There is also "P. Koncewicz, Watchmaker & Jeweler, 454 Milwaukee Ave.," . . . "P. Soboleski, Notary Public at 66 West Randolph Street," . . . "Dr. A. Jakubowski, practical physician, educated in Vienna, who treats all internal and external illnesses, even sends medicine through the mail upon receipt of accurate description of the illness and treats the poor for free, 506 Milwaukee Ave." . . . "F. Nowaczewski, 289 12th

Street, near Halstead, recommends his well-stocked clothing store and tailor shop, as a shop with ready made apparel for Ladies & Gentlemen; willing to take all kinds of orders for church brotherhoods, such as: flags, sashes, rosettes, as well as wedding dresses for girls, at 442 S. Halsted St." Further, in this calendar for 1876, there are advertisements for "A. Sherman's Polish Agency, on the corner of Noble and Bradley Sts." . . . "General Agency of Postal Steamboats of M. Majewski, 519 Milwaukee Ave." . . . also "I. Wendziński Agency, 780 18th St., which is linked with the German consulate and arranges inexpensive crossings by steamboat, issues powers of attorney for the old country, collects inheritances, and so on"—and in far off Waterbury in the State of Connecticut [we read]: "Mieczysław Brzeziński born in Byelorussia in the Mochilewska province recommends his "Groceries store and invites his countrymen living in the area to visit his store, guaranteeing that flour, sugar, coffee, tea, and all other products are sold cheaper than in other stores." But I have written enough of these advertisements from the old *Kalendarz*.[4]

In general, it should be said of the American Polonia that we have too many Polish workers and too little Polish industry! We do not lack traders, and especially "saloonists" or bar keepers, but we have an inadequate number of industrialists. Trade itself, without industry, cannot increase prosperity among our compatriots here. Trade takes money from the workers but gives them very little; that is also why the Polish workers do not have enough work and Polish merchants are not doing big business, because there are not enough enterprises among the Poles to provide work for the Polish workers.[5] But let us return to the issue—to the history of industry among Poles in America.

Tailoring is supposedly the oldest branch of Polish industry in America. That, at least, is what the Milwaukee, Detroit, and Chicago chronicles state. For example, the Detroit chronicle says: "tailoring had the most representatives from the very beginning. Despite thorough research we were not able to find out why it was the tailors who arrived first in America and rose above the other immigrants up to 1874." We think that it was because the Civil War in the United States, which lasted many years, relied heavily on tailoring, due to the need for uniforms for the northern army.

Let us observe the development of Polish industry and trade in the more important Polish settlements beginning with Chicago, the American Warsaw.

Mr. Danisch[6] writes us that the concentration of a substantial number of Poles in the city of Chicago shows that their power is concentrated there and that the Chicago settlement is a sort of mirror in which the various phases of life and work of the Polish immigration in America are reflected. Therefore, anything that can be said about the development and the condition of Polish American trade and industry in the Polish colony in Chicago can also be said of the remaining settlements.

Just ten years ago we did not notice any great movement in the areas of trade and industry in the Chicago Polonia. It was limited to maintaining small retail stores and shops stocking food articles, such as "grocery" and "butcher" shops and taprooms; that was the extent of trade development. At that time there were no large department or industrial stores, and the factory industry, even today, is still in its infant stage.

The population of the Chicago Polonia totals 150,000 souls. It has among the smaller trade shops 39 bakeries, 58 shoe shops, eighteen drugstores, five haberdasheries, nine furniture and home appliance stores, 175 grocery stores, and about 300 taprooms. Industry is limited to a few bigger companies, such as one picture frame factory, one building materials company, and two breweries, with a third under construction.

Wholesale places of any kind are virtually non-existent. A retail warehouse opened by Poles in 1896 did not succeed; nor did a fire insurance corporation. Even a larger clothing store in the center of Polonia, in the northern part of the city, was closed. However, a similar store, which opened in 1901 in the southern part, is developing.

Poles are joining a number of companies that are composed mainly of foreigners. There are a few countrymen at commission houses, as well as a few in the management of the "Milwaukee State Bank." There is a small number of incidental businesses, such as: those that manufacture flags, medals, and so on, for societies; shops for novels and prayer books; stores selling coal and firewood; flower shops; and cigar and tobacco factories.

Lately, the Poles are being swept by an enterprising fervor caused by the constant urging of the press and by the notable success that foreign businesses are enjoying. Because of this, businesses that up until now had not been supported by the Poles themselves are rising and multiplying. Production and wholesale distribution of, for example, so-called bitter wine and other medicinal products; and the opening of photograph studios are the newest signals of the budding entrepreneurial spirit. In comparison with other colonies and even with the work of other nationalities in Chicago, journalism and printing are flourishing among the Poles. In Chicago alone (circa May 1901) there are eighteen papers, of which two are dailies, and there is a multitude of Polish printing shops throughout other cities.

The direct cause of the lack of progress in the areas of trade and industry was and is, for the most part, the attempt to provide for relatives in "the old country," to whom hundreds of thousands of dollars flow annually from the immigrants.[7] Another reason is the purchasing of city "lots" (usually 25 by 125 feet in size) and the building of homes on these lots.[8] These are the two main reasons why the trade-industrial development is suffering. Some of the less significant reasons are the many parties and use of alcoholic beverages among the immigrants.[9] Furthermore, the development of trade and industry is hindered, in part, by the lack of skills or talents in the Poles who have settled in an alien country and who mainly come from farms or from small towns. The younger generation, brought up and educated according to local needs, will undoubtedly fill these jobs in the future.[10]

In 1903, the auditor of the State of Illinois gave permission to organize a new state bank in Chicago, named the "Northwestern Trust and Savings Bank," which is a Polish bank in the fullest sense of the word. The founders are Mr. Jan F. Smulski,[11] Mr. Jan A. Przybysz, and many others.

Another Polish enterprise, the coffin factory in Chicago, is one of the largest coffin makers in the United States because the product is so much better and more suitable than those made in other factories. Of this we have proof and praises from our Polish funeral homes. The following gentlemen have been chosen to administer the company: S. J. Rokosz, president; M. Wojczyński, vice-president; F. P. Kujawski, secretary; L. Wojczyński, cashier; Józef Magdziarz, I. J. Chilewski, J. Pohlman, S. J. Rokosz, M. Wojczyński, B. Rocławski, F. P. Kujawski, L. Wojczyński, and L. Lipecki, directors; Stanisław Ambrożewski, manager.[12]

Since 1904 a Polish trade company has existed in Chicago under the name of "The Ecclesiastical Goods Co." This company supplies devotional products, pictures, frames, altars, church candlesticks, chalices, monstrances, and statues. It is run by local citizens such as Peter Kiołbassa; the manager citizen Augustynowicz, and the secretary lawyer Piotrowski.[13] The sales representative is Ignacy Kowalski.

In Milwaukee in 1894 there were masonry contractors such as Franciszek Nieżorawski, Jan Czaplewski, S. Wabiszewski, and J. Gajewski; land fill contractors such as Jan Weiher and Józef Połczyński; plasterers Franciszek Poznański, W. Kapuściński, J. Różanowski, P. Dason, J.

Cesarz, and S. Osieczonek; carpentry contractors F. Kosecki, T. Łukaszewicz, Maciej Woida, Piotr Woida, and T. Wiśniewski; home movers J. Tuszkiewicz and R. Oparka; stone cutter W. Jesion; painters Jan Walloch, T. Napientek, and Ignacy Sawicki; drainage canals builder Walenty Dargacz; drainpipe installers M. Skowroński, F. Welter, Jan J. Czołnowski, Kopczyński, Zieliński, J. Rudziński, J. Czeżniak, and M. Kwiatkowski. Other enterprises include the publishing of two newspapers, and Klapiński's laundry, which employs twenty Poles. Then there are Polish tailors such as S. I. Sawicki, W. Pietrowski, F. Trock, B. Choiński, A. Dettlaff, W. Zaleski, W. Chmielewski, H. Olszewski, and F. Seroczyński; further, there are Polish cigar producers such as K. Rozmarynowski, M. Wesołek, W. Krysiak, J. Malotke, and N. Ratajczyk; next, Polish blacksmiths such as Jordan and Boiński, and F. Powerski; J. Gruszczyński's brewery of Grodzisko beer and soda water; and F. Mierzejewski, producer of iron fences.[14]

Since 1897 a Polish workshop for stained glass windows for churches, homes, and so on, owned by August M. Gawin, has existed in Milwaukee. But the oldest Polish industrialist was the tailor August Rudziński, who opened his own tailor shop during the Civil War; another was Mr. Wilczewski, who worked for Mr. Zimmermann. In addition to this, in Milwaukee there exist the Independent Brewery, where Mr. Emil Czarnecki is president; the Wenty factory of headstones; and the Wiz and Głysz factory or "machine shop." But lately the most important Polish factory in Milwaukee has been the "Milwaukee Stove and Foundry Co.," whose owner, station master, and superintendent was J. C. Klapiński.[15]

Before 1879 Milwaukee did not have any Polish print shop, or even any Polish typeface. Proof of this was that the printing for the St. Stanislaus Bishop and Martyr Parish was done in German.

It was only in 1879 that Mr. Ignacy Wendziński and Józef Rudnicki moved their print shop "Przyjaciel Ludu" [Friend of the People] to Milwaukee.[16] It was, therefore, the first Polish print shop in Milwaukee. Besides newspapers, school books, missals, and other works were printed. However, because of debts this print shop did not exist for long. In the beginning of 1883 the "Zgoda" [Harmony] print shop was moved from New York, and a short time later it was moved again to Chicago.[17]

In 1885 Mr. Michał Kruszka opened a print shop in which small printing jobs were performed, as well as the Tygodnik Anonsowy [Weekly Announcement]. This was the first and only print shop which began and still exists under the name of "Spółka Wydawniczej Kuryera Polskiego" [Polish Courier Publishing Company]. In addition to this, print shops were opened to Aleksander Giliński, A. Szybczyński, F. Danielski, Ignacy Rajski, J. J. Janecki, and Klafkowski. Of these, however, none is still in existence.

Presently, the following print shops can be found in Milwaukee: Kuryer Polski, Dziennik Milwaucki,[19] W. Maychrzycki, Peksa & Raniszewski & Szybczyński.

Let us now look at the development of Polish commerce in Detroit, Michigan. Here, as in other cities, tailoring developed first and, from the very beginning, had the most representatives. Besides S. and F. Melinów, Jacób Mindah, and two Janów Lemke, a few dozen other tailors arrived and to this day this industry is widespread among the Poles.[20] Likewise, women's sewing developed widely, and it is safe to say that our women workers supply dresses not only to the Polish women, but also to a substantial number of American women. One of the oldest of these shops is that of Mrs. Mroczkowska.

Brewing takes second place among Polish industries. At least 80 percent of the taprooms in Detroit carry Polish beer. The first brewery was founded by Mr. Jan Zynda, who has been in this business since about 1880. With very little capital, Mr. Zynda began to brew beer and even began construction of a gigantic brewery. Mr. Tomasz Żółtowski, observing Mr. Zynda's success, opened a second brewery in 1890 and also achieved a great following. Our countryman Mr. F. Schmidt, a former alderman, bought a brewery with Mr. J. Geiser; he too brews a very good beer which found numerous advocates. And so, Polish beer excels in Detroit.[21]

Baking was the last Polish industry to develop in America. This began around 1888. The first to open a bakery were Mr. Stan Pasternacki and his brothers; then came Józef Prusiński. The success they achieved inspired others. Bakeries sprouted one after the other, and today there is no lack of them.

Shoe making as an industry does not have many representatives in Detroit. However, trade is quite developed. The oldest in this trade among the Poles is Jan Welzand. Butchering developed a long time ago and, for the most part, was successful. Some of the most affluent Poles are butchers, and it can be said that this is the most successful branch of trade among the Poles in America. In addition to this, Detroit has four Polish pharmacies, one photography studio (Sowiński).[22] The cigar and tobacco industry, too, is quite well developed in Detroit, and a great number of Polish women and men are employed there. The pay is still among the best in this industry. We have among the Polish industrialists, however, those who produce cigars and tobacco on their own. Among them the leader is Ignacy Wolf.[23] His shop has existed since 1889, and today his name is known in all the colonies. He has a huge house, steam machines, and he sends his product in wagons to other cities. He produces excellent tobacco for smoking, snuff, and cigars. Besides Ignacy Wolf, his brother Jakób has the same kind of business. Furthermore, there are Juszkowski, F. Strzyżewski (one of the oldest), N. Feldman, Mayer, Kurcewski, Deja, Singer, Braciszewski, Kowalski, Latoszyński, and M. Melin. Clothing shops, picture and wallpaper shops, fabric shops, coal and wood shops, breweries and food shops are numerous in Detroit Polonia and in other Polish settlements.

In Buffalo, New York, Polish industry and trade are also budding. Among many others, K. E. Zawadzki[24] has a drug store; Józef Ślisz[25] a bookstore; M. Usiak a coal and wood shop; clothing is made by tailors including L. Smyczyński and H. Rybarczyk; and cigar and cigarette factories are owned by Józef Jankowski and Fordoński. Contractors and builders include Antoni Stabenau and Habliński; saloons, together with beer bottling institutions, are owned by M. J. Bigosiński, G. W. Tomczak, and others. And beer in Buffalo is supplied by a Polish brewery owned by our countryman A. Schreiber.[26]

Here is how Mr. Schreiber himself describes the history of his brewery:

In the fall of 1898, Mr. Tomasz Żółtowski, a brewer from Detroit, Michigan, first gave me the idea of opening a Polish brewery in Buffalo. He brought my attention to the numerous members of the Polish colony in Buffalo, in which there existed over 100 Polish saloons, all supplied with beer from German and American breweries. He also pointed out that a capital of $16,000 should be sufficient to open and manage such a business. Succumbing to Mr. Żółtowski's urging, I went to Buffalo, N.Y., to canvass the area myself. However, after my investigation, it became clear that existing conditions in Buffalo did not allow for opening a brewery with so little capital; first, because of the huge competition from the long existing breweries, and second because of the financial dependence of a great number of saloon keepers on these breweries. The saloon keepers would virtually have to be bought from the hands of the established breweries, at an average cost of $1,000 apiece.

Seeing such conditions, and knowing at the same time that it was a favorable area for a Polish brewery, I began to work on collecting the needed capital, with the result that on January 30, 1889, a company with a paid capital of $100,000 was incorporated under the laws of New York State under the name "A. Schreiber Brewing Co.," and soon after completing construction we began to brew beer.

The business of our brewery has developed so much lately that its value has increased to $300,000. By 1900 the need to build on and enlarge the brewery already became clear, so that at that time the value of the brewery itself came to over $150,000. The remaining value is in the saloons, in loans, in the saloon keepers' mortgages, and so on. Our brewery has 144 customers, of whom 57 are Poles. The annual production of the brewery exceeds $360,000. We employ 37 people, all Poles, with the exception of positions for which we could not find an appropriately qualified Pole, such as brew master, brewers, and chief machinist.

When considering Polish industry we must also mention another industry that is blooming in America among the Poles; that is the relocating or "moving" of wood and brick houses. Mr. F. Hojnacki does this in Buffalo and there are others in almost every settlement.

Buffalo can also boast about the opening of a Polish factory that produces a product invented by a Pole. A few years ago, when his children returned from school with wet shoes and coughs, citizen Jakubowski began to think about manufacturing some kind of product to repel water on leather. He immediately began to work on it, making various tests, and his efforts were successful. He invented the product he had envisioned and had his invention patented in Washington. It was called "The Electric Leather Oil Filler." Initially he produced his "filler" in small quantities. It became more popular as the magnificent qualities of the product were recognized, and he attracted both Polish and American partners and established a factory.

Another invention by a Pole in America was made in La Crosse, Wisconsin, by our countryman Józef Kubicki, an employee of the North-western Railroad. He invented a shovel for cleaning the grooves between tracks at railroad crossings and had his invention patented.

The most famous invention by a Pole in America was the bulletproof vest of Brother Kazimierz Żeglen, a Resurrectionist from Chicago, Illinois, who had very good relations with the Viennese Company of Jan Szczepanik. Brother Żeglen sent a few examples of his invention to an exhibition of inventions in Lwów in 1902. These samples constituted to some extent the history of the bulletproof vest, and that is why we are describing them here.

The first sample was the original fabric, which was tested at Battery D, in Chicago on March 16, 1897. The second model presented a vest with thick silk strips designed for further testing. The third sample was constructed from fabric made in a weaver's school in Aachen under direction of N. Reiser, according to Brother Żeglen's instructions. The fourth type of fabric was made in Chicago by the inventor himself. One could see on this fabric the places where bullets from a .38 caliber Colt revolver had hit. The fifth sample was a material that had been tested at Fort Sheridan, Illinois, and at the Viennese arsenal. On this material were spots where rifle bullets had hit but not pierced the vest. The sixth sample was similar to the preceding one and was used for further tests at the Viennese arsenal. The next sample was made of a material finished at the weaver's school in Aachen and was provided with a two millimeter thick steel sheet on the surface. Rifle bullets of the newest systems could not pierce this fabric from a distance of 300 paces.

Finally, there was the bulletproof vest itself, designed in the form of an elegant jacket and lined with the weaver's finished material, thus leaving nothing to chance. This jacket was so light that it would be uncomfortable only during a very hot summer. No revolver bullet or sharp dagger could pierce it.

Further examples consist of photographic reproductions of various letters, reports, official documents, patents, and so on. Among them was a photograph of Brother Żeglen at his workbench. This photograph also showed the looms on which the bulletproof material was woven.

We should mention here that the demand for bulletproof vests invented by Brother Żeglen increased more and more. Offers came from various parts of the United States; mainly from bankers, traveling salesmen, policemen, and especially detectives exposed to dealing with criminals.

As in Chicago, Milwaukee, Detroit, and Buffalo, Polish industry and trade is developing in Philadelphia, New York, St. Louis, Toledo, and, on a smaller scale, in the smaller settlements. There was, for example, a Polish brewery owned by Mr. Bójnowski in the small settlement of Antigo, Wisconsin, and another in Danville, Pennsylvania. In Plymouth, Pennsylvania, a group of Poles opened a footwear factory under the name "Plymouth Boot and Shoe Manufacturing Co." In this factory they began production of footwear for men, women and children; however, their specialty was "miners" shoes, designed for miners and coal merchants. Ten thousand dollars was deposited as company capital; then the company became "chartered." In nine months $11,188.50 in merchandise was sold, which constitutes a favorable sign when considering competition from big factories and smaller local factories. This factory produces over one hundred pairs of shoes daily. Only Poles are employed at the factory, and only Poles are employed in the administration. At the last elections the administration was set up in the following manner: Michał Czajkowski, president; Jan Pawlicki, vice-president; Stanisław Motylski, secretary; Kazimierz Szymczak, cashier. The directors are Walenty Riszczek, August Wiśniewski, and Józef Pawlak, who was also the manager.

Polish industry had also developed in Bay City, Michigan, where there were 78 Polish businessmen by 1901. Industrial cooper Jan Bachiński from Bay City is famous throughout America because he made the barrel in which Mrs. Taylor from Bay City went over Niagara Falls on October 24, 1901. This barrel contained 100 pounds of lead on the bottom so that it would stand upright. It was padded with cotton so that Mrs. Taylor would not hurt herself going over the falls, and at the top of the barrel, over the head, were railings for her to grasp.

Other Poles who have accomplished much in America include a lithographer, Mr. W. F. Różycki, of Newton, Long Island and a Polish engineer, Mr. Grodzki, who built the bridge over Niagara Falls and whose statue was erected on the Canadian side.[27]

The Poles did not have great success in exploiting the gold mines. In 1894, a gold mine came into Polish ownership. It was called Quarts Hill in California and was managed by Dr. Kazimierz Midowicz, who followed the unfortunate engineer, Mr. Maryański.[28] At the head of this company were Dr. Midowicz,[29] Father Wincenty Barzyński[30] and Father Wilhelm Grutza,[31] God rest their souls. After two years of hard work at the gold mine, Dr. Midowicz went to Los Angeles, and there in his rich intellect was born the idea of utilizing the power of ocean waves for moving ships. He constructed an instrument called the "Wave Motor" and had it patented, but he hesitated to put larger sums into this invention because no one knew whether it could be perfected in the future.

In Stevens Point, Wisconsin, a Polish company was incorporated under the name of "Automatic Cradle Manufacturing Co." Those who incorporated this company were Jan Bukolt, Jan Langowski, and Jan Józefkowicz. This factory manufactured automatic cradles for children. The cradles have a timing mechanism, which rocks the cradle for a long time after being wound, thus saving time and trouble for the mother.

In America construction was begun on a long railway, which was to join North America with Central and South America. The line, which was to be 17,000 kilometers long, would start at Port Nelson on Hudson Bay, lead through Texas, Mexico, the Isthmus of Panama, Ecuador and Peru, and would end in Buenos Aires. Our countryman, engineer Kazimierz Rechniowski[32] from the province of Minsk, designed a substantial portion of this huge venture which was to cost 1,250,000,000 francs.[33]

There will be more about the development of each individual settlement in Parts Two and Three of this *Historya*.

Chapter 8

Agriculture and the General Economic State of Poles in America

Our immigrants are mainly made up of peasant people. It is, however, strange that these peasant people feel attracted to cities and become townspeople. Whether it is the ease of making a living and having a comfortable life in the city or another reason, it is an indisputable fact that the majority of the Polish immigrants in North America have settled, as much as possible, in the largest cities. Barely one-third went to the farms or agricultural settlements.[1] And even these had to be "lured" by clever agents and special colonizers, since there was a general lack of enthusiasm for agriculture.

Polak w Ameryce [The Pole in America] explains this lack of enthusiasm in the following way:

Usually peasants from the old country who arrived in America had only small pieces of land or none at all. What they had after selling their land was barely enough to pay the cost of travel. After arriving in America they had little money or none at all. Since they possessed no monetary means they could not even dream of travelling to farms and buying land, and so they settled in cities where they soon found relatively well-paying jobs. Working on farms as hired hands also did not appeal to them since that did not pay as much as they could earn in the city and besides lasted only through the summer. Peasants arriving from the old country settled in cities out of necessity, and by the time they saved enough money to buy land they had gotten so used to city living that it would have been difficult for them to move. Poverty, therefore, made our peasants into city dwellers, and all other reasons are only secondary.

Enthusiasm for agriculture was already lacking in those Poles who formed the political emigration [in the early 19th century]. Mr. Thaddeus Wild from Madison,[2] a State Bank Examiner, informs us:

One of the local historical societies, perhaps the Wisconsin Historical Society itself, publishes monographs primarily on the subject of the history of Wisconsin.

One of these monographs fell into my hands in 1893. It had been published two or three years before. The subject was the early settlements in Wisconsin, which at that time was still not a state but a part of Michigan. Among other things the author (I do not remember his name) wrote a detailed account of a huge land grant, passed by Congress in 1831, to be given to a group of Polish emigrants. These lands were located in what was then the territory of Michigan, and if I remember rightly, it fell within the boundaries of the present state of Wisconsin. The pugnacious immigrants, not used to working with their hands, did not measure up to the task. They left this new home in the wilderness and swamps in small groups, and after a few years there was not one Pole left on the lands that had so generously been presented to them. And so, those who had the great opportunity to become true pioneers in the Far West and leaders of the Polish immigrants did not meet the appropriate expectations.

This page is important to the history of Polish immigration if only because it was the first and last time that the Congress of the United States officially took up the matter. This casts a beautiful light on the intellect of those who were members of Congress at that time, because it shows their sympathy for the Polish cause not only in words but also in action as well.[3]

So much for our countryman, Mr. Wild. The lack of enthusiasm for agriculture in our later peasant immigrants was also noted as early as 1887 by a chronicler who wrote in papers left by Father Wincenty Barzyński.

Of those still in Poland who were financially well off, only a small group hastened after the land. But even those who were well settled did not show any particular inclination towards the land. Only people with a gentle disposition desired agricultural property, especially those who had saved so little that there was neither enough to live on nor enough to take back to their home country . . . . Millions of acres of the most fertile land are uncultivated; however, although the Poles grew up on farms, they do not even consider this now. Having once transformed themselves into city dwellers, they believe that they have become a part of the city and that the city has become a part of them. Well! In the city I sit on the first floor or on any one I want. There is water in the kitchen so the woman does not have to trouble herself with carrying it. The street car will drive anywhere one wants to go. In the city there are balls, picnics, theaters, circuses, carousels, and bars. And where is all this on the farm? . . .

The purchase of land for farms does not create any great difficulty. Usually cash is required for farms that are already cultivated; at times, however, the payment is divided into larger installments. Pure virgin land, never touched by a plough, can be bought for payments over a few years. Additionally, the government even gives away land for free (a 160 acre homestead); the settler has only to build a home on the land grant, cultivate a few acres each year, and pay the annual tax, which amounts to a few cents. After five years this land becomes the property of the farmer, and he can manage it according to his own desires.

The geographical division of the land, especially in northern and western states is very simple, straightforward and practical. The state is divided into counties and the counties into towns, which usually form squares with six-mile sides, so that one township covers an area of thirty-six square miles. Each square mile in a town forms one section. Each such section has 640 acres of land, so that an entire town is usually 23,040 acres. Along the length and width of the sectional borders, spacious farm roads are usually marked out. Each section is then divided into four quarters, so-called "homesteads" (of 160 acres), and each "homestead," or each quarter of the section, is divided into four "40s" (of 40 acres). We visualize this division in the following illustration:

6	5	4	3	2	1
7	8	9	10	11	12
18	17	16	15	14	13
19	20	21	22	23	24
30	29	28	27	26	25
31	32	33	34	35	36

The figures designate "sections" in a town and the order in which they are counted.

N.W. Quarter		$^1/_{16}$ section (40 acres)	$^1/_{16}$ section (40 acres)
		$^1/_{16}$ section (40 acres)	$^1/_{16}$ section (40 acres)
S.W. Quarter		S.E. Quarter	

So four 40s, or 160 acres, constitute a quarter of a section or a "homestead." This much, and no more, is offered by the government to one settler in exchange for establishing a "homestead."

The price of private land varies. A chronicle from 1887 stated, "For $500, 40 acres, half or entirely cultivated, can be bought, sometimes even with buildings." This was possible in 1887, but in 1900 the farms were more expensive. For a "40" it was often necessary to pay from $2,000 to $4,000. However, for an acre of wilderness or uncultivated land, payment of between $5 and $9 depended on the soil and location. Land nearer communication routes (railroads), and therefore nearer to cities, was more expensive. Land farther from these routes was proportionately cheaper, ranging from $100 to $120 per acre of cultivated soil.

In woodless areas (there are no forests, for example, in Nebraska and Dakota) a farmer could immediately sow the entire farm in the first year and the harvest gathered would surely be sufficient to support his family. When the area was overgrown by woods (as it usually is in Wisconsin or Michigan) the farming progressed at a much slower pace. First, it was necessary to cut out the trees and burn them or move them to a different location; next, stumps with roots were torn out with the aid of special machines, and only then, on this cleared soil, were crops sown. Clearing usually took place in the winter. It did not progress quickly because two or three persons were able to clear no more than five acres. Because of this it was impossible to immediately feed a family for an entire year from such a small area. The settler did not rely on this, but would go to the city for employment for a certain amount of time.

In the winter they would return and cut the wood. This would be repeated until the homestead could support him and his family. While it was being cleared, the wood did not represent any value for the farmer. If the city or train station was close by, he would transport it to sell. In other cases, he would burn not only large piles, but sometimes the entire woods.[4]

As everywhere, products here also depend on the climate and soil. In Minnesota it is mainly wheat that is harvested. All markets compete for Wisconsin potatoes. The greatest potato district in this state is Portage county, inhabited mainly by Polish farmers; next are the Waushara and Waupaca districts, in which sandy soil can be found. In 1899, 25,026 acres of potatoes were planted in the Portage district; 19,960 acres in wheat Waushara district; and 15,702 acres in the Walupaca district. An average of 100 bushels of potatoes was gathered from each acre. In comparison to potato production of other states, only Maine, in the East, equals Wisconsin. In Texas the Polish farmers grow cotton. However, production in these states is not limited to wheat, potatoes, and cotton alone; the local farmers also grow rye, oats, barley, corn, beets, and other crops. The field of farming also encompasses cattle raising—both bulls and cows—swine, sheep, and poultry raising. Market conditions for animals and products of the earth are not always the same in all locations. In general, it can be said that Polish farmers are well off and that on a small piece of land they are better farmers than those of other nationalities, who usually possess huge areas but neglect them and never become attached to the land. Polish farmers farm only on their own piece of land; for every fifty owners there is hardly one tenant.

How many Polish farmers are there in America and how much land do they own? Only God alone would know that! But we will try to give an approximation. The chronicle from 1887 states: "The number of group agricultural settlements, listed at fifty, will not seem extravagant at all. If we presume that in each settlement there are on the average only fifty owners who own an average of eighty acres each, then we can conclude that there are 2,500 Polish farmers and the land in their hands encompasses an area of 200,000 acres. But that is so little that no one here would believe it" (page 5). It is true that no one would believe that in 1887 there were only 2,500 Polish farms and fifty agricultural settlements. There were then already at least 200 Polish agricultural settlements and 20,000 Polish farmers.

And today in 1901? Today, for 900 Polish settlements in the United States, there are 200 urban settlements (in which the most people live, since about 1,500,000 Poles are employed in trade and industry or work in factories and mines), and about 700 Polish rural or farm settlements; in each of these settlements there is an average of 100 farmers, so there is a total of 500,000 Poles on farms. Polish farmers own 40 to 360 acres of land, and sometimes more. If we presume that there are 700 Polish agricultural settlements, and in each there is an average of 100 farmers, of which each owns an average of eighty acres, we conclude that Polish farmers in the United States own 5,600,000 acres. Therefore, the Poles in America would own, more or less, as much land as the combined acreage of the states of New Jersey and Rhode Island. If we assign each farm made up of about 80 acres—including buildings and inventory—an average minimum value of $3,000, then we will find that the soil in the hands of Poles on American farms represents a value of $210,000,000.

Since we have described the fortunes and the general economic state of the Polish farmers, let us also mention the prosperity of Polish city dwellers in America.

In all of the urban settlements the Poles own their own businesses and buildings, which often take up large areas, creating real Polish sections. These buildings have a diverse value: homes ranging from $1,000 to $5,000 and department stores ranging from $5,000 to $20,000. Let us presume that for 1,500,000 Polish souls inhabiting the cities there are 300,000 property owners, of which the average would be worth $2,000; the fortune of all Polish city dwellers in America would then come to around $600,000.

The Chicago chronicle for 1887 already states: "In Chicago for a building lot of 3,000 square feet it is necessary to pay (in 1887) from $1,600 to $3,000 or more. To set up a simple saloon it costs an average of $500 (in addition to an annual tax of $500); therefore the value of the 100 saloons in Chicago alone is $50,000."

"There are also wealthy people among the Poles," states the chronicle from 1887. "Erazm Jerzmanowski is considered a millionaire.[5] Dr. Biernacki is supposed to be even richer. Andrzejowicz, the owner of a paint factory in Philadelphia, is worth $100,000."[6] In Chicago alone there are a few Poles, each of whom is worth from $20,000 to $100,000. Supposedly there were about 300,000 acres left by a certain Pole in one of the Southern states. In Chicago there is talk of a Polish millionaire who did not want to have anything to do with his own people. The *Tribune*, one of the most serious Chicago dailies, already assessed the private fortune of Poles in Chicago in 1887 at $10,000,000.

The Poles live decently. Furnishings of the poorest cost $50; usually though, they cost from $50 to $300 or higher. In the living quarters of the working class can be found all the things that could once be found only in a rich Polish city dweller's home, that is, carpets, sofas and other trifles—although not always arranged with taste. Residences of workers are not barracks or sheds, but houses or buildings. The worker here lives on the ground or other floor, and if he "bums around," that is, prefers to drink rather than live decently, then he lives in the basement. However, there is a relatively small number of this type.

The most meager place, consisting of one room, a small kitchen with partitions for kitchen utensils and garments, costs $5 per month; but when there is a shop inside it costs more. Such a place is usually occupied by a childless couple or a single person. A family made up of a few people needs two or three rooms, especially bedrooms and cubbies. The monthly rate charged for such a place is $9.

Generally little care is given to the structure and durability of construction when building houses in the city; the main point is that such a house have a good layout and that it bring in six or seven percent of the money invested. On the farms, on the contrary, the issue is not the rent at all, because there are not renters there; thus, the houses are more impressive, sometimes resembling small palaces in the greatest variety of styles.

If the Polish worker lives a hundred times more elegantly than he lived in his home country he also does not neglect his dress. This cost can vary from $30 to $100, and depends on what one can afford. For everyday, clothing is not important. However, in the evening after work or on days off from work, one must be distinguished from the simple mortals, and our Kathy's and Mary's do not differ in any way from the old country countesses. The Poles who arrived here at an older age were probably distinguished by their thick features and awkward movements; however, young people, both male and female, have become acclimated here, both in apparel and appearance, but they especially betray their peasant descent. The male youths are no longer servants; but they are not yet gentlemen and they call themselves "juveniles." The behavior of this youth on the street and in society is coarse, but their physiognomy is close to that of city dwellers. The Polish girls are no longer girls who carry pitch forks, but American ladies and misses, and in Polish "wenches." They differ from rich women probably in that they have less education and social refinement, and in that their dresses, although being of the same style, are not made of such rich fabric.

In general, food comprises meat dishes, fruit, and delicacies. The farmer's nourishment includes poultry, beef, lamb, pork, fruit, sausage, rolls, pies, coffee, and other dishes. They pour out sour milk and feed the swine with sweet milk. For breakfast the workers' meal is made up of a few cups of coffee, a portion of roast beef or other meat, cold cuts, cakes, bread, butter, and so on. Leaving for work, they take with them a special container for lunch—not the clay double pot, as in the old country—but metal "lunch boxes," which have various partitions inside: in the saucer there is coffee, on the top, cold cuts, chicken, eggs, cheese, butter, cakes and dry dishes in general. In America, they do not understand the division into "tables"; they cannot imagine, what "the tail end" is and what "first place" is. The place one sits is for him the "first place." The boarder, the host, and the "servant" sit simultaneously at the same table.[7]

Chapter 9

Poles in American Politics

In the preface to this *Historya,* we wrote that the Polish people established genuine colonies here, because the Poles in America became citizens, not vagabonds or guests living on foreign generosity during exile. They were free citizens and owners of real and personal property; they were political individuals, easily able to take part in representing the government of this country. And, in fact, from the very beginning, the Poles in America have taken an active part in local American politics. They not only elected others, but were themselves elected to various political offices so that the Poles continue to have their Polish representatives, whether in the town wards or district offices, in the city council, or even in the state senates and legislatures.[1]

We still do not have proof as to what part our early political immigration from the end of the eighteenth century and the beginning of the nineteenth played in the politics of the United States. We only heard from Mr. Stanisław Ślisz[2] that, among others, a Mr. Głowacki,[3] the founder of Batavia, New York (near Buffalo), was, at one point, a three-time presidential elector on the Democratic ticket. In Canada, Mr. Kierzkowski[4] was a delegate of Parliament even before 1860.

However, among the peasant immigrants, the first public appointment of a Pole was to the office of justice of the peace in 1868 in the district of Karnes (Helena), Texas, in the oldest Polish settlement of Panna Marya. The first political office for a Pole was secured by storm, under the leadership of a priest. Rev. Bakanowski, CR, at that time the pastor at Panna Marya, writes:

Plundering in Texas decreased only with the aid of military forces. Before rule passed from military to civilian hands (after the Civil War) elections for new officials of the state were announced. Helena, our district city, being on the side of the Southerners, voted for officials from their party who were very unacceptable to us.

The Poles were persuaded and swindled in various ways to vote on the Southerners' side. In the beginning I wanted to be neutral in this, but seeing how many Poles, incorrectly informed, began to bend toward the side of the Southerners, I announced and held a general meeting of all Poles, in which I presented to them our interest in these affairs and what we should do about them. Above all, I wanted to get a Polish judge and laws exclusively for Panna Marya. After presenting the entire matter, I myself gave out tickets indicating for whom they should vote. To be sure that no one would fall short, on the day of the elections I ordered everyone to gather at a certain place so that the Polish cavalry would go together on horses to Helena . . . . Arriving in the city, while yet at some distance, the Americans ran out of their houses to observe this strange army. Finally they recognized the priest at the head of his parishioners. Aha! they exclaimed, the Poles have become smart; now we can no longer count on them! . . . Probably we will try to persuade the priest, with the others, that it is a lost cause! They tried, but for naught; we cast our votes and then returned home in the same order . . . . The elections were successful, we secured our Polish judge, our laws, and our government.[5]

This was the first participation of a priest in American politics. The priest led his parishioners victoriously to the voting box, and from that time on it was not a rare occurrence in American Polish history. At this time (1870) in Milwaukee, Wisconsin, a Pole was appointed as a member of the district council, known here under the English name of "supervisor." The first such elected supervisor was August Rudziński in 1870.[6]

For the first time, Poles were genuinely aroused by politics in the presidential election of 1872. One Pole wrote from Virginia to the New York *Swoboda* [Liberty] on September 6, 1872—"Each nationality wins vested laws for itself. Only the Poles continue to sleep sweetly—quietly, nobody cares for us in America, no one knows about us, because what benefit are mutes? . . ."

"The Chicago community awakened first, but quickly, so as not to be late, it began a partisan war of its own. Was this step political? It appears that it was not. Time is still not lost, communication should have been opened with brothers scattered throughout all the States, an ad hoc committee should have been chosen, and only then could the candidates have been introduced and calmly scrutinized as to what they had to offer. Grant is a representative of militarism, therefore the close relationship with despotism. Greeley brings equality. . . ." Grant and Greeley were candidates for president at the time. Grant was elected. Besides, other Poles supported Grant. A Polish Election Club was formed in New York supporting Grant; and on October 8, 1872, Mr. N. Michalski[7] from Chicago wrote to the New York *Swoboda* (there was still no Polish paper in Chicago):

Seeing the mass of Poles living in America (of which in Chicago alone there are over 20,000 who never took part in matters of politics), we decided to step forward politically, in the current presidential elections, as Poles from Chicago. We took the side of Grant as the good, freedom-loving son of the homeland, of which he gave proof by recognizing the French Republic in the war with the Prussians.

We call attention here to the motives by which our countrymen at that time were moved in politics. From the very beginning of Polish immigration, even in American politics, they came out jointly and in group force as Poles. Their guiding principle, their predominant and ruling principle in politics, was to care about Polish matters first, and not give priority to matters of the American political parties. The following proclamation, issued in the same *Swoboda* on October 9, 1872, stated this principle even more clearly and precisely. Mr. Piotr Kiołbassa[8] wrote at the time:

Seeing the numerous Poles in our Chicago, where there are about 2,000 families who never took part in political issues as a separate nation but always under the protection of the Germans, we have decided to effect this now, with the approaching presidential elections. Why vote for Grant? I know Grant as the righteous son of the homeland, who gave proof during the Civil War that he loves freedom and liberty, and gave more proof in recognizing the French Republic immediately at the conclusion of the war with the Prussians. Did not Greeley support a monarchic government in the matter of annexing Alsace and Lorraine to Germany, and in supporting Austria against the Italians? What are we to say about the disapproving voices regarding the Poles fighting with the Russians? . . . Among this number of Poles, there must be various factions. Still, with the help of organized societies, we can easily come to terms among ourselves with regard to these tendencies that common to our countrymen whether they be from Silesia, Lithuania, Halicz, Mazowsza, Podlasie, or Great and Little Poland. In Chicago we have the following societies: (1) Stanisław Kostka, with 193 members, (2) St. Joseph, 78 members, (3) St. Wojciech [Adalbert], 75 members, (4) Polish Community, and (5) National Guards (Kościuszko Guards), 175 members; this is proof that different parties can exist. But when it comes to Polish matters, all the Poles in Chicago are, in fact, Poles. We founded the Polish Grant Club with 60 members in it. I think that I can assure citizen Wilkoszewski (who opposed Grant) that our club will influence at least 500 votes, not only of our countrymen but also of many other kindred countrymen. To respond to the reproach that not all who belong to the club are citizens, it is true that we have a few of those; but does the Polish Greeley Club comprise entirely citizens? There are those in it who have still not stated their first intention (have not applied for their citizenship papers). So, as the saying goes, he who sits in a glass house should not cast stones.

Such a voice was raised in 1872 by Mr. Piotr Kiołbassa who, from that time on, practiced politics as a craft and is still the head of the local Polonia in Chicago politics. The first Polish alderman in Chicago was Mr. A. J.

Kowalski,[9] elected in the spring of 1888. In 1878, Mr. Antoni Małłek became a justice of the peace in the Manitowac district.

In the meantime, in Milwaukee in 1882, Teodor Rudziński (son of August, about whom mention was made above) was elected alderman, and in 1887 he was elected as deputy to the state legislature. Finally, in 1888 he was elected justice of the peace. Since then, the Poles in Wisconsin have constantly had a Polish delegate to the state legislature. After Rudziński, this office was held by the following: Ignacy Słupecki, Michał Kruszka, Michał Błeński, Andrzej Boncel, Wojciech Wojciechowski, Józef Rechlicz, August M. Gawin, F. Haza, and Jan Szymarek.[10]

Since 1892 Milwaukee Poles have served in all public offices from policeman to state senator and federal official in Washington, D.C. In no other Polish settlement in all of America did the Poles achieve such high offices so early as here in Milwaukee; not in Buffalo, or in Detroit, or even in Chicago, although the largest group of Poles had gathered there. This speaks well of the solidarity of the Milwaukee Polonia and its leaders. Besides this, in 1892, Michał Kruszka became the state senator—an office not held by any Pole in America before him and, in fact, the highest political office held by a Pole in America up until that time.[11]

Nonetheless, in other settlements, the Poles also enjoyed wonderful careers in politics. It is difficult to list them all. Klement Beliński, Kowalski, Laskowski, Geszkiewicz, and Kwidziński from Chicago were delegates to the Illinois state legislature; Mr. Stanisław Kunz was a senator.[12] The young J. Smulski[13] was elected twice on the Republican ticket as alderman and spokesman of the City of Chicago. Franciszek Schmidt, our countryman, was alderman of the City of Detroit three times, and so on. In the state of Minnesota, our countryman Mr. Rosenthal was a delegate to the legislature.

In America our countrymen took an active part not only in peaceful politics and election campaigns, but also in military campaigns. The Poles served in every war conducted by the United States, beginning first with the war for independence (Kościuszko, Pułaski, and others), and ending with the recent Spanish-American War of 1898. When speaking of the participation of our countrymen in the Spanish-American War, it is enough to look through Polish American magazines to be convinced how quickly and actively they answered the call of "Uncle Sam." And so, as Stefan Barszczewski writes in the preface of his melodrama *Cuba Libre*, the first shot in this Spanish-American War was fired from a cannon aimed by our countryman Stanisław Kempiński from the gunboat *Nashville* on

April 22, 1898, in pursuit of the Spanish ship *Buena Ventura* near the shores of Cuba. In June, 1898, so many Poles came forward for the volunteer regiment being formed in Wisconsin that a separate company was formed of 116 people, the Kościuszko Guards, under the command of Tadeusz Wild,[14] a former Austrian army officer. The first lieutenant in this company was Jan Budnik, the second was Piotr Piasecki.[15] A great number of our countrymen were also found in the regiments besieging Santiago. Proof of this is the list of those who died honorably in battles waged near this city: Jakób Wiliński, sergeant of the 1st Regular Cavalry regiment; Pazur and Baranowski, soldiers of the Second Infantry Regiment of the state of Massachusetts; Marcin Kubiak from the Sixth Regular Cavalry regiment; Szymon Wagner, gunner from the Second Artillery Regiment; Jan Babicz from the Seventh Infantry Regiment of the State of New York; Antoni Osuch and Paweł Liwerwicz from the the 25th Regular Infantry Regiment; Ignacy Zielny, Józef Klin, M. Ganecki and Gregorsz Księżopolsi—from the Rough Riders regiment of Colonel Roosevelt (now president of the United States). We are not listing the wounded because there are too many of them.[16] That the American Polish Falconry took an especially active part in this war is proven by the fact that, since most of the comrades joined the army, the nest in Milwaukee was weakened, and in Buffalo the drills were stopped. In South Bend and Chicago the ranks of the Falcons also thinned considerably.[17] Mr. Barszczewski wove his successful melodrama in five acts entitled *Cuba Libre*, based on the Spanish-American War and the Polish Falconry in America.[18]

In the American army in the Philippines, as our countryman Mr. Anthony Thomas, quartermaster sergeant, Co. M. of the Engineers, writes from Manila on January 2, 1905, "There are Poles here to this day; among others, Mr. M. Nowak from Cleveland has the rank of officer of the 22nd Infantry Regiment."

Many Polish nobles arrived in Canada after the uprising in 1863. The most courageous of these Poles was Colonel Kierzkowski, who was a delegate to the Canadian parliament. Rev. Kajsiewicz writes in his letters from 1865:

I left Montreal for the country to visit Mr. Kierzkowski, our countryman who settled there. His father, a soldier from Kościuszko's time, an officer of the Santo Domingo legions and the Duchy of Warsaw, and finally a major in 1830, was ceremoniously buried in the presence of 60,000 people gathered in Poznań three years ago. . . . Mr. Kierzkowski, the son, who went to Paris at age fifteen, was one of the first few, together with Edward Jełowicki, to finish the central school. He obtained the position of engineer on the Beauharnais Canal in Canada. He married Miss de Bartsch, an owner of property in St. Charles, and thus became related to the most illustrious families in Canada, because the second sister of Mr. Kierzkowski's wife was married to Mr. Drummond, the former Canadian minister, and is today in the highest circles; the third is married to Mr. Monk, a judge of the appeals tribunal; finally, the fourth sister was married to our compatriot, Mr. Rottermund, who died many years ago. . . . Mr. Kierzkowski carries the name of an upright and well-behaved person, even in the eyes of the clergy (although he belongs to the liberal or opposing party). He was also a delegate at the diet . . . . We arrived at his house. In the courtyard there was a Polish flag on the mast; in the room hung their embroidered national coat of arms (presented to Mr. Kierzkowski by his electors for delegate), and on this occasion, in the presence of his two sons, he placed a plaque over the family grave with the following Polish inscription: "Kierzkowski, son of a far off, unhappy country, has chosen this grave for himself and his family" [*Kierzkowski syn odległej, nieszczęsnej krainy, Tu grób obrał dla siebie i swojej rodziny*].

Besides Mr. Kierzkowski, I saw two other Poles here. One was a young immigrant who had come from Scotland and was going to upper Canada, having been promised a place there; the other, a Mr. Żmijewski, who is a caretaker for the Tribunal, arrived from France after 1850.

Currently, the chief French consul is Mr. Kleczkowski, who was born in exile.[19] Further, the director of Canadian mining (this position is only subordinate to the ministry of agriculture) is Mr. Obalski, honorary professor of Laval University in Quebec.[20] In the port of Quebec, the American government has an office (for emigrants to the United States), and Mr. Szymański, the former editor of *Górnik* [The Miner],[21] is an official of this office.

Chapter 10

History of Polish Organizations in America

The Union, 1873—The Alliance, 1880—The Częstochowa Alliance, 1878—
The Association, 1889—The League, 1894—The Association, 1896—The
Alliance of Singers—The Union of Youth—The Falcons' Other Organiza-
tions—The Polish Women's Alliance.

Where there is life, soon an organism is born,
an organization, that is group power.

Polish immigration to America can be compared to one giant camp with
innumerable large and small tents. These large and small tents are larger
and smaller organizations, societies, unions, alliances, brotherhoods, circles, clubs, associations, leagues, falcons, and so on. Almost from the
beginning of our immigration (especially from 1874), through the present
times, there have always existed tendencies and endeavors to break up the
huge tent which, when stretched over the entire camp of immigrants,
would cover all of the larger and smaller tents. However, these very ideal-
istic but impractical intentions were never totally realized: because of such
efforts only a few larger tents came into being, a few broader organizations whose history we shall now sketch, leaving the description of minor
little tents or local organizations to the history of individual settlements in
Part II.

The first attempt to create a general organization that would spread its
caring wings over the entire immigration can already be seen in Chicago
in 1866, where the *Gmina Polska* [Polish Commune][1] came into existence
as the first Polish society in America with a wide range of activities. This
Commune, created mainly through the efforts of a Polish Army major,
Mikołaj Michalski, as a result of letters from General Bosak-Hauke and

patriotic appeals published in the weekly *Niepodległość* [Independence], was modelled on the *Gmina Europejska* [European Commune] founded in Switzerland in 1864.[2] A lack of appropriate conditions did not allow it to develop more broadly and encompass the entire United States. In any case, its consistent and undying work contributed greatly to nurturing love for the homeland and creating new national societies. With reason, therefore, it acquired the title of "Mother of National Societies in America."

Seven years later, in 1873, Jan Barzyński, in his weekly *Pielgrzym*[3] [Pilgrim] issued at the time in the small town of Washington, Missouri, took up anew the idea of forming an organization that would encompass the entire American Polonia. Through his initiative, in the following year, 1874, the *Organizacya Polska w Ameryce* [Polish Organization in America] was formed, with 360 members joining immediately. Jan Barzyński (Rev. Wincenty's brother) wanted to enroll the entire Polonia from all parts of America into one circle and create within it a virtually national governing system.

We find this project first mentioned in *Pielgrzym* in October 1873. It came to maturity and fruition in the beginning of 1874 when Jan Barzyński, elected president of the *Organizacya*, appointed illustrious Poles from several Polish colonies as secretaries of various departments, having a range of almost ministerial authority. This plan, especially when existing relations are considered, was outlined too boldly and broadly; so the matter did not develop, but fell through. Contacts with the Polish Roman Catholic Union, whose nucleus was then being formed in Detroit, Michigan, by Rev. Gieryk, did not help. In April or May 1874 a diet was not successful.[4]

For the American Polish community, the model of J. Barzyński's *Organizacya Patryotyczna* [Patriotic Organization] did not continue without consequences. From it, many endeavors were begun which tried to unite the American Polonia into a larger group. Its' outcome [was] the existence of great organizations, such as the Union, the Alliance, the Association, and so on, whose history we will shortly describe, beginning with the oldest.

THE POLISH ROMAN CATHOLIC UNION UNDER THE PATRONAGE OF THE SACRED HEART OF JESUS (ESTABLISHED IN 1873)

Links uniting the Poles to a certain extent in the first years of their stay in America were the newspapers bringing news from various settlements.

From time to time voices would speak up urging a closer contact among various settlements. "Countrymen," stated the *Gazeta Polska Katolicka*,

who do not belong to any society, or even to a parish, are not doing any thing for the Polish cause. . . . If there be only five families living somewhere, they must create a society, if only for lectures, and then as an entire society join the Union. . . . Many people pay dues or taxes to some society for three, five, ten, or fifteen years, and then business or the need for employment forces them to move to another city, and then what happens? Well, these people lose money and aid because they do not live in the city, and other societies do not want to accept them because they are too old, or the newcomers are ordered to pay an entrance fee.[5]

Those and similar arguments were convincing, especially in those times, when settlers often changed their place of residence. There were also other reasons of a moral nature which encouraged unity. Lack of communication and unified action was felt more and more each year. Who would not believe that the Poles, numerous but dispersed throughout the United States and without appropriate leadership, would be absorbed by foreign nationalities? In order to prevent this, a group of clergy and lay people worked with devotion, consulted each other, and considered how to join all the Poles in America through common efforts into one strong link which would stop denationalization. This link joining us in Christian love was to have been the Polish Roman Catholic Union under the care of the Sacred Heart of Jesus.

The idea of founding the Union was first conceived at a congress in Detroit in 1873, where a committee was appointed and authorized to organize a second larger congress or diet in Chicago. This diet took place harmoniously on October 14, 15, and 16, 1874. It was organized by Rev. Teodor Gieryk, Mr. Jan Barzyński, and Mr. Piotr Kiołbassa. This diet was truly magnificent, and the groundwork was laid for the Polish Union in America.[6]

The responsibilities of this Union were to uphold the holy faith and the Polish nationality, to provide fraternal aid, and to undertake educational work. A constitution was drawn up to achieve these goals. However, to ensure that this constitution could be executed faithfully and appropriately, authority was established. To help in this, an official organ, *Gazeta Katolicka*, was established. For the first ten years, it was edited by Jan Barzyński.

Everyone knows that funds are necessary to achieve such great things as encouraging fraternal aid, the spread of education, and the joining of all genuine Poles. Therefore nominal annual dues of $1.00 per member were established. This money, under control of the diet, was utilized for good causes, such as the support of schools for the poor, ophanages, and so on.

The Second Diet devoted much time to the important matter of schools. Proof of this is seen in the fact that the Union, from its very establishment, took care of schools. This diet elected as officers: Rev. Gieryk from Detroit, president; Piotr Kiołbassa from Chicago, vice-president; Jan Barzyński, secretary; August Rudziński from Milwaukee, cashier. Six clergymen were elected as controllers: Revs. Szulak, Rodowicz, Musielewicz, Dąbrowski, Molitor, and Kandyd Kozłowski. Six laymen were also elected: Piotrowski, a bookseller from Detroit; Jan Nowak from Washington, Missouri; Wróblewski from Cincinnati, Ohio; Józef Głosowski from Radom, Illinois; Sonnenberg from Milwaukee; and Niemczewski from Chicago.[7]

The constitution adopted at the first diet was not long; it included only ten short articles. But what was not included in it was etched in the hearts and minds of the gathered delegates.

At the diet in 1886 a decision was made to institute a burial fund. This novelty was looked upon with disbelief. Therefore, immediately after the first case of death, this newly established fund was abolished. In 1887 at the diet in Chicago, the burial fund was organized on a sounder foundation and a greater confidence was thus placed in it. At that time citizen Wojciech Jendrzejek was president, Jan Manna was secretary, and Jan Gniot was cashier.[8]

The burial fund contributed greatly to the growth and development of the Union. From that time on, this common need was the stimulus that encouraged membership in the Union; it was the knot joining hearts in a common labor for the purpose of helping each other more easily; it continued to be a bond of brotherly love: "What happens to you today, can happen to me tomorrow." From the time of its establishment in 1887, the burial fund has paid out about $1,000,000 to widows, widowers, and orphans.

After the burial fund came into existence, the official organ of the Union became *Wiara i Ojczyzna* [Faith and Fatherland], and in later years *Naród Polski* [The Polish Nation].[9]

In 1902 the Union had 12,543 members (6,850 men and 5,693 women). Presently (April 1, 1905), the Union has 18,344 members and $129,877 in its accounts. The officers are the following:[10]

Leon Szopiński, President
Jan Jóźwiak, Vice President
Tomasz Królik, Secretary General
Teodor Ostrowski, Cashier
Rev. Franciszek Lange, Chaplain
Rev. Franciszek Rusin,
   Vice-Chaplain
Rev. K. Gronkowski,
   Vice-Chaplain

Vice Chairmen
Franciszek Ruszkiewicz, Buffalo
W. Korpal, South Bend
A. Górny, Erie
Stanisław Marlewski, Cleveland
W. J. Jóźwiakowski, Chicago

Directors
J. Czerwiński, Chicago
Franciszek Remus, Chicago
S. Grucki, Chicago
W. Follmer, Chicago

(Directors continued)
Ignacy Bogucki, Chicago
Antoni Polenc, Chicago
I. Grocholski, Detroit
A. Stachowicz, Sobieski
A. Amborski, Grand Rapids

Chief Physician
Dr. A. Szwajkart, Chicago

Attorney
Józef Bieliński, Chicago

Legal Committee
Józef Skrzypczyński, Chicago
Jakób Tyrakowski, Chicago
Jan Szczepański, Chicago

Financial Committee
Stanisław Behnke, Chicago
Franciszek Fuhl, Chicago
Leon Szulc, Chicago

THE POLISH NATIONAL ALLIANCE IN AMERICA[11]
(FOUNDED IN 1880)

The first national organization, prototype of the Alliance, 1842; the first November celebration, 1844; the Democratic Society of Polish Exiles in America, 1852; participation of Poles in the Civil War, 1861-65, as well as in the uprising of 1863; the Polish Commune, 1866; the Union of Poles in America and the Alliance of 1870; Poles in America are divided into nationalists and clericalists, 1873; proof of unity with the mother country—the founding of the Polish National Alliance, 1880; crucial congresses in 1895 and 1899; the Alliance house, 1896; paragraph on religion as the apple of discord.

It was worth trying. The Alliance tried to unite all the Poles in America into one great organization, but its efforts were for naught. It tried primarily in the name of religion. Since this attempt failed, it was natural that the desire arose to try again, but under another name—this time primarily in the name of the national cause. If all the Poles did not want to gather under the banner of the church, then maybe a flag of purely patriotic hues would appeal and unite them into one great camp.

Consequently, a purely national flag was hung over American Polonia. In 1880 the Polish National Alliance was founded. In what was until then one American Polish camp, two flags of different hues now began to flutter. The Poles began to gather not only under one, but under both; thus around each the immigrants gathered, at first in clusters, then in constantly larger groups. Finally from one camp there emerged two separate groups that were clearly delineated from each other, and still later, these groups formed adversary and hostile camps. Over each of these camps the idea of unity, union, and harmony was shining as if it were a leading star—but it was shining high above them, and among them in the valley disharmony and conflict were raging in the name of harmony and unity. Isn't this ironic? The *Kuryer Codzienny* [Daily Courier] in Warsaw, correctly writes about this irony in 1887:

> This secession is of no consequence. Two associations for a population of one million could exist freely. Unfortunately, the infamous, ruthless exclusiveness and intolerance bared their jackal teeth, as if to say, "If you differ with me in conviction, then you are not an opponent but an enemy—and not only an enemy, but a scoundrel, a traitor, etc."

This fight between the Alliance and the Union was called "a fractricidal fight." However, we must admit that this very fight created animation, a feeling of unity, a love for the homeland, a desire for education, a need for newspapers, libraries, celebrations, and so on among the American Polonia. Each party, wanting to win over the masses of people, tried to educated (although with its biases), to encourage readership of its newspapers, to gather people into organizational groups that would represent their ideas.

Thus, bad things may have good outcomes. From the very beginning, there existed in the Alliance an aversion toward certain Polish priests who were accused of caring more for the interests of Rome than for the Polish national cause. This aversion finally transformed a party disagreement into outright hatred, which the adversary parties repeatedly spouted. However, despite the fact that these particular priests, the Resurrectionist Fathers, took a very hostile and aggressive position toward the Alliance because it did not deny membership to non-Catholics, through the years many illustrious priests belonged to this national institution and were perfectly able, as they themselves admitted, to reconcile the priestly duties of a fervent servant of Christ with the responsibilities of a Pole, the righteousness of the homeland. One of them, a priest who was at that time very respected by the Alliance, even stated publicly that he was first a Pole because he was born of Polish parents—and only later when he was christened did he become a Catholic. Therefore, the statement that the Polish National Alliance had at any time wanted to remove priests from political activity is erroneous. However, believing primarily in the equality of statuses, it has never recognized privileges in national matters. Thus, in the field of national and civic work, everyone is equal. The enemies of the Alliance often did not understand this premise; they did not want to understand it, or they distorted it totally under the impetus of party fighting.

The Polish National Alliance is the personification of Polish national poliltical thought in America. The birth of the Alliance actually occurred in the year 1880, but its conception in the womb of the past occurred a half century earlier. The first Polish national organization in America, the prototype of the Polish National Alliance, was founded in 1842 under the name of "Society of Poles in America" by a party of former soldiers of 1831.[12] Its chief organizer was Henryk Kałussowski, later the founder of the library and museum of the Polish National Alliance.[13] The first party of insurgents from 1831 landed in New York in May of 1834. Later others arrived, and within a year there were several countrymen here. The Americans gave them a good reception. In order to help these stragglers of the Polish uprising, a group of Americans established a committee bearing the official name of "Polish National Committee in the United States," with a Mr. M. Carey at the head. As a report published in Philadelphia on September 30, 1835, attests, Mr. Carey collected contributions through out the whole of America. Polish soldiers, living from the funds of this committee, considered their stay in America as temporary, while awaiting the call for a new uprising at any moment. Years passed—there was no call. Then they began to disperse throughout all the cities, looking for employment, and out of necessity becoming accustomed to a longer stay in America than they had first expected. The only document that remains from that time, a lithographed appeal "to the Poles in America," explains to us that not until March 20, 1842, did they begin to think about forming an organization at 235 Division Street in New York. They gathered into a Society under the name of *Towarzystwo Polaków w Ameryce* [Society of Poles in America], to which "every Polish immigrant regardless of status or faith can belong." This Society, "having brotherhood and reciprocal help as its foremost consideration, does not manifest an opinion as to which political road to follow. . . . So far there are 63 signatures." This appeal was signed by a committee including: W. Lange, Bazyli Jaroszyński, H. Paięcki, Izydor Czarnowski, Henryk Kałussowski.

We know nothing of the fate of this first Polish national organization in America until 1844. We come across its trail in a brochure printed in Paris entitled *November twenty ninth, 1844 in America*, with a description of the first public celebration of "the 14th anniversary of the Polish revolution" in New York. This first November celebration in America was organized by this "Society of Poles in America," which rented the most appropriate place at the Stuyvesant Institute.

> The celebration began at 7:00 p.m. as soon as groups of Scandinavians and Italians arrived en masse with their flags. The banners presented a magnificent view with the Polish in the middle and around it the American, Scandinavian, Italian, and German. . . . In the audience there were over a thousand of the most beautiful ladies, youth, ranking officials, and well-wishers. G. Theodore Sedgewick, an influential citizen in this country, presided, and next to him were generals, illustrious journalists, and representatives of various nations. There also arrived the Zabryskis or Zborowskis, who were of Polish descent, and who had arrived in America 100-175 years ago; a young Scandinavian exile, Fryd. Stalkerecht, who had lived in Poland for a long time; and Antoni Girard, who fought for our cause. At the end, two commissioners, F. L. Wierzbicki and H. Kałussowski, took their places as speakers. The rest of the commissioners, G. Mass, J. Wodzyński, E. Miller, and N. Łepkowski, took upon themselves the responsibility of receiving guests.

The brochure presents the speeches: Sedgewick in English, Kałussowski in Polish, Foresti in Italian, Harings in German, Howe and Wierzbicki in English. Kałussowski stated: "Let us not discard friendship, let us treasure it, but let us count only on ourselves!" At this gathering the address of one of the members of the Zborowski family was also read, and in it was the following passage: "My fellow citizens! I stand before you this evening in a dual character: first as an American . . . but on the other hand, as a Pole, as a descendent of a Pole, as one related to each of those here who is a victim of arbitrary power. Although my descendants were exiled from Polish soil more than 150 years ago, nevertheless, I look at it as our common mother. . . ."

What happened to this first Polish national organization in America? What was its later fate? That is unknown. To the few hundred exiles from 1831 were added still many more victims from 1846-48 (among them, Professor Boeck and the director Tyssowski in Washington). They dispersed more and more in their search to make a living, and this dispersement and distance made organizational work more difficult. In 1852, a second organization was formed in New York under the name *Towarzystwo Demokratyczne Wygnańców Polskich w Ameryce* [Democratic Society of Polish Exiles in America].

We are paying special attention to this second organization because in it there remains a trace of participation of our countrymen in organizational works of a new American party, the "Republican" party, which brought about the war to abolish slavery, the Civil War (1861-65). The basic tendencies of this new party were: (1) to separate itself from other parties, both the Whigs and the Democrats, and (2) to put an end to the spread of slavery. To the general organization called "Universal Democratic Republicanism" belonged various French, Germans, Italians, Swedes, as well as Americans—and the Poles were represented by the "Democratic Society of Polish Exiles," which included over two hundred members in 1854. Besides supplying fraternal aid, while thinking of homeland and of returning there with arms in hand, this society took an active part in the political movement of this country. Furthermore, being loyal to the ideals of Kościuszko, it was totally sympathetic to those who worked for the freedom of the blacks. H. Kałussowski's records show proof of the existence and activities of this Society from 1852 to 1858. What happened after that is unknown. Whether the Society survived until the Civil War, or whether it was dissolved in 1858, no one knows for certain. Many of its members married American women and died in oblivion; many joined the army and laid down their lives in the Civil War, or later succumbed in "veteran's homes." There were also a few who, hearing about the uprising of 1863 in Poland, left the American army, returned to Poland, and fought against the Muscovites.[14]

Among these last was Ludwik Żychliński, an officer in the service of the Union army. A few hundred Poles took part in the Civil War. Żychliński mentions them in his memoirs on the occasion of President Lincoln's visit to a camp near St. Louis. He writes:

I went, together with a few Poles, as a delegation to the president, who was living in a spacious tent in the camp, to greet and assure him that the spirits of Kościuszko and Pułaski alone brought us into the ranks of regiments of the United States, to fight on the field of battle for noble ideas and to defend the freedom of the endangered republic which our heroes by means of their blood helped from the time of its founding over 100 years before. General Hooker introduced us, praising the courage of the Poles in battles, their conscientiousness in performing duties in service, and their fervent and honest love for freedom. The president shook hands with each of us and stated that every Pole possesses valor for battle in his blood and is a good soldier, that the United States feels a deep compassion for Poland,

and will never deny her sons hospitality and bread. He also asked us how many Poles there were in the army, and he spoke in glowing terms about General Krzyżanowski, Rosenkranz, Szeinic, and many other Poles known personally by him. Then, even for an American, he graciously bid us farewell, saying: "Goodbye gentlemen, and after the war we shall not forget to reward those who have helped us overcome the enemy who strives to keep slavery in the republic and endeavors to break up our entire Union, which is voluntarily united into a strong and solid national entity."

On hearing the news of the 1863 uprising in Poland, the hearts of all Poles fighting in the American army were torn, but to no avail, because before the end of the Civil War no one could be excused from the ranks except under the most extreme circumstances. Only a few were discharged, such as Żychliński—and then only after overcoming unheard of difficulties. Finding out about the outbreak of the uprising, Żychliński writes, "I did not have peace in my soul, because it was yearning unceasingly to be where fraternal blood was being spilt, and I cursed the hour in which I had joined the United States ranks." Knowing that he would not get a discharge or furlough to Europe for as long as the war lasted, he procured a certificate from the doctor stating that he must travel to European springs to heal his wounds, and in this way he was able to leave the American army. Subsequently, he took an active part in the uprising in Poland from June to December 1863.[15]

During the 1863 uprising the Poles in America campaigned to the best of their abilities. Much money was sent to Poland from America and there were many volunteers. In the years 1863-65, a journal, *Echo z Polski* [Echo from Poland], was published in New York providing information to all the Poles who were dispersed throughout the entire region of America about the occurrences in their far-off homeland; the journal also served as a go-between in collecting funds. Meetings were held for the moral and material support of the fighting Poles. Almost all American newspapers wrote in a spirit that was very favorable towards Poland, and also called upon the Washington government to take in a position favorable to the uprising. As we know, the effort was in vain. The soul of everything that was being done in North America for the Polish cause was the Commissioner of the National Government and the Collector of Taxes of the National Fund, Henryk Kałussowski.

After the failure of the uprising, a new wave of political stragglers flowed onto the American shores, and among them could be found the new organizers of the Polish national movement. Polish national political thought in America developed gradually and began to take on more and more distinct shapes: these are the shapes and bodies that it puts on—the shapes of *Gmina Polska* in Chicago (1866) and *Zjednoczenia Polaków* in New York (1870). They were, however, organisms still too frail and undeveloped to be capable of living independently. *Gmina Polska,* founded in Chicago in 1866, initially consisted of a general political organization of a group of Polilsh exiles after 1863, who had been dispersed throughout the whole world. One of the founders of this organization was Julian Lipiński. *Gmina Polska*, although it did not have the gift of expansion, was still the most active national society at the time: it nurtured singing; it kept up a library; paid out death benefits; arranged tours, celebrations, and amateur performances (during one year, from November 1873 to November 1874, it gave five performances and five celebrations). At the November 1873 celebration, these memorable words, far-reaching in consequences, came from the lips of Rev. F. Żwiardowski, CR: "Not the people, as is written on the banner of the *Gmina*, but a miracle will save Poland!" To this, citizen Władisław Dyniewicz answered immediately and appropriately: "Pray, but also work, since prayer is dead without deeds." And citizen Krzemieniecki added: "Poland never forgot, and will not forget, about prayer or God, but it also does not condemn other faiths." These were the slogans that from that time divided Polonia into two camps: the staunch clericalists and the staunch nationalists. The soul of the *Gmina* were, besides the citizens already mentioned: Ignacy Wendziński, Stanisław Kociemski, Michał Majewski, Franciszek Gryglaszewski, Major Zaremba, as well as the poetess Teofila Samolińska.[16]

The two societies founded in New york in 1870—the Polish National Alliance and the Union of Poles in America—had the same goals as the *Gmina* in Chicago. Their leaders were Dr. Maćkiewicz, Dr. Marcinkowski, J. Drozdowski, Edward Kulikowski, Jan Krężałek, F. Latyczewski, Antoni Kopankiewicz, Teodor Janicki, and Ignacy Szczepanowski.[17] They also strove to assemble various other national societies under one banner, but their efforts were in vain. In fact, the existence and activities in Chicago and New York of these types of societies, which were both national and tolerant of others, as well as the formation of similar societies in Philadelphia, Pittsburgh, Milwaukee, and elsewhere, caused an adverse reaction on the part of the clericalists, who, through the initiative of Rev. Gieryk, founded in 1873 in Detroit the Polish Roman Catholic Union. The founders laid down the following tasks for themselves: constructing higher education schools, establishing libraries, founding of a Polish bank for all of America, establishing a teachers' seminary, a girls' monastery, and a Polish hospital. Rev. Gieryk aimed high, and to achieve these noble goals he wanted to unite all Poles. To achieve this end, he made a motion at the congress in 1874 in Chicago that the Union accept Poles regardless of their religious faith. However, this motion fell through and the Union, instead of uniting all Poles, both clericalists and patriots, caused a break in its own clericalist camp. It was then that, due to the uncertain existence of the Union, the thought of creating a general, purely patriotic organization began to take root and mature in the minds of the patriots. And so, from the historical past there emerged in 1880 the powerful Polish National Alliance, which exists to this day [1905].

It should be mentioned that even before founding the Polish National Alliance, Polish patriots in America had provided ample evidence of their unity with the Polish homeland. From the first moment of its creation, the American Poles were interested in the institution of the Museum and National Treasury in Rapperswyl. Even around 1870, *Gmina Polska* in Chicago conducted an active correspondence with the founders of the Museum. The Union of Poles in New York also conducted relations with them, as did the Society of Poles in California beginning in 1874. During the Russian-Turkish War in 1877-78, the Poles were preparing a broad diplomatic action, and Count Plater in Rapperswyl, as a respresentative of Poland to the governments and people of Europe, received mandates from everywhere, including national societies from America. The Polish National Society of Kościuszko from Chicago sent its mandate on March 16, 1877, and the Polish Society of California did so on April 14, 1877, and so on. When the Muscovites began to persecute our countrymen in Turkey, President Dr. L. Pawlicki in San Francisco called an organizational meeting on April 5, 1878. Committees were formed; in San Francisco there were Captain Bielawski, General Krzyżanowski, C. Choiński (a Polish Jew), Professor Elgas, and Captain Lessen; and in Chicago there were M. J. Kucera, Ignacy Wendziński, J. Krzemieniecki, J. Niemczewski, and Władisław Dyniewicz.[18] They explained to the Americans about the disgraceful behavior of Moscow and sent a petition to the president of the United States asking him to take up the defense of those American citizens of Polish descent who were living in Turkey. After the Turkish war, a congress of world powers was held in Berlin. The Poles moved again. On June 27, 1878, *Gmina Polska* in Chicago sent a telegram to Lord Salisbury in Berlin in the name of the Poles in America. It was signed by Kucera, the president, and Pokrzywiński, the secretary, in order to remind the High European Congress that "the partitioning of Poland was a violation of the laws of justice and humanity." A reply came in the form of a telegram on June 29: "Bismarck did not accept the address of the Poles at the congress. Rumania and Czarnogóra gained independence."

Another proof of unity between Poland and American Polonia was given during a jubilee celebration of the fifty years of literary work of J. I. Kraszewski in 1879 when, through the initiative of *Gmina Polska* in Chicago, $73.07 was collected and a silver cup was bought for Kraszewski. The New York Poles sent a collective speech; and our poetess, Teofila Samolińska, in the name of the Polish women of America, honored the celebrator with a beautiful poem, for which Kraszewski thanked her personally by letter. Polonia also gave proof of attachment to its adopted homeland in a magnificent celebration of the 100th anniversary of the Declaration of Independence of the United States on July 4, 1876.

But here is the beginning of the Alliance. "In 1879," as we read in a brochure published by the administration of the Polish National Alliance in 1894, "there appeared in *Ogniwo* [The Link], a weekly published in New York, and later in *Gazeta Polska*, published in Chicago, an article by a famous patriot, Agaton Giller, entitled, 'About the Organization of Poles in America.'" It is a summons to harmony, unity, and activity for the ancestral cause. This article made a great impression, awakening the desire to act and work under the national banner without imposition from above. Additional desires grew; desire to express personal opinions; to show independence; to shout loudly that one was a human being, that one was not only a Catholic but a Pole as well. However, in the face of such a great influence as the clergy possessed, it was risky to raise such a thought, to rise to battle in the name not only of God, but also, the homeland. Thus, everyone waited for the appropriate moment; everyone counted on someone else. Finally that moment arrived. Courageous people were found, and the Polish National Alliance, whose experiences and development we are planning to describe, was founded.

At the beginning of 1880, Śląsk [Silesia] was stricken by famine. News of this crossed the Atlantic and brought sadness to the hearts of immigrants living in the United States. Their obligation was to help their suffering countrymen through a common effort; but how could this be accomplished when the Polish settlements, separated by huge distances, did not have any link and often did not know about their fellow citizens living in the surrounding area?

A group of our countrymen, inhabitants of Philadelphia, asked just such a question of themselves when they gathered on February 15, 1880, to confer over the final fate and position that the Poles in America were to take. The chairman of this group, citizen Juliusz Andrzejkowicz, then developed a suggestion that had been made by Agaton Giller; he proposed joining all of the Polish societies in the United States into one league or society under the general name of Polish National Alliance. The society would be based on the principles of a federation, guaranteeing each of the societies a totally internal self-government. Those present at this conference, citizens Julian Szajnert, Julian Lipiński, Wincenty Domański, Jan Biatyński, Antoni Wojczyński, Jan N. Popieliński, Jan Blachowski, Teofil Kucielski, and Piotr Beczkiewicz, warmly applauded this proposal. Therefore, these people, together with the chairman, citizen J. Andrzejkowicz, are the actual founders of the Polish National Alliance, just as Philadelphia, the cradle of American freedom, is its cradle.[19]

Not losing any time, the founders began to work on realizing the great hope of uniting their countrymen. After a circular was sent out, replies soon began to flow into Philadelphia from various societies agreeing to join the Alliance. The first to answer the appeal were the following societies, which exist to this day: *Towarzystwo Gmina Polska* [Polish Commune Society] in Chicago; *Towarzystwo Przemysłowe Rzemieślników Polskich* [Industrial Society of Polish Tradesmen] in Chicago; *Towarzystwo Harmonia* [Harmonia Society] in Chicago; *Towarzystwo Polskich Krawców* [Society of Polish Tailors] in Chicago; *Towarzystwo Polaków w Kalifornii* [Society of Poles in California] in San Francisco; *Towarzystwo św. Jerzego* [Society of St. George] in Shenandoah, Pennsylvania. In addition to these, there were the PNA in Philadelphia; the Kościuszko Guards in Nanticoke, Pennsylvania; Fraternal Help in Grand Rapids; Polish Club in Chicago; Kościuszko Guards in Milwaukee; Pułaski Society in Brooklyn; Care and Lutnia in New York; Kościuszko Society in Philadelphia; Warsaw Guards in Shenandoah, Pennsylvania; Pułaski Guards in Northeim, Wisconsin; Polish National Society in La Crosse, Wisconsin.

CONGRESS I

Thus emerged a free, independent, and purely national Polish organization in America. The first months of its existence were devoted to preparatory work, formulating statutes, and so on. When this work was completed, citizen J. Andrzejkowicz called together the first congress of the young organization in Chicago on September 20, 1880. The gathering was held at the Palmer House hotel. The meetings were very animated. The following citizens took part in them: J. Andrzejkowicz, S. Kociemski, F. Gryglaszewski, K. Małłek, M. Kucera, W. Domański, J. Borchardt, Ignacy Wendziński, Edward Odrowąż, J. Rewerski, J. Główczyński, F. Sowadzki, R. Stobiecki, W. Dyniewicz, and many others of our country-men who had come to Chicago for the national congress.

At this congress it was resolved that the administration of the Polish National Alliance would be made up of a central committee (this name was later changed to central government, and then to central administration), and a censor, fulfilling the function of the highest official of the Alliance, controlling all activities of the committee (government) and taking care that statutes resolved by the legislative body, that is the congress, were not disobeyed in any way. To familiarize the reader with the main goals that the Alliance traced for itself, we quote directly from the former Alliance constitution, Articles II and III, to point out the paragraphs that became the cause of a battle that lasted many years.

Article II. Goals of the Alliance—paragraph 1. To strive for the moral and material development of the Polish element in the United States by establishing appropriate institutions on the principles of the Catholic church. Such institutions would be Polish homes, schools, and Polish charitable institutions and industry.

Paragraph 2. Care of Polish immigrants.

Paragraph 3. The political settling of Polish immigrants as citizens of the United States with the aid of the organ of the Alliance, and by entering into relations with American papers for the defense of our interests. Every member joining the Alliance will try to obtain United States citizenship papers.

Paragraph 4. The celebration of memorial anniversaries honoring Poland and fulfilling obligations which our national honor prescribes.

Paragraph 5. To support and encourage moderation in using alcoholic beverages.

Article III—paragraph 1. Since the Roman Catholic faith is the predominant faith in the Polish nation, then, we consider it as our obligation to stand by it, live in it, and to be subject to it in everything.

Paragraph 2. The Polish National Alliance is not getting into debates over religious issues, because that is the task of the Apostolic See and the bishops.

Paragraph 3. Since the Polish nation is also made up of a certain number of Poles of different faiths, then, following the Constitution of the Third of May, 1791, we guarantee them the respect of their beliefs and admit them, as Polish citizens, to work on political matters for the good of the Polish nation.

It was especially this last paragraph, or rather its application in practice, that was the cause of prolonged conflict between the Union and the Alliance. After the congress in Cleveland in 1895, this battle again, although for a short time, took on a sharper character. It was at this congress that entrance into the Alliance was prohibited to socialists and so-called "*niezależnym*" [independents]. The congress in Cleveland, however, due to the agitation of *Zgoda*[20] edited by F. H. Jabłoński, espousing "equality for all" after long and animated debates crossed out the paragraphs about religion (as quoted above) and opened wide the gates of his institution when he declared that the "Polish National Alliance accepts all Poles, Lithuanians, and Ruthenians without regard for political, religious, or social convictions." However, official masses were to take place in a Roman Catholic church, since "most of the Polish nation professes the Roman Catholic faith."

We do not see any more mention of religion in the new constitution, which was accepted at a special congress in Chicago, after a new charter was obtained, due to the need for reorganization to ensure the Alliance total protection under the law. Membership was and continues to be prohibited to anarchists and criminals.

As stated above, the sharp party battle that broke out anew after the congress in Cleveland slowly died down after the Alliance, suddenly growing members and assets, won for itself the right to citzenship. Today it is the largest Polish organization in the world in terms of membership and funds. Just as the Alliance formerly felt that the Union was not patriotic enough, now the Union felt that the Alliance was not religious enough. They constantly accused each other of a lack of patriotism on the one side and a lack of religion on the other side. These quarrels and disputes began immediately after the founding of the Alliance, since in 1881 the Alliance created *Zgoda* as an organ for self-protection and for the purpose of propaganda. It was edited by the following: 1881-82, E. Odrowąż; 1882-85, Ignacy Wendziński; 1885-89, Zbigniew Brodowski; 1889-93, Stanisław Nicki; 1893-97, F. H. Jabłoński; 1897-1901, Barszczewski; after 1901, Mr. Siemiradzki, a former professor at the Polish seminary in Detroit.

The Union, seeing the rising Alliance, gathered its strength, joined all church societies anew by joining their common interests, readied itself for battle, and when, in September 1882, the Alliance delegates gathered for the third congress in Chicago, it refused to say mass for the success of the congress deliberations. The Alliance immediately sent a complaint to church authorities, and the case went to the American bishops and even to Rome.

In cases of great importance and in the defense of the good name of Poland, the administration of the Polish National Alliance always took a stand.

Of the goals that the Alliance had traced for itself (establishment of Polish homes, schools, charitable institutions, industry, immigrant houses, and memorial celebrations) only this last one (organizing national celebrations) was achieved completely; the other goals were only partly achieved, and some were not achieved at all. Recently, however, the Alliance has broadened its scope of activities, since the congress in Wilkes-Barre. As an experiment and according to its resources, it has helped create and finance the committees on education, industry and trade, immigration, and colonialization. Within the Alliance there is also a department to aid those touched by misfortune. After completing the battle for survival, other goals that the Alliance has set for itself since its founding may now be achieved. Unprejudiced observers unanimously agree that the Polish National Alliance was the first to begin organizing national celebrations. The Alliance report states, "Let those who make accusations towards us ask our alliance brothers who taught them to love mother Poland, who proved to them that they are Poles; who instilled in them the need to unite in thought and action with this old and poor nation. . . ."

Scheming by our enemies, as well as internal disagreements, brought about the resignation of a few societies from our organization, which brought about a temporary drop in our membership from 455 to 295!! This occurred in 1883. In the following year, 1884, "the censor proves corrupt practices by immigrant agents and recommends the creation of a huge Polish colony under the care of the Polish National Alliance. . . ." And although this case "finally ended in nothing, due to a lack of confidence and capital, we, however, mark it as a proof of work and worthy endeavors.

At the end of 1885

the number of members increases substantially and better times seem to come, since a few Polish priests enter actively into the alliance work. This has an influence so beneficial that at the opening of the sixth congress on July 5, 1886, in Bay City, sixty delegates representing forty-four societies turned out. All in all, then, the Polish National Alliance shows forty-eight societies numbering a total of 1893 members. Following a motion by Rev. D. Majer, citizen Brodowski issues a protest in the name of the congress that denounces violence against our brothers under the Prussian sector. This was sent to Berlin, Vienna and Lwów!!

That same year, 1886, after paying off the stockholders, *Zgoda* became the exclusive property of the Polish National Allliance.

From the very beginning, the founders of the Alliance decided "to introduce into its scope of activities a fund for death benefits, to draw greater numbers of countrymen into the new organization." However, due to the slow development of the Alliance, this fund did not come about until 1886. The sixth congress, "due to the increasing number of members, finally resolves that, in the case of death of a member, the death benefit would come to $500, and in the case of death of the wife of one of the members, it would come to $250." Today [1905] the death benefit in the Alliance is from $300 to $900. Since the reorganizing congress, women, by law, are members of the Alliance with equal rights as men; however, they have taken little advantage of this. In 1886, the Union also introduced the death benefit fund.

The unceasing number of attacks by most of the Polish clergy on the Polish National Alliance forced E. J. Jerzmanowski and W. Żółnowski, from New York, citizens friendly to us, to submit the Alliance constitution to the archbishop of New York and the bishop of Newark for their judgment. Both of these officials of the Catholic church reviewed the submitted copies and approved of them entirely. . . . These approvals had a saving influence on the development of the Polish National Alliance. However, no less important was the behavior of the censor, citizen F. Gryglaszewski, who, upon receiving a government position as inspector of all government buildings in the United States and being forced by his position to travel constantly over the entire territory of the republic, did not overlook the slightest opportunity to spread truth about our Alliance; to encourage gathering under its banner; to muster courage among the frightened; and to enlighten the misinformed.

And so, already in the next year, 1887, the number of members had risen from 1,893 to 3,210.

An important issue also raised by the current (1887) central government was the establishment of the national treasury under the auspices of the Polish National Alliance, whose administration was located in Milwaukee. This treasury, due to the propaganda of *Zgoda,* was transferred at the congress in Cleveland in 1895 to Rapperswyl in Switzerland, and Alliance members are continually replenishing it with monetary contributions.

There then occurred a contact with the *Związkiem Wychodźtwa Polskiego* [Polish Emigrants Alliance] and lately with the *Liga Narodowa* [National League].

In 1886 a Polish seminary was founded in Detroit through the efforts of Rev. Dąbrowski,[21] who "approaches the congress with a request for support of his endeavors." The Alliance members took upon themselves a voluntary per member tax for the seminary.

"The enemies of the Polish National Alliance," we read, "indignant that a few Polish priests joined us, send a memorandum to American bishops presenting our organization in the worst light. That same year (1887), they founded a weekly, *Kropidło*,[22] for the sole purpose of slandering the Polish National Alliance and even destroying it completely. The publishers did not achieve the intended goal. *Kropidło* died after fifteen months. It did, however, leave its mark, because its entire group of advocates came to be known as *kropidlarze*.

"At the beginning of 1888 the central government of the Polish National Alliance made a significant step. It sent to the Prefect of Propaganda in Rome, Cardinal Ledóchowski, a grievance against a certain part of the Polish clergy, which had constantly persecuted our organization unjustly. . . ." This grievance was affixed with 2,470 signatures of Alliance brothers.

The eighth congress held in 1889 in Buffalo "brought about a change in the history of the Polish National Alliance." Three Polish priests also participated in this congress. They were Rev. D. Majer, Rev. W. Domagalski, and Rev. J. Wójcik.[23] "The congress began to make some amendments to the constitution. Rev. W. Domagalski made a motion to add to paragraph 3, Article IV: with the exclusion of notorious non-believers and Jews." The course of this issue is described by an eyewitness, Rev. J. Wójcik, in the following manner: "Regarding this motion of Rev. Domagalski concerning the exclusion of notorious non-believers and Jews the following occurred: the first day in the afternoon, this motion went under deliberation and passed by a majority of votes. The constitution contunued to be read. The next day someone made a motion to return to this paragraph and once more there was debate over the motion that had already been accepted. Then Rev. Majer objected, adding that the priests would leave the Alliance if the motion failed. Therefore, the issue was hushed. But to our surprise, at the afternoon session debates over this motion came up again. We did not say anything more because we could see the manipulations of the leaders. So when this motion was voted down by a majority of votes, we left the room." So much from Rev. Wójcik. However, the Alliance minutes added that citizen Śleszyński from New York "shouted in agitation" after the priests left the room: "Go! The Poles will remain in the Alliance!"

Rev. Majer's motion fell by a vote of thirty-one to eight. Most of the delegates were of the opinion that because of the appeal of the National Government of 1863, the Alliance could not remove Poles of the faith of Moses or any other faith from common effort in the national realm, since this would destroy the foundation from which a purely national organization must emerge. The issue here was one of principle.

Until the congress in Buffalo, Rev. Domagalski was an unpaid co-worker of *Zgoda*. A talented writer, he wrote scathing articles directed against the Resurrectionist Fathers, who had taken up a hostile stand regarding the Alliance. Later, however, Rev. Domagalski switched to the side of the Resurrectionist Fathers and edited *Wiara i Ojczyzna*[24] [Faith and Fatherland], in which more brutally than ably he attacked the Alliance. In the Alliance there was a conviction that Rev. Domagalski, with his motion to exclude Jews and notorious non-believers, wanted to trip Rev. Majer, who had a far greater popularity, esteem, and influence within the Alliance. After Rev. Domagalski's motion was voted down, Rev. Majer, together with the other priests, had to leave the Alliance. He established a new organization, the Roman Catholic Union, and a very sharp party battle erupted.

It could be said that for some time in America there were neither Catholics nor Poles at all, but only Union or Alliance members; he who was not an Alliance member, the Alliance did not consider a Pole; he who was not a Union member, the Union did not consider Catholic. He who wanted to be both a Catholic and a Pole usually found himself between a hammer and an anvil: if he joined the Union, the Alliance would refuse to acknowledge his patriotism; if he joined the Union, the Alliance would not acknowledge his catholicism. So, in their party obstinacy, each one excluded or "cursed" the other.

This situation is much better today [1905]. Times have changed, and the unrest in our still-young society has lessened. At the congress of 1889, Secretary General J. Morgenstern was replaced by citizen A. Małek from Chicago.[25] When the new administration "assumed control over the archives and fund from the former secretary (Morgenstern), it became evident that J. Morgenstern had run off leaving no cash whatsoever. A great panic ensued. To add to the problems, the newly elected vice-censor, K. D. Nowak, took advantage of his position and began to fool the parishioners of St. Wojciech Church in Buffalo. In the name of the Alliance, he tricked them into giving money for various pretexts, such as financing a trip to Rome to present a grievance, and so on.[26] The position of the Polish National Alliance was critical. It was saved by the energy of the central government. The central government removed K. D. Nowak from office immediately and brought Morgenstern's guarantors to trial.

After the congress in Philadelphia in 1897, the Alliance had another problem with the cashier, W. Wlekliński, but it managed to extricate itself successfully due to the effort of the central administration. The losses from Wlekliński's embezzlement were covered.

The Alliance constantly grew and gained power. "Dr. Kałussowski's letter from Washington, in which he offered the Polish National Alliance his library valued at $7,000 and a collection of important documents dealing with national issues and emigration history, under the condition that the Alliance create a public library and a national museum from them, caused a real surprise to those present at the congress in 1891. The congress accepted this gift."

At the pre-congress mass in Detroit in 1891 Bishop Foley blessed the work of the Alliance and was to have said: "I know very well that some priests persecute the Alliance; attention, however, should not be paid to this, because even among priests there are evil people. All unfounded accusations must fall sooner or later." Somehow they did fall.

In 1896 construction on the Alliance House was begun on Division Street in Chicago. The cornerstone was blessed by Rev. Sztuczko, CSC, the pastor of Holy Trinity Parish.[27] The house itself was not blessed. It is worth mentioning an interesting fact here. Rev. W. Kruszka in Ripon, Wisconsin, received a letter from Archbishop Katzer[28] prohibiting the blessing of the Alliance House, although Rev. Kruszka never had the intention of doing so because he had not been asked. Who arranged this? It is easy to guess.

The Alliance House was built according to Flizikowski's plan. It stands on two lots (48 x 100 feet) and has three floors and a basement. The façade is made of the so-called "blue Bedford" stone. The entire building is heated by steam. At the top of the house, the coat of arms of the Polish National Alliance is visible; a similar colorful coat of arms on burnt glass is hung over the main entrance. In the basement are the print shop and shipping room of *Zgoda*; on the first floor the offices of the secretary general, cashier, bookeeper and editor, as well as the conference room of the central government. On the second floor are the National Museum, the Alliance library, and reading rooms, and the apartment for the caretaker. On the third floor is a large hall for general use.

The censors for the Polish National Alliance have been the following: 1880-83, Juliusz Andrzejkowicz; 1883-91, Franciszek Gryglaszewski;

1891-93, Wincenty Przbyszewski; 1893-99, Teodor M. Heliński; 1899-1905, Dr. L. Sadowski.[29]

We can demonstrate the gradual growth of the Polish National Alliance best by means of figures. Numbers are stubborn facts.

Growth of the Polish National Alliance

Year	Number of Groups	Number of Members	Cash in the Fund	Death Benefits Paid Out
1880	9	—	126.30	—
1881	9	—	622.71	500.00
1882	10	455	1,145.06	—
1883	12	448	175.55	2,700.20
1884	10	340	639.52	451.75
1885	10	295	3,660.63	134.00
1886	44	1,893	7,299.09	5,334.00
1887	87	3,210	8,430.05	21,850.00
1888	96	3,682	9,295.97	26,750.00
1889	101	3,398	6,906.57	22,500.00
1890	113	3,426	1,144.73	22,250.00
1891	119	3,856	5,216.83	29,750.00
1892	151	5,077	9,129.32	34,500.00
1893	167	5,654	19,331.38	45,450.00
1894	191	6,107	23,673.36	54,909.00
1895	210	7,515	28,182.71	50,800.00
1896	288	11,077	30,407.51	84,100.00
1897	338	12,231	39,419.29	107,000.00
1898	376	13,513	54,733.79	122,550.00
1899	412	15,288	96,529.86	148,000.00
1900	451	28,358	98,339.05	158,200.00
1901	469	30,355	132,886.30	158,700.00
1902	510	33,255	160,166.24	180,520.00
1903	561	37,104	203,144.62	196,120.00
1904	595	40,035	242,441.53	240,430.00

A total of $1,517,378.95 in death benefits was paid by the end of 1904.

THE UNION OF CZĘSTOCHOWA (FOUNDED IN 1887)

The idea of uniting all Poles into one organization was constantly taking flight, but after each attempt to fly it would undergo a metamorphosis. As we saw, this idea was first embodied in the Chicago *Gmina Polska* (and even in the New York *Zjednoczenie Polaków w Ameryce*), then it turned into J. Barzyński's *Organizacja Polska*; later it took on the form of *Zjednoczenie Polsko-Rzymsko Katolickie*; next it travelled into another form embodied in the Polish National Alliance. But even in these newly created forms there was not enough breathing space for this "idea of general unity." This unity sought other forms, and although it did not yet create larger and more spacious ones than the "Union" and the "Alliance," it becomes apparent that the "idea of general unity" suffered, and still continues to suffer, as an uneasy spirit among the Polish immigrants in America. It is, at least, a symptom of the great vitality of our nation, because only where there is life are organisms born. It would have been better if the idea, the "mother of every action," had given birth to one, huge, comprehensively developed organism, rather than ten infirm and stunted ones—but what can be done? What has happened cannot be undone, and an historian must consider facts as they are and not how he would like them to be.

On June 18, 1887, through the initiative of the Alliance society *Gmina Polska* in Chicago, a funeral service, was organized for the repose of the soul of J. I. Kraszewski, the famous novelist. This, however, met opposition from the local Polish clergy, who refused to say the funeral mass. The initiators, not discouraged by the refusal, went to the Irish church of the Jesuit fathers and there received what they had requested. Thus, this sad service became the reason for dissension within the bosom of the Polish Roman Catholic Union. A few hundred of its members, parishioners of St. Wojciech's Parish, took part in the march, despite the opposition of their pastor. In order to avoid similar cases in the future, several paragraphs were introduced into the statutes of the church societies limiting the scope of activity of the administrations of these societies, and thus increasing the power of the pastors. The parishioners of St. Wojciech, having learned by experience, refused to accept these paragraphs. Because of this they created, together with a few other societies, a separate organization entitled "Polish Roman Catholic Union under the Care of the Mother of God of Częstochowa, The Queen of the Polish Crown."

This organization still exists [1905] and holds its congresses annually. In 1900 it had a total of about four hundred members belonging to ten societies. In its best times, it numbered one thousand members. It had a revenue of $4,699.55 in 1900, and by 1904 this increased to $8,445.20. The official chaplain of this Union was Rev. J. Radziejewski, who died in 1904, and was succeeded by Rev. Olszewski; the president was F. Kamiński; the cashier, W. Jaworski. The official organ is Wojciechowski's *Telegraf*.[30]

THE POLISH ROMAN CATHOLIC UNION (FOUNDED IN 1889)

The desire for general unity would not let the Polish immigrants in America rest long. In 1889 it again flew as high as an eagle's flight, wishing to spread its protective wings over the entire American Polonia. This time, like a bird in a cage, it was too enclosed in the Polish National Alliance, so it left this prison. In 1889, at the eighth congress of the Polish National Alliance in Buffalo, when the priests belonging to the Polish National Alliance made a motion that "all notorious non-believers and Jews be excluded" from the Alliance administration, and when this motion was rejected, the priests, not wanting to fraternize with Jews and atheists, left the Alliance. Under the leadership of Rev. D. Majer[31] in St. Paul, Minnesota, they formed a new organization entitled "Polish Roman Catholic Union," which was to combine harmoniously the principles of the Polish National Alliance and the Polish Roman Catholic Union under the care of the Heart of God. In other words, the Union was to have been the ideal organization, capable of gathering all the Poles in America under its banner. However, this great project did not develop as its creator hoped. In 1904 it had 5,055 members, and its general funds totaled $22,171. In 1904, the administration was made up of the following: S. F. Jarmuż, president of the Union; A. Kubiak; Franciszek Węgliński; W. Malinowiak; Gebler; Antczak; Antoni Wiśniewski; W. Uliński; R. Dewański; J. Zagórski; J. Nagórski; H. Bogacki; K. Urban; P. Koprucki; and X. Kasprzak. The official physician was Dr. F. N. Pitass.

THE POLISH LEAGUE IN AMERICA
(FOUNDED IN 1894—FAILED)

In the Kościuszko Centennial of 1894 the movement toward general unity assumed the form of a "League" modelled on the Polish League established in 1848 in the Poznań region. This League was to have been a "most broad organization" (former ones were also aimed towards this), and was to have "developed a universal representation of the Polish population in America. Its purpose was not to give each other financial support or direct material benefits (that is why it could exist with its head above the clouds, but not on American soil). The purpose of the League was, above all, the preservation of unity here and communication with the homeland. . . . It was ideal work for the common good. . . ." For this goal, the League wanted to unite us all without any factions, without taking away from or doing harm to any of these groups.

The idea of the "Polish League" was fundamentally excellent; it was only necessary to execute this project with an excellance equal to that of its inception. But what could be done when our national flaws stood in the way of this? These flaws can be summarized in this one line: "No one wants to listen, everyone wants to rule."

The Polish National Alliance formally declared itself opposed to such a League, fearing that "the priests would gain power over us." Although the Alliance censor knew that the Polish National Alliance was not, is not, and never will be a general organization, but rather a party one, he nevertheless threw the following naive question out to the world: "Why establish the League with the same goals for which the Alliance is striving and has proven that it sincerely wishes to strive despite obstacles and persecutions?" That same question also could have been put forth at the time by both the Alliance and the Union, and by other more general organizations, but they were not so naive. Although they knew that they were also striving towards the general unification of Poles, in the same way as the Alliance, and perhaps even better than the Alliance, they, however, did not deny the right to exist to a more general organization such as the League was to have been. The most humorous reason that the Alliance censor gave to deter the League was that

those of the Alliance brothers who advise others to support the League may be acting in the best faith, but I ask the advocates of Alliance matters whether they remember those times when it was commanded to make a sign of the cross at the sight of an Alliance man—when it was commanded that every one avoid the Alliance man as a wild animal—and for what? Because we fought for the idea which is to prevail in the League.

Further comments are unnecessary.

The League was established and it functioned for some time, establishing little libraries throughout the settlements, and so on. It received the following monies: for the national treasury $689.61; for the treasury of the *Liga Polska*, $444.42; for a general fund $18.40, bringing the total to $1,152.43. Expenses came to $242.75, therefore $909.68 was left. This money, together with the League itself, was mishandled and disappeared like camphor. The League's funeral probably cost that much.

The League died, but its soul—the idea of general unity—still lives on, and despite so many unuccessful endeavors, there are now attempts to create a "Federation," calling together Union, rallies, congresses, and so on. This idea is undying among our immigrants: although the organizations are dying, the desire for unity lives on.[32]

THE ASSOCIATION OF POLES IN AMERICA, OF THE POLISH ROMAN CATHOLIC ORGANIZATION UNDER THE CARE OF THE HOLY TRINITY (FOUNDED IN 1895)

At the beginning of the summer of 1895, a few Milwaukee societies who belonged to the Polish Roman Catholic Union and were unhappy with the Union for various reasons decided to organize a separate organization with a death benefit fund. The first organizational meeting of the members of various societies was held in St. Jacek's hall on August 4, 1895, in Milwaukee, Wisconsin. It was called together by Tomasz Wesołowski, chaired by Michał Huntowski, and the secretary was Andrzej Hudziński. The second meeting, for further deliberation, was held on September 29, 1895, in St. Stanislaus hall. The third meeting was held on October 27, 1895 in St. Josaphat hall. Here, the first positive steps were undertaken and a committee was chosen for the development of the program of the organization and then the constitution. The following citizens were part of the organizational and constitutional committee: Ignacy Czerwiński, Antoni Danielski, Michał Dettlaff, Józef Rechlicz, and Jan Błochowicz. The next gathering was held on November 3, 1895, in St. Vincent's hall, where Antoni Szymański presided, and then a week later, on November 10, there was a meeting in St. Hedwig's hall. On November 8, the constitutional committee had held its session, accepted the draft of the constitutional, and resolved to call a constitutional convention on November 18, 1895 at St. Stanislaus hall. At the meeting in St. Jadwiga's hall, a temporary administration was chosen, which included the following: Ignacy Czerwiński, president; Ignacy Górski, secretary; and Andrzej Dich, treasurer. The constitutional convention, having officially organized the Association of Poles in America, confirmed this administration, giving it full powers to conduct business for the Association until the electoral congress would be held on January 6, 1896.

This organization constantly, yet slowly, develops and grows, just as oaks grow slowly. In five years of existence it has paid out $82,000 in death benefits alone to widows, widowers, and orphans. The general nature of this organization is made clear by the fact that in addition to the state of Wisconsin, it also encompasses the states of Illinois, Nebraska, Michigan, Ohio, New York, and New Jersey. Furthermore, half of the societies belonging to the "Association of Poles in America" are from Wisconsin.

The second congress of the Association of Poles in America was held in the parish of St. Stanislaus in Milwaukee. The following administration was chosen: Stefan Czaplewski, president; K. Czarkowski, vice-president; Ignacy Górski, secretary; M. Sałaty, treasurer.

At the third congress, in Stevens Point, the following were chosen for the administration: Stefan Czaplewski, president; Emil Czarnecki, vice-president; Ignacy Górski, secretary; M. Sałaty, treasurer.

At the fourth congress at the parish of St. Hedwig in Milwaukee, the same administration was chosen.

At the fifth, at the parish of St. Josaphat, the following were chosen: Stefan Czaplewski, president; Emil Czarnecki, vice-president; Ignacy Górski, secretary; Jakób Leszczyński, cashier.

At the sixth congress, at the parish of St. Jacek, the same administration was chosen.

At the seventh congress, in the parish of St. Stanislaus in Milwaukee, the following were chosen: Stefan Czaplewski, president; Józef Rechlicz, vice-president; Ignacy Górski, secretary; Jakób Leszczyński, cashier.

At the eighth congress, in Detroit, Michigan, in 1904, the following were chosen: F. J. Grutza, president; J. Rechlicz, vice-president; Ignacy Górski, secretary; J. Leszczyński, cashier.

Currently [in 1905], 75 societies, and 3,611 members, belong to the Association. Its monetary assets total $28,000.[33]

POLISH SINGERS ALLIANCE IN AMERICA (FOUNDED IN 1888)

In the field of music, especially in the areas of church and national song, our organists have made great achievements. Throughout parishes everywhere, they organized individual choirs, at first male and female. These later, in 1888, joined into one great Singers' Alliance through the initiative of Antoni Małłek.[34] And so Antoni Małłek, one of many who brought choirs together, organized the following choirs: in 1872 the first choir in the parish of St. Stanislaus Kostka in Chicago; in 1873 the first choir in St. Stanislaus parish in Milwaukee; in 1875 the first choir at St. Casimir in Northeim, Wisconsin, as well as the first male choir incorporated into the Pułaski Guards in Northeim; a mixed choir in Newton, Wisconsin, and a female choir in Memee, Wisconsin; in 1883, a male choir in Holy Trinity Parish in Chicago, and also there in 1888 the female choir "Wanda," the Chopin male choir, and the Foresters choir of St. Wojciech's. Similar organizational activities were undertaken by other organists such as Konstantin Małłek, active in the field of song in America since 1873; Kwasigroch, active since 1875, and others.

In order to develop a program that would unify all singers' societies into one inseparable whole, Antoni Małłek selected an organization committee from the members of the Chopin choir in Chicago. This committee was chaired by Stanisław Pliszka. Delegations of choirs from Chicago, Milwaukee, La Salle, and St. Paul attended the first joint meeting at Holy Trinity School in Chicago on November 29, 1888. The dream of joining together individual choirs into one whole under the name "Polish Singers Alliance in America" began to materialize. From that time, the Alliance held its "conventions" annually; in May 1889, the first convention was held in Chicago, in which Antoni Małłek was chosen the chief conductor of the Alliance, and the administration was moved to Milwaukee. The second convention was held in 1890 in Milwaukee; the third in 1891 in Chicago; the fourth and fifth, attended by the famous composer Antoni Katski, were held in 1892 in Grand Rapids, Michigan, and in 1893 in Chicago; the sixth (1895) and seventh (1896) in Milwaukee; the eighth in 1897 in Grand Rapids, Michigan; the ninth in 1898 in St. Paul, Minnesota; the tenth in 1900 in Chicago. At all of these conventions up until 1897, Antoni Małłek was always chosen the chief conductor. This repetition became boring for many singers, and at the assembly in Grand Rapids in 1897 a new administration was chosen to replace Małłek: some carpenter was chosen as conductor. Małłek did not want to give up his conductor's wand, and this caused a division that lasted until 1903. Two adminstrations were created; the old administration (of the Małłeks) did in fact continue to be powerful because it had possession of the funds, the music, and all the insignias of power; the new administration, although it was considered legal, was in fact powerless. Antoni Małłek remained the conductor of the old Milwaukee administration, which, in 1899, was composed of Ignacy Sawicki, F. Rosenthal, Miss Rehbein, M. Kucera, M. Domiński, and K. Małłek, with a total of twelve choirs, including five from Chicago, two from Milwaukee, two from St. Paul, two from Duluth, and one from St. Louis. Their official publication was Ziarno [The Seed]. Leon Olszewski from Buffalo became the conductor of the new administration in Chicago or Bay City, which comprised K. Sikorski, Weronika Musiał, F. Nowicki, Madaj, Chmieliński, S. Sosnowski, W. Karpus, and Aniela Dardas. In 1902 this group numbered as many as twenty-two choirs with 460 members, including eight choirs from Chicago, three from Buffalo, two from Bay City, two from Toledo, one from Detroit, one from Philadelphia, one from Nanticoke, one from Wilkes-Barre, one from Plymouth, one from Utica, and one from Pullman. The group's monthly organ was *Harmonia* [Harmony]. On February 10, 1902, Leon Olszewski wrote:

It is a fact that the founders of the Singers Alliance are the Małłeks; it is a fact that under their leadership the Singers Alliance was proceeding toward the designated goal for which the Małłeks, and especially Antoni, deserve recognition. But . . . at the assembly in Grand Rapids in 1897, the Małłeks forgot that the "Alliance" created by them is not their property, but a national organization; they forgot that as a father does not have rights over a child who, having reached adulthood, is no longer under his care, so they, the founders, did not have the absolute right of administering this Alliance any more. . . .

Just as discordant tones are sometimes used on purpose in music to create a greater effect, so this disharmony among the singers contributed only to a greater development of the Polish Singers Alliance in America.

Antoni Małłek, the chief conductor of Polish singers in America, was born on May 5, 1851 in Ogorzeliny on Chełmiński land. He received his musical education from his father. Fleeing from the war, he came to stay with his brother Jan in Chicago on March 31, 1871. He worked first at the railroad station of the Illinois Central, then, after 1872-73, as teacher and organist in Chicago, bringing his brother Konstanin to America at this time. He worked from 1873 to 1874 in Milwaukee, and from 1875 to 1880 in Northeim, Wisconsin, where in 1879 he was appointed justice of the peace. In 1880 he quarrelled with his brother, Konstantin and took a position at Holy Trinity in Chicago, where he, has been for the past twenty-five years. In 1884 he bought musical type and began to print Polish songs. By 1900 he had published seventeen works. He was chosen secretary general ofthe Polish National Alliance three times and at his request, in 1892, Antoni Kątski composed the "Polish National Alliance March."

THE POLISH FALCONS ALLIANCE[35]

Although the falconry had already been founded in Chicago, Illinois, in 1888, the first thought of establishing the Polish Falcons Alliance among the immigrants in America was suggested at a modest meeting of friends and fervent advocates of falconry on September 7, 1893, in Pułaski Hall at 800 South Ashland Avenue in Chicago, Illinois.

In accordance with the above resolution, on January 7, 1894, a joint meeting of representatives of the then-existing Falcon nests in Chicago was held in the hall of scout Antoni Groenwald at 668 Holt Avenue. The following representatives came to this first joint meeting of the Falcons. From Nest One: Kazimierz Żychliński, president of this nest, and Alfons

Dziadul. From Nest Two: Leon M. Nowak, Maksymilian Barański, and Antoni Groenwald. From the St. Stanislaus Kostka Nest: Szczęsny Zachajkiewicz, Juliusz Szczepański, and Ignacy Kowalski. From Nest Three: Jan M. Bauer. The purpose of this meeting was to formally establish a single great common organization charged with protecting Polish youth from a total adherence to everything that was American and the relinquishment of evrything that was Polish. Scouts Szczęsny Zachajkiewicz and Kazimierz Żychliński spoke for this cause very convincingly. Those at the meeting elected scout S. Zachajkiewicz as chairman, and scout K. Żychliński as secretary.

With small changes appropriate to the needs of the Poles who had immigrated, the Alliance statute of Polish gymnastic societies in the Austrian empire was adopted. Next, the choice of the first officials for the Department of the newly established "Alliance of Polish Falcons in the United States of North America" was begun, with the stipulation that this Department was only temporary and would discharge its duties only until the first all-Falcon convention which was scheduled to be held in Chicago shortly thereafter. The scouts who were part of the first Department of the Alliance of Polish Falcons in America were the following: Kazimierz Żychliński, president; Szczęsny Zachajkiewicz, deputy to the president; Leon M. Nowak, secretary; Antoni Groenwald, treasurer; Leon Mieczyński, manager; and Maksymilian Barański, Jan M. Bauer, and Juliusz Szczepański, auditing commission.

It was decided that a copy of a report from this meeting would be sent to all Falcon nests in existence throughout the various Polish colonies with the request that these nests join the only common organization, the Alliance of Falcons, as soon as possible. On September 7, 1893, in accordance with the suggestion of scout Zachajkiewicz, it was decided to request gracious support in furthering the Polish Falcons in America from the reverend Polish clergy and the more leading citizens. At this point the first organizational meeting was brought to an end. Nest Number One of the Polish Falcons in Chicago did the most in setting up the Alliance of Polish Falcons. Its members did not spare labor or energy in the cause of interesting other falcon nests to join the praiseworthy Alliance.

The first rally of the delegates of the Alliance of Polish Falcons in the United States was held in Pułaski Hall in Chicago, Illinois, on January 27, 1895. The president of the convention was Jan F. Smulski, and the secretary was Alfons Dziadul. At this time four nests belonged to the Alliance: Nest 1, Chicago; Nest 2, from Chicago; Nest 8 from Chicago; and Nest 4 from Jersey City, New Jersey. There were twelve delegates at the rally: from Nest 1, Alfons Dziadul, Leon Mieczyński, and Adam Osiński; from Nest 2, Jan J. Chrzanowski, Jan Adamowski, and Jan F. Smulski; from Nest 8, Jan Bauer, Andrzej Piotrowski, and Gorywoda; and Nest 4, Jersey City, was represented by Chicagoans Franciszek Marcinkowski, Jan Zawikliński, and Stanisław Cichowicz.

Two telegrams were received during this convention; one came from the Falcons in New York and the other came from M. J. Sadowski, the president of the Falcon Nest 1 in Buffalo, New York. On that day the delegates and Falcons attended a mass (*in corpore*) at Holy Trinity Church. This mass had been specially requested by the Department of the Alliance for the occasion of the rally. The members of the Alliance already numbered 150. A total of $311.65 came into the treasury of the Alliance at the first rally; from it $91.05 was paid out. Therefore, the Alliance had $220.60 after the first rally. Officials of the Alliance chosen at the first rally were the following: president, K. Żychliński; first deputy, L. Czesławski; second deputy, R. Marcinkowski; secretary general, A. Dziadul; treasurer, A. Groenwald; manager, L. Mieczyński; assistant manager, J. Cichowicz. The following were members of the Department: W. Glaza, J. J. Chrzanowski, J. Bauer, and S. Cichowicz; the auditing commisson was W. Żychliński, J. Zawikliński, and A. Piotrowski; the press commission for the propagation of the Falcon idea in the Polish press was L. M. Nowak, K. Żychliński, and A. Błaszczyński. At this rally fifteen dollars was designated for the national treasury in Rapperswyl.

The beginnings of the Polish Falcons were extremely difficult, but through perseverance and quiet, continuing work, the accomplishments of the advocates of falconry were such that today this Polish youth organization, attracting immigrants in America, has a substantial number of advocates of the falcon ideal as well as fervent nationalistic workers. These are mainly young people who were brought up on American soil. This is the exclusive goal of the Falcons—to unite Polish youth under one national banner and preserve it for Poland. The Polish spirit is being reborn in every young person through falconry's development of discipline; love is awakened for everything Polish; the national strength is fortified; Polish children are guarded against denationalization and are prepared and hardened for life's future battles. This is precisely what the falconry is all about.

Scout K. Żychliński was the president of the Falcons Alliance from its founding until January 26, 1900, when he resigned, due to a permanent relocation from Chicago to Grand Rapids, Michigan. The vacancy left by his departure was filled by the deputy to the president, scout Jan J. Chrzanowski, who served as president of the Alliance until July 5, 1901, when the fifth rally of the Alliance moved the headquarters of the Department from Chicago to South Bend, Indiana. At this rally as well as at the sixth in New York, New York, scout G. W. J. Kalczyński was chosen president.

The second rally of the Alliance of Polish Falcons in the United States was held in Pułaski Hall in Chicago, Illinois, from August 1-3, 1896. There were twenty-one delegates present; the alliance already had seven nests with over two hundred members. Rev. Wojciech Furman said mass for the Falcons at St. Casimir Church. On September 1, 1896, at the expense of the Polish National Alliance, the monthly *Sokół* [Falcon], the organ of the Alliance of Polish Falcons, began to be published.

The third rally of the Alliance was held in the parish hall of St. Jadwiga in South Bend, Indiana, from July 3-5, 1897; mass for the intention of the falconry was said at St. Hedwig's church. At this time, the Alliance had 367 members in eleven nests and a treasury of $151.45.

The fourth rally of the Alliance of Falcons was held in Buffalo, New York, on July 3-4, 1899. The Alliance had fifteen nests with 281 members and a treasury of $129.31. A ceremonious unfurling of the banners of the Alliance of Polish Falcons and of the Buffalo nest took place at this rally; the first banner was donated by Polish women of Chicago and the second by Polish women of Buffalo.

The fifth rally of the Alliance of Falcons was held in Pittsburgh, Pennsylvania, in the hall of the German Turners on 13th Street from July 4-6, 1901. There were thirty-three delegates present; the Alliance had twelve nests with 384 members. Its treasury contained $255.52 in cash. During this rally, a majority of delegates resolved to move the headquarters of the Department of the Alliance of Falcons from Chicago, Illinois, to South Bend, Indiana; furthermore, G. W. J. Kalczyński was elected as the third president of this organization.

The sixth rally of the Alliance of Polish Falcons was held in New York city in Beethoven Hall on 4th Street. There were sixty-six delegates present; the Alliance had twenty-five nests with 748 members. Since the fifth rally, $1,646.00 had been received; $744.35 had been paid out; thus, $901.65 remained. Mass for the intention of the falconry was said at St. Stanislaus Kostka church by Rev. Jan H. Strzelecki.

Presently, in March 1905, the Alliance of Falcons has a total of 1,254 members and thirty-eight nests. There are about one hundred in uniform, close to five hundred in training, over two hundred students, and about eighty girls.

The following are the current officials of the Alliance of Polish Falcons: G. W. J. Kalczyński, president, South Bend, Indiana; Paweł Niezgódzki, first deputy to the president, South Bend, Indiana; E. M. Szymorowski, second deputy to the president, Braddock, Pennsylvania; F. J. Karch, third deputy to the president, Chicago, Illinois; L. M. Kucharski, secretary general, South Bend, Indiana; J. W. Papczyński, treasurer, South Bend, Indiana; Ignacy Nowak, manager, Chicago, Illinois; Franciszek Kubiak, first deputy to the manager, Pittsburgh, Pennsylvania; and M. W. Kitkowski, second deputy to the manager, South Bend, Indiana.

Members of the Department are Jan Manikowski, South Chicago, Illinois; Tomasz Dorywalski, Black Rock, New York; N. J. Stachowski, South Bend, Indiana; Jan Deka, South Bend, Indiana; Ludwik Struk, South Bend, Indiana; Stanisław Marszoł, ensign, South Bend, Indiana; Stanisław Niezgódzki, deputy to the ensign, South Bend, Indiana; and E. W. Reichel, editor of *Sokół*, Chicago, Illinois.

THE POLISH YOUTH ALLIANCE IN AMERICA[36]
(FOUNDED IN 1894)

Around 1890 attempts were made to establish a general organization that would encompass Polish youth in all of America. A handful of youth associated with the Patriotic-Scientific Society in Chicago was already making efforts to establish contacts with the dispersed associations of American Polish youth. In 1892-93 these Chicago youths contacted the St. Aloisius Society in New York for the purpose of establishing foundations for one universal "Youth Association." However, after the two groups exchanged some correspondence, the New York group dropped further communication.

Next, the Patriotic-Scientific Society turned to the congress of the Polish Roman Catholic Union under the care of the Sacred Heart of Jesus, which was being held in Chicago (1893). The Patriotic-Scientific Society requested that this organization take over the care of the Polish American youth, which was more and more in danger of denationalization.

The congress ostentatiously accepted the petition and designated a special commission to take up the youth project. The commission, however, did nothing at all to comply with the instructions of the congress. The members of the Patriotic-Scientific Society decided to approach some members of the commission and ask them for help. Moreover, they wanted to take upon themselves the establishment of a youth association.

So, two members of this commission were recruited—Mr. Bolesław Klarkowski and the Rev. Eugeniusz Sedlaczek—who, in communication with the delegates of the Patriotic-Scientific Society, took up the cause of the young people. The result was the calling together of a congress of youth societies in Chicago and the possible establishment, at this congress, of the "Polish Catholic Youth Union in the United States." Six societies immediately joined the "Union." Despite efforts and work toward the development of this new organization, it ceased to exist after a few months, due to the laziness of the societies affiliated with St. Stanislaus Kostka Parish, four of which had joined the "Union."

With the failure of the "Polish Catholic Youth Union" fell the hopes of creating a larger youth organization. After this failure, the Patriotic-Scientific Society ceased to count on the verbal but ineffectual help of the elders and on the commitment of thoughtless and half-Americanized youth. However, it was necessary to save the latter, and in order to do so, it was first necessary to create an appropriate association having this as its goal.

Suddenly, unexpectedly, a letter arrived from Europe, calling for the establishment of a national patriotic organization, the Alliance of Youth. The letter was dated May 26, 1894. A handful of youth gathered at the old rectory of St. Wojciech's church in Chicago on June 20, 1894, to read this letter which had come to the secretary of the Patriotic-Scientific Society of Polish Youth. The gathered youth, seven altogether, listened intently to the secretary reading this letter, which had been signed with a pseudonym. It was not known who had sent this letter or who was calling "Unite Brothers and work for a Poland moaning in shackles!" Therefore, its origins were not considered much, but the attention of those gathered there was given to the contents of the letter. That this letter reached the appropriate hands, the circle of youth wishing to take steps to organize American Polish youth, does not need to be proven, since the existence of the "Polish Youth Alliance in America" attests to results of the letter.

In answer to this letter, youth from the bosom of the Patriotic-Scientific Society, together with their brothers in Europe, wished to work for the good of the national cause and wanted to imitate their forefathers in the battle for freedom.

After an exchange of a few more letters it was decided to establish the Polish Youth Alliance in America, but wishing to insure its strength, members were forbidden to talk about the Alliance. Also, the usual procedure for incorporating entire societies into a larger organization was abandoned, and it was decided to recruit members into the Alliance individually and to create groups called divisions.

Recruitment was slow, but the main concern was for the quality and not the quantity of members. The Alliance was intended to be a school for national service; so, above all, efforts were made to attract youth who were aware of the cause. Broader activities aimed at increasing the members of the Alliance were left to future planning.

The program of the Alliance was described as follows. The guiding objectives were considered to be acting for the good of the Polish cause by contributing to free the homeland from the yoke of captivity, expanding education, and uniting Polish youth throughout the entire world. Besides this, the means to accomplish these objectives were also described. It was decided to awaken the national spirit and the sense of Polish character in our Americanized youth by setting up reading rooms, libraries and evening schools; publishing Polish journals and books, organizing national celebrations and performances, cultivating Polish singing, maintaining the native language, defending the Polish name, and so on. The organization was to have a military character. The members were to become familiar with the use of weapons and drills, as well as with military tactics. The health and the so-called "death benefit" funds were eliminated as not being compatible with the ideal objectives of the Alliance. No membership fee was established, and the monthly tax was a minimum of ten cents per member. Those wishing to could contribute a larger tax. So that the authority would be efficient, concentrated, and modelled on the European organization, a chief administration was established. This administration would direct the organization as an absolute body, would possess both legislative and executive powers, and its members would remain in their positions until they themselves resigned or until they were excluded. Besides this, officials were being nominated for their offices by the higher authorities in Europe, since it had been decided at the time of establishing the Alliance to maintain a close unity with the European organization and, to some extent, to be subordinate to it. The Alliance in America, however, retained absolute independence and total autonomy.

The first members of the Alliance were the members of the administration of the Patriotic-Scientific Society and two members from outside the administration who were considered to be talented and loyal; this brought the number of charter members to nine. After taking the appropriate oath, members were chosen for the chief administration as follows: Stefan J.

Napieralski, president; Leon J. Schultz, vice-president; Franciszek P. Danisch, Commissioner; Franciszek T. Wołowski, secretary; and Józef J. Beliński, treasurer.

The administration went to work. It compiled *Informacye* [Information] for the newly forming division of the Alliance, and the so-called *Akt Połączenia* by which they tied themselves by means of a brotherly knot to the Polish youth in Europe, who possessed an identical program of national acitivity. Another of the activities was to prepare appeals to the youth.

The members of the Alliance worked quietly but briskly on the organization until the end of 1894. Through private correspondence, contact was made with youth in outlying areas to establish divisions. It was not until the beginning of 1895 that the chief administration was publicly described as a "declared representation" of the entire organization in both America and Europe.

In January 1895 the first formal division of the Alliance was officially confirmed in Wilkes-Barre. This was a seed that fell on fertile soil, because several divisions were spawned in Luzerne and Lackawanna counties of Pennsylvania.

As the Alliance grew, it became evident that an official publication was necessary. Thus, in December 1895 the Alliance purchased its own print shop and the weekly *Sztandar* [Banner] from I. J. Migdalski. The first issue of the organ of the Youth Alliance was printed in January 1896.

In March 1895 efforts were made to encourage Polish youth in Brazil to form a similar Alliance, but nothing came of it. Meanwhile, divisions were multiplying in eastern Pennsylvania, and a few were formed in Chicago and Milwaukee. Youth from various cities applied for information about the Alliance.

During this time, the first misunderstandings arose within the administration, but these were quickly and tactfully brought to an end. The administration nominated Władysław Tychewicz as vice-president to replace Schultz.

The Alliance resolved to organize celebrations in honor of the 150th anniversary of Kościuszko's birth, in February 1896, and then to organize public competitive exercises for Polish cadet societies. For these competitions, English commands were used only for the purpose of introducing Polish commands. It was stipulated that only those cadet divisions that used the Polish commands could participate in the competition for a gold medal. The results have been encouraging; from the time of competition until now [1905] the cadets have utilized Polish commands, although not exclusively.

To replace Józef Beliński, who had resigned, Aleksander Dąbrowski from Miners Mills, Pennsylvania, the first member of the Alliance in the East, was appointed treasurer. Also, Jan M. Sienkiewicz from Plymouth, Pennsylvania, was appointed to the newly established position of aid to the secretary. Both resigned from their jobs in Pennsylvania and came to Chicago on January 1, 1897, specifically for the purpose of taking these positions, which were, in fact, unpaid positions.

The youth divisions were constantly multiplying. The campaign of secretary Wołowski turned out to be fruitful. Rev. F. Hodur, who, at this time, had not yet become an independent, also greatly contributed towards forming divisions.

As the Alliance banner was constantly being raised in new settlements, socialist agitators began to force themseves in among the young alliance members; nevertheless, they were not accepted into the Alliance.

In June 1897, for the first time, ominous clouds began to gather over the Alliance. Cabinet crises ocurred; the resignation of secretary Wołowski was legalized and Franciszek P. Danisch, the current commissioner, was chosen secretary. His place was taken by the aid to the secretary, Jan M. Sienkiewicz. The storms did not abate. Demands were made for evidence of unity with the youth in Europe, selection of the administration, and so on. Among these storms, further changes occurred. Vice President Tychewicz and treasurer Dąbrowski resigned. Danisch was chosen president, and Sienkiewicz, in addition to being commissioner, was asked to fulfill the responsibilities of secretary. Jan S. Zawiliński, a member from the seventh division in Chicago, was appointed vice-president and treasurer.

Alliance members called for changes in the statutes and within the administration. For this purpose, the First Convention was called in Buffalo on November 27, 1897. This Convention, which lasted three days, provided the Alliance with new statutes and a new general administration; it established periodic conventions; it established a department of education, a military department, and a department for the administration of *Sztandar*. The administration was made up of F. P. Danish, president; Stefan K. Sass, vice-president; Jan M. Sienkiewicz, commissioner; Franciszek Wołowski, secretary; and Jan S. Zawiliński, treasurer.

An ill turn was done to the Alliance by some journals in 1898. Due to the thunder of Rev. Barabasz, the Baltimore division was dissolved. Later, the divisions in Chicopee were broken up by Rev. Chałupka; in Milwaukee, Rev. Tarasiewicz did the same, as well as in Plymouth, Pennsylvania, in Buffalo, and elsewhere. This persecution only brought about an increase of the anti-church elements. In some cities the priests were aiding, and continue to aid the divisions, by giving them access to school halls for meetings, singing lessons, and social gatherings. There, the members have remained loyal to the church and have continued to respect the priests.

When the Spanish-American War began in the spring of 1898, many of the youth joined the army. Among them, vice-president Sass joined the Milwaukee "Kościuszko Guards." There was a desire to form a Polish division of volunteers, but the army was already large enough, and before long the war ended.

The Alliance went forward, continuing the spirit of its objectives and principles. A press bureau was established, which for some time provided articles about the Poles to American newspapers. Brochures were published and distributed free of charge (*Ruch Narodowy* [National Movement] from 1877); a few travelling libraries were sent to Polish settlements, and so on.

The Second Convention, held in Wilkes-Barre, Pennsylvania, in July 1900, sanctioned the project of uniting the Alliances of Youth, Falcons, and Singers into one Federation of "Young Poland."

After the Second Convention, the divisions became more active; they organized literary evenings, national celebrations and performances, lectures, and evening schools. They continued to supply Polish literature to libraries, and some regularly held military exercises and shooting practices at their shooting ranges.

The Alliance did not grow to the dimensions that the founders had envisioned, but what it accomplished and still accomplishes reflects favorably in general on American Polonia and has a good influence on the Polish cause.

THE "POLISH MOTHERLAND" IN CHICAGO[37]
(FOUNDED IN 1898)

This was intended to be a general organization for Polish youth, but so far it only exists *in spe*, that is, in embryo form. It does not extend beyond the boundaries of its parish. It belongs to the future; thus,we shall leave its history to a future historian. Meanwhile it is enough to say that the founder of this newest organization of Polish youth in America is the courageous Rev. Fr. Gordon, CR, a splendid youth leader, whose work and activity we will frequently meet throughout Polish American history.

OTHER ORGANIZATIONS—THE POLISH WOMEN'S ALLIANCE[38]

Besides the above mentioned, there still exist in America about a dozen other Polish organizations of a broader scope, including the following: (1) Alliance of Poles, established in 1898 in the state of Ohio, with its main administration in Cleveland, Ohio. Its organ of publication is *Polonia w Ameryce*. The administration of 1902 comprised M. P. Knioł, president; Rumiński, vice-president; Sowiński, secretary; Rutkowski. That same year there was $18,000 cash deposited in banks. (2) The Polish Roman Catholic Union in Bay City, Michigan, established in 1892, had, in 1894, 765 members and $25,000. Its organ was *Prawda*. The president was Mateusz Blaszak, and officers included A.E. Cichocki, W. Kazyak, and the cashier, Jan Ślaziński. The economic council included W.V. Przybyszewski, W. Somerfeld, M. Borzewski, Wojciech Filipiak, and Tomasz Matuszewski. The marshal was Ignacy Szulc; the attorney, J. Kopeć. (3) The Polish Roman Catholic Association, founded in 1895 in Detroit, Michigan. The organ was *Polonia*. Members of the administration of 1902 were: F. Klimek, president; J. Świeczkowski, vice-president; Michał Barciszewski, secretary; S. Skrzycki, cashier. (4) St. Joseph's Union in Pittsburgh, Pennsylvania. The organ is *Wielkopolanin*. (5) Polish National League in the East; its main administration is in Jersey City, New Jersey. The organ is *Przyjaciel Ludu*. (6) The Polish Army Corps, with its main administration in Jersey City. The organ is *Patryota*. (7) The Second Polish Army Corps, whose main administration is in Chicago. The organ is *Sztandar*. (8) Polish Women's Alliance, whose main administration is in Chicago. (9) Alliance of Polish Socialists. The organ is *Siła* is Shamokin, Pennsylvania. (10) The Roman Catholic Association in Brooklyn (numbering sixteen groups); Rev. L. Wysiecki, chaplain; W. Norejko, president.

Besides this, we have a few large societies that do not belong to any of the above-mentioned organizations, such as the Society of Kazimierz Pułaski in Chicago; the Central Society of Polish Women in Chicago; and the Society of Polish Women, *Gwiazda Zwycięztwa*, also in Chicago. Of a broader scope, the *Związek Polek* [Polish Women's Alliance] was established in 1900, and holds serious congresses each year. In the first years, the president of the Polish Women's Alliance was Mrs. Chmielińska;

however, at the third congress in 1902, the following were elected: president, Mrs. Neuman, first vice-president, Mrs. Ostrowska; second vice-president, Mrs. Świniarska; secretary, Mrs. Fabiańska; cashier, Mrs. Tomaszewska. Like the Polish National Alliance, the members of the Polish Women's Alliance want to serve their homeland on this foreign soil. The Polish Women's Alliance grows constantly; in 1903, there were twenty-eight groups and 1,406 members; but in 1904 there were already forty groups and 2,040 members; the treasury held $9,310.

There also exist no less than a dozen so-called "Estates" organizations of the Order of Catholic Foresters and Polish regiments of Catholic Knights. However, due to the fact that they are considered to be international organizations, and do not have anything in common with the Polish character,[39] they can not be considered as Polish associations. Despite this, as we can see from the above description, Polish society in America possesses eighteen organizations. Each of these organizations has at least a dozen or so societies; the general number of members gathered under their banners came close to 35,000 at the beginning of 1900, and these were male members only. In 1904 the Association of Polish Pharmacists was founded in Chicago. Stanisław Kuflewski was designated president; Stefan Sass vice-president; Wiktor Bardoński, treasurer; and Stanisław Kossowski, secretary. There also exists an Association of Polish Physicians.

COMMON CHARACTERISTICS OF POLISH SOCIETIES IN AMERICA

Besides organizations in the strict sense of the word, that is, those societies made up of many lesser ones, there exist also in each Polish parish, and even in every settlement that is not yet organized into a parish, many individual societies of the most diverse hues, shades, and names, such as: fraternities, choirs, groups, circles, and clubs, which either form a component part of the above-mentioned organizations or exist by themselves, without being connected to any larger organization. These are strictly local in character, indigenous and private. The American Polonia numbers thousands of such individual societies, from three to four thousand. It would be appropriate to present their general characteristics here. To begin with, our societies are divided into church, secular, and mixed organizations. The church societies, in the best sense of the word, are undoubtedly the parishes themselves. These enter directly into the makeup of the organism of God's institution, the universal church. But in the bosom of each of the individual parishes there exist religious societies, whose members do not concern themselves either with death benefits or with suport in sickness, but who, above all, seek to live virtuous and Godfearing lives, appropriate to their status and calling. These consist of various fraternities and archfraternities, Societies of Ladies of the Rosary, temperance fraternities, Fraternities of a Good Death, Apostolic Prayer and Archfraternities of the Heart of Jesus, whose organs are the so-called *Monthly Intentions*, penny booklets brought over by the thousands from Kraków.

However, besides common prayers in the form of a "Living Rosary" and a mutual commitment to a virtuous and Godfearing life, the Polish Virgins and Women of the Rosary are also concerned about providing honest and decent funerals for their deceased sisters. In order to collect appropriate funds for this, they contribute a monthly tax in the amount of ten cents each. They also contribute cloths for the altars, carpets for the sanctuary, and flowers and other ornaments for the church.

Other societies in the parishes are church choirs, which come under the direction of the male or female organist, who may be either secular or religious. The choirs are engaged in church singing in Latin and Polish, as well as performing outside the church, in national singing. It seems that the most touching songs, which here on foreign soil can move a Pole to the depths of his soul, are Christmas carols and Lenten psalms. The Rosary and Canonical Hours, sung on Sunday before high mass or vespers, can still be heard throughout Polish churches in America just as they were in the old country. At Easter, three processions are held just as they were in Poland; the activities take place throughout the farms around the church, to the accompaniment of explosions from mortars and the hymns *Przez Twoje święte Zmartwychpowstanie, Wesoły nam dziś dzień nastał*, and so on. Before Christmas, in spite of the American custom, the organist distributes the hosts; after Christmas the priest makes house visits, and at Easter he blesses food, although other American Catholics think this strange.

After this small digression (which the reader will forgive) let us return to the church societies. Besides religious, there are also beneficiary societies in the parishes. Beneficiary societies are understood to be those, which, above all, intend to give support to their members in case of illness or to pay a death benefit to orphans left behind. They are commonly called "mutual aid fraternities."

In American Polonia, there also exist literary societies, drama circles, and educational societies, that are divided into "active" and "passive." Elders, the friends of youth, belong to "active"; children and adolescents belong to the "passive." The task of the active educational societies, or the so-called Associations of Friends of Youth, is to advise, encourage, and aid the Polish boys and girls in America who have already left school, to further their good upbringing, education, and learning. The Association strives toward this goal by encouraging literary presentations, concerts, theatrical performances, lectures, free borrowing of books, and evening school divided in such fields as music, singing, recitation, literature, and soon. The ladies gather into Societies of Philanthropic Ladies, whose task is to provide aid to young orphans and poor school children; they pay the children's school tuition, provide them with books, clothing, and so on. For this purpose, the Societies of Philanthropic Ladies give theatrical performances, organize Christmas festivities for the children, and so on. These "active" societies complement the "passive" societies, made up of children and adolescents of both sexes. The purpose of these societies is to supplement the upbringing and education of adolescents from fifteen to twenty years of age. Within the scope of the activities of the Societies of Adolescents are literary presentations, lectures, theatrical performances, and concerts, as well as games and recreation, and physical and spiritual exercises. The Societies aim to make it easier for our adolescents to fulfill the promises they made at their Holy Communion and to prepare them for the Sacrament of Confirmation. Polish boys in America, who ardently like games, sports and baseball, as well as loafing around the streets and "chewing tobacco," are not thrilled to attend the meetings. On the other hand, our adolescent young ladies, although they are also eager to play, do attend the meetings more diligently and are more interested in them in general than are their male peers.

Additionally, there exist throughout our settlements societies that are purely nationalistic, military, and athletic called *Sokoły* [Falcons], as well as political societies which focus attention on local American politics, such as the Democratic, Republican, Populist Clubs, and so on.

Under the date of April 22, 1875, in the old annals of *Gazeta Polska Katolicka*, which were covered with a thick quarter-century layer of dust, we found the following characteristic passage entitled "Activity of Polish Societies in America":

Established as our Associations are today, dissension, empty talk, and quarrels must rule at their meetings. The members come together, and immediately the president, secretary, and cashier begin to collect fees. If the association is numerous, and the secretary is not able to write quickly, then the fee collection drags on for a few hours, until finally the bored members take their hats and slip home.

Then, another time, an extra meeting is called only to dress up in group waistbands and go in procession; another time to organize a ball, then to organize the music; besides collecting fees and enjoying processions, balls, music, and waistbands, what else do our Societies do? Nothing, absolutely nothing. And it is no surprise that the members want to quarrel and talk of their pleasure for fifty or twenty-five cents at a meeting, because what else do they have to do? Without this they would not even know that there had been a meeting. As adults, it is about time that we begin to think about more than fees, waistbands and balls. We must think about education, Polish history . . . about politics and local needs. . . .

So write chronicles from 1875. And how is it today? An historian writes only about what existed in the past; that which exists today does not yet belong to history. We have undoubtedly grown socially and sociably, but have we matured? We will let a future historian answer this question.

However, regardless of the opinion history holds of us in the future, based on what has already passed, it can be stated that from the very beginning of their immigration the Poles in America had an excellent understanding of the importance of fraternal associations. Hardly a Polish settlement emerged where we did not see Polish associations, fraternities, and circles forming, either for specialized purposes or for mutual material aid. At times, individual associations joined together, forming larger organizations, which constituted separate links; then sometimes they operated autonomously with a predetermined goal, by means of joining some other larger federative organization. But all of these societies, through joining and uniting the Poles settled abroad, contributed to spreading the national spirit and the feeling of national solidarity. Directed primarily by the Christian principle of providing fraternal aid, they comply with the provisions of their ancestral faith and their national traditions.

The statutes, or, as they are popularly called here, constitutions, of Polish associations in America are manifold, but in each of them, with small differences, can be found a point attesting to the affection of our immigrants for the Catholic faith and for the land of our fathers. And it must be added that the statutes or "constitutions" do not exist as dead letters on paper. Almost all Polish parishes in various settlements came into existence because of the initiative of the societies; furthermore, many schools, shelters, hospitals, and other institutions are indebted to fraternities and societies for their existence. And hasn't much good been accomplished by various literary associations in the area of education? These associations have set up libraries and reading rooms and hosted celebrations and lectures to familiarize our people with the literature and history of Poland. Then again advocates of singing have gathered under one banner in order to keep alive the Polish religious and national songs and to familiarize the younger generation with them. Without this, the young people would not have had any knowledge of Polish melodies. Finally, the drama circles have familiarized broader classes of our immigrants with Polish dramatic art.[40]

Naturally, at times there were quarrels and disharmonies within these societies, but it is difficult to demand parliamentary maturity from our adolescent immigrants. In any case, the American Polish parlimentarianism is more proper than, for example, the Austrian one in Vienna.

Chapter 11

History of the Polish Press in America[1]

We will continue by writing the history of the Polish press in America. We obtained much of the material for this history from a splendid brochure published in 1894 by Henryk Nagiel entitled *Dziennikarstwo Polskie w Ameryce* [Polish Journalism in America].[2] However, we have our own arrangement for this historical material.

The Polish press in America, thanks to the development of our immigrant society, is already strong, if not in quality, then at least in quantity. This is because we have over two million Poles living in America, and forty-nine Polish periodicals, of which about thirty have an established foundation, since they have been published for many years. In any case, this society of ours, and especially the emigré press which has developed so actively while far from the mother root in Poland, comprises a social and intellectual manifestation that is unusual and interesting, and as such is worthy of research.

Just as every country has its customs, so in each country the press has its specific character, which is always interesting to study. The establishment of the Polish press in America occurred because of the need for unity and communication that emigrés feel when thrown into a foreign way of life on a new soil. Their first impulse is to cluster together. In a group, among themselves, they feel stronger and more capable of resisting foreign influences that may be hostile to them. They gather into organizations and societies in parishes and settlements. The newspaper serves as a link among them. It carries news from one settlement to another; it facilitates organization within a society; it presents news from the old country, which the immigrants miss so much, especially in the first years abroad; it slowly and casually familiarizes its readers with local life and conditions in foreign country; and finally, it serves as a tool for argument, to which our people are so prone.

So wherever larger Polish colonies are created, Polish newspapers slowly appear. On the one hand, they result from a real need; on the other, local social and political conditions facilitate their establishment. There is no other country (with the possible exception of England), where journalism has developed to such an extent as in America. The American needs a newspaper as much as a piece of bread or a glass of water. For him, it is a source of everyday information, an intermediary and a lever in business. There are no restrictions or difficulties whatsoever in establishing or running newspaper here. Thus, there is hardly a town in which a local organ does not exist.

Such conditions could not exist without having a definite influence on the Polish settlers; and so before long, Polish periodicals began to be established. Large resources were not needed, since enough people more or less capable of journalistic work could be found among the stray intelligentsia that made up a substantial percentage of the immigrants. Thus, Polish journalism began.

In time, conditions became more and more favorable. Polonia grew. From it emerged parties. Polish colonies were formed. Competition and fighting thrived and, as needs developed, the newspapers became more numerous and of better quality. Capital was slowly being invested in journalistic enterprises. Next to periodicals of more lasting character, there arose ephemera that were established today and gone tomorrow—and as a result of this, we have reached the present development, which is not, as everyone understands, the last step possible in this area of development.

The above history illustrates the way in which the local Polish press was born. The character of the Polish American press was, is, and for a long time must remain, informational in the broadest sense of the word. A religious spirit will always remain fundamental to its orientation, with few exceptions. Its form always assumed a working-class hue. There was no specialization within our press. There was an almost total lack of periodicals devoted to literature, or to social issues, or to any branch of knowledge, skills, or industry. Even humorous periodicals could not survive on local soil. Indeed, we have newspapers entitled *Górnik* [The Miner], *Rolnik* [The Farmer], and so on, but none of them concentrates either on mining or farming, they are only published in mining or farming districts.[3] Only recently, special periodicals such as *Orędownik Językowy* [The Language Spokesman] by Rev. B. Góral, have made an appearance.[4] All this is very natural.

The mass of Polish immigrants arriving in America first needed information about what was happening in the world, in Poland, and in America; at times, they needed clarification of relations and events, as well as amusement and intellectual food for thought appropriate to their level. The mass of people, honestly and deeply religious, finding their initial support and organizational ties in parish relations and in Polish sanctuaries, needed organs that, above all, would respect their convictions. Finally, their intellectual level required the easiest and most appropriate language and treatment of issues, and sometimes even required avoidance of issues that were too complicated, subtle, or specialized.

For the first seventeen years (from the beginning of *Orzeł Biały* [The White Eagle] in 1870) we had only weeklies or periodicals issued less often than once a week. They were not at all characteristic of weeklies in the European sense of the word. Rather, they were dailies condensed into a weekly issue.

Such is the general character of the American Polish press. It should be added that our newspapers very often, and with very few exceptions, were, and continue to be, serious promoters of education and morality.

One of the traits of the American Polish press is its great capacity for change, variation, and mobility. In the thirty years from 1870 to 1900, about 120 periodicals were established, of which only forty-nine exist today [1905]. This is clear proof that many of these press organs are or were temporary in character.[5] They were established; folded; changed titles, editors, printers, location, often even views and politics. In other words, they changed like chameleons. What is the source of this flexibility and variability?

First, the development of Polish colonies, where these newspapers were established, was changeable and variable. Some of the colonies were established and developed artificially under the influence of speculators to develop them in order to increase the value of the lands. There were colonies (for example, Washington, Kraków, and Union in the state of Missouri) which, after a certain stage of development, declined and disappeared. Another reason for the variability of the American Polish press was the so-called American politics. By politics we mean here party fighting for control of the country and offices. With the aid of money, these political activities were conducted quite openly. Much money is absorbed by U.S. presidential elections every four years, and by state, county, and city elections every year or sometimes twice a year. A significant part of these funds is used for brochures, pamphlets, and propaganda in the press. American politicians are too "smart" not to know that in addition to Americans, Irish, and Germans, a substantial number of votes belong to citizens of Polish, Czech, Italian, Swedish, Slovak, and other origins, and the best means of influencing these people is through propaganda in newspapers printed in their own languages. Thus is created the source of profit for Polish periodicals and for newspapers of other nationalities; thus too, the eagernesss to establish numerous new little periodicals, lasting one, two, or three months, or in other words, for the duration of a political campaign. Sometimes bulletins established in this manner survive longer and even turn into periodicals of a more lasting nature, but this happens very rarely.

It is clear that the uncertain history of the many periodicals was not favorable to their material existence. The first years of every new paper are difficult until it gains wide acceptance. A reader, often already disillusioned, is reluctant to pay for the subscription up front. Others, who are less conscientious, do not even pay for the paper after receiving it. In general, a newly established periodical attempts to build circulation by sending a few thousand copies to any known address in the Polish settlements. Legally, whoever accepts three issues of a newspaper without returning them becomes a subscriber and is then obligated to pay further for the periodical, but from the law to its execution the road is very long. . . . So, the older periodicals, which are based on a more solid foundation send their copies only when they are paid for up front or give credit to permanent subscribers. Daily newspapers collect their fees on a weekly basis or rely on the American-style sales of single copies at newstands.

The unsteadiness of newspapers also has a negative infuence on the fate of American Polish editors. In the first years of development of our journalism they were sometimes paid $2 or $3 per week, either with or without meager board. Mr. Henryk Nagiel writes: "We ourselves know an editor of a weekly in New York who, having complained that such wages are insufficient, was advised to sell flowers on the streets during times when he was free from his editorial duties." Not too long ago, weekly wages from five to seven dollars were still not unusual, and only lately—since 1890—in periodicals having a more certain existence, has the wage scale begun to be set from fifteen to twenty dollars per week, and sometimes even higher (for editors of dailies and more affluent weeklies).

And, one of our readers may ask, what about the fate of the co-worker? The answer to this is simple: there can be no talk of co-workers, because we usually do not have them at all (an exception is found in the older dailies), except perhaps for freelance correspondents—or censors.

The format of our newspapers differs from the European format practiced in Poland. In general, we have adopted the American format as a model. The first page of the weekly or daily contains news, facts, gossip, and telegrams from Poland, Europe, and America. Whatever is the most sensational has one or, in the American style, two or even three headlines—and is placed on page one. This sensational news is sometimes illustrated with plates, which can be obtained here very easily and cheaply. Some perodicals give advertisements on the first page next to the text. In general, advertisements are not placed at the end of the newspaper as in European periodicals, but have the right to exist on almost every page. In this way, each page ending with advertisements constitutes a complete entity in itself, and articles are not continued from one page to another, which creates some difficulty in making up the columns. One of the principles of the format of an American newspaper is also that at least the most important articles begin at the top of the column. Information about the publication, its character, publishers, subscription rate, cost of advertisements, together with the address and other details, is rarely given on the first page near the masthead as in Europe. We inserted this—American style—on the left inside page (the second with four pages, the fourth with eight, and so on) in the first column at the top. Under this information most often the editorial section begins, containing editorials, statements expressing the editor's opinions, so called "paragraphs" (short, but if possible humorous and scathing notes and observations about current issues) and so on. In general, American periodicals carefully distinguish between the description of facts, whether in reporter's accounts or telegrams, and the editor's opinions about them, which are always prepared by editorial writers and located in a specially designated place within the publication. Polish American periodicals generally imitate the American press in this, but not always. However, let us go on to more about the format of the Polish newspaper. The third page is most often, but not always, dedicated to a novel; the last page, to a local chronicle. The personal imagination of the editor, and the needs of the moment, dictate many changes here.

What has been the value of our periodicals? It has been very diverse, depending on the editors, whose scale of talents is very broad. Some among them were complete illiterates, not distinguishing "z" from "rz"; but there were also people with university educations and genuine talent. Finally, we have self-taught people who through hard work and talent, have come to occupy important and respectable positions within the ranks of our editors. Periodicals edited by illiterates have been, it is clear, monstrosities of spelling, style, and sense, not to mention their ignorance and squabbling. The more talented and more honest journalists have edited newspapers not at all inferior to the serious Polish organs in Europe.

To this day, periodicals of one kind and another grow side by side like cockle and wheat, like roses and thistle; nevertheless; generally speaking, with every passing day we have more and more decent, moderate, and intelligent periodicals.

In fact, one thing we can be reproached for is an inclination greater than anywhere in Poland to fight, to storm and rave, as well as having greater polemic sharpness and fierceness, which at times reverts to personal innuendo and indecency. This lack of moderation often occurs among us—and almost everywhere, although in varying degrees. But blood is not water, especially young blood. It boils and bubbles over in a young society. Youth must have its fling, and our society is still young; its relations are neither settled nor stabilized. Anyway, those who are familiar with the condition of our press under the three partitions of Poland know that frequently fighting was not conducted in kid gloves, especially during the time of intermingling of social, political, and academic currents.

At any rate, in this area we see constant progress and improvement. And here the better pens are slowly leaving the wild fighting and the indecent behavior to the journalistic brawlers, whom no one and nothing is capable of changing. However, the latter, who are constantly and stubbornly attracted to mud, have always been condemned by the majority of public opinion.

This is the way literature presents itself in general—but how does the readership look here in America? What is the attitude of the Polish people towards the press here in America? Do they read, and if so how much? These questions are worth answering.

The Polish people from Silesia stand among the most highly educated. It is these people, long forgotten in Poland, upon whom no one relied; whom no one helped in any way; and to whom no one gave any thought. The lowest standing were the Poles of Galicia, who shouted most about the need for education of the people, but for whom, clearly, not much was actually done.[6]

To vindicate Galicia from this reproach it could be said that these immigrants were recruited from the most underprivileged masses, who travelled beyond the sea because they could not support themselves on their ancestral soil. It was a different matter in Silesia. Immigrants from there, who usually left under the pressure of the *kulturkampf*, came from among the most nationally conscious spheres. The same could be said about the Congress Kingdom, which furnished many craftsmen and urban workers, but relatively few peasants for America.

While speaking about readers of newspapers, we should state that the Polish population in America reads far more than that of the Old Country. If one can judge by the quantity of periodicals that are circulated there, no comparison can even be made. The Polish dailies in Poland are actually circulated only among the intellectuals and nowhere in Poznań province.

In Galicia the people read only working-class papers; the dailies are only for the intelligentsia and the enlightened class of craftsmen. There is nothing to be said about the Congress Kingdom. Here in America, the Polish population supports six dailies, which have about 60,000 readers in total, not to mention the weeklies, of which about thirty are regularly published and supported. The number of those who read Polish newspapers will again be three of four times greater.

Generally speaking, this is a quite significant percentage, of which our countrymen in the homeland cannot boast. We cannot, therefore, complain so much about this. On the contrary, in many respects the intelligentsia in Poland, working on the education of the population and on journalism, could learn a number of things from us, despite the fact that any mention of us elicits from them only a scornful smile.

In the first decade, from 1863 to 1873, which Mr. Henryk Nagiel calls the beginning era of the Polish press, four periodicals were established, of which none has survived to the present, with the possible exception of *Pielgrzym* [Pilgrim], the forefather of *Gazeta Katolicka* [The Catholilc Gazette].

In the second decade, from 1873 to 1883, which Mr. Nagiel called the "strengthening period" of the Polish press in America, eight newspapers were established, of which four still exist today.

In the third decade, from 1883 to 1893, which we shall call the "active era" or rather the "era of exuberant development" of the press, approximately sixty new periodicals were founded in addition to those already in existence. Of these, eighteen have lasted to this day, and the rest sooner or later folded. During this era, the years 1887 and 1892 distinguished themselves as being especially productive. Twelve new newspapers were published in 1887 and as many as eighteen in 1892! This later year exceeds all others regarding the development of the press.

From 1893 to 1900, in the period called the "era of maturity" of the Polish press in America, thirty-eight new periodicals were established, of which twenty-seven still exist, in addition to existing ones.

So from 1863 to 1900 there was a total of 121 Polish newspapers established in America, of which forty-nine still exist [1905].

From the summit of a "bird's-eye" view, let us descend to earth to compare the history of individual newspapers in chronological order.

THE FIRST POLISH PERIODICAL IN AMERICA: *ECHO Z POLSKI* [ECHO FROM POLAND][7]

The first Polish-language periodical ever published in America was the very small *Echo z Polski*, whose first issue appeared on June 1, 1863, in New York. It was the organ of the Polish political immigrants, and for this reason it was distinct in nature from all the other Polish periodicals that emerged later in America.

It is a well-known fact that Polish political immigrants, no matter how poor or how small in number, could not do without their own press, the nature of which depended upon local political and legal conditions. The reasons for this are evident and easy to surmise. The mass of our immigrants, whether after 1831 or after 1863, comprised intelligent or at least semi-intelligent people who were taken up with the cause, agitated by the conflict. They were angry, and on the one hand seeking, within the party arguments, explanations for the hopeless riddle and defeat that forced them to leave their homeland, usually never to return; and, on the other hand, they needed, among foreigners, a means of communication with each other or even quarreling. From 1830 to 1870, and even in recent years, the emigré press in France, Belgium, England, and even in Germany and Italy, served as a means of communication; a means for stating a certain amount of more or less bitter truths; a means of propaganda for their ideas; and a place for their battles. These last decades produced a whole series of periodicals, which at the time inflamed minds, but which today are forgotten.

The historiography of this European emigré press does not concern us, especially that portion dedicated to political battles on a broader scale and not based on "business" grounds, as is said here in America. Many of these operations were lucrative, but were supported in their goals through the contributions of individuals, associations, and organizations. We should only point out that the organ of the emigré press, which first appeared in America through the endeavors and energy of a few represen-

tatives of immigration following 1831, 1848, and 1862, has this characteristic.

Echo z Polski was mainly dedicated to issues of the [January 1863]
insurrection. It took into account local matters only insofar as they related
to the issue of fighting in the homeland. Its only objective was political
agitation.

The first issue of this little periodical was printed at the print shop of
Schriftgiesser and Picker at 75 & 77 Nassau Street in New York. Schriftgiesser was a Polish Jew who had emigrated from Poland for political reasons. It is rumored that he was also largely responsible for establishing the
print shop and the newspaper. A group of emigrés were part of the enterprise, and R. J. Jaworowski was listed as editor. Unfortunately, we were
not able to get any other information about him. The address of the editorial office was 926 Broadway.[8]

Echo z Polski was a small periodical with the format of a large quarto
paper with four pages; the paper was absorbent and the print not outstand-
ingly good. In the masthead we see the coats of arms of Poland and
Lithuania, the inscriptions "Polonia," "Lithuania," and "Ruthenia"; at the
bottom, an anchor; and above, banners and the inscriptions *Wolność*
[Freedom], *Równość* [Equality], and *Niepodległość* [Independence] and
the beaming star of hope. It is easy to understand this hope; it was 1863.
The slogan of the periodical, placed next to the masthead, states as follows: "*Znaj najprzód ojczyste sprawy—i jej klęski i jej sławy*" ["First, you
should know your ancestral history—both its defeats and its glories"].

Echo z Polski, at first appeared three times each month, on the 1st, 10th,
and 20th days of the month. Beginning with the seventh issue, that is, after
two months, it began to appear on a weekly basis. The quarterly subscription cost was $1.00 (with mailing $1.25), and later the fee was increased.

In the beginning our little periodical still lacked [Polish] accent type.
Political events in Poland forced it to be printed before the "sculptor"
could complete the accents for it. For this reason, the first and second
issues look quite strange. Only the third issue is printed with accents. An
introductory comment "To the Reader" in the second issue states as follows: "Due to the failure of the sculptor, who is making the letters, we are
still forced to come out with inappropriate orthography and so 'a' is often
used in place of 'an,' 'e' in place of 'en,' and so on; we expect to have the
letters ready for the next issue." And, in fact, they had them.

The nature of *Echo* was strictly political. Its goal was to generate Polish
agitation in the United States in order to support the Insurrection of 1863.

In general, as can be seen from *Echo*, our cause in 1863 won much sympathy from the Americans. Generous contributions for the insurgents were flowing in from Americans everywhere. Committees were formed to aid the uprising, and meetings were held. Therefore, little else could be found in *Echo* about anything but the heroic struggle of the Polish nation against Russia.

For this reason, then, *Echo z Polski* is very interesting not only as an example of the earliest Polish press in America. It also reveals to us the mysteries of the earliest immigrants in America and indicates support for the Polish cause that manifested itself in this era in the United States, undoubtedly through the efforts of Polish emigrés.

The accounts of donations for the 1863 Insurrection are in themselves a measure of the vitality of both this movement and the Polish political emigration at the time. So we read in the second issue of *Echo* that $350 was presented from the committee in St. Louis, Missouri (Colonel Szynkowski belonged to that committee); $21 from the committee in Grand Rapids, Michigan (where there were already Poles to be found); and $50 from Mr. Mateusz Potocki (place of residence not stated). We are omitting smaller contributions. But then in the seventh issue we see a receipt from the Central Polish Society on the shores of the Pacific Ocean, in San Francisco, for the sum of $6,000, which was sent for the benefit of the homeland, and a receipt from the Polish Committee in Cincinnati for the sum of $200. In general, as far as we know from other sources, quite a few thousand dollars were collected for the cause of the uprising in Poland at this time. Whether this money reached Poland, or in what manner, is not exactly known to us.

Echo z Polski also presents an exact picture of the nature of the Polish cause. In the third issue we find a report from a meeting held in San Francisco "to show sympathy for the Polish cause," where Captain Piotrowski and W. Hamil spoke. Further, we find out that on June 1 in West Hoboken, New Jersey, a meeting of English ladies, friends of Poland, was held, at which a permanent committee of ladies was chosen under the leadership of Mrs. J. Robins. Again, on June 3, a meeting organized by the "Ladies Polish Aid Society" under president Mrs. Walter Cook was held at the Cooper Institute [in New York city]. On July 5 in Pythagoras Hall in New York, Poles of the "Mosaic faith" organized a patriotic meeting, and at about the same time in Chicago, a Czech ball was held to raise funds for the Polish cause. In the fifth issue of *Echo z Polski* we read an appeal of the Central Polish Committee to the United States. The committee comprises Dr. Mackiewicz (an exile from 1848 who died in New York in 1894) aw president; Mr. Gacek as secretary; R. J. Jaworowski (editor of *Echo*) as secretary correspondent; and W. Piotrowski as treasurer.

The language of the periodical is not bad, although grammatical and stylistic errors occurred here and there.

National defeats in Poland depressed spirits everywhere and took away from our periodical its reason for existence. *Echo* folded in April 1865.[9] From then until 1870, it seems there was no other Polish periodical in America. Some have mentioned two periodicals entitled *Światło* [The Light] and *Gazeta Nowojorska* [The New York Gazette], which were supposed to have been published in New York during this period. Thus far, this is speculation, unsupported by any authentic proof.

ORZEŁ POLSKI [THE POLISH EAGLE] OF MISSOURI

After the disappearance of *Echo* in 1865, silence reigned in Polish communities for a few years. Schriffgiesser, the publisher, or perhaps only the printer, of *Echo*, moved his print shop all the way to the state of Missouri, and there in 1867 in Washington, Franklin County, he printed one of the oldest Polish publications in America, the constitution of the Society of *Gmina Polska* [Polish Commune] in Chicago.[10]

In 1870, a new Polish newspaper, *Orzeł Polski*,[11] appeared in Washington. With this periodical began the systematic development of Polish journalism in America.

The character of *Orzeł* clearly differed from that of the *Echo*. It did not have political abstractions as its goal; it did not endeavor to be the fighting organ of the intelligentsia. It wanted to accommodate the needs of working-class readers. It was based on real life conditions and sought to make the newspaper a business concern, not only by making ends meet, but eventually by returning certain profits.

Orzeł Polski from Franklin County, Washington (where there were already three Polish settlements), was then the prototype of the prevailing character of Polish newspapers in America. *Orzeł Polski* emerged mainly through the effort of Rev. Matauszek, a Polish Jesuit.[12] The Resurrectionist Fathers from Texas supplied *Orzeł* with their correspondence, attested to by a letter from Rev. Bakanowski dated March 21, 1870.

The first issue appeared on February 22, 1870. From it we learn that *Orzeł* came out every two weeks and that an annual subscription cost $3.00. The format of the periodical was somewhat larger than *Echo z Polski*. Next to the title can be found two versified mottos. One is:

Pamiętaj droga Polsko! że jedności
Ci trzeba;—przez nią osiągniesz nadzieję.
Będziesz posiadała cnotę miłości,
Tem nowe w narodzie utworzysz dzieje.

Remember, dear Poland, that unity it necessary for you;
Through it you shall obtain hope.
You shall possess the virtue of love,
You shall create a new history for the people.

The second poem is as follows:

Bronić zawsze prawdę,
Potępiać zdrożności,
Żadną taić wadę,
Te to Orła dążności.

Always defend the truth,
Always denounce wickedness,
Conceal no fault,
These are the aspirations of the eagle.

As we see, the sentiments are very beautiful, but the rhymes are awkward. In general, the literary value of *Orzeł Biały* [The White Eagle] was far from splendid, and even poor, with many stylistic errors and spelling mistakes occurring. On account of the infantile words, it was difficult to understand the thought. However, it distinguished itself favorable from *Echo z Polski* in working-class form and content. It had a large run and featured regularly some kind of novel; next to that is some kind of moral dissertation, then news, correspondence, anecdotes, and poems. All this interested the reader, relating to him incidents of his times and locality.

Immediately after the first issue of *Orzeł Biały* was published, there was a word from the editorial office criticizing bravely, but lamely, the New York *Echo,* which had not been published for the past five years. It did not make mention of any other newspapers published after *Echo,* from which it maybe deduced that there were none at all.

In the first issues of *Orzeł* there is no publisher or editor listed. However, we know that the periodical was founded by Rev. Aleksander Matauszek, a Jesuit, who had the first Polish type made in St. Louis, Missouri; initially it was edited by a Mr. Aleksander Szczepankiewicz, a former priest, under the pseudonym of Doctor Sacconi (he was born in the Duchy of Poznań in 1840). In the eighth issue he listed himself as the publisher. He was an educated person, but a poor writer. So, after *Orzeł Polski* had existed for two years, Dr. S. disappeared from the scene of Polish

journalism in America and did not return to it any more. Dr. A. Sacconi
went on to live and practice medicine in Pine Bluff, Arkansas.

With the tenth issue it moved from Washington, Missouri, to the neighboring settlement of St. Gertrude, where at that time a small colony from
Silesia was located. Before the move, the enterprising publisher of Orzeł
officially acquired a post office for St. Gertrude and had the name changed
to the more patriotic "Kraków." This name exists to this day, although the
Germans objected. Together with a change of location, Mr. Ignacy
Wendziński, a typical figure of Polish journalism, appeared as assistant
editor in the columns of Orzeł.[13]

With the eleventh issue, Orzeł began to come out every week and therefore increased its subscription rate to $4.00 annually. However, with the
twelfth issue of the second year, Wendziński left Orzeł, and its publisher
immediately made a few uncomplimentary statements (a custom often
practiced here in America). . . . In issue 40 we read that Orzeł had as many
as (!) 297 subscribers, and for this reason the subscription rate was
increased to $6.00. In issue thirty-five of the first year, A. Przybylski was
listed as the owner of the newspaper (was this not still one more name for
Sacconi?). In the second year Orzeł moved to the neighboring town of
Union, also in Franklin County. Here the publisher intended to publish
Czytelnia Polska [The Polish Reading Room], a bi-weekly supplement to
Orzeł dedicated to literary matters and fiction. However, he explained that
if he did not get sixty-three subscribers at the start, this Czytelnia would
not be published. In fact, it did not happen. On the other hand, Orzeł
began to appear twice a week.

And so, slowly and with difficulty, the publishing of Orzeł dragged on
and even began its third year, when suddenly it was discontinued on January 29, 1872. The following week the print shop of Orzeł burned down.
After this catastrophe, it was not published throughout the month of February.

It was resurrected on March 4, 1872. The publisher did not cease battling the fates that persecuted him. With pride he pointed to the fact that
after such a defeat he was capable of publishing a new issue of Orzeł.
Finally, with bitterness, he stressed that it was a difficult time for Orzeł,
since two periodicals were to appear that could become serious competition. Those were Swoboda [(Freedom] in New York and Pielgrzym [The
Pilgrim] in Washington, Missouri. Orzeł finally folded later in 1872.

The two-year battle by the primogenitor of our press with the indiffer-
ence of the contemporary reading public presented a very interesting tragi-

comedy. This battle could be observed in every issue of the newspaper. And this is how Mr. Ignacy Wendziński, a veteran of Polish journalism in America, described to us the contemporary environment of the editorial office: "When W. arrived at St. Gertrude (later Kraków), the editorial and printing staff comprised Dr. Sacconi, his wife—an American typesetter. The difficulties were tremendous, there was little profit, much work, and the salaries were meager." Wendziński, as the editor, was also the correspondent and the typesetter; however, Robert Bernard Zaborowski helped him with typesetting. Zaborowski was born in 1852 in Róg in Pomorze and died in Winona in 1905. Many a time Wendziński would deliver newspapers in a farmer's wagon to the post office of the nearest city of Washington, Missouri. At the time, St. Gertrude included hardly a dozen houses and no one even dreamed of sidewalks, much less of any kind of comforts. The editorial office, theprint shop of *Orzeł Polski,* and its entire staff, not excluding Dr. Sacconi, was located in an old farmer's log house. *Orzeł* is the great-grandfather of the current *Gazeta Katolicka* [Catholic Gazette].

PIELGRZYM [THE PILGRIM]

GAZETA POLSKA KATOLICKA [THE POLISH CATHOLIC GAZETTTE]

The first issue of the weekly periodical of *Pielgrzym,* which was the forefather of the current *Gazeta Katolicka* from Chicago, appeared on March 29, 1872. This occurred a few weeks after the rebirth of *Orzeł Polski* from the ashes of the fire, and not in Washington, Missouri, as had been announced, but in Union, Missouri, the same place as *Orzeł Polski*—and in the same print shop. This happened due to a compromise between Dr. Sacconi, the publisher of *Orzeł,* and Jan Barzyński, the publisher of the new *Pielgrzym.* Instead of competing with each other, they decided to unite. They formed a partnership.

However, this did not last long. In the eighth issue of *Pielgrzym* (on May 17, 1872) we already read an announcement that Dr. Sacconi had not published his *Orzeł* since May 6, 1872, and that he was guilty of various corrupt practices. We discover in the tenth issue of *Pielgrzym* that half of the print shop, which was the property of Sacconi, had been sold at a public auction and that the partnership was dissolved.

That is how *Orzeł Polski* ceased to exist, and how its successor *Pielgrzym* remained. Before we go on to the history of this periodical, let us get acquainted with its publisher and editor, Jan Barzyński.

Barzyński, the brother of Rev. Wincenty, the famous Resurrectionist from Chicago, was born in 1848 in Tomaszów Lubelski in the Congress Kingdom and at twenty-two, he arrived in Texas in May 1870, having been brought over by Rev. Wincenty. Active, energetic, and intelligent, he worked much on his own after his arrival in America and then threw himself into journalism. Already in 1871 we see him on the list of agents of *Orzeł Polski*, and in 1872, with the help of the Reverend Father Matauszek, a priest from Silesia and the pastor in Kraków and Clever Bottom, Missouri, he founded *Pielgrzym*. Jan Barzyński wrote from Union, Franklin County, on June 10, 1872, to Rev. Wincenty and Rev. Żwiardowski, who continue to help me. . . ." And Rev. Wincenty wrote to Rev. Kajsiewicz on March 2, 1872: "Because of my brother and *Pielgrzym*, Rev. Aleksander Matauszek, a Jesuit, writes me a very joyful letter that the Resurrectionists will at last be united with the Jesuits in the field of Polish journalism." From Union, where Jan Barzyński initially published this periodical, he moved to Detroit and then to Chicago. Here he lasted until 1880 in the unrewarding journalistic field at *Gazeta Polska Katolicka*, the successor to *Pielgrzym*. In February of that same year, he moved to St. Paul, Nebraska, having yielded his position to Smulski. There he organized Polish colonies. After a certain time he returned to Chicago, but did not take up journalism again, working in business instead. He died in April 1886.

He was one of the most courageous figures in the early dawn of our journalism. *Pielgrzym*, although a small periodical, was full of information; its language was much better than *Orzeł Polski*, and the content was a hundred times more robust and more interesting. Truthfully, we have already seen in the columns of *Orzeł* the correspondence and articles, news and polemics that mirrored the life of the early Polish communities in New York, Chicago, Milwaukee and other cities, but they occurred there, from time to time, almost accidentally. As to *Pielgrzym*, there was hardly any issue without articles distinctly illustrating the contemporary life of the Polish immigration in the United States at that time. In a letter to Rev. Kajsiewcz, Mr. Jan Barzyński expressed the tendencies of his periodical in the following manner: "Here we shall build such a Poland: a Pole who is born on American soil will never be a European Pole; but we want him to believe in a Catholic manner, let him speak Polish, let him know the tradition and history of Poland—and as far as the rest, let him be a Yankee!" (letter dated June 10, 1872). In the same letter he indicated that he was also printing the English newspaper *Progress*. This was an official organ undertaken for advertisements and judicial employment notices for the local county. This class of people are considered intelligent, but some bums in America point fingers at *Pielgrzym* and accuse it of being a Jesuit paper.

From the very beginning *Pielgrzym* hung out its Catholic banner in spite of *Echo* and *Orzeł,* which did not worry much about religious issues. As can even be seen from its name, *Gazeta Katolicka* has remained faithful to this banner to this day.

In 1874 a congress was held in Detroit that moved *Pielgrzym*, after a few months of suspension, from insignificant Union, Missouri, to Detroit. Here it was first published on September 15, 1874, under the new name of *Gazeta Polska Katolicka*, whose history we shall continue to describe later.

SWOBODA OF NEW YORK

And now we go on to the New York *Swoboda,* which was founded almost simultaneously with *Pielgrzym* in March, 1872. It was preceded by a prospectus published on February 3, 1872, which was printed with type from F. Tomicki's print shop located at 10 William Street in New York. The prospectus announced that the new periodical would be the organ of *Zjednoczenie Polaków* [The Alliance of Poles], a local organization; the publisher would be F. Tomicki; the editor would be Julian Drozdowski. The following promised their collaboration: J. Horain, Dr. Żółtowski, Dr. Maćkiewicz—and other distinguished representatives of New York Polonia.

The format of *Swoboda* was not extensive; the language was quite proper; besides treating general matters, the newspaper also dealt extensively with local issues. With the third issue, Count Piotr Wodzicki became the editor. He had come to America shortly before this and after [his association with *Swoboda*] did not appear on the journalistic scene again. With the twenty-second issue, Julian Drozdowski became editor. *Swoboda* received many letters from Polish colonies in Chicago, Milwaukee, and other areas and quite clearly reflected life in our settlements in America.

After 30 or 40 issues it ceased publication in 1873.

GAZETA POLSKA IN CHICAGO[14]

W. Dyniewicz's *Gazeta Polska* was the first organ of the Polish press that ever appeared in Chicago. Prior to 1870, there existed only a Polish bookstore, whose successive owners were A. Sherman, P. Kiołbassa, and W. Dyniewicz.[15] The latter began to publish a weekly that still exists. After that time, Chicago became the main center of Polish journalism in the United States.

The first issue of *Gazeta Polska* appeared on October 23, 1873, but before we concentrate on *Gazeta*, a word should be devoted to its publisher and creator, Władisław Dyniewicz. Born in 1843 in Miłosław in the Grand Duchy of Poznań, Mr. Dyniewicz received his elementary education in Poland and worked as an apprentice in a machine factory. He came to America in 1866 and first earned a living in a sugar mill in the state of Illinois. In 1867 he went to Chicago and was employed there as a foreman in a locomotive factory. Despite this, something always drew him towards journalism. When we see the first newspapers in the state of Missouri, Mr. Dyniewicz is their agent. In 1872 he purchased a Polish bookstore on Bradley Street from Mr. Kiołbassa, and the following year established a print shop where he intended to print Polish books. Finally, in October, he founded the newspaper.

Mr. Dyniewicz has been less the editor than the actual publisher. He and his entire family worked hard; for this reason he has quite a substantial fortune today. In general, Mr. Dyniewicz is a genuine American businessman and an outstanding example of what hard work can achieve. His newspaper, which began with a few hundred subscribers, today has increased to a few thousand subscribers who have "paid up front."

During its first year the editor of *Gazeta Polska* was Ignacy Wendziński. Then he became the publisher. The newspaper was edited again by Dyniewicz himself and then by his son, Kazimierz. For long years, the editor of *"Dyniewiczówka"* [literally, "Dyniewicz's little tabloid," a popular name for *Gazeta Polska*] was Wiktor Karłowski, an insurgent from [The Insurrection of] 1863.[16]

Gazeta Polska distinguishes itself from all its companions by its extensive format. For this reason it was sometimes called *"Żaglówką"* [sailboat] in the fervor of polemic battles.

Dyniewicz's other publishing activities are also worthy of close attention. His catalogue of publications contained about 400 individual books, of which hundreds of thousands of copies were disseminated. These included novels, educational textbooks, dictionaries, collections of songs and anecdotes, comedies, lives of the saints, dream books—and everything that the human soul could desire. It is true that reprints prevail among his offerings and that he has not inquired about anyone's authorship or publication rights. It is also true that the value of some of the older publications especially were printed, so to speak, "by hobnail"—but with all these negative points one important fact predominates: during the existence of Dyniewicz's print shop hundreds of thousands of Polish volumes and smaller books, brochures and booklets were issued for the American Polish people who had arrived from the Old Country clouded with ignorance. These publications brought light to these people. In order to indicate the extent of the dissemination of his books, it suffices to say, for example, that by 1894 *Podręcznik polsko-angielski* [The Polish-English Handbook] sold about 25,000 copies in six editions.

GAZETA KATOLICKA OF CHICAGO

The second periodical that appeared in Chicago was *Gazeta Katolicka*, which still exists to this day. We already know that it was the successor to *Pielgrzym* and initially was published in Detroit on September 15, 1874, as *Gazeta Polska Katolicka*. As of January 1, 1875, it became the property of the Polish Literary Society, whose president was Rev. Gieryk.[17]

On April 15, 1875, *Gazeta Polska Katolicka* moved to Chicago. The publishing company consisted of a few priests, J. Barzyński, the former publisher of *Pielgrzym* and later Ladislaus Smulski and his son, Jan, the current spokesman of the city of Chicago. From the time of its move to Chicago until 1880 and even later, *Gazeta Katolicka* was the constant champion and defender of the conservative and Catholic principles of the Polish population in America. At that time, the battle was fierce, and was waged with great fervor on both sides, especially in Chicago. *Gazeta Polska Katolicka* took the lead in the vocal journalistic choir of the time. It was always edited with appreciable journalistic talent. Its editors, Jan Barzyński and later Władisław Smulski, were both talented individuals, with powers of no slight measure.

In early 1880, Jan Barzyński resigned the editorshop of *Gazeta Polska Katolicka*, apparently disillusioned by the fruitless battle, and the periodical then came entirely under the editorship of Władisław Smulski, who had been its contributor since 1876. About the same time (after May 20, 1880) the title of the periodical was changed to *Gazeta Katolicka*. In 1884 the Polish Literary Society ceased to exist, and on January 3, 1884, *Gazeta Katolicka* became the property of L. Smulski.

Władisław Smulski, born in 1836 in Gniewkowo, completed his high school education in Trzemeszno and then became an official in the Old Country. He came to America in 1868 and took up journalism for the first time when he edited Dyniewicz's *Gazeta Polska Katolicka*. Still, before returning to Chicago, he had become known through his humorous *"Listy z księżyca"* ["Letters from the Moon"], which immediately revealed him as a courageous and sharp-tongued polemicist. He soon became a contributor and then the editor and publisher of *Gazeta*. This child of his cost him great toil and difficulties. However, he surmounted them all with courage and seriousness and in this manner ensured the existence of the newspaper.

PRZYJACIEL LUDU [FRIEND OF THE PEOPLE]

In 1876 still another newspaper appeared in Chicago. It was very distinctive and active, and left behind outstanding traces in the life of our Polonia. It was *Przyjaciel Ludu* of I. Wendziński and I. Rudnicki.

Ignacy Wendziński, who for seven years was the soul of *Przyjaciel Ludu*, was born on January 23, 1828, in Bydgoszcz in the Poznań region. He was educated in Mogilno, then attended high school and a teaching college in Trzemeszno. In 1846-48 he took an active part in the national movement and belonged to a company of Trzemeszno riflemen. In battle he was taken prisoner and was for some time imprisoned in Poznań and Kistrzyn, after which, due to a general amnesty, he returned to school. Next, he was a teacher and tradesman. After 1863, as a participant in the national insurrection, he lost much financially, and in January 1870, he came to America. From New York he went to Missouri (after purchasing a train ticket with friends' contributions)—and remained with *Orzeł Polski* for about a year. Windziński came to Chicago after the memorable Chicago fire in 1872. Here he taught at the first Polish parish of St. Stanislaus Kostka, then he edited W. Dyniewicz's *Gazeta Polska* for a year, and thereafter he administered a school at the parish of St. Adalbert. Finally, in 1876, he began publishing *Przyjaciel Ludu* with Rudnicki, who provided the capital (malicious people say that old Rudnicki could count publishing expenses on a stick!—anyway this must be a great exaggeration).

Przyjaciel appeared for the first time in May 1876 in Chicago and immediately made a great impression. It was entirely different in both format and content from the other Polish newspapers. We mentioned above that our press in America does not have literary social organs; however, *Przyjaciel Ludu*, in the first year of its existence, aspired to be just such an organ.

It had the form of a daily, but appeared in monthly installments, clearly imitating the so-called "magazines." Each installment cost 25 cents. It was

a popular literary monthly for only ten months. Already in the final installments of 1876, we see a certain note of disillusionment. The people
praised *Przyjaciel*, but they paid little for it. Capital was lacking and the
partners came to the conclusion that *Przyjaciel Ludu* should be modified.

They changed the monthly to a weekly and returned to the informational
type of publication modelled on other Polish periodicals that had already
been published in America prior to and concurrently with *Przyjaciel Ludu*.

From 1877 *Przyjaciel Ludu* took a stand parallel to that of Dyniewicz`s
Gazeta Polska and that of Barzyński and Smulski's *Gazeta Polska
Katolicka*. Within this strategic triangle, local and general homeric battles
among parties, parishes, colonizers, and so on, were played out. *Przyjaciel*
took one side and then the other, but it generally remained on the side of
the liberals.

In May 1879 *Przyjaciel Ludu* moved to Milwaukee, apparently for
financial reasons. *Przyjaciel Ludu* spent its fifth year (from May 1880 to
May 1881) entirely in Milwaukee, and this was the most successful year in
its history. It was specifically during this time that the nucleus of the Polish National Alliance was formed, next to the already-existing [Polish
Roman Catholic] Union. Quite a violent party squabble ensued, especially
in Chicago. Although removed somewhat on the sidelines in Milwaukee,
Przyjaciel Ludu still took an active part in this battle. Every now and then
Wendziński came to meetings in Chicago, took the floor, spoke at celebrations, and worked. This was the culmination of his activity; thereafter the
level of *Przyjaciel Ludu* began to slowly decline.

To add to the financial setbacks, a war broke out between the two partners Wendziński and Rudnicki. As a result, in the middle of 1880 the
name of J. Rudnicki disappeared from the newspaper, and everything
appeared solely under Wendziński's aegis. But fortune travels in a circle:
hardly a few weeks passed, before Wendziński disappeared, and Rudnicki
was back on top. Such are the vicissitudes of life. Explanations were given
first by one, then the other, depending on which of them was in possession
of the print shop and the power; explanations were given about the wrong-
doings of each of them, to whom the newspaper really belonged, and so
on. This was a topic for an operetta or a tragic-comedy! Yet, this was not
enough. One of the partners, not able to cope with the other, sought
recourse in courts. A Polish lawyer, Mr. Borchardt, became the administrator, and he solemnly announced that from that date, subscriptions were
only to be paid to him and not to anyone else. However, his ruling did not
last long either. Rudnicki won the case, took over the newspaper, and pro-

ceeded to give a detailed account in the May 25, 1881, issue of the history of the civil war waged for *Przyjaciel Ludu*.

This, however, was not the conclusion of the fatal business history of this newspaper. Before long, *Przyjaciel Ludu* failed again, while edited by Rudnicki. This occurred because of the betrayal of friends who conducted Rudnicki's case against Wendziński. Having won the case for him, they took away the print shop in payment of legal fees. We learned about this a year later from the second issue of the sixth volume of the newspaper, which appeared, not in Milwaukee, but in Chicago on October 2, 1882. It seems that Rudnicki, ruined by his own defenders, was not discouraged but instead fought, made an effort, and worked and after a year effected the rebirth of *Przyjaciel* at West 18th Street in Chicago in the vincinity of St. Adalbert's parish, popularly known to its residents as "Wojciechowo."

He was conscientious to the extent that he began again with the sixth volume, although he had already published a few issues for that year in 1881. Nevertheless, *Przyjaciel Ludu* did not regain its splendor in Chicago; on the contrary, it went downhill. Despite this, it somehow limped along until the beginning of 1884 and only then disappeared from the horizon forever.

ZIEMIANIN [THE GENTLEMAN-FARMER] OF CHICAGO

This periodical dedicated to farms and rural issues was published for two or three months in 1874 by Dyniewicz's printshop. Władisław Smulski managed it at his own risk. It failed for lack of support.

KURYER NOWOJORSKI [THE NEW YORK COURIER]

Kuryer Nowojorski was founded in mid-1876. Initially, the publisher and editor was A. Zadębowski. Before long, *Kuryer* was moved from New York to nearby Brooklyn, where it folded shortly thereafter. It was resucitated when a partnership was formed, led by Janicki and Zieliński, shoemakers by trade, and Odasz, a tailor. *Kuryer*, thus revived, appeared on December 1, 1876 and, with various changes, existed until 1878. Under the administration of the shoemaker-tailor partnership, the editor was Edward Kulikowski, an enlightened man and an emigré from [The Insurrection ending in] 1831. On March 9, 1878, due to poverty and disillusionment, he poisoned himself in a Brooklyn park. Then Zbigniew Brodowski decided to revive *Kuryer*, but his endeavors did not bring lasting results.[18] Brodowski went to San Francisco and was succeeded at *Kuryer* by Count Ledóchowski, who soon disappeared from the journalistic scene. We later find him in the 1888 election campaign in New York, and later holding the office of consul of the United States. *Kuryer Nowojorski* (still being published in Brooklyn) folded at the end of 1878.

OGNIWO [THE LINK] OF BROOKLYN, NEW YORK

Ogniwo was founded in June of 1879 to replace *Kuryer*. The publisher was T. Janicki and the editor was Stanisław Artwiński, a young lawyer from Galicia. After Artwiński resigned, *Ogniwo* folded in 1881.

ZGODA [HARMONY][19]

After the liquidation of *Ogniwo* in 1881, New York acquired a new publication, *Zgoda*, the organ of the Polish National Alliance which was being formed at that time. This new publication was founded by a group of stockholders who took over the former *Ogniwo* print shop. The first issue of *Zgoda* appeared on November 23, 1881. The editor was Mr. Odrowąż, a man of broad intellectual horizons, who later died of hunger. His assistant was S. Artwiński. Stanisław Szwajkart, the current editor of *Dziennik Chicagoski*, collaborated with the others at *Zgoda*[20] at that time.

After a year, the administration of the PNA (Kucera and Wendziński) relocated *Zgoda* from New York to Milwaukee.[21] There, in early 1883, Wendziński took over the editorship. Later *Zgoda* permanently moved to Chicago. The following worked on it: Zbigniew Brodowski, Nicki, F. H. Jabłoński,[22] Stefan Barszczewski, and Tomasz Siemiradzki.

Zbigniew [Samuel] Edmund Brodowski, a long time editor of *Zgoda*, was born in 1852 in Poznań, studied in Śrem and then at the universities in Leipzig and Wrocław. He came to America in 1876 and immediately began to consider journalistic work. For a short time he edited *Kuryer Nowojorski* and wrote letters to other newspapers. Later the same year, 1876, he left for San Francisco, where he worked hard for a living. In 1884 he returned to Chicago. He edited *Gazeta Chicagoska*, and then *Zgoda* from 1884 to 1889. During the era of the heaviest party battles, Brodowski was the soul of *Zgoda*. During his tenure, the Alliance began to grow in numbers and strength. After 1896, Brodowski served as a consul of the United States in Germany, where he died in 1901.

GAZETA CHICAGOSKA [THE CHICAGO GAZETTE]

This newspaper was published by Klupp beginning in 1885. Its first editor was Z. Brodowski, and later it was M. I. Sadowski. Klupp, a common clerk, made it to the top in America through cleverness and was on the road to fortune. He conducted a land office and waged an obstinate battle with other colonizers. This very circumstance prompted him to found *Gazeta*. The newspaper was successful, but in the second half of 1885 Klupp died and the entire business enterprise, which had been maintained by his energy, tumbled to ruins, taking *Gazeta* with it. *Gazeta Chicagoska* introduced two new journalistic powers into American Polonia: Brodowski and Sadowski. *Gazeta Chicagoska* again appeared in 1901, under the editorship of F. Danisch, but soon disappeared from the scene.

Michał Józef Sadowski (Pankiewicz) was born in Warsaw on June 22, 1857. After completing high school he entered Warsaw University, studying first medicine and then law. In 1881 he left for America. At first he edited *Gazeta Chicagoska*, then consecutively *Kuryer Chicagoski* (1887), *Polak w Ameryce* (1888), and *Echo* (1888-1891). Thereafter he was the editor of *Dziennik Narodowy* until his death in April 1900. He was the secretary general of the PNA and also published the humorous periodical *Kukuryku* [Cock-a-doodle-do].

GAZETA NARODOWA [THE NATIONAL GAZETTE] OF DETROIT

In 1874 Jan Barzyński's *Gazeta Polska Katolicka* had been appearing in Detroit for a few months. After that, however, there was no newspaper there for the next ten years. Only I. Piotrowski's bookstore existed. In September 1884, just before the national elections, the weekly *Gazeta Narodowa* appeared in Detroit, published by Piotrowski and edited by Zawisza.[23] Zawisza was also one of the more interesting journalistic figures in America. He was an absolute radical who came from Galicia and was a socialist. The extreme radical tone of the periodical and the lack of funds soon caused the *Gazeta Narodowa* to fail in the same year it was founded. Hieronim Derdowski, a famous Kaszubian folk writer who had come to America at that time, also worked for *Gazeta Narodowa*.

PIELGRZYM POLSKI [THE POLISH PILGRIM] OF DETROIT

Pielgrzym Polski was a joint stock publication. The president of the company was Rev. Paweł Gutowski, the secretary was A. Kołakowski, and the treasurer was K. Nowakowski. Hieronim Derdowski took over the editorship of *Pielgrzym*. Misunderstandings occurred and in 1888 Derdowski left the newspaper and went to Winona, Minnesota. Kazimierz Olszewski, later the publisher of *Pawda* [The Truth] in this city, took over as the editor of *Pielgrzym*; it folded in 1888.[24]

KRYTYKA [THE CRITIQUE] OF MILWAUKEE[25]

The founder of *Krytyka* in 1885 was Michał Kruszka. By 1905, twenty years had passed since he began his first publication, *Tygodnik Anonsowy* [Weekly Announcement], which had been replaced by *Krytyka* on November 7, 1885, and by *Kuryer Polski* on June 28, 1888.

Quite simply, *Tygodnik Anonsowy* was very small in format, and its title described its character. However, at that time any periodical had a right to exist, even if fun was poked at it. Writing about the proposal for "the first convention of Polish American journalists" in 1885, M. J. Sadowski, at that time the editor of Klupp's *Gazeta Chicagoska*, mentioned Michał Kruszka in passing. Kruszka was still little known at the time, and Sadowski asked humorously in his newspaper whether the *Tygodnik Anonsowy* would send its "editor" to the planned "convention." Later Sadowski changed his conviction about M. Kruszka and his newspaper.

Krytyka, since it was not much larger in size than *Tygodnik*, did not yet impress others, because the Czech *Slavie* from Racine, Wisconsin, a newspaper of Karol Jonas, labelled it "malicka Kriticka" [Pint-sized Critic], since *Krytyka* had condemned *Slavie* for accosting it.[26] Later, Jonas became an acquaintance and good friend of M. Kruszka when Jonas was lieutenant governor and Kruszka served as Wisconsin state senator.

Other editors of *Krytyka* included Antoni A. Parysso [Paryski] in 1886, Stalisław Ślisz in 1887, and F. H. Jabłoński in 1887-1888.[27]

Being totally under the direction of young men, *Krytyka* naturally could be nothing but radical in every respect. At the time M. Kruszka was twenty-five and A. Paryski and F. H. Jabłoński were both younger than he. Only S. Ślisz, who also edited *Krytyka* for a few months, proved more conservative than they, although in various respects he was also radical. Since that time each of them has changed considerably.

It could be said that *Krytyka* was the first Polish "people's" newspaper, and it declared itself vehemently on the side of the interests of the working class.

The first issue of *Krytyka* appeared in a small format. But in January, 1886, *Krytyka* enlarged its format, and by October of that year it had increased its size threefold, finally reaching seven columns of print.

When writing about *Krytyka*, it is also necessary to mention its demise. It surrendered its role as the first experiment in Polonia publication to *Dziennik Polski*, a Polish daily periodical in Milwaukee, Wisconsin, founded by a joint stock company. Despite Jabłoński's talented editing, *Dziennik Polski* did not stand on its feet for long, because each shareholder—as is usual for us Poles—gave much advice but little money. M. Kruszka gave the company its entire print shop, and all the other shareholders gave a total of $175 in cash!

Quarrels and disarray hastened the demise of *Dziennik* and *Krytyka*, and the print shop of both newspapers was taken by their creditors, who founded a weekly newspaper, *Orzeł Biały*[28] [The White Eagle], which Jabłoński again edited for some time.

However, even though Michał Kruszka had lost everything, having come out of this company without a cent or without a single bit of printer's type, he had not lost his inborn energy and hope. With $125 borrowed from supporters, he established *Kuryer Polski*, which, although it had only a miniature format, was actually the first Polish daily in America.

OJCZYZNA [HOMELAND] IN BUFFALO

The first Polish newspaper in Buffalo began publishing on July 22, 1885. It was controlled by a stockholders' company consisting mainly of Americans. The guiding spirit behind the publication was one George Bork, a German by birth, but a person sympathetic and well disposed toward Poles.

The editor, Stanisław Ślisz, was given complete freedom on Polish and especially on Polish American matters, but the publishers stipulated that the editor support the Democratic party. In 1887 *Ojczyzna* was transformed into *Polak w Ameryce* [The Pole in America].

TYGODNIK NAUKOWO-POWIEŚCIOWY
[LITERARY AND SCIENTIFIC WEEKLY]

Founded in Chicago, Illinois, in 1885, it soon folded.

ZIARNO [THE SEED]

This publication first appeared in Chicago in July 1886. Its masthead describes it as a periodical "dedicated to lovers of music and national song." Its editor and publisher was Antoni Małłek, one of the better Polish musicians in Chicago. Born in Wałdów, West Prussia, he arrived in America in 1871, after which he served as an organist at the church of St. Stanislaus Kostka and later at Holy Trinity. In 1889 he was the secretary-general of the Polish National Alliance. *Ziarno* folded in 1903.[29]

LEKARZ DOMOWY [HOME PHYSICIAN]

This was a weekly dedicated to hyguiene. It appeared in Chicago for a short time under the editorshop of Doctor M. P. Kossakowski, but folded in the same year it was founded—1886.

OSA [THE WASP]

This was the first humorous Polish periodical in America. Published in New York in 1886, *Osa* was enthusiastically accepted and its humor, though based on local situations, had universal appeal. This, however, did not stop it from folding after three months. The publisher and editor of was Dr. Julian Czupka, who was born in the Czartków district in Galicia in 1854. He attended high school in Tarnopol, and in 1879 received his doctor of laws degree. He came to America in 1882.[30]

WIARUS [THE OLD GUARD]

This first Polish periodical in the state of Minnesota had, for a time, quite a wide-ranging sphere of influence. *Wiarus* appeared in mid-1886 in the Kushubian settlement of Winona through the efforts of the local pastor, Rev. Byzewski.[31] Initially, it was a joint stock enterprise with H. Derdowski hired as editor. Derdowski had recently left the Detroit *Pielgrzym* and had been looking for a position in the various Polonian enclaves—it is rumored that he had travelled on foot from one to another. Initially Derdowski's pen produced only one issue of *Wiarus*. He resigned the editorship and was replaced by the typesetter Paryski. This revolution was followed by a counter-revolution in which Derdowski returned to his position, and from that time on his rule was unquestioned at *Wiarus*.

The newspaper was quite interesting. Derdowski's talent as a folk writer was already known in the Old Country. In America his writing style proved more appealing to readers than others. He wrote expressively, strongly, and on occasion too strongly; he did not beat around the bush. This is precisely what, at times, appealed to readers who were accustomed to abstract statements and smooth talk. It is clear that it is only one step from this style of writing to unpleasant vulgarity and slander that can occur when lack of restraint takes precedence over the editor's intellect.

Wiarus, which for some time carried the nickname *"Katolik,"* was always fortunate regarding its volunteer contributors. Anyone who had a sharp pen and wanted to employ it to annoy his opponents would go quickly to *Wiarus*; if his article was spicy enough, he found a friendly reception. So, for example, L. Heilpern, a Jew with a rather wretched personality, often published in *Wiarus*. After 1889 the mainstay of *Wiarus* was Rev. K. D. Domagalski, one of the most talented Polish writers in America. He used several pseudonyms, including "Cyrulik" [the barber], and unquestionably possessed a satirical talent.[32] Rev. Franciszek Król later inserted very spicy "marzipans" in *Wiarus*, but interest in the publication completely vanished a few years prior to Derdowski's death from paralysis.[33]

GAZETA POLSKI W NEBRASCE
[THE POLISH GAZETTE OF NEBRASKA]

This publication was founded in Elba, Nebraska, in 1887, and was published by a company. It never rose above the level of a local newspaper and closed in 1890. Since that time Nebraska has not had any other Polish newspaper.

WSZYSTKO PRZEZ SERCE JEZ. I MARYI [EVERYTHING
THROUGH THE HEARTS OF JESUS AND MARY]

This first periodical in Manitowoc, Wisconsin, served mainly to support and encourage contributions to Rev. Łuczycki's institutions. Sustained by Rev. Łuczycki's energy, they included a monastery, home for the elderly and orphans, and a polytechnic school. Many books were also printed, mainly of a religious character. The publication began in 1887 and folded in 1890.[34]

POLAK W AMERYCE [THE POLE IN AMERICA]

As we already know, *Ojczyzna* ceased publication in Buffalo in 1887. Actually it was transformed; that is, in March of that year Rev. Jan Pitass purchased *Ojczyzna* and changed its name to *Polak w Ameryce*, a conservative newspaper.[35] After first paying off the former shareholders, he then began to publish *Polak w Ameryce* on a bi-weekly basis. The first editor of was J. M. Sadowski, who also edited *Echo* and served as secretary-general of the Polish National Alliance. However, since occasionally as editor he unintentionally exhibited "too liberal principles," he had to make way after a few months for Zygmunt Słupski, a railroad official in Washington who also did not remain long.[36] Finally, on December 29, 1889, S. Ślisz took over the editorship of *Polak w Ameryce*.[37] In 1895 it became a daily; prior to that it had been appearing bi-weekly.

GŁOS WOLNY [FREE VOICE]

Founded by J. Zawisza in Buffalo in 1887, this organ was the prototype of an unrestrained periodical with socialist and even anarchist tendencies. *Głos Wolny* later passed into the hands of M. I. Sadowski and was transformed into *Echo* in the same year it was founded.

DZWONEK [LITTLE BELL]

Published in Buffalo in 1887 by Rev. Antoni Klawiter,[38] and edited by R. Dobrzelewski, this weekly was literary in character. It folded after six months.

OGNISKO [CAMPFIRE]

Founded in mid-1887, *Ognisko* was a typical New York newspaper. It clearly reflected the life of the local Polish community, which differed greatly in character from the other Polish settlements in America. It created in its bosom a fireside for the "Bohemian intelligentsia," as Mr. Henryk Nagiel phrased it. *Ognisko* emphasized the propagation of progressive ideas. The red paper on which it was printed further illustrated the hue of its convictions. It was published by the "Ognisko" Society, known for its ultra-radical principles. Antoni Lewandowski was its first the editor; he was succeeded by J. J. Chrzanowski. The company included: Leon Wild, later the editor of *Nowe Zycie* [New Life]; Jan Zychliński; K. Sieciński; Suskind, the author of a scandalous comedy *Po amerykańsku* [American Style]; Dr. Gruenberg, a physician from the University of Munich, who came from Prasmysz in the Congress Kingdom and who, though a Jew, contrary to the practice of the Israelites in America always considered himself a Pole; Dr. Czupka; Bernolak, the author of American couplets; J. Goldschmidt, known in the Congress Kingdom for various brochures; the young socialists W. Fischler and A. Moren; and Stanisław Nawrocki, a talented poet. These collaborators actually provided *Ognisko* with considerable activity. At first it was issued in its own little print shop (bought on credit); but later it moved to Schroeder's print shop. Its shareholders changed daily. Their joint stock company consumed the small capital of some of the newly arrived "greenhorns" in America, including a Mr. Myśliwiec from Galicia. Life at *Ognisko* was generally cheerful. Wild, the chief adminstrator, often had to win the money for paper in poker games or at the races. The members of the Polish Bohemia in New York were constantly hanging around the editorial office and the newspaper's print shop. They slept on mail bags on the premises for lack of better bedding. At any rate, they did not work for profit, but for an idea. The paper folded in 1889.[39]

DZIENNIK [DAILY NEWS] AND *KURYER CHICAGOSKI* [CHICAGO COURIER]

At the beginning of 1887, Władisław Smulski began publication of the daily *Kuryer Chicagoski* and Dyniewicz published two or three issues of *Dziennik*, all on a trial basis. These were the first endeavors to create a daily newspaper in America. *Kuryer*, edited by M. J. Sadowski in cooperation with F. J. Jabłoński, lasted three months before it failed.

CZAS [TIME]

Near the close of 1887 Ślisz, with the help of Łobarzewski, founded a small daily entitled *Czas* in the neighborhood of St. Adalbert's Parish in Chicago. After a few weeks it folded. This was the third unsuccessful attempt to create a Polish daily in America.

DZIENNIK POLSKI [POLISH DAILY NEWS] OF MILWAUKEE

The fourth attempt to create a daily newspaper occurred in Milwaukee. *Dziennik Polski* first appeared in November 1887 and lasted until May 1888. It was founded by a company headed by fifteen directors. Its first editor was Franciszek H. Jabłoński.

KROPIDŁO [THE ASPERGILLUM] OF CHICAGO

The battle for the principles, rights, and interests of the [Polish] Catholic populace [in America] was to be waged by *Kropidło* beginning in 1887. And it did so for a year! The title of the periodical itself proved that it was not to pardon, but to "sprinkle." And this "sprinkling" editor was Stanisław Ślisz. His two main adversaries, Z. Brodowski at *Zgoda* and J. Derdowski at *Wiarus,* also sprinkled. The battle was so unrelenting that occasionally it reached the courts. The battles ceased when *Kropidło* was closed on June 22, 1888.

WIARA I OJCZYZNA [FAITH AND FATHERLAND] OF CHICAGO

NARÓD POLSKI [THE POLISH NATION]

Initally, beginning in 1887, this was a well-edited Catholic working-class periodical. It was edited by Rev. Jan Radziejewski,[40] the brother of the publisher of *Katolik* in Upper Silesia. It became the publication of the [Polish Roman Catholic] Union in 1888.

Both periodicals, *Kropidło* and *Wiara i Ojczyzna*, were founded in 1887 as organs of the Polish Publishing Company established at that time in Chicago. This company came to occupy a very prominent position in America. For a long time it published the organ of the Polish Roman Catholic Union under the protection of the Sacred Heart of Jesus—*Wiara i Ojczyzna* and *Dziennik Chicagoski* founded in 1890. The company also published the weekly periodical *Polacy w Ameryce*, in 1890; and over several years it produced thousands of copies of educational textbooks, as well as books of religious, fictional, and other content.

The formation of the Polish Publishing Company gave rise to the following circumstances: when a relative calm ensued after the factional battles, *Gazeta Katolicka*, the clericalists' organ, became the private property of W. Smulski. But after some time, the need again arose to defend the rights of the clerical faction against the attacks of the opposition. The company was formed to create press organs for this defense and, in general, to promote the publication of Catholic works. It consisted of the following priests: Rev. W. Barzyński and the Resurrectionists; Rev. J. Radziejewski; and lay men such as Piotr Kiołbassa, W. Jędrzejek and others. The administrator of the company was Rev. W. Barzyński, and later Rev. Franciszek Gordon, CR.[41]

For a time in 1892, Rev. Domagalski edited *Wiara i Ojcyzna*. He previously had used the pseydonym of "Cyrulik" in *Zgoda*—sheared and shaved until everything decrepitated. His *"Bakcyle"* [The Bacterium], a type of polemic chronicle published in *Zgoda*, was biting and poisoned his opponents' peace of mind. In 1893 he left American soil and returned to the grand Duchy of Poznań, where he died two years later. In addition to Rev. Domagalski, *Wiara i Ojczyzna* was edited by Rev. Zaleski, Mr. Szwajkart, and Ignacy Machnikowski. It later became *Naród Polski*.

KURYER POLSKI [THE POLISH COURIER] OF MILWAUKEE[42]

This daily was established by Michał Kruszka in 1888. The previous dailies had been only experiments. This newpaper was really the beginning of the daily Polish press in America. It survived as such due to the energy, work, and perserverance of Michał Kruszka. Founded with borrowed capital of $125, it first appeared in a small format and successively grew. After only four months it had enlarged its format. In the beginning, Kruszka did everything—he was the publisher, editor, collector, and even typesetter. Through this work he was able to build his newspaper.

At that time, the entire staff—of *Kuryer*—apart from the publisher consisted of only two adults and two delivery boys. Naturally it was difficult, but somehow they pushed on until they slowly overcame the hardships.

Kuryer also encountered favorable political conditions. Out of a total population of 200,000 inhabitants, Milwaukee had 30,000 Poles at that time. The requirements for securing the right to vote in the state of Wisconsin were so simple that the majority of Poles availed themselves of it. This greatly contributed to the success of *Kuryer* which could speak to the Polish population.

"One must admit," wrote Henryk Nagiel, "that Mr. Kruszka is a good politician, and he knows how to follow events so well that in cooperation with others he can gain important political benefits for the Poles."

Kuryer initially cost ten cents per week and $5.00 per year. In 1890 Kruszka lowered the price to six cents and $3.00, respectively, winning many subscribers in the process.

Three years after its founding, when *Kuryer* already had about 3,000 subscribers, the Wisconsin state legislature voted that municipal government notices should also be published in the Polish language. In 1896 *Kuryer* moved its headquarters to the Montgomery Building in the middle of town at the corner of Milwaukee and Michigan Streets.

In 1899 an incorporated "Kuryer Publishing Company" was organized consisting of Michał Kruszka, president; Józef S. Kruszka, vice-president; M. S. Cyborowski, secretary; and Leon Drwenski, treasurer. The initial capital of the company amounted to a nominal $20,000 divided into shares.

In the ranks of Kuryer's contributors, who also helped to improve it or who contributed to its development, we should first include W. Maychrzycki. A well-known printer, he was the mainstay of the mechanical department in the beginning, because he had only one typesetter, A. Giliński, and one boy to help him. The next important individual undoubtedly was the late Kazimierz Owocki, who had begun to work for the *Kuryer* in November 1888 and whom Kruszka considered his right-hand man; he wrote everything for the newspaper, supervised shipping, and even did the printing if the need arose. On Kruszka's recommendation, Owocki established an agency of *Kuryer Polski* in Chicago in 1890 and within six months obtained over 900 subscribers. The publishers of *Wiara i Ojczyzna*, seeing that Kruszka's daily was so popular in Chicago, founded *Dziennik Chicagoski* [Chicago Daily] at that time and immediately acquired almost half of *Kuryer's* readers. Thus, *Dziennik Chicagoski* owed its success to the preparatory work of *Kuryer Polski*.

Those affiliated with *Kuryer* were quite numerous. During K. Owocki's time, there were K. Neuman and Jan Kuk (1891), followed by Józef S. Kruszka (1893), Tadeusz Wild (1893), Stanisław Osada (1899), and later Franciszek H. Jabłoński, J. J. Chrzanowski, W. Halicki, and Stefan Rachocki.[43] It could be said that they were permanent editors because they worked with *Kuryer* for years. They were assisted by temporary editors: Łuczyński from Chicago, W. Ziemiński from New York, B. Dalkowski from Toledo, and J. Kwaśniewski and Dr. Machnikowski from Milwaukee. In 1905 the editorial staff of *Kuryer* consisted of J. J. Chrzanowski, S. Rachocki, M. S. Cyborowski and J. Wedda.

In the beginning the business department had only one clerk, who also doubled as a sales person. It seems that the first such clerk was Wincenty Sławski, and his assistant and delivery person on the east side [of Milwaukee] was Max Dorszyński. Dorszyński later became a theology student, and following his ordination he became pastor of St. Vincent's Parish. The clerks and collectors at *Kuryer* included the following: The late F. Danielski, E. Pawłowski, Leon Drwenski, M. S. Cyborowski, T. Czerwiński, I. Przybyła, and L. Kotecki. In 1905 the business department of *Kuryer* employed five travelling agents, two advertising agents, four bookkeepers, a cashier, four sales people and one supervisor of delivery personnel. The manager was Józef S. Kruszka.

The heads of foremen of the print shop included the following: W. Maychrzycki, T. Zagórski, A. Szybczyński, F. Raniszewski, L. Muehleisen, M. Cyborowski, A. Giliński, and Franciszek H. Cichocki.

In 1888 *Kuryer* had 360 readers, while in 1905 (together with the weekly) it had 18,000 readers. In 1888 it employed a total of six people, and by 1905 had grown to employ twenty-seven adults and seven minors, as well as eighty-seven delivery people, for a total of 121 people. The average weekly payroll in 1888 came to $31; and in 1905—$570.00. In 1900, *Kuryer* acquired expensive machines for typesetting letters.

In May 1905 the Kuryer Publishing Company raised the institutional capital from $20,000 to $50,000, spread over 500 shares at $100 per share. The value of the entire *Kuryer* enterprise was assessed by experts at between $40,000 and $55,000. The company had virtually no debts. The present company president (1905) and the chief administrator of publishing is Michał Kruszka; the secretary is M. S. Cyborowski; the treasurer and manager is Józef S. Kruszka.

ORZEŁ BIAŁY [THE WHITE EAGLE] AND OPIEKUM [THE GUARDIAN] IN MILWAUKEE

These two weeklies were published by the same company. They were similar in content, size, print, and so on, and actually comprised one periodical, which was published twice a week under two different titles in order to utilize postal conveniences. They were founded in 1888 and failed in 1890. The company consisted of A. Boncel and S. Hanyżewski, who had taken over the print shop of two failed publications, *Krytyka* and *Dziennik*. At first F. H. Jabłoński was the editor, followed by Thomas Łobarzewski, a young technician or mining engineer from Galicia, and then Kazimierz Neumann. Both weeklies folded in 1890.

PRAWDA [THE TRUTH] OF DETROIT

This was a local periodical founded in 1888. It was published by Kazimierz Olszewski, a locksmith by profession from Połock. His helper was a typesetter, Jakubowski. From 1893 *Prawda* became the property of the young and talented Dr. Laskowski, a former professor of the seminary in Detroit, Michigan, who had received his degree in Rome. Dr. Iłowiecki, a Polish physician living in Detroit at the time, often wrote for *Prawda*. He later was the publisher of the daily *Swoboda* and the author of many competent poems. *Prawda* moved on later to Bay City, Michigan, where it became the property of Przybyszewski.[44]

GWIAZDA [THE STAR] OF TOLEDO, OHIO

In 1888, the Polonia of Toledo, Ohio, had felt the need for its own publication. *Gwiazda* was published by Czarnecki and edited by A. Paryski. It began in 1888, but in 1889 *Gwiazda* disappeared from the Toledo horizon and thereafter appeared anew in Detroit.

GWIAZDA [THE STAR] OF DETROIT

When Czarnecki got tired of subsidizing the newspaper in Toledo, he closed it. Paryski went to Detroit, where he and Skupiński founded the new *Gwiazda*, which glowed in 1889. As long as Paryski had worked on *Gwiazda*, it was an average publication. It was still acceptable under Linde and Topolnicki; but when Skupiński, the publisher, began to administer it personally, the paper became a "pure horror" in substance, style, and spelling.[45] Not only a journalist or writer but even a third year high school student would have been able to ascertain this. We note this fact, however unpleasant, to emphasize that it is an exception in American Polish journalism, and that sometimes our countrymen in Poland mistakenly have made a "rule" out of such exceptions. After a few years *Gwiazda* ceased to appear.

AMERYKA [AMERICA] OF TOLEDO, OHIO[46]

Henryk Nagiel wrote this about *Ameryka*, which was founded in 1889:

Here a few words should be devoted to Mr. Paryski, whose name has already been brought up several times in this brochure. Mr. Paryski (a pseudonym) was a native of Warsaw. In Poland he was a court clerk. He came to the United States while still very young—in 1882 or 1883—and at first learned typesetting in the print shop of *Gazeta Narodowa* in Detroit and later with Dyniewicz in Chicago. In 1886 he served as the temporary editor of *Wiarus* and in that same year, in the era of the famous anarchistic disturbances, he engaged in vociferous, radical agitiation among the Polish workers in Chicago. As a result, he edited *Krytyka* for few months and likewise agitated among the workers in Milwaukee. He came to Toledo in 1887. On June 30, 1888, he took over the editorship of *Gwiazda* founded by Czarnecki. Following its demise he lived in Detroit; however, shortly thereafter he returned to Toledo, where he established *Ameryka* in 1889.

Paryski's newspaper was among the ultra-progressive ones. He was an active businessman. He knew how to speculate in politics. He encouraged his readers either by selling sewing machines cheaply or by offering bonuses on soap, books, pictures, etc. He likewise issued two or three editions of his periodical in various cities. In 1891 Paryski published his newspaper in a Cleveland edition entitled *Kuryer Clevelandski*; during the 1892 elections he put out a special Detroit edition of his *Ameryka*; and in 1894 he sent his paper to Pittsburgh under the title of *Gazeta Pittsburska*.

Such publishing maneuvers may have caused surprise in Europe, but here in America it was nothing new. In 1905 Paryski published his periodical, *Ameryka-Echo*, after buying out the weekly *Echo* in Buffalo, New York.

KOŚCIUSZKO OF WINONA

Mr. Derdowski began to publish a smaller periodical entitled *Kościuszko* as a supplement to his *Wiarus* in 1889. It was devoted to fiction and was mainly intended for young people. It failed in 1891.

NIEDZIELA [SUNDAY] OF MILWAUKEE

This was a weekly devoted to fiction; it was considered something of a supplement of the daily *Kuryer Polski* from 1889 to 1892.

ECHO OF BUFFALO

M. J. Sadowski bought the radical and anti-religious *Głos Wolny* from Zawisza in March 1889 and then converted it to the moderately progressive *Echo*. For some time this newspaper even appeared on a daily basis. The editors were Henryk Nagiel (until 1890), Łucyan Dewoyno, and Mr. Litwin, a scathing polemicist and the American correspondent of the Warsaw *Głos*.

In 1904 *Echo* merged with *Ameryka* in Toledo, where it was published as *Ameryka-Echo*.

BOCIAN [THE STORK] OF BUFFALO

This was the second humorous periodical in America. The publisher, editor, and illustrator was Z. Słupski, the director of *Polak w Ameryce*. After a few months of publishing in 1889, *Bocian* failed.

KUKURYKU [COCK-A-DOODLE-DO] OF BUFFALO

Kukuryku crowed and then died in 1889. When Słupski's *Bocian* died of anemia, Sadowski published *Kukuryku,* the third consecutive humorous periodical in America. H. Nagiel edited it and Dr. Czupka published his *"Kącik Osy"* ["Wasp Corner"] in it.

GŁOS WOLNY [THE FREE VOICE] OF CHICAGO

Having sold Sadowski his *Głos Wolny* in Buffalo, Mr. Zawisza immediately went to Chicago. For what purpose? It was clearly to found a new *Głos Wolny,* which soon occurred in 1889. The printshop of *Czas,* a daily that had just folded under the editorship of Ślisz, was for sale. Zawisza bought it and immediately established *Głos Wolny*. Zawisza, however radical, knew how to adapt to conditions, and consequently *Głos* even became the organ of the Polish Roman Catholic Union under the care of Our Lady of Częstochowa, a Chicago organization with about six hundred members. This confrontation of Catholicism with the surfacing of Mr. Zawisza's radical tendencies constituted a unique situation. This bolstered him to the extent that he even attempted to transform *Głos* into a daily periodical. However, these efforts ended in a fiasco and the newspaper ceased publication in 1890.

Through *Głos*, Zawisza introduced two new journalists of a rather radical orientation: one was M. I. Szameit, a technician from Galicia, and the other was the typesetter, F. Szczerbowski.

SŁOWO [THE WORD] OF BUFFALO

Through the efforts of M. Makowski, *Słowo* began to appear in 1890 under the editorship of the eternal wanderer, Zawisza, who in this periodical had to moderate his socialist outbursts. *Słowo* stopped appearing in 1891. However, for a short time, Zawisza irregularly still published the previously discontinued *Głos Wolny* (for the third time!).

PRZYJACIEL LUDU [FRIEND OF THE PEOPLE]

This weekly, a local periodical, began to appear in 1890 through the efforts of Rosiński. It was edited by various individuals: Antoni Zawisza (Józef's brother), Professor Kuk from Galicia, typesetters Zacharewicz, Abczyński, and others, and then by Rosiński himself. He hailed from the Poznań region and came to America in 1866. It also ceased publication.

GAZETA Z NANTICOKE [NANTICOKE GAZETTE]

This was a periodical of local character founded in 1890. It had two editors, Tomasz Łobarzewski and Zygmunt Twarowski. It failed in 1892.

PATRYOTA [THE PATRIOT] OF PHILADELPHIA

Zygmunt Słupski founded this weekly in July 1890. Its initial issues were worthy of attention; however, it did not continue to fulfill the hopes placed in it. In 1891 Teo. Wąsowicz bought it. The editor was Romanowski. *Patryota* was still being published in 1905. It had its own unique spelling and very few local readers.

KURYER NOWOJORSKI I BROOKLYŃSKI [THE NEW YORK AND BROOKLYN COURIER]

This publication was founded in August 1890 by Henryk Nagiel in cooperation with K. N. Złotnicki [Korngold], who had just arrived from Warsaw. Of the issues *Kuryer* discussed (1891), the following stirred much commotion: Polish colonization in Argentina (New Poland) and the question a Polish bishop in America. Through a strange coincidence exactly ten years later (in 1901 and 1902), these same two issues were again raised by the press. In September 1891 Nagiel sold *Kuryer* to a company consisting of Kołakowski and Złotnicki, and he himself went to Chicago. *Kuryer* thereafter was edited by Złotnicki, W. Ziemiński, and Józef Rybakowski, a Galician engineer. Finally, in June 1892 the paper was acquired by Rev. Fremel and Mr. Reiner, and J. J. Chrzanowski took over the editorship. The 1892 political campaign so invigorated the *Kuryer* that on December 11 of that year it began to come out on a daily basis. However, this did not prevent its failure in February 1893; it came to life again after a few months. The periodical was still being published in 1905.

NOWE ZYCIE [NEW LIFE] OF CHICAGO

Nowe Zycie can be considered the successor to Zawisza's *Głos Wolny*. Mr. Niemczewski bought the *Głos Wolny* printshop and relocated it to Bridgeport. There he began to publish *Nowe Zycie* in 1890, first under the editorship of Zawisza, then of Henryk Nagiel, and later under the direction of his pupil, F. Szczerbowski. In 1891 M. Wild took over the editorship. Stanisław Osada later served in that capacity. The tone of the periodical was atheistically socialist, and under Mr. Osada it went bankrupt.

POLACY W CHICAGO [THE POLES IN CHICAGO]

Through the efforts of the Polish Publishing Company, the weekly entitled *Polacy w Chicago* appeared in Chicago at the beginning of 1890. It was the predecessor of *Dziennik Chicagoski*.

DZIENNIK CHICAGOSKI [CHICAGO DAILY][47]

Through the efforts of this same company the first issue of *Dziennik Chicagoski* appeared in December 1890. Its first editor was Stanisław Szwajkart. Born in 1857 in Tarnopol (Galicia), Szwajkart was educated in Stanisławow and Lwów. While still in Poland he wrote and printed short stories and poetry. He came to America in 1881 and contributed radical articles to the German newspaper *Staats Zeitung*. Then, in Chicago, he worked as a teacher, an official, etc. Only in 1889 did he become F. Kaczorowski's assistant at *Wiara i Ojczyzna*. In December 1890 he took over the editorship of the newly founded *Dziennik Chicagoski*, which he ran until November 1892, when he was succeeded by Mr. Henryk Nagiel.

Henryk Nagiel was born in Warsaw in 1859. He attended local schools and at age twenty-one completed the law faculty of Warsaw University. In 1885 he became a certified lawyer with the Warsaw judicial chamber. Three years later he went to Paris and in 1889 he came to America and settled in Buffalo, where he edited *Echo*. He remained in America until the end of 1896, and throughout his entire stay he occupied himself exclusively with journalism, editing various periodicals, lately *Telegraf* and *Dziennik Chicagoski*. Henryk Nagiel had already begun his journalistic work at age fifteen when he wrote various poems from humorous Warsaw periodicals. During his university studies he edited *Wędrowiec* [The Wanderer], wrote for *Dziennik dla Wszystkich* [Everyone's Daily], *Kuryer Warszawski* [Warsaw Couries], *Kolce* [Thorns] and *Muchy* [Flies]. From among a large group of Polish American journalists, Nagiel was definitely the most talented, because he possessed all of the necessary attributes: knowledge, extraordinary ease at understanding a situation, and a still greater capability of transferring his thoughts to paper. He could embellish all this with humor, thanks to which his publications were gladly read even by those who held opposing views. In the last years of his stay in Chicago, he edited *Dziennik Chicagoski*, and although he had to adhere to the pubishers' principles, it should be ackowledged that he administered the newspaper as honestly as he was able.

In 1896 Nagiel left Chicago for Lwów, where he was the co-editor of *Słowo Polski* [The Polish Word], one of the largest Galician dailies. He died in Lwów in 1900. We are mainly indebted to him for compiling this section of the "History of Polish Press in America."

As of 1896 *Dziennik* was again edited by Szwajkart, together with Kazimierz Neumann.

NIEDZIELA [SUNDAY] OF DETROIT

This was a working-class, literary weekly established in 1891. It was published by the Polish seminary and its rector, Rev. Dąbrowski. Its first editor was Rev. Barabasz, a professor at the seminary, who was a worthy priest and a talented writer. Rev. Paweł Ćwiąkała took over the editorship of *Niedziela* in 1892. He was a young priest from Galicia who was born in the Sanok region, educated in the town of Sanok, and ordained in 1892 in Przemyśl. *Niedziela* folded in 1904. It did appear later in a reduced format.[48]

DZWON [THE BELL] AND *GOŚĆ* [THE GUEST] OF MANITOWAC, WISCONSIN

This was Rev. Z. Łuczycki's publication that replaced his previously issued *Wszystko przez Serce Jezusa i Maryi* [Everything through the Sacred Hearts of Jesus and Mary]. Founded in 1891, these periodicals were devoted to religious writings and popular fiction. They folded with Rev. Łuczycki's departure to Europe in 1894.

PISMO DALKOWSKIEGO [DALKOWSKI'S PERIODICAL] OF TOLEDO, OHIO

At the end of 1891 a tolerably good local periodical was founded, whose editor for a few years was Bolesław Dalkowski, a young Pole educated in America. The publisher was Mr. Brzeczka.

POLONIA [POLONIA] IN BALTIMORE, MARYLAND

The Polish press in Baltimore, on the shores of the Atlantic, had its beginning in 1891 when *Polonia* became the first periodical published there. Mr. Welzant, the publisher, was a clever businessman. The first editor was Czupka. Bernolak later served as editor from 1894 until the failure of *Polonia* in 1898. Bernolak published *Strażnica* [The Watchtower] in Baltimore for six months, then worked in a musical instrument factory. After January 1901 he was active with *Echo* and *Polak w Ameryce* in Buffalo.

KURYER CLEVELANDZKI [THE CLEVELAND COURIER][49]

The Polish press in Cleveland, Ohio, also had its beginning in 1891. Paryski of Toledo founded *Kuryer Clevelandzki* and ran it with the help of a Mr. Kempiński until it failed in 1892.

ROLNIK [THE FARMER] OF STEVENS POINT, WISCONSIN[50]

The Polish organ *Rolnik* appeared here for the first time in 1891. It was a local periodical which did not play politics. This newspaper was established by Messrs. Hutter and Krutza, but a year after its founding Hutter

bought out his partner and thereafter ran it on his own. The publishers are
J. Worzała and sons.

REFORMA [REFORM] OF CHICAGO

Reforma was founded at St. Adalbert's Parish in 1891 by the renowned
Alfons Chrostowski with inherited or borrowed money. If not for his
moral shortcomings, Chrostowski could have occupied a certain position
in the literary field, not only here in America but also in Europe. But he
instigated, slandered, brought ruin everywhere, fomented parish discord,
and finally in 1894 contributed to the creation of a church schism. He did
not last long at *Reforma*. The only result of his disheveled anarchistic
ideas was that copies of the periodical were returned to the publisher. As a
result, *Reforma* became the property of Messrs. F. A. Satalecki (president
after September 1891 of the Central Administration of the Polish National
Alliance), S. Rokosz, and A. Stefanowicz. These gentlemen appointed H.
Nagiel as editor. He gave *Reforma* a moderately progressive orientation
and raised its circulation to a few thousand paid subscribers. *Reforma* even
became the organ of the Polish Roman Catholic Union under the patronage of Our Lady of Częstochowa, Queen of Poland. *Reforma* folded under
the next editor. Only later was it resurrected as the organ of the Independent "Bishop" Kozłowski and subsequently renamed *Lud* [People], published by G. F. Biba.[51]

GŁOS WOLNY [THE FREE VOICE] AND *SOCYALISTA* [THE SOCIALIST] OF BUFFALO

Zawisza's *Głos Wolny* was heard for the third time in 1891 and immediately thereafter fell silent in the same year. Furthermore, Zawisza's
Socyalista soon gave up its spirit as well. The titles of these periodicals are
the best indication of their direction. They failed, as did everthing else that
Zawisza touched.

WIEK [CENTURY] OF BUFFALO

Wiek did not last one hundred years, or even one year. It was founded in
1892 and failed in the same year. This political periodical was published
by Makowski and was edited by T. Łobarzewski. It was distinguished by
the fact that one of its pages was printed in English.

GAZETA POLSKA [THE POLISH GAZETTE] OF NEW YORK[52]

The *Gazeta Polska* of Ludwik Niemojewski and K. N. Złotnicki published two or three issues in 1892 before it folded. Its format even attracted the attention of the Polish press in Europe.

POSTĘP [PROGRESS] OF NEW YORK

The year of the presidential elections—1892—brought to life many new periodicals that were mainly ephemeral and without any future. In June of that year *Postęp* appeared as the dissenting political periodical of A. Chrostowski and Dr. Lewandowski; it lasted through the elections.

POSIEW [SOWING] OF NEW YORK

Posiew was Mr. Kornobis' pleasant political organ. Founded in 1892, it was edited by the always pleasant poet, S. Nowrocki, but failed in the same year.

ORZEŁ BIAŁY [THE WHITE EAGLE] OF NEW YORK

This literary organ was founded in 1892 but lasted only a short time, failing in the same year. The publisher was Mr. Segers and the editor was J. Goldszmidt.

ŚWIATŁO [THE LIGHT] OF NEW YORK

This was a socialist organ unfurling its banner under the management of Fischler, Jentys, and Bombiński. It flashed in 1892 and burned out in 1893.

GOŚĆ [THE GUEST] OF MILWAUKEE

Mr. Karchut, the owner of a popular bookstore in Manitowoc, founded this friendly little popular periodical and moved it to Manitowoc. The Milwaukee *Gość* failed in 1892, the same year that it first appeared.

POLANIN [THE POLE] OF MILWAUKEE

This was a small political periodical was circulated by E. I. Słupecki and edited by the typesetter, A. Surdela. Its name was taken from the name of a Slavic tribe inhabiting Poland prior to 900 A.D. It first appeared in 1892 and was transformed into *Praca* [Work] in the same year.

PRACA [WORK] OF MILWAUKEE

This periodical was founded in 1893 and failed in the same year.

OJCZYZNA [FATHERLAND] OF CLEVELAND

This was quite an eccentric publication, edited in 1892 first by Łabędzki and then by Alfons Chrostowski. It then became the property of Mr. Gostomski, a carpenter, who owned it until it burned down in the summer of 1893.

POLONIA W AMERYCE [POLONIA IN AMERICA] OF CLEVELAND

This periodical was founded in 1892 by a group of the most distinguished citizens of Cleveland. Its first editor was Małkowski, followed by L. Dewojno. Teodor Dłużyński was the publisher.[53]

ŚMIECH [LAUGHTER] OF TRENTON, NEW JERSEY

This was the fourth consecutive humorous periodical founded by the Poles in America, although it is true that there is no lack of humor in every newspaper in America. It began and ended in 1892.

GŁOS POLSKI [THE POLISH VOICE] OF PHILADELPHIA

Głos Polski was begun in 1892 in response to church disturbances. One of the instigators, a certain Wyruchowski, established this newspaper as a combatant organ. It was initially edited by Łopatyner, who even went to Rome complaining about the matter of these disturbances. The next editor was Nowicki, a typesetter and musician.[54]

TELEGRAF [TELEGRAPH] OF CHICAGO

Telegraf was a daily founded in 1892 by a company consisting of Messrs. Cyborowski, Tarkowski, Groszkiewicz, and Szulc. H. Nagiel first edited it until September 1892, when he took over the editorship of *Dziennik Chicagoski*. *Telegraf* subsequently failed, due to J. Rybakowski's overly radical editorship. Later it appeared as a weekly and belonged to a printer named Pettkowski.[55]

GAZETA HANDLOWA [BUSINESS GAZETTE] OF CHICAGO

This was a small business periodical intended for advertisements. It was published for some time in 1892 by Mr. Nalepiński.

PRZEGLĄD [THE REVIEW] AND *TYGODNIK* [THE WEEKLY] OF MILWAUKEE

These two small periodicals each appeared once a week as supplements to *Kuryer Polski* in 1892 and 1893. They presented a synopsis of the contents of the daily *Kuryer*.

ROBOTNIK POLSKI [THE POLISH WORKER] OF MINNEAPOLIS

This publication was founded and failed in 1893.

GAZETA WISCONSIŃSKA [THE WISCONSIN GAZETTE] AND KURYER TYGODNIOWY [THE WEEKLY COURIER] OF MILWAUKEE[56]

These weeklies, founded in 1893, presented the most important news in abbreviated form. In addition, *Gazeta Wisconsińska* contained much information about agriculture, and *Kuryer Tygodniowy* featured good, new political articles.

SŁOWO [THE WORD] OF MILWAUKEE

It was founded in 1893 in opposition to *Kuryer Polski* and was circulated by Kazimierz Newman, the former editor of *Kuryer*. It failed in 1895.

SZTANDAR [THE BANNER] OF CHICAGO[57]

Sztandar was founded at St. Adalbert's Parish in 1893 through the efforts and under the editorship of J. I. Migdalski. Initially it was the organ of the [Polish Roman Catholic] Union under the patronage of Our Lady of Częstochowa, Queen of Poland, and later the organ of the Youth Alliance. In 1901 it became the property of Mr. Danisch, who sold it to the Youth Alliance. After a year *Sztandar* ceased publication.

PRZEGLĄD TYGODNIOWY [THE WEEKLY REVIEW] OF CLEVELAND

This socialist newspaper was again published by the untiring and relentless Mr. Zawisza, naturally—for only a few weeks in 1893.

JUTRZENKA [THE DAWN] OF CLEVELAND

This was a newspaper of the most radical kind, which first was published in Pittsburgh. Alfons Chrostowski then wandered with it to Cleveland, where he immediately created disturbances in the local [Polish Roman Catholic] parishes and was responsible for the development of a religious schism. *Jutrzenka* was the organ of the independent "Union of the Most Sacred Heart of the Holy Virgin Mary" in Cleveland, as well as of the "Holy Cross Society" and the "Union of Polish Armies" in Brooklyn. A. Wielowiejski was the editor.[58] A. Chrostowski later wrote for *Jutrzenka*, the organ of the Independents.

NOWINY NOWOJORSKI [NEW YORK NEWS]

FILADELFIJSKIE [PHILADELPHIA NEWS] AND Z WILKES-BARRE [NEWS FROM WILKES-BARRE]

This periodical endeavored to appear in three cities at once. It was issued by the former publishers of *Śmiech* [Laughter] in Trenton, New Jersey. The attempt to publish three editions of one newspaper for three cities was not successful. After a few months in 1893 it lost its spirit and failed.

GÓRNIK [THE MINER] OF WILKES-BARRE, PENNSYLVANIA[59]

Górnik was first published in September 1893 under Messrs. Strużewski and Sieniewicz. From the outset it was a peaceful local organ of an informational character.

ŚWIAT POLSKO-AMERYKAŃSKI [POLISH-AMERICAN WORLD] OF ALBANY, NEW YORK

This periodical was published by a company and edited by T. Łobarzewski. After the first issue in 1894 the printshop burned down and everything went up in smoke. It was not published again.

GAZETA ROBOTNICZA [THE WORKER'S GAZETTE] OF CHICAGO

This wildly anarchistic newspaper appeared in January 1894. However, it folded in May when its editor, Rybakowski, began to organize Polish divisions of Coxey's "Army."[60]

BIBLIOTEKA LUDOWA [THE PEOPLE'S LIBRARY] OF TOLEDO

The so-called *Biblioteka Ludowa*, consisting of reprints starting with Brodziński's *Wiesław*, began to appear in 1894. It was published by A. Paryski, the founder of *Ameryka*. It failed in the same year.

GAZETA LUDOWA [THE PEOPLE'S GAZETTE]
OF MAHONEY CITY, PENNSYLVANIA

This was a small local organ that appeared in 1894. Bączkowski, a Lithuanian, was its editor.

DZIENNIK POLSKI [THE POLISH DAILY] OF CHICAGO

Dr. Ignacy Machnikowski, adroit with a pen, was the editor of *Dziennik Polski*.[61] He was born in Łekno (Grand Duchy of Poznań), completed high school in Poznań and the University of Wrocław [Breslau]. He received a gold medal for Hebrew from Pope Pius IX at the Collegium Romanum. At the request of Rev. Semeneńko, the General of the Resurrectionist Order, Machnikowski, went in 1898 to Adrianople, Turkey. There he raised a school with four classes to the rank of a high school, so that its diploma was considered on a par with its European counterparts. One of Machnikowski's students, Chrystofor Kessjakow, was the public prosecutor in Bulgaria and was famous for his splendid translation into Bulgarian of Słowacki's *Ojca Zadżumionych* [Father of the Stricken Plague]. Dr. Machnikowski later became a government engineer in Dedeagacz, after which he was transferred to Bayazid in Asia Minor. In 1888, the late Rev. Wincenty Barzyński brought him to America, where he was a teacher in Chicago and then a doctor and editor of *Dziennik Polski, Kuryer Polski,* and *Dziennik Milwaucki*. Finally, in 1901 he became a professor at the Polish seminary in Detroit. The *Dziennik Polski* began in 1895 and failed in 1896.

PRZYJACIEL MŁODZIEŻY [FRIEND OF YOUTH] OF CHICAGO

This publication was edited by Kazimierz Neuman, later editor of *Dziennik Chicagoski*, from its founding in 1895 until its failure in 1897.

PRZYJACIEL DOMU [FRIEND OF THE HOME] OF BALTIMORE

The publisher of this periodical was Rev. Barabasz, DD. It was founded in 1895.

SWOBODA [FREEDOM] OF DETROIT[62]

In the beginning, *Swoboda* was a weekly when it was founded in 1896. Later it became a daily but failed in 1898. It was edited by Dr. Iłowiecki, who in 1898 returned to the Old Country, where he died in Skalmierzyce on February 22, 1902. He had been born around 1850 in the Poznań region. Having completed his medical studies in Wrocław, Dr. Iłowiecki fervently dedicated himself to his profession. He came to Amercia as a young man and settled in Detroit, Michigan, where tens of thousands of people found him to be a very talented physician. Gifted with rare literary talents, he wrote articles, poetry and prose pieces distinguished by their elegant form, humorous content, often satirical bluntness and sometimes touching nostalgia. An example is his poem *"Smutno mi Boże"* ["God, I am Sad"], which imitates Słowacki in form, but conveys a totally unique idea. In his journalistic articles, a satirical element prevailed, and misfortunes and setbacks sharpened the tone of his writings. A kindhearted person, he was often generous and obliging to the point of forgetting about himself. However, when disheartened, he would slash with his satirical whip regardless of the fact that he might miss the target. For some time he published the weekly *Swoboda* and he also temporarily issued a daily with the same title. In addition to journalistic works, he devoted his talents to more serious and lasting literary ones, which will be further discussed in the following chapter.

WARTA [THE WATCH] OF BUFFALO

Warta, founded in 1896, was the publication of the Independent "Bishop" Stefan Kamiński.[63]

SŁOŃCE [THE SUN] OF BUFFALO[64]

The editor of *Słońce* was "Count" Jerzy Mirski, for some time an advocate of the Independents, but later a convert. *Słońce* belonged to the category of migratory periodicals. From Buffalo it moved west to St. Paul, and from there east again to Milwaukee and back again to Buffalo. *Słońce* rose in 1896 and set in 1904.

PRZYJACIEL LUDU [FRIEND OF THE PEOPLE] OF PHILADELPIA

This was the organ of the Death Benefit Fund and other societies in Philadelphia. It was founded in 1897. The publishers were W. Wendt and his son.[65]

PRZEGLĄD [THE REVIEW] OF NANTICOKE, PENNSYLVANIA

This publication was like a hammer beating the *Hodurczyki* [the followers of the Independent Bishop Hodur] on the anvil of Catholic principles. It was published by a company headed by Rev. Gramlewicz.[66] It was founded in 1896 but failed in 1901.

STRAŻ [THE GUARD][67] OF SCRANTON, PENNSYLVANIA

The auxiliary organ of Hodur and his "National Church," *Straż* found itself between the devil and the deep blue sea. Dangiel was its editor. It was founded in 1896.

ECHO Z ST. LOUIS [ECHO FROM ST. LOUIS][68]

GONIEC POLSKI [THE POLISH MESSENGER] OF SOUTH BEND[69]

A local, Catholic publication.

KATOLIK [THE CATHOLIC] OF MILWAUKEE

When it began in 1897, *Katolik* was published three times a week by a partnership of Milwaukee priests. Later it became the property of Rev. Grutza, who transformed it into a weekly, edited by Professor Kuk. Initially Dr. Jawornicki had edited *Katolik*.[70] With Rev. Grutza's death in 1901, *Katolik* folded, or rather it was sold, just as Smulski's *Źródło* [The Source] had been.

ŹRÓDŁO [THE SOURCE] OF MILWAUKEE

Published by Rev. Grutza beginning in 1898, *Źródło* consisted entirely of reprints. It dried up in 1901. Jan Kuk edited both *Źródło* and *Katolik*. He had been in America since 1891, but returned to Galicia in 1902. He was born in the Jasło in 1841.

MACZUGA [THE MACE] OF WILKES-BARRE, PA.[71]

SOKÓŁ [FALCON] IN CHICAGO[72]

This is the organ of the Polish Falcons Alliance of America.

POLONIA [POLONIA] OF DETROIT[73]

Edited by Stanisław L. Kapcia, it was the official organ of the Roman Catholic Association. It began in 1898.

KURYER NOWOJORSKI [THE NEW YORK COURIER][74]

Mr. Momidłowski was the editor of this newspaper. It was founded in 1899 and incorporated on January 14, 1905. Its directors were L. Korybski, J. L. Struś (editor), and A. Gronicki. It was the organ of the Polish National Alliance of Brooklyn.

GAZETA PITTSBURSKA [PITTSBURGH GAZETTE][75]

A newspaper with an Independent religious orientation, it folded in 1903.

WIELKOPOLANIN [HE FROM GREAT POLAND] OF PITTSBURGH[76]

The official organ of the Union of St. Joseph in Pittsburgh, founded in 1899 and edited by Leon Machnikowski.

DZIENNIK NARODOWY [NATIONAL DAILY] OF CHICAGO[77]

This newspaper encompassed not only local but also broader national horizons. It was founded in 1899 and edited successively by Sadowski, F. H. Jabłoński and J. J. Chrzanowski. *Dziennik* belonged to the publishing partnership composed of the following directors (1902): Dr. Kazimierz Midowicz, president; M. Rzeszotarski; K. Łagodziński; M. Durski; L. M. Wild; C. Dużewski; C. Brukwicki; J. Chmieliński; W. Tobiński, and later W. Jaworowski.

The late Kazimierz Midowicz was born in 1858 in Turza, in the vicinity of Tarnów, Galicia. He attended elementary and high schools in Nowy Sącz, from which he graduated. He completed his medical studies at the University of Kraków in 1884. In his last year of medical studies, he fulfilled his military obligation by volunteering for army service. He thereafter set up practice in Husiatyn, and later in Tarnów, where he was the second in charge at the district hospital. He rendered great service as the president of the Tarnów *Gwiazda,* proving that even though medicine was his profession, he did not shy away from civic duties and was above all a Polish patriot.

In 1890 he came to Chicago. Until his death in 1902, he worked in the Polish American sphere. Not only was he a talented physician; he was also a co-organizer of the unfortunate "Liga Polska" [Polish League]. He was an entrepreneur in a California gold mine and the co-founder of *Dziennik Narodowy.* On June 24, 1902, he died in State Line, Mississippi, where he is buried.

DZIENNIK MILWAUCKI [MILWAUKEE DAILY][78]

This publication emerged in opposition to *Kuryer Polski* in 1899. It aspired to be very pugnacious under the editorship of Dr. Ignacy Machnikowski and "Count" Jerzy Mirski. For some time it was peacefully disposed.

Beginning on June 10, 1901, Stanisław Osada was the editor-in-chief of *Dziennik Milwaucki*. Following his arrival in America in 1893, he worked at a tannery in Buffalo. A year later, however, he joined the ranks of Polish American journalists. He worked successively for *Reforma* in Buffalo, *Sztandar*, *Dziennik Polski* and *Nowe Życie* in Chicago, as well as for *Kuryer Polski* in Milwaukee.

The next editor of *Dziennik Milwaucki* was Ignacy Kowalski. Scandals published in *Dziennik* ill-disposed the public towards it. Business was bad, and after sinking $56,000 into this enterprise, the publishing company declared involuntary bankruptcy in August 1905.

GŁOS POLSKI [THE POLISH VOICE] OF GRAND RAPIDS, MICHIGAN[79]

TYGODNIK [THE WEEKLY] OF MINNEAPOLIS[80]

KOMAR [THE MOSQUITO] OF CHICAGO

Komar was a humorous periodical founded in 1900. It was edited by S. Zahajkiewicz, who for many years was a poet and literary man in the fullest sense of the word.[81] *Komar* folded in 1901.

KURYER ŚWIĄTECZNY [THE HOLIDAY COURIER] OF CHICAGO

This was also a humorous periodical, founded in 1900 and edited by Złotnicki. Through jest and humor it drove *Komar* into a corner, but not always with honorable tendencies. *Kuryer Świąteczny* failed, but was revived in 1903 as *Dzwon Niedzielny* [The Sunday Bell]. It stopped ringing in 1905.

N.K. Złotnicki, editor and publisher of *Dzwon Niedzielny*, was born in Zamość, Lublin district, in the Congress Kingdom. He received his education at the University of Warsaw and at a commercial school in Gdańsk.

His journalistic debut occurred in *Nowiny* [News], edited at the time by A. Świętochowski, and later in *Kuryer Codzienny* [Daily Courier]. For a year he managed *"Echa"* (a chronicle) in *Przegląd Tygodniowy* [The Weekly Review]. He wrote for *Kolce* [Thorns] and *Muchy* [Flies]. In 1890 he came to America and a week after his arrival he established *Kuryer Nowojorski* with Henryk Nagiel, a colleague from Warsaw University. Złotnicki also edited the Buffalo *Kukuryku*, published by the late M. J. Sadowski. In 1897 he moved to Chicago and edited *Djabel* [The Devil] and *Kropidło* [The Aspergillum]. In 1895 he became editor-in-chief of *Dziennik Narodowy*, but after fifteen months he left it to begin publication of *Kuryer Świąteczny*, which was later transformed into *Dzwon Niedzielny*.

MACIERZ POLSKA [THE POLISH ALMA MATER] OF CHICAGO[82]

A scientific and literary monthly founded in 1899. Published under Rev. Gordon's management, this periodical had a religious and patriotic character.

SIEROTA [THE ORPHAN] OF CHICAGO[83]

Founded in 1900, it was oriented toward religion and science.

TYGODNIK MILWAUCKI [THE MILWAUKEE WEEKLY][84]

Founded in 1901.

KURYER OHIOSKI [THE OHIO COURIER] OF TOLEDO, OHIO[85]

This weekly Catholic periodical was published in Toledo, Ohio, beginning in 1901, and was the property of a publishing partnership comprising Rev. A. Suplicki of Toledo, president; Rev. Paweł Ćwiąkała, DD, of Berea, Ohio, vice-president; Rev. K. Łaziński of Cleveland, manager; and K. J. Benkowski, a lawyer, as secretary and treasurer. Ludwik Haduch was the editor.

TYGODNIK KATOLICKI [THE CATHOLIC WEEKLY] AND *PROMIEN* [BEAM] OF LASALLE, ILLINOIS

Rev. Bernard Marya Skulik, DD, the local pastor, was the founder, owner, and editor of this periodical, which began publication in early 1902 and failed in 1905.[86]

DZIENNIK POLSKI [THE POLISH DAILY] OF DETROIT, MICHIGAN[87]

This is the sixth of the existing Polish dailies. It was founded in 1904 and belongs to the "Polish-American Pubishing Company" comprising Jan Welzand, president; M. Domzalski, secretary; A. Skoczek, treasurer; and J. Wedda, manager. W. Halicki is the editor. He had worked previously at *Kuryer Polski* in Milwaukee.

GŁOS KANADYJCKI [THE CANADIAN VOICE]

This was the first Polish newspaper in Canada. It was founded in 1904.

WSCHÓD [THE EAST][88]

A weekly begun in 1904 in Providence, Rhode Island.

ORĘDOWNIK JĘZYKOWY [THE LANGUAGE SPOKESMAN][89]

This publication cultivates language and was begun in 1905. The editor is Rev. B. Góral of St. Francis, Wisconsin.

HARMONIA [HARMONY]

The periodical of the Alliance of Polish Singers. It is published in Milwaukee.

This, then is the listing of the titles, histories and fates of those Polish newspapers in America that were founded before 1905.

Chapter 12

History of American Polish Literature

Samolińska—Wendziński—Karłowski—Szwajkart—Rev. K. Kozłowski—
Czupka—Ślisz—Dr. Machnikowski—Rev. Marcinkiewicz—Nagiel—Derdowski—Jabłoński—Iłowiecki—Rev. Słomiński—Zahajkiewicz—Mańkowska—Rev. Barabasz—Sawicka—Paryski, etc.—Artists—Theater.

American Polish literature is still in its infancy. Although still in dia-
pers, nevertheless it already does exist and has established a foundation.
Just as all beginnings are small and not immediately recognized as great,
so too, in our mother country, Poland, Kraków was not built in a day and
literature did not immediately reach the heights where it stands today. Its
development spanned centuries. As oaks grow slowly, so did Polish literature. It can be no different with Poland in America.

"Thus far our entire output in the field of author's creativity," writes
Stanisław Osada, "is very modest; it cannot be considered literature."[1] It is
true that it cannot be regarded as fully developed literature. And so, the
American Polish community does not even consider it literature. However, it can be said with certainty that it already exhibits the beginnings of
literature. And with a newly developing society, this is what is important.

As early as 1876 those in the Old Country recognized the beginnings of
American Polish literature. This is what was written about us on November 18, 1876, in *Ruch Literacki* [The Literary Movement], a weekly published in Lwów and devoted to literature, fine arts, science and social matters:

The development of Polish literature in America is an event of great significance. Thousands of Poles, driven to the land of the United States by persecution
or poverty, would have quickly lost their Polish national character among the alien
population if they were living without any organization and without literature, living in isolation, and occupied only with their own survival. The formation of
numerous Polish associations, especially parishes and Polish schools, which join

the diaspora into a unified whole, guarantees that they will preserve their nationality and will be saved for Poland; a second guarantee of preserving their nationality is their creation among them of this Polish literature.

Literature developed there [in the United States] spontaneously. The writers who created it were not authors in Europe. The need for Polish intellectual work, which manifested itself among the Polish colonists, put pens in their hands and inspired their thoughts. Therefore, they are authors out of necessity, and not by profession, and their works reflect the nature of this need; there is no art in them and the writers' proficiency is not great, but there is good will, conscientiousness and a desire to be useful to their brothers. As this literature continues to develop, talents will emerge and the works of American Poles will open a road to the homeland and will affect the general development of Polish literary output.

This was what the Lwów *Ruch Literacki* wrote about our germinating literature in 1876. Whether out literary works since then have "opened the road to the homeland," and to what extent, we will leave to the judgment of our motherland. Meanwhile, let us examine superficially, but objectively, the development of American Polish literature.

We already found in *Orzeł Polski* in 1870 the first traces of work by one of our literary forces in America who is worthy of attention. This force was Teofila Samolińska, later a prize-winner at a drama contest in Warsaw for the comedy *Trzy Flory* [Three Flora], which she submitted from Chicago about 1880.[2] In the second issue of its first volume (March 8, 1870), *Orzeł Polski* published what was probably Samolińska's first printed poem. This work, sent from Cincinnati, was entitled *Do rodaków!* [To the Countrymen]. For the purpose of characterizing it, we will quote the following verse:

> W tym to tu kraju Zjednoczonych Stanów
> Tu możem płakać nad stratą Ojczyzny,
> Tu nas nie sięgnie okrutność tyranów,
> Tutaj się zatrą zadane nam blizny!

> In this country of the United States
> We will not be reached by the tyrants' hates
> Here we can mourn the loss of our Fatherland
> And heal the scars of our wounded band.

It is appropriate to point out that the form of Samolińska's later works is many times more splendid than that which was probably one of her first poems.

Later, about 1878, she wrote letters to *Przyjaciel Ludu,* about which Henryk Nagiel commented as follows:

Hers is an energetic pen; not a feminine one, but more masculine. The Chicago relations presented in her letters take on plasticity; her humor and sarcastic comments at times elicit sharp protests by those whom they touched; at any rate, the correspondent does not fear battling with them. She fences energetically with her pen and she sometimes wins.

At that time Ignacy Wendziński also prepared two booklets, published in the print shop of *Orzeł*: These were *Definicya o nieomylności Papieża* [A Definition of Papal Infallibility; 1871] and *Nauka o jubileuszu* [A Lesson about the Jubilee; 1871].[3]

Wiktor Karłowski, an 1863 insurgent, later a soldier of the French Foreign Legion in Mexico and Algiers, and finally a *franc-tireur* in the Franco-Prussian War of 1870-1871, subsequently came to America and was elected to the Illinois state legislature. He described his experiences during his stay in Europe and Mexico in a small book entitled *Z przygód tułacza* [From the Adventures of a Wanderer], which was published in Chicago in 1884. He is also the author of a short story entitled "W oczach śmierci" [In the Eyes of Death], published in 1885.

Stanisław Szwajkart, the editor of *Dziennik Chicagoski*, wrote a story entitled "Lila" in the columns of *Zgoda* in 1881.

Rev. Kandyd Kozłowski[4] from Lamont, Illinois, was the author of a few small works including *Antychryst* [Antichrist], *Przeniesienie—Domku Loren-tańskiego* [The Relocation of the House of Our Lady of Loretto], *Sobieski pod Wiedniem* [Sobieski at Vienna], a drama called *Św. Mikołaj* [St. Nicholas], and a tragedy titled *Powstanie 63 roku* [The 1863 Uprising].

Dr. Julian Czupka broke his pen and hurled himself into the industrial field a long time ago because here in America literature is still not profitable.[5] However, he is the talented author of many humorous and serious poems. His song in which the verse "Bo ta Ameryka to śliczny wolny kraj" [Because this America is a beautiful free country] repeats itself will undoubtedly outlive him and will resound on the lips of our local youth as long as there is Polish speech "in this beautiful free country." Here are excerpts from *Piosnka o Ameryce*:

Song of America

1. Gdy w domu ci jest źle,
   Wolności ci się chce,
   Porzuć ten brzydki dom
   Jedź do naszych stron.
   Tu ci błogi los
   Napełni złotem trzos
   Zaświta szczęście ci
   Wesołych dni!

   Chór: Bo ta Ameryka
   To śliczny, wolny kraj,
   Wszystkiego dosyć ma,
   To ziemski raj!

2. Gdy skradniesz chleba kęs
   By zaspokoić głód,
   Zamkną cię na rok
   Nie wypuszczą wprzód—
   Lecz skradnij złota trzos,
   To świetny zrobisz los
   Postawisz tylko bejl
   Otworzą ci wnet dżejl

   Chór. . . .

3. Gdy mieszkać nie ma gdzie
   Przespać możesz się
   W parku którymbądź
   Na ławce sobie siądź.
   I gdy strudzony już
   Toniesz w smacznym śnie
   Wtedy anioł stróż
   Pałką budzi cię.

   Chór. . . .

4. Zarobku pełno tu
   I pracy wielka moc
   Szukasz jej bez tchu
   Biegając dzień i noc,
   A gdy świadectwa masz

1. When things go badly in your house
   And liberty is on your mind
   Then leave that place behind
   And come to our shores.
   Here a good fortune's dawn
   May fill your purse with gold
   Good luck will then take hold
   And happy days shall be your own!

   Chorus:
   Because America beckons sweet
   With its lovely open land
   And with everything on hand
   It's a paradise on earth indeed.

2. When you swipe a piece of bread
   To take care of hunger's pain
   A year's jail may be your gain
   And liberty will not be had.
   But steal a purse with gold
   Good fortune will take hold
   Merely put up a bail
   And you will soon leave jail.

   Chorus. . . .

3. And if you find no place to stay
   A bench will do in a park someway
   Where you find comfort at its best
   To stretch your tired bones and rest.
   When you are finally sound asleep
   Someone will wake you with a beep
   This angel guardian who is a cop
   May also hit you with a club.

   Chorus. . . .

4. Wages here are plentiful on sight
   And prospects of work are surely
   bright
   But when applying for it, they get tight
   Even when you chase them day and
   night.
   And when you come with
   certificates

Aż z dwóch fakultetów,	From as many as two faculties
Posadę dadzą ci	You will get a job alright
Do dojenia krów!	To milk the cows at night.
Chór. . . .	Chorus. . . .

5. Pożartuj z panną raz
   Choć w biały, jasny dzień,
   To choćby piorun trząsł
   Już się bratku żeń!
   Bo sprawiedliwy sąd
   Nie pyta: ktoś i skąd?
   Czyś rad jej czyś nie rad
   Żeń się bratku z nią!

   Chór. . . .

5. Having some fun with a young lady
   You are expected to go steady
   And suddenly on a clear bright day
   You have to marry her right away!
   Because the righteous court will not
   Ask who, where from or what
   You better like her the way she is
   And enjoy life in married bliss!

   Chorus. . . .

Stanisław Ślisz, an outstanding journalistic force in America, also left his mark in the literary field.[6] He wrote *Podręcznik wojskowy* [A military textbook], and novels such as *Z miłości* [Out of Love], *Obcy w rodzinnym kraju* [A Stranger in the Homeland], *Emigrant* [The Emigrant], *Pod Pokładem* [Under the Deck], and a few shorter stories which were printed in the semi-weekly *Ojczyzna* published in Buffalo during the years 1885-1887. The Old Country newspapers accepted his stories with favorable reviews. Besides this, Ślisz translated a few novels from foreign languages. In Galicia he wrote letters to *Samorząd* [Self-government].

Dr. Ignacy Machnikowski, a lover of astronomy and exact sciences, wrote, among others, a novel depicting customs, which was set against a religious background, entitled *Szkaplerz Matki* [Mother's Scapular].[7] He distinguished himself by his great ease of writing, but he did not make adequate use of his talent, because he did not make his living through literature.

Kazimierz Neuman, editor of *Dziennik Chicagoski*, wrote a few short stories including "Mój spadek w Ameryce" [My Inheritance in America], "Moi trzej przyjaciele" [My Three Friends], "Cerkiew w Rypinie" [The Orthodox Church in Rypin] and others which were published under the pseudonym of "Janusz" or "Dada," and so on.[°]

Rev. Adam Marcinkiewicz, the pastor at Czarna Skałka [Black Rock] in Buffalo is a talented writer. The following are some of the titles of his works: *Redaktor w zalotach* [The Courting Editor] (a work that received an award at a literary contest), *Dziekan i Żaby* [The Dean and the Frogs] (a free translation of Lafontaine), *Kłopoty Gracza* [The Problems of a Card

Player], *Wanda* [Wanda] (a poem), *Kazania okolicznościowe* [Sermons for Different Occasions], and so on.

Henryk Nagiel has completed his service and has moved to a better world, but his name, both in the field of Polish journalism in America and in Polish American literature, will be remembered with appreciation.[9] As an author he did not write much because he did not have the time, but he had plenty of talent. Through the report *Dziennikarstwo Polskie w Ameryce i jego 30-letnie dzieje* [Polish Journalism in America and Its Thirty-Year History], which covered the years through 1894, he rendered a great service to those who would occupy themselves with the future developments in this field.

His largest American work was a novel based on local relations, entitled *Kara Boża idzie przez oceany* [God's Punishment Transcends Oceans]. In it the author was concerned only with sensation, with kindling curiosity and attempting to be entertained. He was either unable to, or did not want to, introduce other elements into the novel that would have given it greater moral and artistic value. In this regard the novel does not differ much from *Tajemnic Nalewek* [The Secret of Making Liquors with Herbs and Berries], which he had written while he was still in Poland. At any rate, he did possess an outstanding talent.

Hieronim Derdowski, author of the history *O panu Czorlińścim* [Of Mr. Czorliński] and of *Emigrancyi żydów do Palestyny* [The Emigration of Jews to Palestine], wrote hardly anything in the last years of his life.[10] To *Czorlińści* he added only a few insignificant pieces in the Kaszubian dialect. The volumes of *Wiarus* will also remain as his legacy.

Rev. Hieronim Jabłoński wrote a few novels here in America that were printed in *Dniu Święty* [The Holy Day].[11] One of them is *Dzieci Wisielca* [Children of a Hanged Person]. His *Kłopoty Pana Bencwała* [The Troubles of Mr. Bencwal][12] is full of wit and humor.

Dr. Józef Iłowiecki splendidly translated Byron's "Giaur," some of Heine's songs, and Cervantes' *Don Quixote*. His original works, beside many fine lesser poems, include the completion of Słowacki's unfinished, or rather damaged, five- act drama "Horsztyński." We wish to note here that, of the few critical works on this beautiful drama, the best is the work of Dr. Iłowiecki, which was recognized by such an expert on literature as St. Tarnowski. Dr. Iłowiecki dedicated himself to literature, especially to poetry, with full fervor, and it is a shame that he did not publish his works and did not let the public get to know him on a wider scale. Ideas would come to him suddenly and he would take pen in hand and create. In this manner the parody of Shakespeare's "Tymon, the Athenian" emerged, in which the author criticizes contemporary relations through the eye of an inside observer. Dr. Iłowiecki, though irregularly, wrote letters to friends and acquaintances in beautiful poetic form. In other words, he possessed a great talent, but due to his struggle for survival in a difficult profession, he dedicated too little time to the muses; rather, he sought tranquility and solace in them after his toils in the gray background of daily life.

Dr. Iłowiecki was born in 1850 in Rycz, in the Wągrowa district. He completed his studies in the then-famous *gimnazyum* in Trzemeszno, which was to the history of the Prussian sector [of partitioned Poland] more or less what the Marymount school near Warsaw was for the Polish Kingdom, the school in Nowogrodek was for Lithuania, and the school in Niemirow was for Russia. For many years a special patriotic spirit existed in these schools, and with each generation they produced several outstanding workers.

To continue our look at Polish American literature, Rev. Słomiński was the author of beautiful dramas such as "Narzędzie Szatana" [Instrument of Satan] and others which were performed on parish stages.[13]

Szczęsny Zahajkiewicz was the most famous Polish poet in America.[14] His talent was unquestionable and his pen was precious. Zahajkiewicz was born in 1861 in Stanisłowo, Galicia. He was educated in Kołomyja and Stanisłowo, and thereafter worked as a teacher. While living in Stanisłowo and Lwów he wrote much verse and prose in Polish and Ruthenian, especially for youth. He contributed to *Szkoła* [The School], a pedagogical publication, as well as to periodicals for the common people and for youth. In Lwów he edited *Światełko* [The Little Light] and wrote humorous poems for *Szczutka* [The Fillip] and *Śmigus* [Easter Monday].[15] Departing Galicia for America in mid-1889, he left behind in the Old Country a collection of poems entitled *Rymy* [Rhymes], a dozen or so pamphlets and fictional works, and other works designed mainly for youth. Some of these include: *Dwie baśnie* [Two Fairytales], *Pamiętniki mądrej muchy* [Memoirs of a Smart Fly], *Wśród Indyan* [Among the Indians], *Sassacus* [Sassacus], *O Janie Karolu Chodkiewiczu* [Of John Carl Chodkiewicz], and so on. His Ruthenian works include the following folk tales: *Nad Dniestrem* [On the Dniester], *Dziadek Iwaś* [Grandpa Iwaś], *Czarownik* [The Sorcerer], *Michał z Korostowa* [Michael from Korostow], and many more. As of 1889, Zahajkiewicz's literary activity in Chicago was very lively. There he began to write for the stage. Through the efforts of the Polish Publishing Company he published his novels and dramatic works in *Biblioteka Ludowa*. These works include: *"Wieczór wigilijny"* [Christmas Eve], *"Trzy ziarnka grochu i syn dziadowski"* [Three Peas and the Beggar's Son], *"Powiastki dla małej dziatwy"* [Stories for Little Children], *"Dzieci Izraela"* [Children of Israel] (a dramatic picture), *"Noc Czarodziejska"* [Sorcerer's Night], *"Powinszowania"* [Best Wishes], and *"Książę Czarnoksiężników"* [Count of the Sorcerers]. Besides *"Dzieci Izraela"* and *"Noc Czarodziejska,"* the following dramatic plays were presented on stage in Chicago: *"Jasnogóra"* [Bright Mountain], *"Powrót łaty"* [Papa's Return], *"Oświadczny przez telefon"* [Proposal over the Telephone], *"Niespodzianka"* [A Surprise], *"Akademia Smorgońska"* [The Smorgonska Academy], *"Jadwiga"* [Hedwig], *"Perła Cyllejska"* [The Silesian Pearl], and others. In 1894 he published what was referred to as a "small collection of his poetry." In 1897 he published *Złotą Księga* [Golden Book], a description of Polish parishes and priests in Chicago and the vicinity. He was a genuine writer of the purist kind.

A Polish woman, Marya de Mańkowska, also achieved recognition in the literary field.[16] English newspapers appearing in Houston, Texas, wrote favorably about her works including the translation of novels from her native language into English. To former works by Julian Jasieńczyk that had enjoyed great popularity, such as *Dziesięć lat w niewoli u Kozaków* [Ten Years in Cossack Slavery] and *Czarna Rosya* [Black Russia], one more was added in 1902. This was *Faraon* [The Pharaoh], translated by de Mańkowska with extremely colorful language and with extraordinary accuracy. A note inserted by Abbé Press at the beginning of this new work attests to the great popularity of our countrywoman among Americans. The inscription reads as follows: The lady, whose previous works are known to you, translated this from the Polish language." Mrs. de Mańkowska, although born on American soil, brings us great honor through her work and her effort to exalt the Polish name in America.

Stefan Barszczewski is the author of a few lesser works and the melodrama *Cuba Libre*.[17] He distinguished himself with his unmistakable talent, but worked too little as an author in the creative field to appropriately shape public opinion. *Cuba Libre* has a few good scenes, but it is deficient where the author does not curb his fantasy. In addition, its literary value is impeded by a somewhat provincial tendency to place one organization in the forefront and agitate too much on its behalf. *Cuba Libre* is undoubtedly better than Brodowski's *Związkowiec* [The Unionist], but only because it has more scenes in which these tendencies are forgotten and life and its manifestations are observed. If Barszczewski wanted to develop his talent he could have contributed to what we should all be striving for—the creation of Polish American literature.

The Rev. Barabasz was a poet.[18] His translation in verse of Rev. Coppe's "Ojcze Nasz" [Our Father], published in *Niedziela* [Sunday], was worthy of attention in all respects.

Szymon Modrzewski, a "poet-carpenter," besides possessing a certain ease of verse, distinguished himself by his most radical views.[19] The print shop of *Nowe Życie* published a small collection of his poems in 1893.

Tomasz Siemiradzki came to America as a professor of the Uniwersytet Ludowy [Polish People's University], having been brought to this country by the Education Department of the Polish National Alliance. As long as this university existed, he taught history. Thereafter he taught at the Polish seminary in Detroit until 1901, then edited *Zgoda* in the spirit of an "historian" or a "specialist in the philosophy of history." He also wrote as an historian; his extensive work *Porozbiorowe Dzieje Polski* [The History of Poland Following the Partitions] is not only informative about dates and occurrences, but also asserts the national strength and establishes a belief in a better future for the nation.

Rev. Wacław Kruszka, besides his numerous and fortuitous newspaper articles, wrote *Rzym* [Rome], *Neapol i Wezuwiusz* [Naples and Vesuvius], *Hymny Wielkopostne* [Lenten Hymns], *O Piękności* [On Beauty], *Anarchizm i jego stosunek do socyalizmu* [Anarchism and Its Relation to Socialism], *Które rządy najlepsze?* [Which Regime Is Better?], and *Wrażenia z wycieczki missyjnej* [Impressions from a Missionary Tour], as well as the English text *The Unbeliever Before the Tribunal of Reason.*

Until 1905 Helena Sawicka had admittedly not written and published very much, but even in those fragments, novels, scenes, and so on, published from time to time in one newspaper or another, she showed much talent and originality.[20] Sawicka was probably the only representative in America of one of the newer trends in literature—symbolism. She wrote picturesquely, very carefully choosing harmonious sounding phrases; she wrote poetry based on the most prosaic language, but did not fall into decadence—writing "nonsensical nonsense"—which would be understood only by so-called "supermen."

Alfons Chrostowski was a totally deranged but nevertheless talented person.[21] Today [in 1905] no one is interested in him, but Henryk Nagiel has already noted that "if not for his moral shortcomings he could occupy a certain position in literature not only in America but also in Europe." He wrote a few skillful dramas such as *Nihiliści* [The Nihilists], *Śmierć Uli-*

janowa [The Death of Ulijanow], *Uwiedziona* [The Seduced Woman], and so on. He also began many works he did not complete. Unfortunately, his was a totally wasted talent.

Rev. Stefan Dąbkowski, CR, was the author of a small work titled *Pierwszy Zakon z łona Polski* [The First Order from the Womb of Poland].[22]

Rev. Stanisław Siatka, CR, wrote *Krótkie wspomnienie o śp. ks. W. Barzyńskim* [Brief Reminiscences about the Late Rev. W. Barzyński].[23] Other fruits from his pen were published in the monthly *Sierotka* [The Orphan], which he edited.

The Rev. Bernard Marya Skulik, author of *Sznaps* [Schnapps], *Stolica Mądrości* [The Capital of Wisdom], *Teologia Pastoralna* [Pastoral Theology], *Luter i Djabeł* [Luther and the Devil], *Kielnia Masońska* [The Mason's Trowel], and other works, is undoubtedly the most productive Polish writer in America.[24] It is enough to say that he wrote and published forty-six greater and lesser works on a variety of subjects. He is also a multilingual writer. Besides twenty-two books in Polish, he published two works in Slovak, five in German, eleven in Italian, three in Latin, and three in English.

Of the works of Stanisław Osada, we should mention a few scenes from the life of Colonel Miłkowski (printed in *Reforma* in 1895). He also wrote "Literatura polsko-amerykańska" [Polish American Literature] (printed in *Kuryer Polski*), and "Liberum Veto," a work awarded first prize at a contest of the Education Department of the Polish National Alliance and printed in *Zgoda* and elsewhere. Further, he also wrote *O Stronnictwie Demokratyczno-Narodowem i Lidze Narodowej* [On the Democratic National Faction and the National League] and *Historya Związku N.P.* [The History of the Polish National Alliance].

Dr. Franciszek E. Fronczak is the author of many medical papers in both Polish ("Stosunki lekarskie w Stanach Zjedn. Półn. Am." [Medical Conditions in the United States of North America], a reprint from *Przegląd lekarski* [The Medical Review; Kraków, 1900]) and English ("Compound Dislocations," 1899; "The Pathogenesis of Chloelithiasis," 1899; "The Resuscitation of Apparently Dead Newborns," 1900; "Lands Across the Seas," or medical impressions from a trip throughout Europe, 1900; "Alcoholism," 1900; "Plica Polonica," 1898, a paper about matted hair, is the broadest and the only serious medical work on this subject in the United States).[25]

This young physician-writer, Dr. Franciszek Eustach Fronczak, A.M.,

M.D., LL.B., was born in Buffalo, New York, on September 20, 1874, the son of Wojciech and Wiktoria Jaworska Fronczak. He attended the local parish school of St. Stanislaus from 1879 to 1887, then Canisius College from 1887 to 1894. He received his Bachelor of Arts degree *summa cum laude* and other awards on June 21, 1894. He then took up graduate education and received his Master of Arts degree in 1895. He received the degree Doctor of Medicine from the Medical Department of the University of Buffalo on April 28, 1897. He was awarded first prize for his paper "Plica Polonia" (matted hair). This is the only exhaustive paper on the subject in English and is currently used as a textbook in a few medical schools. He attended the Law Department of The University of Buffalo from 1897 to 1899 and received his LL.B. degree. Dr. Fronczak was a collaborator on a few medical journals and was generally very active in the field of medicine.

During his ten year stay in America (1892-1902), Jan Kuk, a retired teacher from Galicia, published his *Wiersze ulotne* [Transitory Poems], as well as the valuable *Poemat dydaktyczny* [Didactic Poem], in which he presented special teaching instructions for Polish schools in America.[26] There also appeared a didactic-moral poem entitled *Smutne Przygody* [Sad Adventures] bearing the signature J.K.; however, J. Kuk was not the author of this as some said. *Smutne Przygody*, despite its so-called moral tendencies, can be considered to be pornographic literature.

Ignacy Kowalski wrote a piece about "*Szkoły Polski Parafialna*" [Polish Parish Schools].

Stefan Rachocki was talented at creating rhymes.

During the past year, Rev. F. Hodur's "novel" *Faryzeusze i Saduceusze* [The Pharisees and the Saduccees] appeared together with his "drama" *Zbrodniarze* [The Criminals].[27] In *Zbrodniarze* crime follows upon crime, which is followed by still more crime. Even the only "honest" hero of the drama murders people and finally takes his own life. In *Faryzeusze i Saduceusze* the author maintains that Christ appeared to him and clearly commanded him to form the Polish "independent" church. In the brochure *Nowe Drogi* [New Roads] he presents the history and characteristics of the "national church" which he created. More characterization is unnecessary; what I have said is sufficient. In general his periodicals abounded in dishevelled atheistic and socialistic ideas.

A. Zdziebłowski[28] and Antoni Jax[29] are two interesting types of Polish American playwrights. Both do not accurately know orthography and both write dramas and comedies that are extremely popular on our amateur stages. Furthermore, both are tradesmen by profession and write during free time from their hard work.

Stanisław Łempicki is the author of "Sonata Duchów" [Ghost Sonata].[30] Further, the following literary forces are of great dimension and worthy of mention here: Dr. Gawrzyjelski (poet), Zygmunt Brodowski (author of Związkowiec), St. Nawrocki (poet),[31] and many others.

It seems to me that the list of those who have made efforts in the literary field, or of those who are actually working on it, is complete, although it is probably not quite accurate. Nevertheless, in addition to the talented journalists and publishers who were acquainted with their profession so thoroughly that they had few equals even in Poland—such as M. Kruszka, Szwajkart, Neuman, S. Ślisz, A. A. Paryski, Władisław Dyniewicz and others—we still have here a substantial group of writers who, if not excessively impeded by the constant exertion of all their intellectual faculties in order to support and develop business, could have effectively tried their hand at writing.

Such journalists as J. J. Chrzanowski, Leon T. Wild, Leon Machnikowski, S. Horbaczewski, F. P. Danisch, Józef Kruszka, F. Szczerbowski, Dr. Gruenberg, L. Olszewski, Z. Chrzanowski, Z. Olszanowski, and others, as can be determined from their lesser works, from journalistic articles, and so on, still have enough strength to dare to attempt still one more step forward. Many of them would undoubtedly try if not for the fact that many things impede rather than encourage this work.

In America there is no lack of Polish masters both in literature and in the fine arts. In the field of painting there are first-rate artists—Żukotyński[32] from Chicago, Żabiński[33] in Milwaukee, and Modrakowski[34] in New York. In the field of construction there is Bernard Kołpacki,[35] the architect of a million-dollar postal building in Milwaukee and of many churches in Wisconsin. In the theater, Helena Modrzejewska[36] from California enjoys undying fame. There will be more about her in the description of Poles in California. In virtually every parish there is a theater hall where amateur actors perform beautiful dramatic plays, but despite numerous efforts, a permanent Polish popular theater has not yet been organized in America. In song and music one sees Antoni Małłek[37] from Chicago, the renowned composer of many musical works, as well as B. J. Zalewski[38] from Chicago, who generously covers expenses for publishing Polish musical works in America. There is also Jadwiga Smulska,[39] wife of the well-known spokesman for the city of Chicago, Jan Smulski. In 1900 Mrs. Smulska received a gold medal from the Chicago Musical College at a competitive singing performance; she also received a diploma for graduating from that institution. There are as many Polish preachers and political speakers shining in the firmament of American fine arts as there are stars in the sky.

Chapter 13

The American Polish Dialect

To the great distress and indignation of our *purystów* [purists] or language experts, the Poles in America, much the same as the Poles from Silesia or Kaszubia, created their own dialect, or American-Polish speech, which they use on a daily basis. A *grynhorn* [greenhorn; a person newly arrived from the Old Country], of course, has difficulty understanding such a dialect and is often appalled by it, reproaching his immigrant countrymen for corrupting the native language with adopted words and for distorting it beyond recognition. But soon the same *grynhorn* who recently was so appalled by the American Polish dialect slowly begins to express himself by saying that today he will go to the city by *karą* [car; in Polish, *wagon kolejowy*] for *biznesem* [business; in Polish, *interes* or *sprawunek*]. A *grynhorn* begins with these expressions, but before long he does not stop there; for a person becomes like those with whom he associates. He soon learns to polonize other English words and says that he was in a *salunie* [saloon; in Polish *karczma*] where at the *barze* [bar] stood the *barkiper* [barkeeper; *szynkarz*] who served *wiski* [whiskey; *gorzałki*], and next they had *luncz* [lunch; *przekąska*] and *potrytowali* [treated; *częstować*] each other to a beer.[1]

This same newcomer, after these experiences, stops being a *grynhorn*, he stops being *zielonym* [green] and becomes a mature American who will *wotował* [vote; *głosować*] in the next *elekszen* [election; *wybory*]. He goes to the *sztoru* [store; *skład*], to the *groserni* [grocery store; *skład korzenny*], to the *buczra* [butcher; *rzeźnik*], to the *drajguds-sztoru* [drygoods store; *skład łokciowy*] to buy himself an *owerkot* [overcoat; *palto*], *kendów* [candies; *karmelki*] for his *bebi* [baby; *dziecie*], on the *kornerze* [corner; *róg*] three *bloki* [blocks; *ulicami odgraniczony czworobok domów*] near the *eli* [alley; *zaułek*].

He received *pejdę* [pay; *wypłacone*] in *kiesz* [cash; *gotówką*]. Then he went to the *ofisu* [office; *biuro*], asked for the *klerka* [clerk; *kancelista*, *sekretarz*], and then the *bas* [boss] came in. He requested the *bil* [bill; *rachunek*].

In America there are no peasants or country folk, there are only *farmerzy* [farmers]; there are no villages, only *farmy* [farms]. One speaks of *korna* [corn], *kaunty* [county], *kryka* [creek], *taun* [town], the *wardy* [wards] in cities, *kerrycze* [carriages] and *bogi* [buggies]. Anyone who is a homeowner has a *dyd* [deed] and money is borrowed for a *morgecz* [mortgage]. No one competes for an office, rather he *leci* [runs] for an office.

A Pole in America says *strajk* and *strajkować*, not *strejk* and *strejkowac* as the Poles in Europe erroneously say and write. These words come from "to strike" and are pronounced as *strajk*.

Bojkotować [to boycott] is a new word in both Polish and English because it has been used only since 1881. During agrarian disturbances in northern Ireland in 1880-1881 a captain named Boycott, who was a tenant on lands belonging to Lord Erne, compromised himself with the Irish peasants so much that no one wanted to gather grain from his fields. Because of this the phrase *bojkot* or *boykotować* first achieved civil law status during these disturbances and meant the same as ostracism or banishment did to the Athenians, that is banishment of someone from the social circle to which he belonged and the dispossession of all social rights. Therefore, to *boykotować* someone means to consider him a social outcast with whom, as with anyone cast out of society, no one should have any relations. He should not be given material or moral support, but should be considered stripped of all human rights. Therefore, the idea of *boykot* expands further than the idea of *strajk*: to strike is to refrain from work, to stop according to a previously devised plan, but a boycott goes further because it not only prohibits offering the worker's services, but it also endeavors to keep others from working and effectively cuts off the boycotted person from the rest of the world, placing him outside social rights. A strike hits and injures the employer, but a boycott kills him socially, or at least attempts to kill him.

The Poles in America like to eat *paje* [pie] and *pudingi* [pudding] no less than the rest of the Americans. Let the purists wrack their brains about how to polonize the two words *paj* and *puding*. We, as practical Americans, will not only continue to eat pies, but will call them *paje* and not *placki* or *plastry* [cakes or tarts].[2] Thus also our people in America favor the word *pentry* [pantry] in place of *szafarnią* or *spiżarnia* [pantry]. Why did our people abandon the traditional names? Why do they assimilate the new ones? Well, why? Ask the people themselves. They themselves do not know, because they do it by instinct. A living language would not be alive if it did not undergo constant changes and transformations, especially when the people speaking this language find themselves in a new environment and different circumstances. The acceptance of the new and the abandonment of the old words should be considered a totally natural occurrence in a living language; on the contrary, it would be an unnatural occurrence and a sign of language torpor if a language always remained the same without assimilating any new phrases or eliminating any old, used and antiquated phrases.

Who will succeed in eliminating from the Polish language the word *tajprajter* [typewriter], designating a mechanical machine for writing or printing? Of the Poles in America, who will call an alderman something other than that, or a mayor something other than a mayor? An overseer of a ward, something other than a *superwizor* [supervisor]? Who here will have someone arrested and not *wyciąga no niego warantu* [post a warrant; *rozkaz uwięzienia, list gończy*]?

A *forman* [foreman] in America has much in common with a *furman* [wagon driver] in the Old Country in that a *forman* supervises the workers in a factory, typesetters in a printshop, just as a *furman* controls horses.

A Pole in America refers to an official who is investigating the deaths of those murdered or who died of unnatural causes as a *koronerem* [coroner].

This is only a *blof* [bluff], it means something only to the eye, to pull the wool over the eyes. In America there are no *prawodawczych* [law-giving bodies] or *parlamentów* [parliaments], only *legislatury* and *kongressy*. *Doraźny sąd* [martial law] and punishment carried out by a mob do not exist, only *lyncz* and *lynczowanie* [to lynch]. The lower part of a house or church with rooms half below and half above the ground, which in the Old Country is called *sklep*, is called *bezment* [basement] by a Pole in America. In America the Poles are not familiar with *morgi*[3] but with *akry* [acres].

A Pole in America will not call an Irishman anything other than *Ajrysz*,[4] because the Irishman both writes and calls himself "Irish" and pronounces it "*ajrysz*." A Pole in America always and unequivocally says *stary kraj* [old country; with the adjective being *starokrajski*] when referring to Poland and Europe in general, because no English speaker here will refer to Europe other than as "the Old Country." A statement sworn before a *notaryusz publiczny* [notary public] is called an *affidavit*.

In our opinion these words, perhaps not all of them but at least those generally accepted as polonized and used widely by the Polish population of one million, must be considered by anyone who wants to draw up an accurate and complete Polish dictionary in the future. The above-mentioned words could and should be eliminated from books or literary language; however, they should not, because they cannot, be eliminated from everyday speech or from the people's dialect. Not to allow a living language to assimilate new words from the environment in which it finds itself would be to cut the roots it has struck in a new, foreign ground where it has been transplanted; this would mean that the language was destined for extinction. If the Polish language, transplanted on American soil, is to continue to live and develop, it naturally has to draw the vital juices from this soil where it has been transplanted; it must breathe the surrounding atmosphere and must assimilate foreign words, altering them an becoming enriched by them. If it did not possess this capacity, so to speak, to become acclimated, this would be a sure sign of its torpor. But on the contrary it is precisely in this acclimatization that the vitality of a language is exhibited, and that it is capable of adapting itself to new though foreign living conditions. Not to allow language, which has been thrust out of the Polish soil and transplanted to English soil, to take root in this English language and to assimilate English words would be the same as digging up a tree from the earth, hanging it with its roots in the air and expecting it still to live and grow!

The ideal written or literary language is something else; it is not spoken in conversation; it is only written in books. As a fine but lifeless art, it can daydream, it can hang like a beautiful painting in a museum or like a painted, artificial flower it can adorn walls and rooms. However, as time goes by and its form of speech becomes old and drab, even this literary language, the artificial language, changes to a new and fresh form, discarding antiquated words and exchanging them for new ones. A living, natural, real language, which is spoken every day, needs this change even more. This day-to-day language, in order to live, must seek nourishment from the environment in which it lives, must constantly take in and absorb new elements, and eject and expel the old, worn out and used ones. The natural process of growing and living indispensably requires this.

It could be that this process of transformation of the Polish language of the people in America should have taken place according to totally different rules, but it is not our place to dictate the rules here! An historian must write down the manifestations of life as he observes them, not as he thinks they should be. We are not writing what the American Polonia should be, according to the ideals of some, but what it was and still is in reality. History should be a mirror, accurately reflecting its visage: let her look into it, and if she sees spots and flaws somewhere, let her cleanse herself of them!

Thus, it seems to me that the objections put forth by some when this chapter on "American Polish dialect" was first published in the newspaper are dispelled. However, we were criticized by a certain editor from Buffalo, New York, who wrote in a private letter: "The Reverend Father praises, as it were, the dialect used by the Poles in America. This will be a collection of words whose meaning will only be understood by an American Pole. By justifying the use of such a dialect, the American Polonia is only encouraged to denationalize, which the Reverend Father surely does not desire . . . ."

We surely do not desire this. But with the obligation of an historian we have ascertained a fact that cannot be denied, that the Polish language of the people in America has undergone a change. And also as an obligation of an historian, we have explained this fact by a rule, which seems to be a general historical rule; that is, that the language of a people, not only Polish, but any other language when coming in close proximity with a foreign language, is naturally modified, especially on the lips of simple people. By explaining this fact, we do not by any means intend to encourage Poles to denationalize. Most certainly, and with reason, we believe that quoting these Americanisms in *Historya* will be a frightening rather than an encouraging example to the Polish reading public. The public will look into this "dictionary" as into a mirror, will be convinced that the image it sees does not look good, and will say with indignation: "Do I look like that? I must look differently!"—and it will improve.

Notes

INTRODUCTION

1. Anthony Kuzniewski, SJ, *Faith and Fatherland*; Edward Kantowicz, *Corporate Sale*, pp. 6-8.

2. Jay Dolan, *American Catholic Experience*, pp. 172, 184-85.

DEDICATION

1. Rowland Blennerhassett Mahany (1864-1937): diplomat; Republican member of Congress from Buffalo (1895-99); lawyer; harbor commissioner of Buffalo (1899-1906); member of the Wilson administration in various capacities dealing with labor, foreign trade, and immigration matters. Mahany replaced Rev. Jan Pitass of Buffalo as Kruszka's fellow delegate to Rome, leaving in June, 1903, to negotiate with the Vatican for a Polish bishop in the United States. They were acting on instructions from the Executive Committee of the Polish Catholic Congress. See: *Biographical Dictionary of the American Congress 1774–1961* (Washington, D.C.: Government Printing Office, 1961), p. 1254; Joseph J. Parot, *Polish Catholics in Chicago* (DeKalb, Illinois: Northern Illinois University Press, 1981), pp. 156-57; Anthony J. Kuzniewski, *Faith & Fatherland: The Polish Church War in Wisconsin, 1896-1918* (Notre Dame, Indiana: University of Notre Dame Press, 1980), pp. 49-53.

PREFACE

Original Preface

1. Kruszka attributes this quotation to words spoken by Bishop Spalding of Peoria, Illinois, on August 14, 1892. Bishop John Lancaster Spalding (1840-1916) had once been associated with the Americanizing wing of the American Catholic hierarchy led by Archbishop John Ireland and Cardinal James Gibbons but had become, as Kruszka implied, more tolerant of ethnic persistence. See: David Francis Sweeney, *The Life of John Lancaster Spalding, First Bishop of Peoria: 1840-1916* (New York: Herder and Herder, 1965), p. 286.

2. In an effort to counter the influences of Catherine II of Russia, Polish reformers organized the anti-Russian Confederation of Bar. Following a Russian invasion of Poland, Russia, Prussia, and Austria cooperated in seizing large portions of Polish territory in the First Partition of 1772. A long period of legislative reform resulted in a new Polish constitution on May 3, 1791. This prompted the Russians to intercede once again and precipitate the Second Partition in January, 1793. Polish troops under Tadeusz Kościuszko fought a bitter campaign against the Russians in 1794-1795, but were unable to prevent the fall of Warsaw and the elimination of Poland from the map of Europe in the Third Partition (October 1795). Polish

political refugees fled throughout Europe, many of them joining forces with Napoleon I in the hope of liberating their homeland. Throughout the nineteenth century, Polish political exiles continued to flee overseas, especially following the Polish revolts of 1830-1831, 1846, and 1863. Many of these émigrés eventually migrated to the United States.

3. For analyses of the reasons for Polish emigration see: Victor R. Greene, "Pre-World War I Polish Emigration to the United States: Motives and Statistics," *The Polish Review*, VI (Summer, 1961); M. Lucille, "The Causes of Polish Immigration to the United States," *Polish American Studies*, VIII (1951); J. Zubrzycki, "Emigration from Poland in the 19th and 20th Centuries," *Population Studies*, V-VI (1953).

4. In the original text, Kruszka uses the words *kolonia* and *osada* to describe Polish places of habitation. Although both words could be translated similarly, there is a difference in emphasis. *Kolonia* is translated here as "colony" and *osada* as "settlement."

5. "Almanac" is generally the best English-language equivalent of the Polish *kalendarz*.

6. *Orzeł Polski* [The Polish Eagle] (1870-1872); Washington and Krakow (St. Gertrude), Missouri, was the first newspaper in America directed to and about the new mass Polish immigration. It was founded by the Jesuit missionary, Rev. Aleksander Matuszek.

7. Rev. Marcin Możejewski (1827-1899): missionary priest in Latin America, Argentina, and the United States (Texas, New York, Wisconsin). Kruszka also sometimes spells the name as Możewski.

8. *Gazeta Katolicka* [The Catholic Gazette; 1874-1913, Detroit and Chicago], and *Wiara i Ojczyzna* [Faith and Fatherland; 1887-1891, Chicago] represented a conservative Roman Catholic and Resurrectionist viewpoint in Chicago Polonia.

9. Szczęsny Zahajkiewicz (1861-1917): editor of *Naród Polski* [The Polish Nation], official organ of the Polish Roman Catholic Union, and associated with *Dziennik Chicagoski* [Chicago Daily News], both supported by the Congregation of the Resurrection, at whose request he came to Chicago in 1889. He was also a prolific writer, poet, and teacher.

10. Kruszka's original citation for this quotation read: "See annals of *Wiara i Ojczyzna* from 1890."

11. Ignacy Wendziński (1828-1901): teacher, Polish national activist, and editor; fled to the United States after the insurrection of 1863-1864 and there edited *Orzeł Polski* [The Polish Eagle], *Gazeta Polska* [The Polish Gazette], *Przyjaciel Ludu* [Friend of the People], and *Zgoda* [Harmony, 1882-1885], the voice of the Polish National Alliance.

12. This is a reference to the post-partition period in Poland. See note 1 above. Kruszka's original citation indicates that the information came from the 1890 issues of *Wiara i Ojczyzna*.

13. Zdzisław Łuczycki (1858-1927): priest, publicist, editor-publisher and historian of American Polonia; author of *Album opisowo-obrazkowy emigracyi polskiej w Ameryce* (Manitowoc, Wisconsin: Dzwon: Gość Printery, 1893). See: *Polski Słownik Biograficzny* [Polish Biographical Dictionary], 18, p. 517; Casimir Stec, "Pioneer Polish-American Publisher," *Polish American Studies*, XVIII, No. 2 (1961), pp. 65-83.

14. Szczęsny Zahajkiewicz, *Księża i parafia polskie w St. Zjednoczonych A. P.* [Polish Priests and Parishes in the United States of North America] (Chicago: Privately printed, 1897).

15. In the original text, Kruszka uses "de or II.c.9" as his citation for Cicero. It is not clear from available sources on what Kruszka drew for Cicero. A standard English rendering of his "quotation" is: "And as History, which bears witness to the passing of the ages, sheds light upon reality, gives life to recollection and guidance to human existence, and brings tidings of ancient days, whose voice, but the orator's, can entrust her to immortality?" Cicero, *De Oratore*, translated by E. W. Sutton and H. Rockham (Two volumes; Cambridge: Harvard University Press, 1942), I, p. 225 (II, ix, 36).

16. The original citation in Kruszka's text reads "de or II.c.15." A standard English translation of this would be: "For who does not know history's first law to be that an author must not dare to tell anything but the truth? And its second that he must make bold to tell the

whole truth?" Cicero, *De Oratore*, II, xv, 62 in the Sutton and Rockham translation, pp. 243, 245 (see note 16 above).

17. On the *Kalendarz* (here dated to 1877), see note 5 above; for Zahajkiewicz, see note 9 above; for Łuczycki, see note 13 above; Henryk Nagiel, *Dziennikarstwo polskie w Ameryce i jego 30-letnie dzieje* [Polish Journalism in America and its Thirty-Year History] (Chicago: Polish Publishing Company, 1894); Antoni Małłek, *Dzieje parafii św. Trójcy* [History of Holy Trinity Parish] (Chicago: n.p., 1898); *Związek Narodowy Polski w Stanach Zjednoczonych* [The Polish National Alliance in the United States] (Chicago: Zgoda, 1894); Bernard M. Skulik, *Historya parafii św. Jacka w La Salle, Illinois, 1874-1900* [History of St. Hyacinth's Parish in La Salle, Illinois, 1874-1900] (Chicago: Gazeta Katolicka, 1900); Paweł Smolikowski, *Historia Zgromadzenia Zmortwychwstania Pańskiego* [History of the Congregation of the Lord] (Kraków: Kięgarnia Spółki Wydawniczej, 1892-1896, four volumes); Hieronim Kajsiewicz (1812-1873), one of the founders and a superior-general of the Resurrectionists. It is not clear whether Kruszka referred to the printed works of Kajsiewicz—*Pisma: Rozprawy, List z Podróży, Pamiętnik o Zgromadzenia* [Writings: Treatises, Letters from Travels, Remembrance of the Congregation] (Berlin, B. Behra, 1872, three volumes)—or to the material he found in the Resurrectionist Archives during his stay in Rome in 1903-1904. On the feud with the Resurrectionists that followed the use of their unpublished materials, see Joseph J. Parot, *Polish Catholics in Chicago, 1850-1920: A Religious History* (DeKalb, Illinois: Northern Illinois University Press, 1981). pp. 156-57. Walery Przewłocki, superior-general of the Resurrectionists.

18. Kruszka cites "de or II.c.9" incorrectly. A standard English translation would be: "The nature of the subject needs chronological arrangement and geographical representation: and since, in reading of important affairs worth recording, the plans of campaign, the executive actions and the results are successively looked for, it calls also, as regards such plans, for some intimation of what the writer approves, and, in the narrative of achievement, not only for a statement of what was done or said, but also of the manner of doing or saying it; and, in the estimate of consequences, for an exposition of all contributory causes, whether originating in accident, discretion, or foolhardiness; and, as for the individual actors, besides an account of their exploits, it demands particulars of the lives and characters of such as are outstanding in renown and dignity." Cicero, *De Oratore*, II, xv, 63 in the Sutton and Rockham translation, p. 245 (see Note 16 above).

19. "World history is the world's judgment."

Preface to the Book Publication in 1905

1. *Kuryer Polski* [The Polish Courier]; June 23, 1888-September 23, 1963; Milwaukee, Wisconsin], daily (1888-1961), weekly (1962-1963); *Gazeta Wisconsińska* [The Wisconsin Gazette; title varies, 1892-1914], weekly except for twice per week in 1908; *Kuryer Tygodniowy* [The Weekly Courier; title varies, 1892-1911], weekly except twice per week in 1910. *Gazeta Wisconsińska* was a newspaper for rural Wisconsin, *Kuryer Tygodniowy* a weekly edition of *Kuryer Polski*. All three were published by Michael Kruszka.

2. The first members of the Polish colony in Texas arrived in December 1854, and celebrated mass at Panna Maria on Christmas Eve. However, the formal anniversary of the colony—and the beginnings of continuous Polish community life in the United States—dated from the blessing of the cornerstone of the church at Panna Maria the following summer. For August 14 as that date see: T. Lindsay Baker, *The First Polish Americans. Silesian Settlements in Texas* (College Station, Texas: Texas A&M University Press, 1979), p. 60.

CHAPTER 1: THE DISTINCT TYPE OF POLE IN AMERICA

1. The Polish word *ziomek* can be translated as "countryman" or "compatriot," one who, as Kruszka puts it, is born in a certain territory. The word *rodak* may be rendered as "fellow-citizen," someone bound to other citizens by virtue of closer social, cultural, and spiritual

ties. Poles, a large number of them at any rate, were preoccupied with the definition of their nationality in the late nineteenth century. The distinction is reminiscent of another long-standing one in Polish speech and social thought: that between *lud*, the folk or the masses of people, and *naród*, the one-time majority of politically conscious and enfranchised persons who constituted the Polish nation.

2. At this point Kruszka launches into a vision of America that would only later become popular as the concept of "cultural pluralism."

3. Kruszka's use of Muscovite (*Moskal* in Polish) reflects a Polish and East European perspective. It clearly distinguished Moscow, i.e. "Great" or ethnic Russians, from the peoples to their west. The distinction has particular meaning for Ukrainians (Ruthenians or Rusins in eastern Galicia in the nineteenth century) and Byelorussians (also White Russians or White Ruthenians). Since at least the eighteenth century, Moscow had treated them as culturally derivative of itself, as children of "Mother Russia." In Polish see, for example, the poetry of Cyprian Norwid (1821-1883):

> Jeśli mi Polska ma być anarchizna
> Lub socjaliz mu rozwinąć pytanie
> To ja już wolę tę panslawistyczną
> Co pod Moskalem na wieki zostanie!

> If Poland is to be anarchy
> Or is to eleborate the question of Socialism
> Then I prefer that Pan-Slav (system)
> Which would stay for centuries under the Muscovite!

Quoted in Norman Davies, *God's Playground. A History of Poland* (New York: 1982), II, p. 77.

4. Karol Fryderyk Libelt (1807-1875): philosopher, political activist, nationalist, and publicist; active principally in Poznań. See Adam Galos and Andrzej Walicki, "Karol Fryderyk Libelt," *Polski Słownik Biograficzny*, XVII (1972), pp. 174-279.

5. This paragraph alludes to the dismemberment of Poland by Russia, Prussia, and Austria in 1772, 1773, and 1795. When Kruszka penned his history, Poland had been occupied by foreign powers for over a century; yet, despite attempts by the occupying powers to eliminate the Polish language and culture, the concepts of Polish nationalism enjoyed extreme popularity. Kruszka describes being Polish as a sense of shared tradition, culture, and hope derived from the century of national suffering under the partitions. Piotr Wandycz, in his study of American-Polish relations, notes that throughout the period of the partitions, Poles clung to the common bonds of culture, language, historical consciousness, opposition to foreign rule, and reliance on the Catholic faith. The whole experience, he suggests, produced a distinctly Polish nature characterized by "oscillation between hope and despair," a highly developed sensitivity and "a tendency to think in extremes." See Piotr Wandycz, *The United States and Poland* (Cambridge: Harvard University Press, 1980).

6. Kruszka implies an innate recognition of ethnic consciousness among Poles abroad. Victor Greene, in a pioneering case study on the development of ethnic consciousness among Poles and Lithuanians, suggests that the original immigrants had no strong ethnic feeling or interest in politics. These grew gradually as the immigrants adjusted to their new environments. See: Victor Greene, *For God and Country: The Rise of Polish and Lithuanian Ethnic Consciousness in America* (Madison: The State Historical Society in Wisconsin, 1975).

7. Włodzimierz Czerkowski.

8. Rev. Marian Morawski, SJ See chapter 5.

9. Adam Mickiewicz (1798-1855), the most influential of the romantic Polish writers, author of the national epic *Pan Tadeusz*, and an ardent Polish nationalist, who spent most of his adult life in exile in France.

10. Note Kruszka's explanation that the negative image of Poland that Polish Americans had was of their own creation.

11. "Anioł Pański" [Angel of the Lord] is a prayer normally said before meals. Church bells in Poland, particularly in the countryside, were rung at noon to inform the people of the time. Thus the term came to be associated with these activities as well as with the prayer itself.

12. Silesia had been part of the Czech, Austrian, or Prussian domains since the fourteenth century. It had long since ceased to identify itself with the Polish state, though many country folk (later urban workers in Upper Silesia) spoke a Silesian dialect of Polish until the eighteenth century and a more standard Polish since the nineteenth century, but it was far from complete as the plebiscite for incorporation with the new Poland after the First World War seemed to prove. After 1945, the expulsion of Germans and resettlement of Poles from the eastern border lands made the question largely academic.

13. F. Banaszyński. See chapter 5.

14. Helena Jadwiga Modrzejewska (1840-1909): actress, active in Polish literary and artistic circles; frequent performer on the American stage from 1876 as Helena Modjeska. Though she played most of the major heroines of nineteenth-century romantic European drama, she was best known for her performance in Shakespeare. See Jerzy Got, "Helena Jadwiga Modrzejewska," *Polski Słownik Biograficzny*, XXI (1976), p. 528-34. Ignacy Jan Paderewski (1860-1941): pianist and composer; politician and diplomat; prime minister of Poland in 1919. See Roman Wapinski, "Ignacy Jan Paderewski," *Polski Słownik Biograficzny*, XXIV (1979), pp. 795-803.

15. These are the major regions of central and southwestern Poland. The differences among them, except for some regionalisms in speech and the preservation work of folk culture groups, have largely disappeared in the twentieth century.

16. Rapperswyl, Switzerland, was a haven for Polish nationalists and revolutionaries in the late nineteenth century. The National Treasury had been established in 1894, during centennial commemorations of Kościuszko's Insurrection, to gather funds for national Polish cultural and political causes.

17. Józef Chociszewski (1837-1914), the author of many popular works dealing with Polish history, especially for younger readers.

18. The allusion to Września, a village in the Prussian Partition, refers to a school strike by parents and children against attempts to eliminate Polish and substitute German in the teaching of all subjects. The strikes, which reached the level of a mass movement in 1906-1907, ultimately failed. See John J. Kulczynski, *School Strikes in Prussian Poland, 1901-1907: The Struggle over Bilingual Education* (Boulder, Colorado: East European Monographs, 1981).

19. Sarmatia is the classical name for Poland. The term is often used to describe the style of the Polish gentry in the seventeenth and eighteenth centuries as they cultivated what they assumed were the ancient Polish ways of life. Kruszka implies that the long history and unique traditions of Poland are a unifying, nationalizing factor among Poles in distant lands. See: Czesław Miłosz, *The History of Polish Literature* (Toronto: Macmillan, 1969), chapter IV.

20. On the national fund, see note 16 above.

21. Aleksander Fredro (1793-1876): Poland's greatest comic dramatist. The best introduction in English is in Aleksander Fredro, *The Major Comedies of Alexander Fredro*, translated by Harold B. Segal (Princeton: Princeton University Press, 1969), pp. 3-62.

22. This passage alludes to the long conflict between the national and clerical parties in Chicago, represented institutionally by the Polish National Alliance and the Polish Roman Catholic Union. The nationalists were mostly Catholic, but did not identify Poland exclusively with the Catholic Church; the clericalists linked Catholicism with nationalists, ranking the spiritual mission of the Church first. It was a matter of emphasis; the dispute gradually diminished after 1900. See chapter 10 for further information.

23. Kruszka compares the organization of Poles in the United States to that in Poland. In both cases there was, at that time, no separate Polish government. Despite this, both Poles and Polish Americans retained their sense of nationality and identity as Poles.

24. This is a reference to the three partitioned sections of Poland plus the Polish diaspora abroad, the latter being the "Fourth Province of Poland."

25. During the nineteenth century, large numbers of Polish political exiles attempted to locate a permanent Polish settlement in Brazil. The idea did not materialize, but Brazil did become a haven for individual Poles.

26. The Dunikowski's were Polish journalists who frequently wrote with contempt and satire about the growth of Polish colonies in the United States.

27. The *Kuryer Lwowski* [Lwów Courier] was a newspaper published in Lwów, Poland. It carried commentaries and letters on the Polish communities in the United States, many of them none too complimentary.

28. The flow of money from immigrants to their families and friends in Poland was constant and widespread. Indeed, Polish aid to their comrades in Europe generally surpassed that of any other immigrant group.

29. The reference here is to a group of Polish politicians who were critical of Polish emigrants and their communities abroad. Kruszka took great care to emphasize the significance of the contributions to Poland made by the Poles in North America.

CHAPTER 2: WHEN DOES POLISH IMMIGRATION TO AMERICA REALLY BEGIN?

1. The census of 1900.

2. During the 1860s, 98.4% of all European immigrants came from the northern and western areas of the continent. This proportion fell to 91.6% in the 1870s and to 80.2% in the 1880s. In 1896, for the first time, immigration from northern and western Europe was overshadowed by the arrival of peoples from southern and eastern Europe. By the end of the 1890s, some 51.6% of European immigrants originated in these "new" areas of the Old World, a proportion that rose to 76.7% in the first decade of the twentieth century.

3. This is an allusion to the thesis of Adam Mickiewicz that the emigration is the "soul of the Polish nation" as outlined in *Księgi narodu polskiego i pielgrzymsta polskiego* [The Book of the Polish Nation and the Polish Pilgrims], published in 1832. He frequently compared the modern Polish nation to the ancient Jews—a people destined, despite their travails, for a leading role in the emancipation of humanity from oppressive political power. See: Manfred Kridl, *Adam Mickiewicz. Poet of Poland* (New York: Columbia University Press, 1951), pp. 9, 27.

4. Kruszka alludes to some of the nineteenth-century Polish authors who popularized the nation of pre-Columbian Polish exploration in America: Wacław Aleksander Maciejowski, *Piśmiennictwo polskie od czasów najdawniejszych aż do r. 1830* [Polish Literature from the Earliest Times to 1830] (Warsaw; 1851-1852, three volumes); Piotr Czarkowski, *Krótki wykład geografii powszechnej* [Short Lectures on Universal Geography (Warsaw; 1855, the third of several editions); Antoni Oleszczyński (1794-1879), illustrator of many books of Polish literature and history; [Józef?] Supiński. See: Janina Wiercińska, "Antoni Oleszczyński," *Polski Słownik Biograficzny*, XXXII (1978), pp. 751-53; Juliusz Bardach, "Wacław Aleksander Maciejowski," *Polski Słownik Biograficzny*, XIX (1974), pp. 71-74.

5. From *Kaszube pod widnem* ["The Kaszubs before Vienna"] by Hieronim Derdowski (1852-1902). The Kaszubs are a slavic people living south and southwest of Gdańsk in Western Prussia and Pomerania. Derdowski was one of the literary leaders of the revival of their language in the late nineteenth century, as well as an associate of many of the major Polish writers of his day. He spent the last part (1886-1902) of his life as editor of *Wiarus* [The Old Guard] in Winona, Minnesota. This long poem deals with Kaszub participation in the Battle of Vienna where, in 1863, King John III Sobieski of Poland led the forces that repelled a

major Turkish threat to the city. The allusion to John of Kolno comes early in the poem. The canto cited was translated for the editors by Mr. Joseph L. Ziarnik. For the remainder of the poem, see *Wiarus*, April 12, 1888, p. 2 and April 19-May 17, 1888. Also see Andrzej Bukowski, *Działalność literacka i społeczna Hieronima Derdowskiego w Ameryce* [A Literary and Social History of Jerome Derdowski in America] (Gdańsk: Gdańskie Towarzystwo Nankowe, 1961).

6. Kruszka's original citation is *Catholic Education in the United States*.

7. Albrecht Zaborowski was born in Poland about 1638 and arrived in New Amsterdam in 1662. A Lutheran, through marriage and business acumen he acquired large tracts of land along the Passaic River in New Jersey and became the progenitor of a family that spread widely through Virginia and the Midwest. See: Rev. Francis Bolek, *Who's Who in Polish America* (New York: Harbinger House, 1943), p. 510; Mieczysław Haiman, *Polish Past in America, 1608-1865* (Chicago: Polish Museum of America, 1974), pp. 17-19; Joseph A. Wytrwal, *Poles in American History and Tradition* (Detroit: Endurance Press, 1969), pp. 21-24; Mieczysław Haiman, *Poles in New York in the 17th and 18th Centuries* (Chicago: Archives and Museum of the Polish Roman Catholic Union, 1938), p. 43.

8. Tadeusz Andrzej Bonawentura Kościuszko (1746-1817); Polish volunteer appointed colonel of engineers in Continental Army, October 18, 1776; fortified American lines at Saratoga, October, 1777; designed and constructed fortress at West Point, 1777-1779; served with southern army after 1779; led unsuccessful Polish revolt against Catherine II of Russia, 1794; author of *Manoevres of Horse Artillery* (1800) used at the U.S. Military Academy. Kazimierz Pułaski (1747-1779); military commander in the Confederation of Bar, 1768-1772; volunteer aide at Battle of Brandywine, 1777; appointed brigadier general in the Continental Army, September 15, 1777; mortally wounded at the Siege of Savannah, October 11, 1779.

9. The legality of Kościuszko's American will was successfully challenged by European claimants, thus precluding its use for the intended purpose. See: James S. Pula, "The American Will of Thaddeus Kosciuszko," *Polish American Studies*, Vol. XXXIV, No. 1 (Spring, 1977), pp. 16-25.

10. Julian Ursyn Niemcewicz (1757-1841); writer, poet; aide-de-camp to Kościuszko in 1794; traveling companion and confidant of Kościuszko in America, 1796-1797; married Elizabeth Lewinston Kean and became U.S. citizen; Secretary of State of the Grand Duchy of Warsaw, 1807-1831; political refugee in Paris, 1831-1841. For reminiscences of his American travels see: Julian Ursyn Niemcewicz, *Under the Vine and Fig Tree: Travels Through America in 1779-1799, 1805 with Some Further Account of Life in New Jersey* (Elizabeth, New Jersey: Grassman Publishing, 1965), translated and edited by Metchie J. E. Budka.

11. A reference to the formation of Polish military units under General Jan Henryk Dąbrowski which fought on the side of the French Revolution in the hopes of freeing their homeland from foreign occupation. The marching song of Dąbrowski's "Polish Legion," written by Józef Wybicki, was later adopted as the Polish national anthem.

12. Demetrius Augustine Gallitzin (1770-1840); son of Prince Dmitrii Aleksievich Gallitzin, a Russian diplomat and associate of the *philosophes*, and the devoutly Catholic Amalia von Schmettan; reared as an Orthodox Christian; emigrated to the United States in 1792 where he was ordained a Roman Catholic priest; promoter of Catholic colonization and a missionary priest in western Pennsylvania from 1799. In addition to Polish and his native Russian, Gallitzin spoke Dutch, German, French, Italian, and some English. His family's roots were in the Byelorussian provinces of the old Polish-Lithuanian Republic; his cultural heritage was correspondingly cosmopolitan and not narrowly national in the modern sense. See: *Dictionary of American Biography*, VII, pp. 113-15.

13. Rev. Ladislaus Sebastyański, SJ, arrived in Nebraska from Poland in 1884. He is credited with building six churches and directing sixty missions spanning ten states. See: Bolek, *Who's Who*, p. 402.

14. Władysław Franciszek Konstanty Jabłonowski (1769-1802). The legionnaires probably died of yellow fever. See: Jan Pachoński, "Władysław Franciszek Konstanty Jabłonowski," *Polski Słownik Biograficzny* (1962-1964), pp. 243-46.

15. The Society of Jesus was dissolved by Pope Clement XIV in 1773. However, the decree was never promulgated in the Russian Empire and the Society survived there legally. Byelorussia, which came under Russian control through the First Partition of Poland in 1772, was the home of a significant Polish Jesuit community. Pope Pius VII (1799-1823) granted members of the suppressed order in the United States and Europe the right to affiliate with the Byelorussian province.

16. Rev. Norbert Korsak (1773-1846); Rev. Boniface Krukowski (1777-1837); Rev. Franciszek Dzierożyński (1779-1850); Rev. Philip Sacchi (?-1850). These Jesuits contributed significantly to the revival of their Society in the United States. Dzierożyński, who was either superior or provincial of the Maryland Jesuits in the period 1823-1848, and played a major role in the revival of Georgetown University and the College of the Holy Cross.

17. In 1830-1831, a Polish rebellion against Russian rule occurred. With its failure, hundred of political refugees fled throughout Europe, some venturing as far as the United States. In 1834, 234 Polish prisoners in Austria were set free on the condition that they migrate to the United States. They arrived in New York harbor on March 28, and within two years grew in number to 425. See: Jerzy Jan Lerski, *A Polish Chapter in Jacksonian America: The United States and the Polish Exiles of 1831* (Madison: University of Wisconsin Press, 1958).

18. Henryk Kałussowski (1806-1895): Polish political activist; participated in insurrections of 1830-1831 and 1848; represented the insurrectionary Polish government of 1863 in the United States; helped found several major organizations that promoted the Polish cause, including the Polish National Alliance.

19. Paweł Sobolewski (1818-1884): journalist, teacher, and writer; edited the monthly magazine *Poland* in New York City in 1842; published *Poets and Poetry of Poland* in 1880.

20. Kazimierz Bielewski [Bielaski, Bielawski] (1815-1905): engineer; emigrated to the United States in 1850 following the disturbances in Austrian Poland in 1846; long employed as a surveyor by the United States Land Office in California.

21. Ignacy Domejko (1801-1889): major contributor to Chilean education and science; author of many books including a study of the Indiana of southern Chile, *Araucania and the Araucaniana*.

22. Rev. Antoni Rossadowski, OMC (?-1865): chaplain in Polish insurrection of 1830-1831 and in the Seminole War; pastor in Panna Maria, Texas, 1856-1860.

23. Kruszka's claim that they were "sent" to Florida distorts the matter somewhat. Exiles of 1830-1831 enlisted in units fighting the Seminoles in Florida. Their exact number is unknown, but there were at least 54 who were discharged in Florida in 1836-1842.

24. Kruszka's original citation reads: "Annual volume for 1887." The reference is to the periodical *Polak w Ameryce* [Buffalo].

25. Leopold F. Boeck (1826-1896): teacher, mathematician, and engineer; active among Poles of Philadelphia from 1877; he had participated in the Hungarian uprising of 1849.

26. Jan Tyssowski (1811-1857): active in insurrection against Russia in 1830. During a short-lived insurrection in the free city of Kraków in 1846, he proclaimed himself "dictator." The Austrians quickly occupied the city and annexed it to their empire. Exiled to the United States in 1847, Tyssowski was employed by the U.S. Geodetic Service and the Patent Office.

27. Rev. Gaspar Matoga, SJ (1823-1856).

28. Rev. Antoni Lenz, SJ (1823-1888).

29. Ignacy Peukert (1821-1878).

30. Kruszka's original citation reads: "See *The Official Year Book of 1902*."

31. A reference to the January Insurrection (1863-1864) of Poles against Russian rule. For its implications on U.S. foreign policy and public opinion during the American Civil War, see Joseph W. Wieczerzak, *A Polish Chapter in Jacksonian America* (New York: Twayne Publishers, Inc., 1967).

CHAPTER 3: THE GRADUAL GROWTH AND HISTORICAL DEVEL-
OPMENT OF POLISH SETTLEMENTS, SKETCHED IN THEIR
GENERAL OUTLINES

1. This statement is somewhat misleading if one reflects on the secular nature of the organizations founded by Polish exiles between 1834 and 1880. Some of these included the Polish Committee in America (1834), the Polish Slavonian Literary Association (1846), the
Democratic Society of Polish Emigrés in America (1852), The Polish Commune (1866), the
Kościuszko Society (1871), and the Polish National Alliance (1880).

2. The Polish priests active in the 1850s and 1860s may be viewed in various lights. All,
as Kruszka emphasizes, were founders or builders of the first Polish parishes in the United
States, but some were more adept at that task than others. The most striking examples are
Rev. Franciszek Xavier Szulak, SJ, who traveled tirelessly throughout the Middle West in
the last decades of the nineteenth century, and Rev. Wincenty Barzyński, CR (1838-1899), of
Chicago. See: Rev. Franciszek Szulak, *Journal* (1863-1903), a microfilm copy of the manuscript in the Immigration History Research Center of the University of Minnesota; Joseph J.
Parot, *Polish Catholics in Chicago, 1850-1920* (DeKalb, Illinois: Northern Illinois University Press, 1981), chapters 3-5. About half of these pioneer priests were members of religious
orders: the Friars Minor Conventual, in the cases of Revs. Leopold Moczygęba (1824-1891)
and Antoni Rossadowski (?-1865); the Jesuits in the cases of Revs. Szulak and Aleksander
Matuszek; and the Resurrectionists in the cases of Revs. Adolf Bakanowski (1840-?), Wincenty Barzyński, Jan Wołłowski, Szymon Wieczorek (?-1901), Franciszek Breitkopf, and
Feliks Żwiardowski (1840-?). The remainder were secular priests: Revs. Jan Polak (?-1862),
Piotr Kruk, Juljan Przysiecki (?-1863), Bonawentura Buczyński (?-1872), Adolf Śnigurski,
Józef Juszkiewicz, T. A. Węglikowski, Klemens Kucharczyk, Teofil Bralewski, Felix Orzechowski, and Jan Frydrychowicz (?-1874). From the viewpoint of the American bishops, the
secular priests were the most difficult to control and were a source of instability in the communities they served. Rev. Frydrychowicz is considered a forerunner of the independentism
of the 1890s, and Rev. Wieczorek had difficulty with the bishop of Detroit. Many of these
pioneers had also participated in the Polish insurrection of 1830-1831 (Rossadowski) or 1863
(Bakanowski, Barzyński, Śnigurski). The Congregation of the Resurrection itself was
founded by participants in the 1830-1831 uprising and long had a distinctly national mission
to Poles abroad.

3. In 1876 Sienkiewicz toured America, briefly joining Helena Modrzejewska and her circle in California, where there was a plan to establish a utopian community at Anaheim. One
lasting result of this journey was a series of letters published in the Warsaw and Lwów press
from 1876 to 1879. A selection of these letters has appeared in English: Henryk Sienkiewicz,
Portrait of America. Letters of Henry Sienkiewicz, edited and translated by Charles Morley
(New York: Columbia University Press, 1959). See pp. 184-86 for a longer account of the
episode Kruszka mentions. It was an early skirmish in the long conflict between the clerical
and the nationalist parties for influence in Polonia. The two colonies Sienkiewicz described
retained their Polish character for a long time—Warren Hoino, now Marche, in Arkansas and
New Posen, now Farwell, in Nebraska.

4. To convey the expression "beat," Kruszka uses the word zbitowała, a word constructed
by adding a Polish verb ending (*owach*) to the phonetic equivalent of the English word
"beat" (*bit*).

5. Kruszka's original citation reads: "See the 'Kronike Polonii w Ameryce' [Chronicle of
Polonia in America] in the *Kalendarz* for 1877, pages 98-106."

6. Here Kruszka uses the word *byznesistami*, a polonization of the English word "businessman."

7. The reports of the United States Commissioner-General of Immigration, as cited in the
reports of the United States Immigration Commission, Volume 3, indicate that 448,572 peo-

ple migrated to the United States in 1900, including 304,148 men and 144,428 women. While these figures vary only minutely from those cited by Kruszka, the latter's figures for specific groups are considerably different from those cited by the Commissioner-General. The official figures for 1900 include 46,938 Poles, 1,200 Russians, 12,615 Finns, 10,311 Lithuanians, 2,832 Ruthenians, and 29,682 Germans.

8. In the foregoing paragraph, Kruszka cites data for professional and skilled immigrants arriving during 1900. The correct data provided by the Commissioner-General of Immigration, and cited in the reports of the United States Immigration Commission, Volume 3, are as follows: Professionals—196 Germans, 45 French, 351 English, 360 Italians, 253 Jews, 29 Poles, 16 Spanish, 6 Slovaks, and 2 Ruthenians; Skilled—21,047 Jews, 13,791 Italians, 4,660 Germans, 1,865 Poles, 1,793 Japanese, 993 Croats, 147 Russians, and 33 Ruthenians.

9. Kruszka's statistics were probably inflated by the cause that stimulated the writing of his history; the more Poles there were, the greater the need for Polish priests and bishops in the United States. He was not the first to exaggerate the number of Polish Americans (see, for example, Sienkiewicz's comments on Polish American editors in the 1870s in *Portrait of America*, p. 284); however, he gave credibility to a practice that has persisted within the ethnic community to this day. For specific commentary on Kruszka's population data, see the notes in chapter 4.

10. Kruszka's original footnote reads: "We have taken into consideration in the present edition all corrections sent to us."

CHAPTER 4: STATISTICS ON POLISH SETTLEMENTS AT THE BEGINNING OF THE TWENTIETH CENTURY

1. The question "Who is a Pole?" is an important consideration in determining statistical information. It is obvious that Kruszka regarded anyone born of Polish parentage in the United States as Polish. Such a judgment suggests a nineteenth-century definition of nationality, based on blood ties rather than cultural affinities, thus precluding any suggestion of an American nationality. There is no question, as Kruszka argues, that the U.S. census undercounted Poles by identifying many of them as Germans, Russians, Austrians, or native Americans. Kruszka, on the other hand, falsely assumes that Poles alone constitute the population of his parish surveys and that Polish family size is larger than it is. Some of the evidence that he admits into his text shows overcounts as indicated in succeeding notes for chapter 4. See also notes 7, 8, and 9 in chapter 3.

2. Data from the Commissioner-General of Immigration, cited in the reports of the United States Immigration Commission, Volume 3, pp. 53, 57, 62-63, indicate that between 1899 and 1910 some 18.6% of Austro-Hungarian immigrants were of Polish origin, as were 9.5% of those from the German Empire and 29.4% of those from the Russian Empire. It thus appears that Kruszka's assertion that 40% of these groups were of Polish origin is an arbitrary and inflated figure.

3. Throughout this statistical survey, Kruszka relied on the official census of 1900, but his figures must have been derived from an earlier, uncorrected version of that census which produced different figures, though the differences were statistically insignificant. For example, the final official count of immigrants from Poland, according to the *Abstract of the Twelfth Census of the United States, 1900*, third edition (Washington: 1909), p. 9, is 383,407. Such minor discrepancies occur throughout the chapter.

4. Kruszka's basic source of information, besides the official census, was the *National Catholic Directory* for 1901. This source is fairly accurate on the total Catholic population in each diocese and the total number of churches and priests. However, the *Directory* did not and could not make a distinction between *de jure* and *de facto* ethnic parishes. Kruszka obviously and properly included in his statistics parishes that were territorial parishes *de jure* but functioned in a Polish community whose language was Polish and whose liturgical language was therefore Polish. These parishes were *de facto* Polish parishes. In a significant number of

instances where, because of the mixed ethnic character of communities, especially in Wisconsin, Minnesota, and Michigan, it was impossible to determine the ethnic identity of the parish. Kruszka labeled the parish as Polish if Polish was used as a liturgical language in some of the services. This tended to inflate his figures on the number of Polish parishes significantly. Thus, for the Archdiocese of Chicago, the *Directory* for 1901 listed 18 *de jure* Polish parishes. but there were four more parishes that were regarded as *de facto* Polish. These 22 parishes were served by 44 Polish priests. These figures differ significantly from those of Charles Shanabruch, *Chicago's Catholics: The Evolution of an American Identity* (Notre Dame, 1981), p. 235, and those of François Houtart, *Aspects Sociologiques du Catholicisme Americain* (New York, 1978), p. 195.

5. Kruszka's original reference reads: "K. Nowacki, in a letter dated October 4, 1901, counts 50 Polish families in Kenosha, comprising a total of 239 people."

6. Kruszka's original reference reads: "Wincenty Szprejda from Sheboygan reports that there are only 50 Poles there, and the rest are Lithuanians, who total 150 men, not including women and children (from a letter dated December 5, 1901)."

7. The *National Catholic Directory* for 1901 lists 13 Polish parishes in the Archdiocese of Milwaukee served by 17 priests.

8. The figures for the Diocese of Green Bay for 1901 are: 23 Polish parishes served by 24 Polish priests. The total number of priests in this diocese was reported at 151. The discrepancy with Kruszka's figure of 35 Polish priests may be explained by his tendency, with this diocese as well as others, to include priests of Czech, Slovak and Slovenian ancestry with the Polish priests.

9. For the Diocese of La Crosse, the *Directory* for 1901 reported eleven Polish priests serving seven Polish parishes and ten parishes of mixed nationality.

10. In 1901 Wisconsin contained 28 *de jure* Polish parishes and 24 *de facto* Polish or mixed parishes attended by 52 Polish priests.

11. The *National Catholic Directory* reports a total Catholic population in the three diocese of Milwaukee, Green Bay and La Crosse as 467,000, but Kruszka's figure of 598 Catholic priests does not agree with the *Directory*'s figures for Milwaukee (289), Green Bay (150) and La Crosse (136), a total of 575 for all of Wisconsin.

12. A total of 52 Polish priests in Wisconsin would, therefore, amount to 9% of the total number of Catholic priests.

13. The figure given for Wisconsin by the twelfth census in 1900 is 2,069,042. The error is statistically insignificant.

14. There were only three clearly recognizable Polish priests in the Diocese of Winona.

15. Kruszka surely exaggerated at least the number of Polish parishes in the Diocese of St. Cloud, which in 1901 was 13 churches served by 10 priests.

16. The Kruszka argument against Bishop Trobec's assertions is plausible. The *Cathedraticum* is a church tax levied on parishes for the support of the bishop and the diocesan offices.

17. Kruszka included in these figures some 5,000 Poles of Lutheran persuasion, but did not offer the source of this information. Moreover, the sixteen priests of Polish ancestry whom he claims must have included priests of other Slavic, non-Polish backgrounds. The number of priests of indisputably Polish background was probably ten.

18. Kruszka's summation for Minnesota is clearly exaggerated. The *National Catholic Directory* for 1901 lists only nine *de jure* Polish parishes. Sixteen additional parishes that Kruszka placed in the Polish column were *de facto* mixed parishes, reflecting the ethnic mix of many Minnesota communities of that time. The percentage of Polish priests in Minnesota amounted to only 5% of the total.

19. The inaccuracies for North Dakota are glaring. The census of 1900 reported a total population of 319,146 for North Dakota, a figure that significantly alters Kruszka's calculations. Thus, assuming the relative accuracy of Kruszka's claims of 16,600 Poles in North Dakota, this amounted to 9% of the total population. Moreover, the *National Catholic Direc-*

tory for 1901 claimed only 27,000 Catholics which would have calculated to a Polish population of 61% of the total Catholic population, as assertion difficult to defend inasmuch as there were only three *de facto* Polish parishes served by three Polish priests. The inaccuracy extends to the number of Catholic priests: the *Directory* reported only 55 Catholic priests which would amount to one priest for every 491 Catholics. Every Polish priest, according to Kruszka's claim, would therefore serve over 5,500 Polish Catholics, an unlikely conclusion.

20. The official figures reported for South Dakota are 401,570 inhabitants, of whom 35,000 were Catholics, and 76 priests, of whom one was Polish.

21. The Kruszka figures for Nebraska are all accurate except a typographical error which placed the number of Catholics in the Diocese of Lincoln at 24,340, whereas the *Directory* reported 25,340.

22. Kruszka's figures for Nebraska require some correction. The *National Catholic Directory* recorded only ten parishes that were *de facto* Polish, not a single one being *de jure* Polish. Poles were scattered in many communities where their presence must have necessitated some Polish liturgical services in mixed parishes, but it would be an exaggeration to claim these as Polish parishes.

23. These figures are presently unverifiable. All the Polish or mixed parishes are of somewhat later foundation in Sioux City, Clear Lake, and Clutier, Iowa.

24. There were probably twelve Polish settlements in Missouri but only three Polish parishes, only one of which acquired *de jure* status (St. Stanislaus Kostka in St. Louis).

25. It is curious that Kruszka failed to elaborate on two sizeable Polish communities in Kansas, both of which produced rather large Polish parishes (St. Joseph's in Kansas City and St. Casimir's in Leavenworth, the latter acquiring and maintaining *de jure* Polish status).

26. Rev. Seweryn Niedbalski was ordained in 1898. He served as pastor in Panna Maria, Texas, 1898-1903, and thereafter at Holy Trinity Parish in Erie, Pennsylvania. Later he was director of the Polish Theological Seminary in Orchard Lake, Michigan.

27. Kruszka's original citation read: "Excerpt from a letter of September 30, 1901." Only six of the Polish settlements listed by Kruszka in the Diocese of San Antonio succeeded in founding and maintaining Polish parishes, not one of which acquired *de jure* status: Panna Maria, Bandera, San Antonio, Yorktown, Częstochowa, and Meyersville. On the other hand, there were parishes already functioning at Granger and La Grange in the Diocese of Galveston, which Kruszka did not mention. On this basis, his calculations would have to be viewed with skepticism.

28. Among the six priests said to be Polish were some Polish-speaking Bohemians.

29. The town of Thurber in 1901 founded a parish, but its priests were Bohemian and German.

30. The Kruszka figures for Texas are in need of considerable correction: There were only twelve Polish churches served by twelve Polish priests. According to the *National Catholic Directory*, the three dioceses of San Antonio, Galveston, and Dallas had 181 Catholic priests serving 137,000 Catholics in 1901.

31. The official census figures for the eight states and three territories listed by Kruszka as the so-called "Wild West" in 1900 total 4,308,942 inhabitants. The discrepancy amounts to 276,506 inhabitants fewer than the official figures reported. For so vast an area, this would seem to be statistically insignificant, an average of six inhabitants fewer per square mile than officially reported.

32. The figure for the total number of Catholic churches in the "Wild West" is completely out of line with that reported in the National Catholic Directory. Excluding Hawaii, which was not included in the Directory's survey for 1901, the number of Catholic churches was 851, with a total of 790 priests.

33. Kruszka's original citation read: "Rev. St. Sosnowski wrote that in Sheboygan there were only 355 Poles and only 245 Poles in Mullet Lake."

34. The figures as reported by the *National Catholic Directory* show 70,000 Catholics in the Diocese of Marquette, with 68 priests of whom only two were Polish.

35. The corrected figures for Michigan should read thus: 46 Polish churches, served by 32

Polish priests; a total of 370 Catholic priests in all of Michigan for 367,530 Catholics. The census of 1900 reported 2,420,782 inhabitants in Michigan within 57,430 square miles of territory, discrepancies which are insignificant.

36. The official census of 1900 and the National Catholic Directory for 1901 recorded the following for Indiana: 16 Polish churches, served by 15 Polish priests; 314 Catholic churches served by a total of 362 Catholic priests; and 185,000 Catholics in Indiana out of a total population of 2,516,462, living in an area of 36,350 square miles.

37. The Kruszka figures for Ohio are surprisingly accurate with only this exception, that the official census lists the size of the state at 40,760 square miles.

38. The statistics for the five diocese of Pennsylvania need considerable revision. The Archdiocese of Philadelphia had seven Polish priests in 14 Polish parishes; the Diocese of Harrisburg had four Polish parishes served by two Polish priests; the Diocese of Scranton had 25 Polish parishes and 16 Polish priests; the Diocese of Erie had six Polish parishes and five Polish priests; and the Diocese of Pittsburgh had 21 Polish parishes served by 14 Polish priests.

39. The previous changes in the Kruszka figures considerably alter the total picture for Pennsylvania: 70 Polish churches served by 44 Polish priests. Therefore, for every 26 Catholic priests, there was one Polish priest. A case can be argued here for an acute shortage of Polish priests, but Kruszka's objectives led him to claim far more than reality dictated.

40. The actual figures for New York State, as reported by the *National Catholic Directory* for 1901 present this picture: Archdiocese of New York had nine Polish churches and seven Polish priests; Diocese of Brooklyn had four Polish churches and five Polish priests; Diocese of Albany had three Polish churches and three Polish priests; Diocese of Syracuse had two Polish churches and two Polish priests; Diocese of Rochester had two Polish churches and two Polish priests; and Diocese of Buffalo had 15 Polish churches and 21 Polish priests. These figures total 35 Polish churches served by 40 Polish priests which averages to one Polish church for every 29 churches and one Polish priest for every 40 priests.

41. There were seven Polish churches in the Diocese of Newark and five in the Diocese of Trenton, served by four and five Polish priests respectively. The Kruszka figures taken from the census of 1900 are accurate except the area of the state, which was reported at 7,525 square miles.

42. The Kruszka figures for Maryland, Delaware, and the District of Columbia cannot be challenged. For West Virginia, there was no Polish church in Monongah.

43. The Archdiocese of Boston in 1901 had one Polish church served by two Polish priests, whereas the Diocese of Springfield had five Polish churches and four Polish priests. Kruszka claimed churches established in 1901 for Haverhill (1910), Salem (1903), Bondsville (1910), Lowell (1904), and Westfield (1903). It is probable that parishes were anticipated in these towns in 1901, but were not yet functioning.

44. The Diocese of Providence in 1901 had only one Polish parish (St. Stanislaus in Fall River) and one priest. The parishes listed by Kruszka in New Bedford (1905), Taunton (1909), Providence (1902), and West Warren (1908) were founded later than 1901, but were probably in the process of formation when he wrote his *Historya*. Moreover, the Polish churches in Thorndike and Three Rivers refer to the parish of St. John the Baptist in Three Rivers, founded in 1903, but located in the Diocese of Springfield. Thorndike, like Three Rivers, is in Palmer Township, Massachusetts, and never anticipated or founded a parish, but was included in the Three Rivers parish.

45. There was only one Polish priest in the Diocese of Providence in 1901.

46. The *National Catholic Directory* for 1901 lists Polish parishes in Meriden, New Britain, and Bridgeport. All the other parishes listed by Kruszka were founded at later dates: Hartford, 1902; Ansonia, 1926; Norwich, 1904; Waterbury, 1913; New London, 1904; Middletown, 1903; and Bristol, 1919. Moreover, there were never any Polish parishes established in Rockville or Portland, whereas Union City founded its Polish parish in 1906, and New Haven in 1902.

47. In 1901 there were only four Polish priests in the entire state of Connecticut. By 1910

that number increased considerably, and inasmuch as Kruszka listed parishes of later founda-tion, one must question whether he was faithful to his original plan to use the figures of the *National Catholic Directory* for 1901.

48. There is no better example of Kruszka's inflated figures. In 1901, all of New England had ten Polish parishes and eleven Polish priests. Inasmuch as his figures for the total number of Catholic parishes and Catholic priests in New England is accurately drawn from the *National Catholic Directory* for 1901, we must assume that all his data was drawn from that source. From this conclusion, it is evident that Kruszka's figures for Polish communities and churches were larger than justified.

49. The statistics drawn from the official census of 1901 are all verifiably accurate. How-ever, there is no way to verify either the number of Poles in the United States in 1900, nor the number of Polish settlements. As for the number of Polish churches and priests, Kruszka's figures are undoubtedly inaccurate. A more believable figure for all the United States in 1901 would be 328 parishes and 330 priests.

50. While many Poles were no doubt listed as Austrians, Germans, or Russians, there is no evidence to suggest that the proportions were anywhere near those cited by Kruszka in the two paragraphs above.

CHAPTER 5: HISTORY OF THE POLISH
CHURCH IN AMERICA

1. On the growth of the Roman Catholic Church in the United States in the nineteenth century see: John Tracy Ellis, *American Catholicism* (Chicago: University of Chicago Press, 1956); Thomas T. McAvoy, *A History of the Catholic Church in the United States* (Notre Dame: University of Notre Dame Press, 1969). Though McAvoy made a start in that direc-tion, it is only since the 1960s that historians have begun to comprehend the American Church as something more than an institution reacting to Protestant America. For example, see: Philip Gleason, ed., *Contemporary Catholicism in the United States* (Notre Dame: Uni-versity of Notre Dame, 1969).

2. The tradition of Old Country criticism of the material and cultural shortcomings of its immigrant offspring is an old one. The quotation is from *Księgi Pielgrzymstwa Polskiego* [The Book of the Polish Pilgrims], Book X, and can be found in Adam Mickiewicz, *Dzieła* [Works] (Warsaw: Czytelnik, 1956), VI, p. 31.

3. Kruszka's original citation is: "Lwów, *Gazeta Kościelna*."

4. The charge that American bishops, by failing to deal appropriately with the immigrants of the late nineteenth century, were responsible for great losses in church membership stirred debate that was difficult to resolve. An answer of sorts, based on presumably "scientific" immigrant statistics, was provided by Gerald Schaughnessy, *Has the Immigrant Kept the Faith? A Study of Immigration and Catholic Growth in the United States 1790-1920* (New York: Macmillan, 1925). Schaughnessy's slim discussion of Poles and other Slavs is based on statistics that he does not understand. His conclusion is a panegyric to the hierarchy for its success in absorbing nearly all immigrants into a single American church. Kruszka, as a close observer of a decade of religious independency among Poles, saw things differently.

5. There was an affinity between the Czechs and the early emigrants from adjacent west-ern Poland, evident in the sharing of church facilities and priests. It had a parallel in the 1890s and later in relations between emigrants from eastern Poland and the western Ukraine (Ruthenia). See: Frank Renkiewicz, "The Poles," in Jane Holmquist, ed., *They Chose Min-nesota* (St. Paul: Minnesota Historical Society, 1981); Joanna Matejko, "Polish Farmers in Alberta," in Frank Renkiewicz, ed., *The Polish Presence in Canada and America* (Toronto: Multicultural History Society of Ontario, 1982), pp. 47-50, 56-59. On Rev. John M. Gartner (1820-1877) see: Henry Hooper Heming, ed., *The Catholic Church in Wisconsin* (Milwau-kee: Catholic Historical Publishing Company, 1896?), p. 1026.

6. A reference to the period when Christianity was introduced into Poland under Duke Mieczyslaw I (Mieczko, reigned ?-992) and King Boleslaus I the Brave (reigned 992-1025).

7. There have been many associations of Polish Catholic priests. Barzyński's Association of Polish Catholic Priests in the U.S.A. was the first, founded in 1875 to support the Resurrectionist policy of accommodation with the Irish hierarchy. The Association of Priests in Minnesota (also known as the Allied Priests) was founded in 1886 by Rev. Dominic Majer of St. Paul to accommodate more nationally minded priests who were dissatisfied with some but not all aspects of the program of the Polish National Alliance. See: Parot, *Polish Catholics in Chicago*, pp. 134-38, 152-53, who assumes that the Association that Rev. Nawrocki headed in 1902 was descended from Barzyński's. As Kruszka's name for it implies, the Resurrectionists appear to have been excluded from the Association of 1902. Rev. Nawrocki was chaplain to the Polish National Alliance, president of the Association for 1903 and pastor of St. Mary of Perpetual Help in Chicago.

8. Eventually American bishops recruited reliable secular priests through European institutions like the University of Louvain, the Polish Seminary in Detroit, and, of course, their own diocesan seminaries. At first only the religious congregations could consistently provide priests whose training and character made them reliable pastors. Hieronim Kajsiewicz (1812-1873) was a founder and a superior-general of the Congregation of the Resurrection. Kruszka cites, as the source of the quotations, *"Letters of Father Kajsiewicz*, pp. 220, 401."

9. Bartosz Głowacki (1758-1794) was the peasant hero whom Kościuszko promoted to the rank of officer at the Battle of Racławice during the Insurrection of 1794. Głowacki and the peasant soldiers, who were armed with no more than scythes, have become one of the enduring legends of Polish history—representatives of the virtue and nationalism of the common folk, a sign of the road not taken in relations between the aristocracy and the peasantry in modern times.

10. Kruszka's original citation reads: "See page 232 about the vision of Rev. Breitfopf." The reference is to the *Letters of Father Kajsiewicz*.

11. Rev. Piotr Semeneńko, CR (1814-1886), one of the founders and a superior-general of the Congregation of the Resurrection.

12. Rev. Walenty (Valentine) Czyżewski, CSC (1846-1913), first pastor and long-time leader of Poles in South Bend, Indiana.

13. The Third Plenary Council of Baltimore in 1883 codified many of the administrative procedures Kruszka mentions. Diocesan consultors and irremovable rectors were supposed to nominate three candidates for filling a vacancy in their see; the bishops of an archdiocese then met to approve or disapprove (with explanation) the list before passing it along to Rome. In practice the process could be manipulated by the bishops, for example, by the order in which the candidates were listed for consideration by Rome. Ordinarily one-tenth of the pastors of a diocese were to be designated irremovable rectors. On these and other matters (education of Catholic youth, rules governing church property and finances) that touched sensitive chords in relations between Poles and American bishops see: Peter Guilday, *A History of the Councils of Baltimore* (New York: Macmillan, 1932), pp. 230-32, 237-39, 242.

14. On the origins of the Polish Roman Catholic Union (PRCU) see: Mieczyzsław Haiman, *Zjednoczenie Polski Rzymsko-Katolickie w Ameryce 1873-1948* [The Polish Roman Catholic Union in America 1873-1948] (Chicago: Polish Roman Catholic Union, 1948), pp. 23-42. Note, however, that Haiman frequently relies on Kruszka for information. On Gieryk and Kiołbassa see the notes to chapter 11. Józef Dąbrowski (1842-1903) founded the Polish seminary in Detroit (now at Orchard Lake), Michigan. On Dąbrowski and the other priests noted here, see: Bolek, *Who's Who*.

15. Rev. Kazimierz (Casimir) Stuczko, CSC (1867-196?), was appointed pastor of Holy Trinity Church in Chicago in a settlement that resolved the long conflict between the nationalist party and the Resurrectionists for control of the parish. His successful accommodation with the nationalists foreshadowed the approach of the next generation of Polish American pastors.

16. The most recent discussion of the Polish Catholic congresses is in Parot, *Polish Catholics in Chicago*, pp. 126-28, 144-50, 258 n. 30.

17. Rev. Adalbert Mielcuszny (1830-1881) was nominated successfully by the nationalist

and anti-Resurrectionist party as pastor of Holy Trinity Church in Chicago in 1877. He was dismissed by Bishop Feehan in 1881 for violating diocesan regulations in deeding the church property to himself and the parish as well as to the bishop. When Mielcuszny remained obdurate, Holy Trinity was closed and not reopened except briefly until 1893. See: Parot, *Polish Catholics in Chicago*, pp. 69-73.

18. On this schism see: Kuzniewski, *Faith and Fatherland*, pp. 24-25, who gives 1872 as the year Rev. Jan Frydrychowicz arrived and 1874 as the year of his death.

19. *Żelaźni* was a popular short form for the Polish "independents" (*niezależni*).

20. Rev. Dominik H. Kołasinski (1838-1898), as priest and pastor in Detroit from 1882 to 1896, because the focus of issues and events that foreshadowed the pattern of religious independency in all large and many small Polish American communities from 1894 to 1914. The major issue, aside from Kołasinski's personality, was the right of Polish Catholics to nominate their pastors and hold title to the land on which their church was built. See: Laurence Orton, *Polish Detroit and the Kołasinski Affair* (Detroit: Wayne State University Press, 1981).

21. Rev. Antoni Kozłowski (1857-1907) led a secession from St. Hedwig's parish in Chicago in 1895 that resulted in the formation of All Saints, the first parish in the Independent Polish Catholic Church of America (later the Polish Old Catholic Church). Though the immediate issues were personal rivalry between Kozłowski and his pastor (Józef Barzyński, brother of Wincenty), the break reflected the pent-up frustration with Resurrectionist policies in Chicago. See: Parot, *Polish Catholics in Chicago*, pp. 102-20.

22. Rev. Antoni Kozłowski was consecrated bishop in 1897 in Berne, Switzerland, by bishops of the Old Catholic movement. The Old Catholics were founded in 1871-73 in opposition to the decrees of the First Vatican Council, particularly the declaration of papal infallibility. The heirs of the Schism of Utrecht, a small, Jansenist group founded in the early eighteenth century, consecrated their first bishop. All Old Catholic churches are national but none is an established church. It is easy to understand their appeal to dissident Poles, since they could provide a validly ordained clergy and episcopacy while allowing members to function in autonomous national units. Prior to his ordination in Italy in 1885, Kozłowski had been influenced by Old Catholic thinking, but the early teachings of independent Polish churches in America (which Kruszka illustrates here) did not at first coincide with the Old Catholics' basic statement of belief, the Declaration of Utrecht of 1889. When Kozłowski died in 1907, the old Catholics consecrated Rev. Franciszek Hodur (1866-1953), who consolidated most of the independents in America into the Polish National Catholic Church. The P.N.C.C. subscribes to the Declaration of Utrecht. See: Parot, *Polish Catholics in Chicago*, pp. 103-104, 121; "Old Catholics," *New Catholic Encyclopedia*, X, pp. 672-73, though its summary of the history of the P.N.C.C. is wholly inadequate; Laurence Orzell, "A Minority Within a Minority: The Polish National Catholic Church, 1896-1907," *Polish American Studies*, Vol. 36, No. 1 (Spring, 1979), pp. 5-32.

23. The maintenance of the rule of clerical celibacy emphasizes the conservative nature of the independent movement once the goal of Polish autonomy had been achieved. Clerical celibacy was also reaffirmed by the National Catholics centered in Scranton at their second synod in 1906. See: Orzell, "A Minority Within a Minority," p. 30.

24. Joseph René Vilatte was a former priest who brought together some dissident parishes in what he claimed was an Old Catholic diocese centered in Green Bay, Wisconsin. Though consecrated by a Swiss Old Catholic bishop in 1885, his ties with the movement were tenuous. He was also consecrated bishop for America in 1892 by Jacobite bishops in India and Ceylon who were associated with the patriarch of the Syrian rite. His views are not clear, but quite possibly he hoped to bring dissident Poles under his leadership. See: Orton, *Polish Detroit*, p. 125; Parot, *Polish Catholics in Chicago*, pp. 103-104, 109.

25. Rev. Hodur had been elected bishop by the first synod of the Polish National Catholic Church in 1904. His all-important consecration by the Old Catholics had to await the death

of his Chicago rival, Bishop Antoni Kozłowski. See: Orzell, "A Minority Within a Minority," pp. 7, 28, 31.

26. Alliancists (*Związkowy*) were members of the Polish National Alliance.

27. Kruszka cites *Nowe Drogi* [New Ways], pp. 7-8, an early magazine of Rev. Hodur's.

28. *Jura Stolae* is a reference to "stole fees," the payment that priests receive for performing ceremonies such as marriages and baptisms. The term derives from the stole worn by the priest on such occasions.

29. American bishops usually saw the Polish movement for representation in the hierarchy as a threat to their authority, to the future unity of the American Church, and to native American acceptance of the legitimacy of the Catholic Church. They classed the Polish movement with those of other national groups—Germans, Italians, French, and Ruthenians—and with few exceptions opposed them bitterly. The willingness of Poles to use the political influence of Presidents Grover Cleveland and Theodore Roosevelt or of the Polish government (in 1920) probably only increased their fears and anger. On the 1891 episode see: James H. Moynihan, *The Life of Archbishop John Ireland* (New York: Harper, 1953), pp. 71, 74. Also see: John Tracy Ellis, *The Life of James Cardinal Gibbons. Archbishop of Baltimore, 1834-1921* (Milwaukee: Bruce, 1952; 2 vols.), I, p. 384; Coleman J. Barry, *The Catholic Church and the German Americans* (Milwaukee: Bruce, 1953), p. 275; note 33 below.

30. Mieczysław Ledóchowski (1822-1902) was imprisoned for urging passive resistance to restrictions upon religious instruction in Polish enacted in Germany during the *Kulturkampf* in the early 1870s. He was made a cardinal during his imprisonment and later released in a bargain that allowed him to settle in Rome. Prior to that, as archbishop of Poznań-Gniezno, he had compromised in the Germanization of the Polish church. He was himself largely a Germanized Pole. As Prefect of the Congregation of the Propaganda of Faith from 1892 to 1902, he wielded jurisdiction over the American church (considered a mission church until 1905). In that position he was consistently opposed to Polish efforts to secure representation in the American hierarchy. See: Kuzniewski, *Faith and Fatherland*, pp. 14-15, 48-49; Parot, *Polish Catholics in Chicago*, pp. 137-40; *Catholic Encyclopedia* (1913), IX, pp. 111-12.

31. The opposition of Majer, Molitor, and Bratkiewicz may be easier to understand if one assumes that Barzyński had a Resurrectionist mind as Apostolic Vicar for Polish Catholics in America.

32. On the Cahensly movement see: Barry, *The Catholic Church and German Americans*.

33. Proposals for a Polish Catholic jurisdiction in the United States had been discussed for some time, but the Cahensly movement gave them new life. On the petitions of 1890-91 see: *Wiarus* [The Old Guard], January 30, 1890,, June 12, 1891, June 19, 1891, June 26, 1891, and July 10, 1891; Parot, *Polish Catholics in Chicago*, pp. 137-38; Kuzniewski, *Faith and Fatherland*, pp. 32-33.

34. John J. Keane (1839-1912) was the first rector of the Catholic University of America (1889-1896), Archbishop of Dubuque (1900-1911), and a leading member of the progressive, Americanizing wing of the American Catholic Church.

35. Leo XIII died July 20, 1903. His successor, Pius X, was elected August 9, 1903.

36. The opposition is explained below as American—possibly the Resurrectionists and the assimilationist wing of the American church. See: Parot, *Polish Catholics in Chicago*, pp. 150-52, 154-55.

37. The duke of Norfolk was the traditional lay leader of English Catholics. Most of the English bishops were then Irish.

38. The decision to appoint a Polish bishop was not made until 1907, three years later. Finally, on the recommendation of the clergy, and the archbishop of Chicago, Rev. Paul Rhode, was appointed and on July 28, 1908, and consecrated an auxiliary bishop of Chicago.

CHAPTER 6: HISTORY OF THE POLISH
EDUCATIONAL SYSTEM IN AMERICA

1. The standard work on the subject is Józef Miąso, *Dzieje Oświaty Polonijnej w Stanach Zjednoczonych* (Warsaw: Polish Scientific Publishers, 1970). Miąso's work was translated by Ludwik Krzyżanowski under the sponsorship of the Kościuszko Foundation. See Józef Miąso, *The History of the Education of Polish Immigrants in the United States* (Library of Polish Studies,VI, Eugene Kusielewicz, General Editor. New York: Kościuszko Foundation, 1977/Warsaw: PWN—Polish Scientific Publishers, 1977). Pagination in the following notes refers to the English translation. For complimentary studies on the subject of Polish education in the United States, see Ladislaus John Siekaniec, *The Polish Contribution to Early American Education, 1608-1865* (San Francisco: R & E Research Associates, 1976); Sister Ellen Marie Kuznicki, "A Historical Perspective on the Polish American Parochial School," *Polish American Studies*, XXV (Spring-Autumn, 1978), pp. 5-12, and "The Polish American Parochial Schools," in *Poles in America: Bicentennial Essays*, Frank Mocha, ed. (Stevens Point, Wisconsin: Worzalla Publishing Company, 1978), pp. 435-60; Anthony J. Kuzniewski, "Bootstraps and Book Learning: Reflections on the Education of Polish Americans," *Polish American Studies*, XXXII (Autumn, 1975), pp. 5-26; Andrew M. Greeley and Peter H. Rossi, *The Education of Catholic Americans* (New York: Anchor Books, 1968).

2. For a thorough history of the Panna Marya settlement, see T. Lindsay Baker, *The First Polish Americans: Silesian Settlements in Texas* (College Station, Texas: Texas A&M University Press, 1979); also, Baker's *The Early History of Panna Marya, Texas* (Lubbock: Texas Tech Press, 1975); also, Edmund Dworczyk, *The First Polish Colonies of America in Texas* (San Antonio: The Naylor Company, 1936). For a primary source on Panna Marya, see Ks. Adolf Bakanowski, CR, *Mjoe Wspomnienia* (Lwów: Nakładem X. X. Zartwychstańców, 1913), pp. 24-70. For a brief sketch of Resurrectionist involvement in Texas missions, see John Iwicki, CR, *Resurrectionist Studies: The First One Hundred Years: A Study of the Apostolate of the Congregation of the Resurrection in the United States* (Rome: Gregorian University Press, 1966), pp. 24-25. Each of the above works deals with the pioneer figures in the Panna Marya settlement and in other Texas areas.

3. For a discussion regarding the subject of the oldest Polish school in America, see Miąso, *History*, pp. 101-106; 120; also see Sister M. Nobilis, S.S.N.D., "The First Polish School in the United States," *Polish American Studies*, IV (January-June, 1947), pp. 1-5. Sister Nobilis argues that St. Stanislaus Bishop and Martyr in Milwaukee established Polonia's first school, a claim that Miąso disputes. Miąso argues that the Panna Marya school house was the first Polish school in America. As for the Buffalo community, one might consult works listed in Walter Drzewienicki, *Polonica Buffaloensis. Annotated Bibliography of Source and Printed Materials Dealing with the Polish-American Community in the Buffalo, New York, Area* (Buffalo: Buffalo and Erie County Historical Society, 1976); also see, Maxine Seller, "The Education of Immigrant Children in Buffalo, New York, 1890-1916," *New York History*, 57 (1976), pp. 183-199.

4. Kruszka's original reference cites page 23, but there is no identification of the specific source. Microfilm copies of manuscript materials pertaining to the Rev. Wincenty Barzyński, CR, are housed in the Archives of the Congregation of the Resurrection, Chicago Province, Winnetka, Illinois. See: Wincenty Barzyński's *Listy z Ameryki, 1886-1898* [Letters from America, 1886-1898]; Antoni Lechert, CR, *Listy do O. Barzynskiego, 1883-1887* [Letters to Rev. Barzyński, 1883-1887]; also see, *Reports to the General Chapters from the North American Delegates, 1857-1947*. None of the above listed materials were available to Kruszka when researching and writing his *Historya*.

5. Kruszka, of course, did not have access to Census Manuscript Schedules for the Twelfth Census of the United States (1900) when making his estimates. Nor did he know of the Chicago Board of Education, *School Census for the City of Chicago, 1898* (Chicago,

1898), which listed the ethnic composition of the entire school system. For more on this subject, see James W. Sanders, *The Education of an Urban Minority: Catholics in Chicago, 1833-1965* (New York: Oxford University Press, 1977); also, Timothy George Walsh, "Catholic Education in Chicago and Milwaukee, 1840-1890," unpublished Ph.D. dissertation, Northwestern University, 1975.

6. Kruszka's original footnote reads: "In addition to the school tax for the support of public school."

7. Ladislaus Dyniewicz (1843-1928) maintained the largest and most significant publishing house in Chicago Polonia in the 1873-1898 period. Much of Dyniewicz's business was devoted to newspaper publishing and to the printing of textbooks and religious hymnals. But in the late 1890s, the Polish Publishing Company, owned by Jan Smulski (later a mayoral candidate in Chicago and political adviser to President Woodrow Wilson) surpassed in volume the printery of Ladislaus Dyniewicz.

8. See note 7 above. Also see Helene Chrzanowska, "Polish Book Publishing in Chicago," *Polish American Studies*, IV (January-June, 1947), pp. 37-39.

9. The Rev. Franciszek Wojtalewicz (1861-1942) was pastor of Immaculate Conception Parish in Chicago from 1895 until his death. See: Bolek, *Who's Who*, p. 500.

10. For studies of the curriculum and textbooks used in Polish schools, see Miąso, *History*, pp. 125-38; 176-96, and *passim*; also, Rev. Felix Ladon, CR, *Podręcznik dla Nauczycielek Szkół Parafialnych* (Chicago, 1914); and the Rev. Ladon's *Zarys Ogólny Dogmatyki* (Chicago: Dziennik Chicagoski, 1920); also, *Dzieje Parafii Św. Trójcy w Chicago. Na Pamiątkę 25-letniego Jubileuszu Założeniam Parafii Ś. Trójcy* (Chicago, 1898), which tells, in passing, of education developments at Holy Trinity Parish in Chicago; *Dyniewicza Druga Czytanka dla Szkół Polskich w Stanach Zjednoczonych* (Chicago: W. Dyniewicza, 1910), a standard reader published by the Dyniewicz Publishing Company, which was used throughout Polish parochial schools in Chicago (see note 6 above) along with the *Dzieje Polski dla Użytku Szkół Polskich w Ameryce* (Chicago, 1906) and the *Mała Historia Polska dla Szkół Polskich* (Chicago, 1910), two standard history texts. Finally, for interpretations of Miąso and the subject of curriculum and texts, see Kuznicki, "Polish American Parochial School," *passim*, and Kuzniewski, "Bootstraps and Booklearning," *passim*.

11. See note 10 above; Miąso, *History*, pp. 125-38; 176-96.

12. A major work on the overall educational efforts of Polish teaching nuns is Sister M. Tullia, "Polish Sisterhoods and Their Contributions to the Catholic Church in the United States," in *The Contributions of Poles to the Growth of Catholicism in the Untied States* (Francis Domański, editor, Volume VI of the *Sacrum Poloniae Millenium* series. Rome: 1959), pp. 371-612. For abbreviated treatments of the same subject, consult the following: Sister M. Ligouri, C.S.F.N., "Polish American Sisterhoods and Schools to 1919," *Polish American Studies*, XIII (July-December, 1956), pp. 71-76 and "Imported Polish American Sisterhoods," *Polish American Studies*, XIV (July-December, 1957), pp. 91-102. For an annotated bibliography of Catholic sisterhoods in the United States, see John Tracy Ellis and Robert Trisco, *A Guide to American Catholic History*, second edition (Santa Barbara, California: ABC-Clio, 1982), pp. 137-47.

13. Correspondence of the Rev. Feliks Żwiardowski, CR (died 1895 in Częstochowa, Texas), is contained in his *Listy z Ameryki (1866-1895)*, microfilm copy available in the Chicago Province Archives of the Congregation of the Resurrection, Winnetka, Illinois.

14. See notes 2 and 4 above.

15. Mother Marcelline Darowska and Mother Josephine Karska founded the Immaculate Conception Sisters (European Branch) in Rome in 1857. Shortly thereafter, an attempt was made by the Congregation of the Resurrection to amalgamate the European and American branches. Of note is that Rev. Feliks Żwiardowski, CR, authored the rule of the Immaculate Conception Sisters, patterning the rule after the Congregation of the Resurrection. In 1881, after a brief six-year mission in the United States, the Immaculate Conception Sisters merged with the Sisters of the Incarnate Word. See Iwicki, *Resurrectionist Studies*, pp. 34-35 and

passim; also, Rev. Władisław Kwiatkowski, CR, *Matka Marcelina Darowska* (Wieden: Nakładem Księży Zmartwychwstania Pańskiego, 1952).

16. Kruszka's original citation is a letter dated April 20, 1875.

17. See Rev. Bronisław Przewłocki, CR, *Listy z Ameryki, 1877*, microfilm copy of the original housed in the Chicago Province Archives of the Congregation of the Resurrection, Winnetka, Illinois. Rev. Przewłocki died in Bandera, Texas, in 1879.

18. The Rev. Eugene Funcken (died in Berlin, Kansas, in 1888), was the first non-Polish candidate admitted into the Congregation of the Resurrection. He was ordained in 1857 and served as Regional Superior of Canada and the United States for the Congregation of the Resurrection from 1865 to 1888. See Rev. Eugene Funcken, CR, *Letters to the Roman Motherhouse, 1868-1888*, microfilm copy of the original in the Chicago Province Archives of the Congregation of the Resurrection, Winnetka, Illinois.

19. Rev. Tyszkiewicz served as pastor of St. Hedwig Parish in Martinez, Texas, 1877-1881. See Iwicki, *Resurrectionist Studies*, pp. 40-43.

20. Earlier in the chapter, Kruszka indicates that the Sisters of Providence were the first order teaching in Polish schools in the United States, beginning in Texas in 1872. Consult Sister M. Nobilis, "The School Sisters of Notre Dame in Polish American Education," *Polish American Studies*, XII (July-December, 1955), pp. 77-83.

21. Kruszka's footnote reads: "In the middle of 1901 the Polish sisters from this convent left it and founded a purely Polish order with a motherhouse in Stevens Point, Wisconsin."

22. For additional materials on these various sisterhoods mentioned in Kruszka, see Sister M. Tullia, "Polish Sisterhoods," *passim*; Sister M. Ligouri, "Polish American Sisterhoods," pp. 71-76.

23. Bibliographic sources on the Felicians are generally more abundant than for other Polish American sisterhoods: Sister M. Amandine, "Seventy-Five Years of Felician Activity in America," *Polish American Studies*, VI (July-December, 1949), pp. 65-79, an article noted for its comprehensive compilation of all Felician-sponsored educational and social service institutions in the United States (pp. 76-79); Sister M. Angela Betke, "The Felician Sisters and Social Service," *Polish American Studies*, III (January-June, 1946), pp. 21-29; Sister M. Feliciana, "The Chicago Province of the Felician Sisters," *Polish American Studies*, XVIII (July-December, 1961), pp. 100-106; Sister M. Feliciana, compiler, *A Memoir of the Fifty Years—Fiftieth Anniversary of the Mother of Good Counsel Province of the Congregation of the Sisters of St. Felix* (Felician Sisters) (Chicago, 1960); Sister M. Charatina Hilburger, "Writings of the Felician Sisters in the United States," *Polish American Studies*, III (July-December, 1946), pp. 65-97, an article distinguished for its comprehensive coverage devoted to textbooks, theses, periodicals, religious books and catechisms, readers, and voluminous pedogogical works published by the Felicians; Sister M. Theophania Kalinowski, "The First Decade of the Sisters of St. Felix in America, 1874-1884," M.A. thesis, Loyola University, Chicago, 1956, as well as Sister M. Theophane's *Felician Sisters in the West* (Ponca City, Oklahoma: Bruce in cooperation with the Felician Sisters of the Southwest, U.S.A., 1967); Sister Ellen Maria Kuznicki, "An Ethnic School in American Education: A Study of the Origin, Development, and Merits of the Educational System of the Felician Sisters in Polish American Catholic Schools of Western New York," unpublished Ph.D. dissertation, Kansas State University, 1973; *Magnificat: A Centennial Record of the Congregation of the Sisters of St. Felix (The Felician Sisters), 1855-1955* (privately printed, 1955); Mary Alma Postulka, "History of the Felician Sisters in Buffalo under the Administration of Provincial Mothers (1900-1926)," unpublished M.A. thesis, Canisius College, 1949; Ellen Maria Ryba, *Response (Felician Sisters Centennial in America): 1874-1974* (privately printed, 1974).

24. Kruszka's citation reads: "The above history was sent to us by the Superior of the Felician Sisters from Detroit in 1901."

25. The literature on the Sisters of the Holy Family of Nazareth is likewise voluminous. See: Mary Jane Menżenska, *Guide to Nazareth Literature 1873-1973: Works by and about the Congregation of the Sisters of the Holy Family of Nazareth* (Philadelphia: Sisters of the

Holy Family of Nazareth, 1975). In addition, see Sister M. DeChantal, C.S.F.N., *Out of Nazareth: A Centenary of the Sisters of the Holy Family of Nazareth in the Service of the Church* (New York: Exposition Press, 1974); Sister M. Ligouri, "Seventy Five Years of Religious Growth," *Polish American Studies*, VIII (January-June, 1951), pp. 1-11, which lists all institutions served by this sisterhood (pp. 10-11); Sister M. Theophane, "The Nazareth Way in America," *Polish American Studies*, XVII (January-June, 1960), pp. 49-52.

26. For material on the Resurrectionist Sisters, see Iwicki, *Resurrectionist Studies, passim*; also, Sister Beatrice Wiech, CR, "The Resurrection Sisters—Fifty Years for God and Country," *Polish American Studies*, VI (July-December, 1949), pp. 99-105 and "The Resurrectionist Pedagogical System," *Polish American Studies*, XX (January-June, 1960), pp. 34-39; Annette Chmielewska, "A History of the Educational Activities of the Sisters of the Resurrection in the United States from 1900 to the Present," unpublished M.A. thesis, Fordham University, 1958. For materials on the foundress, Mother Celine Borzęcka, see Teresa Kalkstein, *Witness to the Resurrection: The Servant of God Mother Celine Borzęcka Foundress of the Congregation of the Resurrection of Our Lord Jesus Christ* (Castleton-on-Castle Hudson, New York: Sisters of the Resurrection, 1967); Sister M. Catherine, CR, "Mother Celine Borzęcka CR, Foundress of the Resurrection Sisters," and Sister Ligouri CR, "Mother Hedwig Borzęcka CR, Co-Foundress of the Resurrection Sisters," *Polish American Studies*, X (July-December, 1953), pp. 95-103, 103-111.

27. Sister Mary Edwina, "The Franciscan Sisters of St. Joseph," *Polish American Studies*, V (January-June, 1948), pp. 8-13, carries a brief sketch of this sisterhood.

28. See Miąso, *History*, pp. 176-96 for a survey of higher education developments; also see the extremely significant piece done by Rev. Joseph Swastek, "The Formative Years of the Polish Seminary in the United States," in *The Contribution of Poles to the Growth of Catholics in the United States*, pp. 39-150; Francis Bolek, *The Polish American School System* (New York: Columbia University Press, 1948); Mary Edwin Bozek, "Early History of SS. Cyril and Methodius Seminary," unpublished M.A. Thesis, University of Notre Dame, 1943; Valerian Jasiński, "A Polish Seminary in Contemporary America," *Homiletic and Pastoral Review*, XLI (October, 1940); A. Karr, "History of St. Mary's College, Orchard Lake, Michigan," in *Studies in the History of Higher Education in Michigan* (Claude Eggertsen, editor, Ann Arbor: University of Michigan, 1950); Arthur Prudden Coleman, "Alliance College: American Cradle of Polish Heritage," *Zgoda*, August 15, 1957; A. Piwowarski, *Historia Seminarium Polskiego w Detroit i Orchard Lake, Michigan* (1910); finally, for a detailed investigation of curriculum and educational activities at St. Stanislaus College in Chicago, see *St. Stanislaus College—Weber High School, 1890-1940* (Chicago, 1940), the golden year jubilee album of this institution.

29. The preceeding paragraph originally appeared as the penultimate paragraph in the chapter. It has been moved to this location for clarity and consistency.

30. See note 28 above, especially Swastek, "Formative Years," pp. 39-150.

CHAPTER 7: POLISH INDUSTRY AND
COMMERCE IN AMERICA

1. This sentence did not appear in the original. It was added to improve the sense of the introductory paragraph and set the parameters of the chapter.

2. Hieronim Kajsiewicz, CR (1812-1873), veteran of the 1830-1831 insurrection and one of the founders of the Resurrectionist order. He was a leading advocate of the position that the order should commit itself to ministry to Poles abroad. He arrived in the U.S. in 1871 to accept a Polish mission in Chicago from Bishop Foley and to negotiate an agreement to give the order the right to administer all non-diocesan Polish parishes in the archdiocese for ninety-nine years.

3. Kruszka's original citation reads: "*Letters*, p. 351." This is a reference to the published letters of Rev. Hieronim Kajsiewicz (see Note 2 above) which appeared in: Hieronim

Kajsiewicz, *Pisma, rozprawy, listy z podróży. Pamiętnik o zgromadzeniu* [Writings, Discourses, Travel Letters, Memoirs of the General Meetings] (Kraków: privately printed, 1872); Hieronim Kajsiewicz,*Wyciagi z listów i notat zmarłego* [Extracts from the letters and notes of the deceased], edited by Bronisław Zaleski, in Rocznik Towarzystwo Historyczno-Literackiego w Paryżu [Annual of the Historical-Literary Society of Paris], 1 (1873?), pp. 254-419.

4. Small businessmen such as these were the founders of the Polish American middle class. Their social origins are not clear, but they often provided an alternative to clerical leadership in the early immigrant communities. Particularly important were tavern owners or grocers, who also rendered services in connection with travel, transfers of money, land or legal transactions, and employment. Maximillian J. Kucera (?-1904), for example, was one of the organizers of the *Gmina Polska* in Chicago in 1866 and the Polish National Alliance in 1880. See: Bolek, *Who's Who.* Anthony Sherman (Antoni Smarzewski-Schermann), Piotr Kiołbassa, and Józef Niemczewski were respectively president, vice-president, and secretary of the St. Stanislaus Kostka Society when it was organized in Smarzewski's Chicago home in 1864. See: Parot, *Polish Catholics in Chicago,* pp. 23-24. On Smarzewski and Kiołbassa, see notes for Chapter 11 below. Sometimes printers or publishers functioned like the early tavern-keepers, either personally or through their newspapers. Ignacy Wendziński, the editor, seems to fit this category in part. See text and notes for Chapter 1 above and Chapter 11 below. P. Soboleski was probably the well-known writer and journalist Paweł Sobolewski (1818-1884). See: Bolek, *Who's Who.*

5. Kruszka's argument in this chapter, that Polish industrial capitalism would strengthen the immigrant worker as well as the ethnic community ("our nationality"), expands on the popular campaign for economic self-sufficiency. The cry had already been raised in Europe and America for Poles to buy from Poles, but that had been at the retail level, where Jews traditionally provided many of the services and goods required by peasants and workers. It is interesting to note that Ukrainians adopted a similar approach to the Polish merchants among them. Kruszka would carry the argument for economic self-improvement one step further.

6. Adalbert Danisch. A Chicago businessman and political figure. Owner of the Chicago Badge and Banner Works. He was a captain in the Pulaski volunteers, and a member of the Polish Educational Aid Society, the Board of Holy Trinity High School, Polish Falcons, PRCU and PNA.

7. The impact of immigrant remittances was not geographically uniform. That fact encouraged widely divergent opinions about their importance. Remittances were significant in the wooded Kurpie region in the northern Russian partition, where 15% to 20% of the inhabitants of some villages had gone to America by 1914. In Galicia on the eve of the First World War, 25% of the population relied in some way on income from the emigration. See: Krzystof Groniowski, "The Socio-Economic Base of Polish Emigration to North America, 1854-1939," in Frank Renkiewicz, ed., *The Polish Presence in Canada and America* (Toronto: Multicultural History Society of Ontario, 1982), pp. 4-6.

8. Polish immigrants invested an unusual portion of their income in real property, be it their homes or their churches. See: Parot, "Ethnic versus Black Metropolis: The Origins of Polish-Black Housing Tensions in Chicago," *Polish American Studies,* XIX (1959), pp. 18, 24-25; Julius John Ozog, "A Study of Polish Home Ownership in Chicago," unpublished M.A. Thesis, University of Chicago, 1942.

9. The belief that the progress of Poles was hindered by excessive consumption of alcohol stimulated a temperance movement led by the clergy in both Europe and America. See: Wepsiec, P*olish American Serial Publications,* p. 98, Item 593; Frank Renkiewicz, "The Polish Settlement of St. Joseph County, Indiana: 1855-1935," unpublished Ph. D. dissertation, University of Notre Dame, 1967, pp. 227-35.

10. Kruszka was too optimistic about the possibility of producing a well-educated younger generation and assuming an important position in trade and industry. A survey done shortly after Kruszka's study showed only 100 Polish American high school students in Chicago. See: Antoni Karbowiak, *Dzieje edukacyjne Polaków na obczyznie* (Lwów, 1910),

p. 54. The 1911 W.S. Congregational Report, *The Children of Immigrants in Schools*, showed Poles had rates of persistence beyond the sixth grade lower than those for native born whites, Blacks, and other ethnic groups in the cities surveyed. In fact, they were lowest in the sample. Quoted in John Bodnar, "Morality and Materialism: Slavic Immigrants and Education, 1890-1940" *Journal of Ethnic Studies*, (Winter, 1978), p. 9-12.

11. John F. Smulski (1867-1928), banker, publisher, civic leader, and politician. Founder and owner of Smulski Publishing Company. Served as alderman and city attorney in Chicago and State Treasurer of Illinois. Leading Polish Republican in Illinois. Smulski was very active in Polish War Relief during and after World War I and was the organizer and President of the Polish War National Council in Chicago. See: Edward Kantowicz, *Polish-American Politics in Chicago, 1888-1940* (Chicago: University of Chicago Press, 1975), pp. 29, 60-64.

12. "The Polish Coffin Factory" was quickly reorganized as the Standard Coffin and Casket Manufacturing Company with Mr. Józef Magdziarz (1868-1939), one of the original directors, as president. Mr. Magdziarz was born in Poland in 1868 and died in Chicago in 1939. He served as treasurer of the Polish National Alliance between 1915 and 1924. The S. J. Rokosz referred to as first president of the company was probably Stanisław Rokosz (d. April 20, 1921) who served as vice-president and president of the PNA at the turn of the century and was later active as a labor organizer.

13. Nicodemus L. Piotrowski (1863-1932), lawyer, teacher, Democratic politician, active in Polish American organizations, especially the Polish Roman Catholic Union. See: Bolek, *Who's Who*; Kantowicz, *Polish-American Politics*, pp. 63, 84, 105-6. On Kiołbassa, see below Chapter 11.

14. Of this group of small entrepreneurs, only Sylwester Wabiszewski achieved some prominence later. In 1920 he founded the Maynard Electrical Steel Casting Company, which became one of the largest industrial firms in Milwaukee. He was born in Poland in 1866. See: Bolek, *Who's Who*.

15. Of the foregoing, only August Rudziński and August Gawin achieved prominence. Rudziński arrived in Milwaukee from Poznań in 1858 and was one of the pioneers of Milwaukee Polonia. After successfully launching his tailoring business through military contracts as Rev. Kruszka notes, he became active in politics. In the 1870s he served two terms on the Milwaukee city council. He was one of the organizers and first captain of the Milwaukee Kościuszko Guards. He died in 1891. August Gawin also went into politics from tailoring. He served as Milwaukee city controller from 1908 to 1910 and was later elected to the state assembly from Milwaukee.

16. The *Przyjaciel Ludu* appeared in Milwaukee between 1880-1882. It was a liberal weekly founded in May, 1876, in Chicago. It appeared in Chicago between 1876 and 1880 and 1882-1884. Its founder was Ignacy Wendziński (1828-1901) writer, editor, and publisher. Józef Rudnicki was his partner in the printing end of the business.

17. *Zgoda* was the official organ of the Polish National Alliance. In its early days it took a strongly anti-clerical line. After four years in Milwaukee it was moved to Chicago.

18. Michał Kruszka (1860-1918), publisher and editor. Came to United States in 1880 and Milwaukee in 1883. Founded the weekly *Krytyka* in 1885 and the daily *Kuryer Polski* in 1888. Elected assemblyman in 1890 on Democratic ticket and served one term. In 1892 was elected to state senate and served two terms. Switched to Republican party in 1898. He was the leader of the struggle to get equal rights for Poles in the Catholic Church and obtain the appointment of a Polish American Bishop. Older brother of Wacław Kruszka. See: Kusniewski, *Faith & Fatherland*. On the Kuryer Polski Publishing Company, see: Kruszka, below, Chapter 11 under *Kuryer Polski*.

19. On *Kuryer Polski* and W. Maychrzycki, see below, Chapter 11, under *Kuryer Polski*. On *Dziennik Milwaucki*, see Kruszka, below, Chapter 11, under *Dziennik Milwaucki*. The latter, published in Milwaukee from 1899 to 1905, was associated with the Democratic party and bitterly opposed the Kruszka brothers. Its editor was Ignacy Czerwiński.

20. These men are generally considered the founders of Detroit's Polish community. Sta-

nisław Melin, from Bydgoszcz in Prussian Poland, arrived in Detroit in 1857. In 1858 his brother (or cousin, according to one source) Franciszek and Franciszek's brother-in-law Jakub Mindak arrived. In 1859, Jan Lemke, a Kashub from Koscierzyna near Gdańsk, came to Detroit with his wife, three sons, two cousins, and sister-in-law. Stanisław Melin married Augusta Rohr, Lemke's sister-in-law, in 1860. These men were among the original founders of St. Albertus Parish, the first Polish parish in Detroit. All became very prosperous, with Lemke emerging as the patriarch of Detroit Polonia. He developed wide real estate investments, grocery and hardware stores, and other commercial interests. His son, Rev. J. Lemke, was probably the first Polish American ordained a priest in the United States. The older Lemke eventually owned a chain of grocery and hardware stores as well as considerable real estate. He played a patriarchal role in the formation of Detroit Polonia, analogous to that of Antoni Smarzewski in Chicago. See: Orton, *Polish Detroit*, pp. 11-12, 171-72, 198 note 4, and elsewhere; Allan R. Treppa, "John A. Lemke: America's First Native-Born Polish Priest?" *Polish American Studies*, XXXV, No. 1-2 (Spring, 1978), pp. 78-83.

21. Jan Zynda began his brewing business by leasing an old German brewery, the Endriss Brewery. In five years he had accumulated $18,000 in cash. He built a new "White Eagle" brewery in the late 1880s. By 1908, the plant was valued at $28,000. Tomasz Zołtowski, who founded the second Polish brewery, was called "The King of the Poles" by English speaking papers because of his wealth and ambition. In addition to his brewing interest, he amassed a vast fortune in real estate. One of the founders of St. Albertus, he also donated the land for St. Josaphat's Church (1889). He was deeply involved in the Kołasiński affair which split Polish Detroit in the 1880s. Alleging immoral conduct, he emerged as the principal accuser of Rev. Kołasiński. On this affair, see Orton, *Polish Detroit*.

22. Józef Sawiński opened his photography shop in 1899.

23. Ignacy Wolf began the White Eagle Tobacco Company in 1889.

24. Kazimierz E. Zawadzki, druggist. He was active in Polish American fraternal and community life and Buffalo civic affairs.

25. Józef Slisz (1864-?), publisher. Came to America in 1885 and settled in Buffalo, where he found work as a printer for the daily newspaper *Polak w Ameryce*. In 1896 established first Polish store in Buffalo. In 1907 became president of the Polish Daily News Company and publisher of *Polak Amerykański*.

26. For brief biographies of members of the Usiak family, members of the Stabeneau family, Bolesław W. Tomczak, and Antoni Schreiber, see: Bolek, *Who's Who*. Schreiber established a national reputation among Poles for his work in the Polish National Alliance and as champion of Polish National causes.

27. This is a reference to Sir Kazimierz S. Gzowski (1813-1898), refugee of the Polish insurrection of 1830, settled in Toronto in 1841, civic leader, engineer, and railroad builder responsible for many projects in Canada including the International Bridge across the Niagara River between Fort Erie, Ontario, and Buffalo, New York. See: *Polski Słownik Biograficzny*, 9, pp. 209-211.

28. Modest Maryański, see: Bolek *Who's Who*.

29. Kazimierz Midowicz (1818-1902), physician, inventor, and publisher. Received his medical education late in life, graduating from School of Medicine in Kraków in 1884. After six years of practice in Poland, he migrated to U.S. and settled in Chicago. Co-founder of daily newspaper *Dziennik Narodowy* in 1899. On the "Kościuszko Quartz Hill Gold Mine" see note 30 below.

30. Rev. Wincenty Barzyński, CR (1838-1899). Ordained a priest in 1861, took part in the insurrection of 1863 and joined the Resurrectionist order in Rome in 1866. He was sent to the Polish colonies in Texas in the same year. In 1874 he moved to Chicago and became pastor of St. Stanislaus Kostka Parish which he built into the largest parish in the United States. Organized twenty-five other parishes. Founded and edited *Dziennik Chicagoski*, and other newspapers. Founded printing houses, religious societies, a bank, orphanages, and St. Stanislaus Kostka College. He was co-founder of the Polish Roman Catholic Union. In 1898,

became first Resurrectionist provincial for United States. He was supporter of Democratic party in Chicago. The mine venture was another in a series of unsuccessful business ventures, a speculative investment of $41,000 in gold mine stock from the Parish Bank (*Bank Parafialny*). The Bank had been established by the Chicago Resurrectionists in 1875 as a safe place for the funds of parishioners of St. Stanislaus Kostka. By the late 1880s it had over extended itself with loans to support construction in new parishes, the operations of a printery, and the purchase of lands for a Polish farm colony in Nebraska. The investment in the gold mine in California was designed to rescue the bank from bankruptcy. The mine was not productive and never paid any dividends. See: Parot, *Polish Catholics in Chicago,* pp. 87-90.

31. Rev. Wilhelm Grutza, writer, publisher, priest. The organizer and first pastor of St. Josaphat's Parish in Milwaukee, Wisconsin, in 1888. Established a short lived high school attached to the parish. Published the newspaper *Katolik* from 1897 until his death. Built the magnificent and inordinately costly St. Josaphat's Church modeled on St. Peter's in Rome. Died August 24, 1901, in Milwaukee. Kruszka was assistant pastor at St. Josaphat's under Rev. Grutza shortly after his ordination in 1905. Michał Kruszka was an outspoken critic of Grutza's decision to burden St. Josaphat's parish with the cost of the basilica dedicated in 1901. See: Kuzniewski, *Faith & Fatherland.*

32. For Kazimierz Rechniowski, see: Bolek, *Who's Who.*

33. The line was completed in 1904.

CHAPTER 8: AGRICULTURE AND THE GENERAL ECONOMIC STATE OF POLES IN AMERICA

1. About twenty years later, when the urban orientation of Polish immigrants was still more pronounced, Mieczyłsaw Szalewski, the Polish vice-consul in New York, estimated that about 500,000, or 16%, of the Polish American population of 3,000,000 depended on the land for a livelihood. The usual explanation is greater and easier economic opportunities in industry. Szalewski's analysis was based on the United States census of 1920 and the tabulations of Poland's Bureau of Statistics. Though all statistics of Polish immigration are a matter of dispute, Szalewski's are considerably lower than Kruszka's, both here and later in the chapter. Poles were no more than 1% of the total American farm population. See: Mieczysław Szalewski,*Wychodźtwo Polskie w Stanach Zjednoczonych Ameryki* [Polish Emigration in the United States of America] (Lwów: Ossolineum, 1924), pp. 202-24 and p. 24 n. 2 for comparison to Kruszka.

2. Thaddeus Wild had been a member of the staff of Michał Kruszka's *Kuryer Polski* and captain of the Kościuszko Guard, Company K of the Wisconsin National Guard. See: Kuzniewski, *Faith & Fatherland.*

3. The reference in this account is to the act of Congress on June 30, 1834, which granted public lands to the Polish refugees who first arrived in the United States in significant numbers in 1834. Land was selected in Illinois but consideration was given to land in Michigan Territory. See: Florian Stasik, *Polska Emigracja Polityczna w Stanach Zjednoczonych Ameryki 1831-1864* [Polish Political Emigration in the United States of America 1831-1864] (Warsaw: State Scientific Publishers, 1973), pp. 95-105, 118-123; Jerzy J. Lerski, *A Polish Chapter in Jacksonian America* (Madison: University of Wisconsin Press, 1958), pp. 126-55.

4. Poles were well known for slowly preparing wooded, swampy, or otherwise difficult to farm land for agriculture in the Midwest. Creditors considered them reliable risks. Their technique of farming was conservative; their goals self-sufficiency as well as modestly valuable cash crops. See: U.S. Immigration Commission, *Reports* (Washington, D. C.: Government Printing Office, 1911), Vols. 21-22; T. Lindsay Baker, *The First Polish Americans: Silesian Settlements in Texas* (College Station, Texas: Texas A&M Press, 1979); Frank Renkiewicz, "The Polish Settlement of St. Joseph County, Indiana: 1855-1935," Ph. D. Dissertation, University of Notre Dame, 1967, Chapter I.

5. Erasmus Jerzmanowski (1844-1909), a refugee from the January Insurrection, made a

fortune in the gas-lighting industry in the United States in the 1870s and 1880s. He was active in the efforts to organize the Polish American immigration in the 1880s. In 1896 he retired to Austrian Poland where he became renowned for this philanthropic support of Polish national and cultural projects. See: *Polski Słownik Biograficzny*, Vol. 11, pp. 178-180.

6. Julian Andrzejkowicz (1821-1898), a manufacturer of paint who settled in the United States in 1854. He was a leader in the formation of the Polish National Alliance in 1880 and was elected its first censor. See: Bolek, *Who's Who*.

7. The account emphasizes social redivision in America according to economic achievement, not according to birth as was still the case for most Poles in Europe. For a starker description of the material condition of Poles in some of the same neighborhoods at about the same time, see: Joseph J. Parot, "Ethic versus Black Metropolis: The Origins of Polish-Black Housing Tensions in Chicago," *Polish American Studies*, Vol. 29, No. 1-2 (Spring, 1972), pp. 7-14.

CHAPTER 9: POLES IN AMERICAN POLITICS

1. On the history of Polish American politics, see: Angela Pienkos, ed., *Ethnic Politics in Urban America* (Chicago: Polish American Historical Society, 1978); Edward Kantowicz, *Polish Politics in Chicago 1888-1940* (Chicago: University of Chicago Press, 1975).

2. Stanisław T. Ślisz, (1856-1909), editor, writer, and publisher. Graduate of Jagiellonian University in Law. Arrived in Buffalo in 1885. Editor of *Ojczyzna* (Buffalo 1885-1887), *Krytyka* (Milwaukee 1887), *Wiara i Ojczyzna* and *Kropidło* (Chicago 1887-1889), *Polak w Ameryce* (Buffalo 1889-1908), and *Polak Amerykański* (Buffalo 1908-1909). Also author of a number of books and short stories.

3. Henryk Głowacki (1816-1891), jurist and politician. Participated in 1830-31 insurrection and was interned in Austria. Deported from Trieste in 1834 to New York. A founder of Batavia, New York. Prominent in Democratic party, he served as presidential elector four times and was elected to State Assembly.

4. Aleksander E. Kierzkowski (1816-1870), civil engineer. Fought in 1830-1831 insurrection and went into exile in France, where he studied civil engineering. Migrated to Canada in 1841. Served as Civil Engineer to Public Works and Assistant Quartermaster General of 5th Military District of Lower Canada. Became active in politics in 1858 when he was elected first to Legislative Council and then to the Legislative Assembly. After confederation in 1867, was elected to the Canadian House of Commons, where he sat until his death.

5. Rev. Adolph Bakanowski, CR (1840-?), priest and missionary. Ordained a priest in 1863. Joined the rebellion of 1863 as a chaplain. After the rebellion was crushed, he made his way to Rome where he entered the Congregation of the Resurrection. In 1866 he came to Panna Maria, Texas, where he served as pastor and the order's vicar general for United States missions. Was pastor of St. Stanislaus Kostka in Chicago from 1870-1873. Returned to Rome in 1873. Spent the remainder of his career in Europe. Was an accomplished pianist and composer and a renowned preacher. Kruszka credits the quotation to Bakanowski's memoirs of his stay in Texas, pp. 79-81.

6. See Chapter 7, note 8.

7. Mikolaj (Nicolaus) Michalski, fought as a major in the insurrection of 1863. Came to the United States to help rally support for the Polish struggle for independence in 1866. Settled in Chicago, where he was one of the organizers of the *"Gmina Polska"* in Chicago, whose purpose was to rally Polish immigrants in support of the National Polish Government in Rapperswill, Switzerland, and the Polish National cause. Michalski was one of the founders of the Rapperswill group.

8. See Chapter 7, note 4.

9. August Kowalski, politician. First Pole to hold elective office in Chicago. Elected alderman for one term as a Republican from the 16th Ward in 1888. Little is known about his background. Kowalski was married to the daughter of Francis Schermann, early Polonia

leader in original Polish northside settlement in Chicago. Kowalski ran unsuccessfully for the same seat in 1899 as a Democrat against Jan Smulski.

10. See Chapter 7, note 8 and note 11.

11. See Chapter 7, note 11.

12. Stanisław Kunz, (1864-?), public official, politician, and civic leader. Graduate of St. Ignatius College and Metropolitan Business School in Chicago. Active in Democratic party. Member, Illinois State House 1888-1890, State Senate 1902-1906. Chicago city council 1891-1925. Second Polish American to serve in U.S. Congress, 1921-1927. Delegate to Democratic National Conventions 1916 and 1925.

13. On Smulski, see Chapter 7, note 4.

14. Tadeusz Wild (1867-?). After service with Company K (Kościuszko Guard) during the Spanish-American War, he was also called up to active service during the Mexican border problem with the First Wisconsin Infantry and served in the Southwest in 1916. Was first president of the Polish Educational Society of Milwaukee (1896), the purpose of which was to promote Polish language and culture in public school.

15. Peter Piasecki (1876-?), public official. After service in the Spanish American War, he served as First Lieutenant of First Wisconsin Infantry on Mexican Border and later during World War I. End service as Colonel of Infantry, U.S. Army. Postmaster of Milwaukee 1923-1936. In 1938 became business manager of Kuryer Publishing Company and in 1939 appointed member of City Tax Review Board.

16. For a lengthier, modern summary of the history of Polish Americans in service during the Spanish-American War and especially on the Milwaukee Kościuszko Guard, see: Joseph Wytrwal, *Poles in American History and Tradition* (Detroit: Endurance Press, 1969), pp. 175-281.

17. The Polish American Falcons was founded in Chicago, June 17, 1887, by Feliks L. Pietrowicz as a paramilitary patriotic organization to prepare Poles in America to assist in independence struggle and to preserve Polish heritage in America. Falcons were established in 1867 in Lwów in emulation of the gymnastic, patriotic German *Turner Verein*. Polish Falcons in America remained in union with Falcons in Poland until 1939. A women's branch of Polish American Falcons was founded shortly afterwards by Theophila Samolińska, a leader of Polish suffragettes. In 1912, headquarters of the Polish Falcons was moved to Pittsburgh. Falcons were crucial to the recruiting of the Polish Army abroad in World War I.

18. Stefan Barszczewski (1870-1937), writer-editor. Came to United States in 1887 and became an editor of *Dziennik Chicagoski* [Chicago Daily] until 1890. From 1890 to 1897 edited *Sokol* [The Falcon] organ of Polish Falcons of America. From 1897-1901 was editor of *Zgoda* [Harmony] organ of the Polish National Alliance. In 1901 returned to Poland to become editor of *Kuryer Warszawski*. Besides his play *Cuba Libre*, he is remembered for an 1894 monograph on the Polish National Alliance in Chicago.

19. Wojciech Kleczkowski (d. 1911), French consular official. Entered Franch Consular Service in 1891, served in Montreal from 1894 to 1906. Subsequently was assigned as plentipotentiary minister in Central America.

20. Józef Obalski (1852-1915), mining engineer and professor. Superintendent of Mines for Province of Quebec, Canada, 1881-1909. Professor, Laval University. Associated with several important mineral discoveries in Province of Quebec. He was elected vice-president of Canadian Mining Institute, awarded Gold Medal by Louisiana Purchase Exposition. Author of numerous papers and monographs.

21. *Górnik* newspaper published between 1893 and 1948 in Wilkes-Barre, Pennsylvania. It was a weekly at the time that Kruszka was writing. It became a daily in 1923. *Górnik* was the organ of the Polish Union of the United States [*Unia Polska w Stanach Zjednoczonych*]. Except for a brief period in 1909 when it followed an independent Republican line, the newspaper was independent politically. There is no record of a Mr. Szymański as the editor of the paper. He presumably served in some lesser capacity.

CHAPTER 10: HISTORY OF POLISH ORGANIZATIONS
IN AMERICA

1. The founder of the Chicago *Gmina Polska*, Ladislaus Dyniewicz, published a brief account of the commune's early years. See Ladislaus Dyniewicz, *Ustawy Gminy Polskiej* (Chicago: W. Dyniewicz, 1988), a work that contains the first constitution of the Chicago *Gmina*. Another helpful account, though a generation removed from the birthdate of the Chicago *Gmina* (1866), is Stanisław Osada, *Historya Związku Narodowego Polskiego i Rozwój Ruchu Narodowego w Ameryce Północhej* (Chicago: Polish National Alliance, 1905), pp. 34-36; 58-66. Note that Dyniewicz was still alive (he was 52 years old at the time) when Osada published his history of the Polish National Alliance.

2. General Józef Bosak-Hauke (1834-1871), a Polish aristocrat with only a slight knowledge of the Polish language, took an active part in the Insurrection of 1863, serving under General Romauld Traugutt until the latter's execution in 1864. Bosak-Hauke then took refuge in Galicia, and still later in Switzerland. He was killed in the Franco-Prussian War. See Piotr Wandycz, *The Lands of Partitioned Poland, 1795-1918* (A History of East Central Europe, Vol. VII. Seattle: University of Washington Press, 1974), pp. 177, 209; R.F. Leslie, *Reform and Insurrection in Russian Poland, 1856-1865* (London: University of London, The Athlone Press, 1963), p. 241. For a brief sketch of Army Major Nicholas Michalski, see Francis Bolek, *Who's Who*, p. 296. Michalski emigrated to the United States and went to Chicago after the Insurrection of 1863; he assisted Dyniewicz in organizing the Chicago *Gmina Polska*.

3. Jan Barzyński (1848-1886) was editor and publisher of *Pielgrzym* (1872-1874). He later edited *Gazeta Polska* in Detroit and Chicago. See Bolek, *Who's Who*, p. 30. *Pielgrzym* issued a call for a national organization of Poles in the United States, which brought about the *Organizacya Polska w Ameryce*, to which 360 applied for charter membership. See Jan Iwicki, *Resurrectionist Studies*, pp. 133-35, 197-201; 228-30. See also, Eugene P. Willging and Hertz Hatzfield, "Nineteenth Century Polish Catholic Periodical Publications in the United States," *Polish American Studies*, XIII (January-June, 1956), pp. 19-35, especially pp. 26-27; Mieczysław Haiman, "Barzyński, Jan (1848-1886)," *Polski Słownik Biograficzny*, Vol. I (Kraków, 1935), pp. 347-48.

4. The Rev. Theodore Gieryk (1837-1878) is generally recognized as the founder of the Polish Roman Catholic Union of America. See Bolek, *Who's Who*, p. 127; Iwicki, *Resurrectionist Studies*, pp. 200, 228; *Polski Słownik Biograficzny*, VII, pp. 446-47; and all standard histories of the PRCU, especially, Karol Wachtel, *Z.P.R.K. Dzieje Zjednoczenia Polskiego Rzymsko-Katolickiego w Ameryce* (Chicago: L. J. Winiecki, 1913); and Mieczysław Haiman, *Zjednoczenie Polskie Rzymsko-Katolickie w Ameryce 1873-1948* (Chicago: PRCU, 1948).

5. Kruszka's original citation reads: "See annual of the *Gazeta Polska Katolicka*."

6. See notes 3 and 4 above for information on Jan Barzyński and Theodore Gieryk. Peter Kiołbassa (1837-1905) was born in Swib, a small Silesian town in Prussian Poland. He came to the United States in 1855, where he taught school at Panna Marya, Texas. He fought in the American Civil War, and after the war moved to Chicago, where he was one of the organizers of St. Stanislaus Kostka Parish, the first Polish church in Chicago (1867). Kiołbassa later became involved in real estate in Chicago Polonia. His many outside contacts brought him into the Republican party in Chicago, where he served as city treasurer in 1893-1894. His efficient tenure in public office (he had once served in the Illinois legislature) earned him the title "Honest Pete." For biographical details, consult the following: Helen Busyn, "The Political Career of Peter Kiołbassa," *Polish American Studies*, VII (January-June, 1950), pp. 8-22, and "Peter Kiołbassa—Maker of Polish America," *Polish American Studies*, VIII (December, 1951), pp. 65-84; *The New World* (Chicago, Illinois), October 27, 1900; *Naród Polski*, June 28, 1905; Joseph Parot, *Polish Catholics*, pp. 23-24; 36-46; 53-54; *Polski Słownik Biograficzny*, XII, pp. 409-10.

7. Several of the more prominent members of the PRCU at the Second Diet include Gieryk, Kiołbassa, Jan Barzyński (see notes 4 and 5 above) and the Rev. Józef Dąbrowski (1842-1903), whose lengthy clerical career has been studied thoroughly by a number of scholars. For a list of works on Dąbrowski, consult Irene Paczyńska and Andrew Pilch, *Materiały do Bibliografii Dziejów Emigracji Oraz Skupisk Polomijnych w Ameryce Północnej i Południowej w XIX i XX Wieku* (Zeszyty Naukowe Uniwersytetu Jagiellońskiego, DXI, Prace Polonijne, Zeszyt 3. Karków: Nakładem Uniwersytetu Jagiellońskiego, 1979), items 2213-2242 on pp. 190-91, hereafter cited as Paczyńska and Pilch, *Materiały*. For some of the lesser-known figures at the Second Diet, consult the following: August Rudziński (?-1891), Bolek, *Who's Who*, p. 387; Kandyd Kozłowski (1836-?), *ibid.*, p. 231, and the *Polski Słownik Biograficzny*, XV, p. 15; Józef Glossowski (1834-1886), *Polski Słownik Biograficzny*, VIII, p. 114; Jan Rodowicz (?-1896), Bolek, *Who's Who*, p. 378; Józef Piotrowski (n.d., Detroit), *ibid.*, p. 90; Józef Musielewicz (n.d.), *ibid.*, p. 310; the Rev. Szulak, a Jesuit priest who served in Chicago in the last 1860s, *ibid.*, p. 451, and Parot, *Polish Catholics*, pp. 43-44; the Rev. Molitor, who served Polish immigrants at the Bohemian church of St. Wenceslaus in Chicago in the last 1860s; however, material on the remaining participants was not obtainable in the *Polski Słownik Biograficzny*, Bolek, or standard histories.

8. For further details on the PRCU during the 1880s, see Haiman, *Zjednoczenie, passim*. Material on Wojciech Jendrzejek and Jan Gniot is lacking in the standard biographical sources. However, a brief note on Jan Manna (1845-1899) is included in Bolek, *Who's Who*, p. 285.

9. *Wiara i Ojczyzna* published its first weekly issue on May 3, 1887. On October 31, 1888, it became the official journal of the PRCU. Published by the Polish Publishing Company, owned and operated by the Resurrectionist Congregation, the newspaper had a run of twelve years, emphasizing the close connection between religion and society throughout Polonia. After January 11, 1898, it was succeeded by *Naród Polski*, which carried the *Proceedings* of the PRCU and other news of interest to Polish Catholic readers. See Iwicki, *Resurrectionist Studies*, pp. 203-04; also, Willging and Hatzfield, "Polish Catholic Periodical Publications," pp. 22-23.

10. Haiman, "Barzyński"; Wachtel, *Z.P.R.K., passim*; note, also, the turbulent history of the Polish Catholic congresses in the last 1890s and early 1900s, during which the PRCU officers played significant roles. For this story, see Wacław Kruszka's *Siedm Siedmioleci Czyli Pół Wieku Życia: Pamiętnik i Przyczynek do Historji w Ameryce*, 2 vols. (Poznań, Milwaukee: Nakładem Autora Czcionkami Drukarni Św. Wojciecha w Poznanu), I, pp. 441-44 and *passim*. Haiman, *Zjednoczenie,* and Osada, *Historya,* likewise follow these congress/fraternal organization ties. Leon Szopiński, president of the PRCU, is credited with bringing about greater stability within that fraternal as well as setting the PRCU on a solid financial base. Jan Jozwiak, (1864-?) a Bay City, Michigan, businessman, organized the Polish Business Cooperative Association in his hometown; Jozwiak served as vice-president of the PRCU for a lengthy period. His experience in banking and financial circles in Michigan also served the PRCU well while on the national executive board (see Bolek, *Who's Who*, p. 184). The chaplains of the PRCU were all of national prominence: the Rev. Franciszek Lange (born 1857 in Domatowo, Poland) was longtime pastor of St. Joseph's Parish in Chicago; he also served as diocesan consultor in the Chicago archdiocese. The Rev. Franciszek Rusin (1867-1939) was founder of Sacred Heart Parish in Syracuse, New York, where he served his entire priestly life. The Rev. Kazimierz Gronkowski (born 1873) served for nearly a half century as pastor of St. Adalbert's Parish in Chicago near southwest side. He, too, was a diocesan consultor in the Chicago archdiocese. See Bolek, *Who's Who*, pp. 146, 255, 387-88.

11. Kruszka's original footnote reads: "Reviewed and supplemented by F. H. Jabłoński." For additional information, see: Victor Greene, *For God and Country: The Rise of Polish and Lithuanian Ethnic Consciousness in America* (Madison: State Historical Society of Wisconsin, 1975), pp. 69, 81, 128; Bolek, p. 168; Osada, *Historya, passim*.

12. The most extensive and thorough scholarship on Polonia in the United States prior to

the American Civil War was conducted by Mieczysław Haiman (1888-1949). The authoritative Jagiellonian University bibliography edited by Paczynska and Pilch (*Materiały*—see Note 6 above) lists 73 items by or about Haiman. Perhaps the most popular English language work by Haiman on the pre-Civil War period is his *Polish Past in America 1608-1865* (Chicago: Polish Roman Catholic Union Archives and Museum, 1939). The work contains much valuable information on early organizational efforts of Poles, which preceded the major Polish National Alliance struggle to ally all Poles in America under a single banner. Other helpful English language works that can be read alongside Haiman's scholarship include: Bogdan Grzeloński, *Poles in the United States of America, 1776-1865* (Warsaw: Interpress, 1976), which contains information on the prototypes of the PNA, notably the Democratic Society of Polish Exiles in America (1852-1860). Grzeloński claims that the group reached a total membership of 157; also see Jerzy Jan Lerski, *A Polish Chapter in Jacksonian America: The United States and the Polish Exiles of 1831* (Madison: University of Wisconsin Press, 1958); Joseph A. Wytrwal, *Poles in American History and Tradition* (Detroit: Endurance Press, 1969); Frank Renkiewicz, *The Poles in America, 1608-1972: A Chronology and Fact Book* (Ethnic Chronology Series, Number 9. Dobbs Ferry, New York: Oceana Publications, 1973). Each of these four works can be consulted should one need to trace obscure names and events in the history of Polonia prior to 1880 and the founding of the Polish National Alliance. The bibliography on the Polish National Alliance is too voluminous to list here. The reader should consult Paczynska and Pilch, *Materiały*, pp. 279-86. The Jagiellonian bibliography contains 114 separate items (items 3579-3692) on the PNA (as well as 104 items [items 3454-3557] on pp. 271-78 on the PRCU). In any event, Osada's *Historya*, listed previously, is the standard Polish-language work for the PNA and the best English-language treatment in Donald Pienkos' *PNA: A Centennial History of the Polish National Alliance of the United States of America* (Columbia University Press, 1989).

13. Kruszka's original citation was Osada's *Historia*.

14. Henryk Kałussowski (1806-1895) is generally regarded as the "Father of the Old Polish Immigration," that is, the first wave of immigration following the Insurrection of 1830-1831. In 1842, Kałussowski organized the Society of Poles in America, a prototype and forerunner of the Democratic Society of Polish Exiles in America (see Note 11). In the late 1870s, Kałussowski worked in tandem with Agaton Giller in organizational efforts bringing about the PNA. For biographical materials on Kałussowski, see Lubomir Gadon, *Emigracja Polska*, 3 vols. (Kraków, 1901-1902); Agaton Giller, *Album Muzeum Narodowego w Rapperswylu, Wieniec Pamiątkowy* (Rapperswyl, 1881); Bolek, *Who's Who*, p. 188; *Polski Słownik Biograficzny*, XI, pp. 505-07; Haiman, *Polish Past, passim*; Grzeloński, *Poles, passim*; Lerski, *Polish Chapter*, pp. 156-59. Each of these sources contains brief sketches on the Society of Poles and the Democratic Society of Polish Exiles.

15. For materials on Polish participation in the American Civil War, see note 12 above. Ludwik Żychliński (?-1891) attained the rank of captain in the Union Army, serving under General Hooker. He authored a memoir of the American Civil War, published in 1862. Żychliński participated in the 1863 Insurrection and was subsequently deported to Siberia along with other Polish officers. See Bolek, *Who's Who*, p. 530; Grzeloński, *Poles, passim*.

16. Ladislaus Dyniewicz, the founder of the Chicago *Gmina Polska*, was born in Chwalków, in the Prussian sector of Poland, on June 13, 1843. He emigrated to the United States in 1866 and moved to Chicago. Here he founded a publishing firm which became a springboard for *Gmina* activities in the St. Stanislaus/Holy Trinity parish area. In October 1873, he and his son, Kazimierz, began publication of *Gazeta Polska*, Chicago's first Polish language newspaper. Dyniewicz and his friend, Juljan Lipiński (1834-1898), were instrumental in bridging the gap between the Chicago *Gmina* and the Polish National Alliance in later years. Dyniewicz, whose publishing company had brought him great prosperity and much social acclaim in Chicago by 1900, gradually assimilated into Chicago's high society. His mansion on 5917 West Diversey was frequented by numerous prominent journalists and businessmen, a far cry from his earlier battles with the clerical party in Chicago during the

1866-1880 period. See the *Dziennik Chicagoski*, February 28, 1929; Helena Chrzanowska, "Polish Book Publishing in Chicago," *Polish American Studies*, IV (January-June, 1947), pp. 37-39; John Drury, *Old Chicago Houses* (Chicago: University of Chicago, 1941), pp. 384-87; Dyniewicz, *Ustawy, passim*; Osada, *Historya, passim*; Bolek, *Who's Who*, pp. 109; 168; Parot, *Polish Catholics*, pp. 35-43, 50-69; 83-84; 130; 207. The Rev. Feliks Żwiardowski, a Resurrectionist priest, who is discussed earlier in this volume, served as pastor of St. Stanislaus Kostka in Chicago from September 1873 to July 1874. He was a vigorous opponent of the *Gmina Polska*. See Iwicki, *Resurrectionist Studies*, pp. 26-45. After leaving Chicago, Żwiardowski was called to the San Antonio, Texas, diocese, where he served as Vicar-General. See Iwicki; also Bolek, *Who's Who*, p. 528; Parot, *Polish Catholics*, 56-57; 71, 80; Rev. Władysław Kwiatkowski, D.R., *Historia Zgromadzenia Zmartwychwstanis Pańskiego na Stuletnią Rocznicę Jego Założenia, 1842-1942* (Albano, 1942), pp. 276; 287; 336. "Citizen" Krzemieniecki was a member of Dyniewicz's *Gmina*. For sketches of other *Gmina* members, see Bolek, *Who's Who*: Ignacy Wendziński (1828-1901), p. 485; Stanisław Kociemski (1827-1904), p. 211; Francis Grzylaszewski (1852-1918), p. 148; Teofila Smolińska (died 1913), p. 397. Bolek gives no information on the others.

17. The only leader of the Polish National Alliance and Union of Poles in America covered in Bolek is Antoni Kopankiewicz, who was president of the Union of Poles and the New Union of Poles in 1872. Kopankiewicz was also active in New York City parish affairs in 1873. See Bolek, *Who's Who*, p. 218.

18. For brief sketches on Dr. L. Pawlicki, Kazimierz Bielawski, M. J. Kucera, and Ignacy Wendziński, see Bolek, *Who's Who*, pp. 339, 243, 245, 485, respectively; also, Haiman, *Polish Past, passim*, which includes several photographs and numerous bibliographic citations pertaining to California and to biographical and autobiographical accounts on leading figures. On General Włodzimierz Krzyżanowski, see: James S. Pula, *For Liberty and Justice: The Life and Times of Wladimir Krzyżanowski* (Chicago: Polish American Congress Charitable Foundation, 1978).

19. Osada's *Historya* and Francis Barc, "The Polish National Alliance," *The Polish Review*, VI (April 11, 1946) cover most of the details on the historic Philadelphia meeting. Brief sketches in Bolek, *Who's Who* include: Juljan Szajnert (died 1928), p. 445; Wincenty Domański (1849-1935) p. 97; Piotr Beczkiewicz (1857-1934), p. 32; J. Andrzejkowicz (1821-1898), p. 18. Also see note 11 above, paragraph two, for citations pertaining to the PNA's history in Paczynska and Pilch, *Materiały*, many of which give extensive coverage to details given on pp. 222-23 of this Kruszka translation. Finally, see the roster of delegate membership on Osada, *Historya*, pp. 624-25, and the PNA "Honor Roll" on p. xv of Osada's appendices.

20. *Zgoda* [Harmony] began publication on November 23, 1881; the first issue is in the *Dziennik Związkowy* editorial library in Chicago. This newspaper is still in publication after 100 years marking the longest single run for any Polish newspaper in Chicago (and one of the longest runs for Polish papers in the United States). See Edmund Olszyk, *The Polish Press in America* (Milwaukee, 1940); Robert Park, *The Immigrant Press and Its Control* (New York, 1922). By 1920, *Zgoda* reached a circulation of 124,000 (*American Newspaper and Annual Directory, 1919*).

21. The list of works on the Rev. Józef Dąbrowski is quite extensive. See Paczynska and Pilch, *Materiały*, pp. 190-91, (items 2213-2240).

22. *Kropidło* [Aspergillum] began publication on January 24, 1887, and ceased publication on June 22, 1888. Edited by Stanisław Slisz, a member of the clerical party at St. Stanislaus Kostka parish in Chicago, *Kropidło* consistently and vehemently attacked the PNA point of view, and *Zgoda* in particular. See Iwicki, *Resurrectionist Studies*, 204-06; also Willging and Hatzfeld, "Nineteenth Century," pp. 20-21. An aspergillum is a sprinkler used in Catholic religious ceremonies, hence the title is sometimes rendered as "The Sprinkler."

23. The Rev. Dominic Majer (1838-1911) is said to have been the first Polish monsignor in the United States. A charter member of the PRCU, Majer also organized the Polish Union

of America (Buffalo). For most of his career, the controversial Majer was pastor of St. Adalbert's parish in St. Paul, Minnesota. He remained a staunch supporter of the PNA, and in 1886 attempted to organize PNA sympathizers in the clergy into an adjunct group known as the Allied Priests. See Iwicki, *Resurrectionist Studies*, 204-05; Bolek, *Who's Who*, p. 179; Kruszka, *Siedm Siedmioleci, passim*. The Rev. Konstantin Domagalski (died 1895), in addition to writing for *Wiara i Ojczyzna*, also wrote columns in *Wiarus* (Winona, Minnesota). The reasons for his switch from the pro-PNA faction of the clergy over to the pro-PRCU faction controlled by the Rev. Wincenty Barzyński are not clear. See Bolek, *Who's Who*, p. 97.

24. See note 9 above.

25. Antoni Małłek (1851-1917) of Holy Trinity Parish in Chicago was a prominent spokesman for the PNA point of view. An organist and music teacher in Chicago, Małłek served as secretary general of the PNA in 1889 and for three terms thereafter. He took part in writing a celebrated petition to the Vatican criticizing the Resurrectionist management of Polish parishes in Chicago in 1891. See Parot, *Polish Catholics*, pp. 84-85 and *passim*; Osada, *Historya*, 624-25; *Lakeside Directory* for the City of Chicago (1890; 1900). Małłek also published a brief history of Holy Trinity Parish in Chicago, *Dzieje Parafii Św. Trójcy, 1873-1898* (Chicago, 1898), a work that highly praises the close connection between that parish and the PNA.

26. Kruszka's original citation reads: "See the Alliance minutes."

27. Father Kazimierz Sztuczko, CSC, came to Holy Trinity Parish as pastor in 1893 and served there for more than a half century. His only biographer is Brat Maxymus, who penned a golden anniversary album (for Sztuczko's fiftieth year in the priesthood) entitled *Pamiątka Złotego Jubileuszu Kapłaństwa Wielebnego Ks. Kazimierza Sztuckzki, CSC, Proboszcza Parafii Świętej Trójcy w Chicago* (Chicago: Holy Trinity Parish, 1941.)

28. Archbishop Katzer was one of Polonia's most avid supporters in the struggle with Americanist bishops who wished to deny Polish and Slavic representation in the American hierarchy. Katzer died in 1903, during Kruszka's celebrated mission to the Vatican in support of Polish representation in the American hierarchy.

29. See the brief sketches in Bolek for the following: Franciszek Gryglaszewski (1852-1918), p. 248; Wincenty Przybyszewski (d. 1923), p. 365; Teodor Heliński (1856-1931), p. 159; Dr. Leo Sadowski (1868-1927), pp. 395-96. All four were credited with dedicated service to the PNA.

30. The Rev. Jan Radziejewski (1844-1905) served as pastor of St. Adalbert's parish in Chicago from 1884 until his death. He served as national chaplain of the PRCU for several terms. He was known for his close support of the Rev. Wincenty Barzyński and the Resurrectionists in the Chicago archdiocese. Commemorative albums celebrating the anniversaries of his parish (and of many other Polish parishes in Chicago) can be located at the PRCU Museum of America, albums that often detail the rise of various local organizations such as the Częstochowa Union. Note that William I. Thomas and Florian Znaniecki in their *The Polish Peasant in Europe and America*, 2 vols. (New York: Knopf, 1927) make extensive use of these parish albums (which are translated into English in *The Polish Peasant*), especially in volume two.

31. See note 23 above.

32. For materials on the Polish League, see Greene, *For God and Country*, pp. 90-95; Parot, *Polish Catholics*, pp. 92-94; 105-06. The *Liga Polska* was opposed by the PNA because it had been organized by the Rev. Wincenty Barzyński, a staunch opponent of the PNA throughout his clerical life in Chicago.

33. For material on the origins of the Milwaukee Polonia, see Thaddeus Borun, *We, the Milwaukee Poles* (Milwaukee, 1946); Kuzniewski, *Faith & Fatherland, passim*.

34. See note 25 above.

35. Kruszka's original footnote reads: "Compiled by L. M. Kucharski, South Bend, Indiana." For further information on the Polish Falcons, see Arthur L. Waldo, *The Origin and Roles of the Falcons: An Outline of Their Mission of Yesterday and Today* (Pittsburgh: Fal-

con Institute of Historical Research, 1965); *Diamond Jubilee of the Polish Falcons of America 1887-1962* (Pittsburgh: Polish Falcons of America, 1962).

36. Despite the Resurrectionist origins of the Polish Youth Alliance (via the Rev. Eugene Sedlaczek, CR), none of the standard histories, directories, bibliographies, or finding aids on Polish Americana or Chicago Polonia contain information on this group or its affiliate, the Patriotic Scientific Society. But see note 37 below.

37. The *Macierz Polska* was formally organized on December 10, 1897, under the Rev. Franciszek Gordon (1860-1931), later the pastor of St. Stanislaus Kostka and St. Mary of the Angels parishes in Chicago. Known officially as the Polish Alma Mater, this major Polish youth organization introduced a broad scope of activity: theatrical productions, lectures, dramatics, forensics and debate, gymnastics, music programs, and a cadet corps. See *Album Jubileuszowy Macierzy Polskiej, 1897-1917* (Chicago, 1917); Iwicki, *Resurrectionist Studies*, 246-47.

38. The standard history of the Polish Women's Alliance is Jadwiga Karlowicza, *Historia Związku Polek w Ameryce* (Chicago: Polish Women's Alliance, 1938).

39. Kruszka's original footnote reads: "The Polish press has always sharply reproved, and still does, those countrymen who, instead of joining Polish organizations, join foreign ones."

40. For a dated, but still valuable, comparative account of Polish organizational life in America, see Thomas and Znaniecki, *Polish Peasant*, II, especially pp. 1511-1644.

CHAPTER 11: HISTORY OF THE
POLISH PRESS IN AMERICA

1. Kruszka's original footnote reads: "Reviewed and supplemented by J. J. Chrzanowski." John Joseph Chrzanowski (1867-1933), editor of newspapers with a nationalist orientation, including *Kuryer Polski* of Milwaukee in 1901. See: Bolek, *Who's Who.*

2. Henryk Nagiel, *Dziennikarstwo Polskie w Ameryce i jego 30-letnie dzieje* [Polish Journalism in America and Its Thirty-Year History] (Chicago: Komitet Centralny Obleslania Wystawy Lwowskiey przez Polonię Amerykańska,1894). Kruszka's debt (or Chrzanowski's) to Nagiel was greater than he admits. For examples of plagiarism from the older work, compare the accounts of *Echo z Polski* in Kruszka, *Historya*, in Volume 4, pp. 98-102, with Nagiel, pp. 31-36. Kruszka, however, carries Nagiel's chronicle through 1905 and, not surprisingly, adds a long account of his brother's *Kuryer Polski* in Milwaukee. Kruszka also provides an interpretation that distinguishes the ethnic Polish press in America from its European counterparts. Also, he does not include Lithuanian and Ruthenian publications in his account as Nagiel did. The omission reflects the growth of exclusive nationalism in the three major components of the old Polish Republic in the intervening decade. Nagiel adopts a more traditional (and European) approach to what it means to be dealing with what Kruszka saw as a new ethnic press.

3. *Górnik* [The Miner], published in Wilkes-Barre, Pennsylvania, 1893-1948; *Rolnik* [The Plowman], published in Stevens Point, Wisconsin, 1891-1960. See below, notes 59 and 51.

4. *Orędownik Językowy* [The Language Advisor] (1905-1909), a journal on correct Polish usage and Polish literature, published first in St. Francis, Wisconsin, and then in Milwaukee, Wisconsin. It was edited by Rev. Bolesław Góral with the aid of Stanisław Osada and others.

5. There were 50 Polish American newspapers publishing during 1901; eight were dailies. The Polish American press reached its peak about 20 years after Kruszka wrote. The largest number of newspapers, 90, appeared in 1927; and of daily newspapers, 25, in 1921. The best available guide is Jan Wepsiec, *Polish American Serial Publications: 1842-1966. An Annotated Bibliography* (Chicago: Privately printed, 1968). It has been used extensively for the notes in this chapter.

6. Kruszka touches on a major regional distinction in modern Polish history. The portions of Poland under Prussian administration—Silesia had been in that class longest—had benefitted from compulsory school attendance and had the highest rates of literacy. Galicia, i.e.

Austrian Poland, had the lowest literacy rate of the three partitions. The difference was reflected in the immigration and in attitudes of Poles toward each other in America.

7. The newspaper was known as *Echo Polskie* [Polish Echo] from October 8, 1864, after the January Insurrection was suppressed.

8. Józef Schriftgiesser is a pseudonym for an otherwise mysterious person. Romauld J. Jaworowski is better known, though only for the period of his editorship. See: Joseph Wieczerzak, *Polish Chapter*; Maria Copson-Niećko, "The Poles in America from the 1830s to the 1870s," in Frank Mocha, ed., *Poles in America. Bicentennial Essays* (Stevens Point, Wisconsin: Worzalla Publishing Company, 1978).

9. The last issue may have been in June 1865. See: Copson-Niećko, pp. 124, 248, note 417.

10. The *Gmina Polska* [The Polish Commune] was founded in 1866 by lay Polish nationalists and was soon embroiled with conservative clerical forces for leadership in Chicago Polonia. See: Joseph J. Parot, *Polish Catholics*, pp. 36-37.

11. *Orzeł Polski* [The Polish Eagle] (1870-1872) is available on microfilm at the Immigration History Research Center, the University of Minnesota, St. Paul, Minnesota.

12. On Rev. Alexander Matouszek, see Chapter 3, note 2.

13. Ignacy Wendziński (1828-1901), journalist and teacher, participant in the insurrections of 1848 in Poznań and of 1863 in Russian Poland. See: Bolek, *Who's Who*.

14. *Gazeta Polska w Chicago* [The Polish Gazette in Chicago] known as *Gazeta Polska Narodowa* [The Polish National Gazette] in 1915-1917, was published in Chicago from 1873 to 1917. It was independent in politics except in 1903-1904, when it supported the Republicans. It opposed the influence of the Resurrectionists and supported the Polish National Alliance. A partial file is available on microfilm at the Immigration History Research Center, University of Minnesota, St. Paul, Minnesota.

15. Ladislaus Dyniewicz (1843-1928), founder of Chicago's most important Polish publishing house, led the nationalist faction in early Chicago Polonia. Antoni Smarzewski-Schermann (sometimes Sherman) (1818-1900), grocer, tavern-keeper, and earliest organizer of Chicago Polonia in the 1850s and 1860s. See: Joseph J. Parot, *Polish Catholics*, pp. 19-24; Bolek, *Who's Who* under Smagorzewski. Piotr Kiołbassa (1837-1905) was political leader of Chicago Polonia and an ally of the Resurrectionists in the development of the community. See: Helen Busyn, "Peter Kiołbassa," pp. 65-84; Helen Busyn, "The Political Career of Peter Kiołbassa," pp. 8-22.

16. Ladislaus Smulski (1836-1897), editor and publisher; Wiktor Karlowski, soldier, civic leader, and editor. See: Bolek, *Who's Who*.

17. Rev. Teodor Gieryk (1837-1878) initiated the movement in Detroit in 1873 that led to the formation of the Polish Roman Catholic Union of America. The foundation and movement of newspapers often reflected shifts in ideological outlook and personal leadership. *Gazeta Katolicka* (it was known as *Gazeta Polska Katolicka* from 1874 to 1880) was transferred to Chicago as the Resurrectionists of that city became a dominant force in Polish Catholic organizations like the PRCUA. It ceased publication there, probably in 1913. Some sources give 1873 as the first year of publication under the direction of Rev. Gieryk. On this and the origins of the Polish press in Detroit, see: Laurence Orton, *Polish Detroit and the Kołasiński Affair* (Detroit: Wayne State University Press, 1981), pp. 191-219, note 85, 222 note 86; Wepsiec, *Polish American Serial Publications*, p. 50.

18. Edmund Zbigniew Brodowski (1852-1901), editor, active in the Polish National Alliance, U.S. consular official in Germany. See: Copson-Niećko, "The Poles in America," pp. 115-243, note 352; *Polski Słownik Biograficzny*, 2, p. 446.

19. *Zgoda* [Harmony] has been published since 1881, in Chicago since 1888, weekly until 1947, and biweekly since 1948. It is the official organ of the Polish National Alliance of North America. It is available on microfilm for 1887-1906, 1908-1974 at the Immigration History Research Center, University of Minnesota, St. Paul, Minnesota.

20. Stanisław Szwajkart (1857-1918), teacher, writer, editor. See: Bolek, *Who's Who*.

21. M. J. Kucera (?-1904), active in the organization of the Chicago *Gmina Polska* in 1866 and the Polish National Alliance in 1880. See: Bolek, *Who's Who*.

22. Francis Jerome Jabłoński (1863-1908), author, leader in the Polish National Alliance and editor of major Polish American newspapers including *Kuryer Polski* of Milwaukee in 1901-1905. See: *Polski Słownik Biograficzny*, 10, pp. 255-56.

23. Julian Piotrowski, printer, was one of the pioneer leaders of Detroit Polonia. See: Orton, *Polish Detroit*, pp. 21-22, 172, 191. On Józef Zawisza, see: Orton, *Polish Detroit*.

24. *Pielgrzym Polski* [The Polish Pilgrim] was founded in opposition to the controversial Rev. Dominic H. Kołasiński by a group headed by Rev. Paweł Gutowski, the pastor of St. Casimir's church on the west side of Detroit from its beginning in 1882 until his death. Kazimierz Olszewski, to whom Kruszka refers, probably was Leonard Olszewski who established *Prawda* in 1888. See: Orton, *Polish Detroit*, pp. 31-32, 183, 191, 200, note 56.

25. On the beginnings of the Polish press in Milwaukee, see: Anthony J. Kuzniewski, *Faith & Fatherland*, p. 23. *Krytyka* [The Critique] had a moderately pro-labor orientation during the troubles of 1886. See: Kuzniewski, *Faith & Fatherland*, pp. 28-29, 144, note 38.

26. *Slavie* (Racine, Wisconsin) is available on microfilm for 1861-1862, 1865, 1870-1918 at the State Historical Society of Wisconsin at Madison and the Immigration History Research Center, University of Minnesota, St. Paul,Minnesota.

27. Antoni A. Parysso, pen name for Antoni A. Paryski (1865-1935), publisher best known for his association with *Ameryka-Echo* of Toledo. On Francis Jabłoński, see note 22 above.

28. *Orzeł Biały* [The White Eagle], June 30, 1888 to April 1890, Milwaukee, Wisconsin. It was published alternately with *Opiekum* [The Guardian].

29. Antoni Małłek (1851-1917), musician, composer, teacher, and publisher; organized the Polish Singers Alliance of America in 1888 and held major office in the Polish National Alliance. See: *Polski Słownik Biograficzny*, 19, pp. 474-75; Leon T. Blaszczyk, "The Polish Singers' Movement in America," *Polish American Studies*, 38, No. 1 (Spring, 1981), pp. 50-62.

30. Julian Czupka (1854-?), lawyer, editor, and poet. See: Bolek, *Who's Who*.

31. Rev. Jan Romuald Byzewski, OFM (1842-1905), pastor of St. Stanislaus Kostka church in Winona from 1875 (?) to 1890. See: Bolek, *Who's Who*; Orton, *Polish Detroit*, pp. 187-188.

32. Rev. Konstantin Domagalski (?-1895?), writer and editor. See: Orton, *Polish Detroit*, pp. 56-57; *Polski Słowniok Biograficzny*, 5, p. 292.

33. Jerome Derdowski (1852-1902), poet, editor, and major contributor to Kaszubian as a literary language. See: Andrzej Bukowski, *Działalność Literacka i Społeczna Hieronim Derdowskiego w Ameryce* (Gdańsk, 1961); Helen Derdowska Zimniewicz, "Polish Troublemaker—Pioneer Trouble Shooter," *Gopher Historian*, 4 (November, 1949), pp. 2, 4, 13. *Wiarus*, which ceased publication in 1919, is available on microfilm at the Minnesota State Historical Society in St. Paul.

34. On Rev. Łuczycki, see original preface, note 13.

35. Rev. Jan Pitass [Pitas} (1844-1913), the foremost leader of Buffalo Polonia in the early immigrant generation. See *Polski Słownik Biograficzny*, 26, pp. 584-85.

36. J. M. Sadowski is the same as M. J. Sadowski noted earlier in the chapter.

37. Stanisław Slisz died in 1908. See: Bolek, *Who's Who*.

38. Rev. Antoni Klawiter (1839-?), a Roman Catholic priest who eventually joined the independent Polish church movement in America. See: Stanley L. Cuba, "Rev. Antoni Klawiter: Polish Roman and National Catholic Builder-Priest," *Polish American Studies*, 40, No. 2 (Fall, 1983).

39. The persons noted in this paragraph are mostly shadowy figures associated with the beginnings of Polish socialism in America. The biographies of Józef Bernolak, Alphonse Chrostowski, Jan J. Chrzanowski, and Juljus Szupka in Bolek, *Who's Who*, and Kruszka, *Historya*, 5, pp. 23, 65, suggest that the *Ognisko* group was an ideologically mixed one

including viewpoints best described as liberal or progressive. *Ognisko* is available on microfilm at the Immigration History Research Center, University of Minnesota, St. Paul, Minnesota.

40. Rev. Jan Radziejewski (1844-1905), assistant and pastor at various Chicago churches.

41. Rev. Franciszek Gordon, CR (1860-1931), priest and pastor who succeeded Rev. Wincenty Barzyński as the leading Resurrectionist clergyman in Chicago in the early 1900s. See: *Polski Słownik Biograficzny*, 8, pp. 301-302. *Wiara i Ojczyzna* for part of 1891 and 1896 is available on microfilm at the Immigration History Research Center, University of Minnesota, St. Paul, Minnesota.

42. *Kuryer Polski* [The Polish Courier] was published in Milwaukee daily from 1888 to 1861 and weekly from 1962 to 1963. The most recent account of the early years of *Kuryer Polski* and its founder, Michał Kruszka, is in Kuzniewski, *Faith & Fatherland*. It is available on microfilm at the State Historical Society of Wisconsin at Madison and the Immigration History Research Center, University of Minnesota, St. Paul, Minnesota.

43. Kazimierz Neuman (1843-1907), editor and writer, co-edited *Kuryer Polski* with Michał Kruszka until 1893, when they quarreled about supporting the international exhibition in Lwów. Neuman founded *Słowo* [The Word] in 1893 and engaged in a press war with *Kuryer Polski* until his newspaper closed in 1895. See: Bolek, *Who's Who*; Kuzniewski, *Faith & Fatherland*, p. 31. Stanisław Osada (1869-1934), journalist, editor, writer, historian. See: Bolek, *Who's Who*. Stefan Rachocki, see: Bolek, *Who's Who*.

44. *Prawda* [The Truth] continued publication in 1893 as *Nowa Prawda* [The New Truth], in Bay City until 1913. Some sources give 1887 as the beginning of publication. It was the organ of the Polish Roman Catholic Union of America. See: Wepsiec, *Polish American Serial Publications*, p. 92; Orton, *Polish Detroit*, p. 191. On Józef Ilowiecki (1851-1902), physician, editor, writer, see: *Polski Słownik Biograficzny*, 10, p. 157.

45. *Gwiazda* ceased publication in 1891. See: Orton, *Polish Detroit*, p. 191.

46. *Ameryka* absorbed *Echo* of Buffalo in 1903 to form *Ameryka-Echo* [America-Echo]. It was published in Toledo, 1889-1961, in Chicago, 1961-1971, and in various regional editions from time to time; daily in 1912-1919, 1929-1934, twice weekly in 1920-1928, weekly in 1889-1911, 1935-1971. Independent politically and in its orientation within Polonia, *Ameryka-Echo* devoted considerable space to literature. A complete file on microfilm is available at the Immigration History Research Center, University of Minnesota, St. Paul, Minnesota, and at the Northwest Area Research Center, Bowling Green University, Toledo, Ohio.

47. *Dziennik Chicagoski* [The Chicago Daily News] was published from 1890 to 1971 in Chicago. It was founded by Rev. Wincenty Barzyński and the Resurrectionist Fathers and represents their major journalistic effort to shape Polish opinion along Catholic lines. *Dziennik Chicagoski* supported the Democratic party through 1919 except for 1907-1914; thereafter it was independent. It is available on microfilm through 1941 at the Immigration History Research Center, University of Minnesota, from 1941 at the Library of Congress, and from 1890 to 1971 at the Polish Museum of America in Chicago.

48. *Niedziela* [Sunday] was temporarily suspended in 1904 and resumed publication in a new format until 1907 or 1908. See: Wepsiec, *Polish American Serial Publications*, p. 191. It was edited by a succession of professors at the Polish seminary, e.g. Rev. Barabasz (1863-?), who later became a pastor in Baltimore, and Rev. Paweł Ćwiąkała (1865-?), teacher, editor, pastor.

49. The name of this newspaper was *Gazeta* [The Gazette], published in Toledo from 1891 to 1896 (?). See: Wespiec, *Polish American Serial Publications*, p. 49.

50. This was a regional edition of *Ameryka* in Toledo.

51. *Rolnik* [The Plowman] was published from 1891 to 1960 in Stevens Point, Wisconsin, the center of a large Polish (and Polish-Kaszubian) farm community, by Worzalla Brothers (later the Worzalla Publishing Company). When *Gwiazda Polarna* was begun in 1908, *Rolnik* usually reprinted part of the newer newspaper. It was independent in viewpoint and

emphasized rural conditions. Available on microfilm at the State Historical Society of Wisconsin in Madison and the Immigration History Research Center, University of Minnesota, St. Paul, Minnesota.

52. The most recent account of Rev. Antoni Kozłowski's independent church movement in Chicago makes no mention of *Reforma*. See: Parot, *Polish Catholics*, chapter 5. For a summary of the tangled history of *Reforma*, see Wepsiec, *Polish American Serial Publications*, p. 136.

53. *Polonia w Ameryce*, a weekly until 1923, continued as *Monitor Clevelandzki* and *Monitor*, a daily from 1923 to 1938. See: Wepsiec, *Polish American Serial Publications*, p. 86.

54. *Głos Polski* [The Polish Voice] probably ceased publication in 1893. See: Wepsiec, *Polish American Serial Publications*, p. 55.

55. *Telegraf* was published in Chicago, daily from 1892 to 1905, weekly from 1906 to 1939. It had a Catholic orientation and normally supported the Democratic party. See: Wepsiec, *Polish American Serial Publications*, p. 154.

56. *Kuryer Tygodinowy i Gazeta Wisconsińska* [Weekly Courier and Wisconsin Gazette] was published from 1892 or 1893 possibly to 1914. See: Wepsiec, *Polish American Serial Publications*, p. 80.

57. *Sztandar* [The Banner] was published until 1901. Publication resumed in February 1906 as a section in *Zgoda*. See Wepsiec, *Polish American Serial Publications*, p. 153.

58. *Jutrzenka* [The Morning Star] was probably published until 1923.

59. *Górnik* [The Miner] was published from 1893 to 1948 in Wilkes-Barre, Pennsylvania. Local and independent (except in 1909 when it supported the Republicans), it was the organ of the Polish Union of the United States of America with headquarters in Wilkes-Barre. Only a few scattered issues have survived. See: Wepsiec, *Polish American Serial Publications*, pp. 37-38; Frank Renkiewicz, comp., *Immigration History Research Center, Polish American Collection*, 2d ed.; (St. Paul: University of Minnesota, 1977), pp. 9, 14.

60. Kruszka neglected several socialist newspapers that appeared in the 1890s, principally *Robotnik Polski* [The Polish Worker]. See: Wepsiec, *Polish American Serial Publications*, pp. 52, 137-38; Orton, *Polish Detroit*, p. 192.

61. Ignacy Machnikowski (1847-1935), engineer, physician, teacher, editor, and author. See: Bolek, *Who's Who*.

62. On *Swoboda* [Freedom] see: Orton, *Polish Detroit*, pp. 192, 220 nn 88-89. Unlike most of his audience, Dr. Ilowiecki was an ardent Republican. That and his caustic comments on all factions contributed to the failure of the newspaper.

63. Stefan Kamiński (?-1911) was the second name of Frederick Raeder, who assumed leadership of the independent Polish church movement in Buffalo in 1896. See: Lawrence Orton, *Polish Detroit*, pp. 93, 147-48. Warta ceased publication in 1911.

64. *Słonce* [The Sun], was published in Buffalo, St. Paul, and Milwaukee from 1895 to 1905. It was the organ of the Polish Union in America, a fraternal federation which took a middle-of-the-road Catholic position between the Resurrectionists and the nationalists in the 1890s. It is available on microfilm for 1898-1900 at the Immigration History Research Center, University of Minnesota.

65. *Przyjaciel Ludu* [Friend of the People] began publication in 1895 according to some sources. It was known as *Gazeta Niedzielna* [Sunday Gazette] from 1929 and published in Camden, New Jersey, from 1926 until it shut down in 1934.

66. Rev. Franciszek Hodur (1866-1953) was the leader of the independent Polish church movement in northeastern Pennsylvania in the late 1890s and throughout the United States after the death of rival leaders in Chicago in 1907 and in Buffalo in 1911. Rev. Benvenuto Ignacy Gramlewicz (1837-1925) was Catholic pastor in Nanticoke, Pennsylvania, in 1875-1925. See: Bolek, *Who's Who*.

67. *Straż* [The Guard] has been published weekly in Scranton since 1897. It was begun by Rev. Franciszek Hodur to publish news and opinion of his movement for Polish autonomy

within the Catholic church. *Straż* became a major source of news of the Polish National Catholic Church and the fraternal Polish Union of America, both of which Rev. Hodur founded. The first editor was Stanisław Dangiel (1873-1938). See: Bolek, *Who's Who*. It is available on microfilm or in hard copy for most years at the Immigration History Research Center, University of Minnesota.

68. This may be the same as *Echo St. Louiskie* [St. Louis Echo] published from 1899 to 1900. See: Wepsiec, *Polish American Serial Publications*, p. 45.

69. *Goniec Polski* [The Polish Messenger] was published in South Bend, Indiana, from 1896 to 1964.

70. *Katolik* was founded as a Catholic alternative to Michał Kruszka's *Kuryer Polski*. Rev. Wilhelm Grutza (?-1901), founder and pastor of St. Josaphat's parish, was its guiding spirit. Rev. Grutza's *Zrodło* [The Source] seems also to have died with him in 1901. See: Kuzniewski, *Faith & Fatherland*, p. 40, 41.

71. *Maczuga* [The Mace] was published in 1898 in Wilkes-Barre, Pennsylvania, but no more is known about it.

72. *Sokoł* [The Falcon], published in Chicago from 1896 to 1912, was merged in 1913 into *Sokoł Polski w Ameryce* published in New York from 1909 to 1913; it in turn was absorbed in 1913 by *Sokoł Polski,* published in Pittsburgh by the Polish Falcon's Alliance of America. It is available on microfilm and in hard copy from 1910 at the Immigration History Research Center, University of Minnesota.

73. *Polonia* was published in 1911 when it was superseded by *Rekord Niedzielny* [Sunday Record]. It was the organ of the Polish Roman Catholic Association, a regional secession from the Polish Roman Catholic Union.

74. The sources present conflicting evidence about this newspaper and its relation to *Kuryer Nowojorski* described above (Kruszka, 5, pp. 59-60). See Wepsiec, *Polish American Serial Publications*, pp. 79, 157.

75. *Gazeta Pittsburska* [The Pittsburgh Gazette] was a regional edition of *Ameryka* published, according to most sources, from 1893 to 1903. See Wepsiec, *Polish American Serial Publications*, p. 51.

76. *Wielkopolanin* [He from Great Poland] was published weekly in Pittsburgh from 1899 to 1935. It was a Catholic newspaper.

77. *Dziennik Narodowy* [The Polish National Daily] was published from 1898 or 1899 to 1923, except for the period from October 11 through December, 1899. It was founded with a Polish nationalist orientation in opposition to the Polish National Alliance and *Dziennik Związkowy* [Alliance Daily]. During 1909-1914, it was owned by Michał Kruszka of Milwaukee and embroiled in his controversies, and during World War I, it was a semi-official organ of the National Department. See: Wepsiec, *Polish American Serial Publications,* pp. 40-41; Kuzniewski, *Faith & Fatherland,* pp. 90, 114. See: Bolek, *Who's Who* for biographies of early editors: Michał Sadowski (nicknamed Pankiewicz) (1857-1900); Józef J. Chrzanowski (1867-1938); Franciszek H. Jabłoński (1863-1908); Kazimierz Midowicz (1858-1902); on Midowicz, also see: *Polski Słownik Biogaficzny*, 20, pp. 722-23.

78. *Dziennik Milwaukee* was founded as a Catholic and Democratic rival to Michał Kruszka's *Kuryer Polski.* The two newspapers engaged in a bitter rivalry until *Dziennik* was forced into bankruptcy in 1905. See: Kuzniewski, *Faith & Fatherland,* pp. 40-41, 44, 58-59.

79. *Głos Polski* [The Polish Herald] was published in Grand Rapids from 1899 to 1900.

80. *Tygodnik* was published in Minneapolis in 1900.

81. Szczęsny Zahajkiewicz (1861-1919), poet, teacher, writer, active in the Falcons movement. See: Bolek, *Who's Who.*

82. *Macierz Polska* [The Polish Alma Mater] was published until 1936 by the Polish Publishing Company. It was the organ of the Polish Alma Mater.

83. *Sierota* [The Orphan] was published through 1906 and absorbed by *Macierz Polski.* Oriented to Catholicism and social problems, it was part of the Resurrectionist press in Chicago.

84. The publication dates according to some sources are 1900-1905. See: Wepsiec, *Polish American Periodical Publications*, p. 157.

85. *Kuryer Ohioski* began publication in 1900. It was known as *Kuryer Katolicki* in 1909-1924, and as *Kuryer Toledoski* from 1925 until it ceased publication in 1926. It was the organ of the Polish Roman Catholic Union in the state of Ohio.

86. Rev. Skulik lived from 1867 to ?. See: Bolek, *Who's Who*.

87. *Dziennik Polski* [The Polish Daily] published in Detroit since 1904. Independent in American politics, it supported the Piłsudski-ite Committee for National Defense during World War I, the Piłsudski government of Poland in the inter-war period and its successor, the *sanacya* wing of the Polish government-in-exile in World War II. It is available through 1941 on microfilm at the Michigan State Library in Lansing and at the Immigration History Research Center, University of Minnesota; and from 1941 at the Library of Congress.

88. *Wschod* [The East] was probably published in Providence until 1930.

89. See above, note 4. Rev. Bolesław Góral (1876-?), a professor of languages at the Milwaukee diocesan seminary, was the most formidable Catholic opponent of the Kruszkas. He was the founder and first editor of *Nowiny Polskie* [The Polish News] in 1906. See: Wepsiec, *Polish American Serial Publications*, pp. 94-95; Kuzniewski, *Faith & Fatherland*, p. 65.

CHAPTER 12: HISTORY OF
AMERICAN POLISH LITERATURE

1. Stanisław Osada (1868-1934), journalist, editor, writer. Came to the United States via Germany and Switzerland in 1893. Edited a number of Polish American newspapers, among them *Dziennik Milwaucki* [Milwaukee Daily] and *Tygodnik Milwaucki* [Milwaukee Weekly], and authored books and pamphlets on Polish American history and affairs: *Historia Związku Narodowego Polskiego, 1880-1905* [History of the Polish National Alliance, 1880-1905], Chicago, 1905; *Literature polska i polsko-amerykańska* [Polish and Polish American Literature], 1910; *Sokołstwo Polskie* [The Polish Falcon Movement], 1929; *Prasa i publicystyke polska w Ameryce* [The Polish Press and Journalism in America], 1930; *Jak się kształtowała dusza wychodźtwa w Ameryce* [How the Soul of the (Polish) Emigration Was Formed in America], 1930.

2. Teofila Samolińska (1848-1913), poet, writer, club woman. Active in Chicago in the last quarter of the nineteenth century. Agaton Giller's reply to her letter written to him in 1879 provided the impetus for the organization of the Polish National Alliance a year later. In 1887 she became a founder-member of the *Centralne Towarzystwo Polek w Ameryce* [Central Society of Polish Women in America] and that same year became the first Falconette in America. Her poetry appeared in two Polish American newspapers, *Orzeł Polski* and *Przyjaciel Ludu*. In 1876—not in 1880—she submitted her comedy, "Trzy Flory" ["Three Flowers"], to a contest for new theatrical works in Kraków, while her four-act comedy, "Emancypacja Kobiet" ["Female Emancipation"], was staged in Chicago, Kraków, and Poznań. See: Karol Estreicher, *Teatry w Polsce* [Theaters in Poland]. In 1879 the Polish American Committee asked her to write a rhymed address to the Polish novelist Józef I. Kraszewski to celebrate his golden anniversary as an author.

3. Ignacy Wendziński (1828-1901), journalist, editor, teacher, writer. Veteran of the 1848 and 1863 insurrections in partitioned Poland. Editor in 1871-1872 of *Orzeł Polski* in Kraków, Missouri, and subsequently of *Pielgrzym* in Union, Missouri, published by Jan Barzyński; later a teacher at St. Stanislaus Kostka parish school in Chicago. Edited *Gazeta Polska* (1873, Chicago), *Przyjaciel Ludu*, which he founded (1876-1882, Chicago and Milwaukee), *Zgoda* (1882-1884). In Milwaukee, Wendziński later ran a steamship ticket agency for Polish immigrants and was active in the local Polish amateur theater.

4. Rev. Kandyd Kozłowski (1836-?), writer, painter, architect, clergyman. Elementary and secondary education in Warsaw, theological studies in Bologna, Italy. Ordained in 1863 and participated as a chaplain in the January Insurrection that same year against czarist Russia.

Fled via Palestine and Egypt to the United States in 1872, where he founded several parishes: St. Rose of Lima (Cincinnati, 1872-1877), St. Hyacinth's (LaSalle, Illinois, 1877-1884), and St. Josaphat's (Chicago, 1884-1889). He built one of the first Polonia orphanages in the United States at LaSalle in 1877.

5. Czupka, see chapter 11.

6. Stanisław Thomas Slisz (1856-1908), editor and writer. Secondary education in Jasło; law school at the Jagiellonian University, Kraków. Came to the United States in 1885. Elder brother of Józef Slisz, who served for twelve years as foreman of the print shop of *Polak w Ameryce* and who in 1896 established the first Polish bookstore in Buffalo. After editing *Krytyka* in Milwaukee and *Wiara i Ojczyzna* and *Kropidło* in Chicago, Stanisław Slisz returned to Buffalo in 1889 and took over the editorship of *Polak w Ameryce* for the next nineteen years until 1907, when it became *Polak Amerykański* [The Polish American].

7. Ignacy A. Machnikowski (1847-1935), engineer, physician, professor, author. University studies at Kraków and Wrocław. Engaged by the Turkish government as engineer of bridges and railroads. Received M.D. degree and later practiced in Milwaukee. Came with his family in 1890 to Chicago where he edited *Wiara i Ojczyzna*. In 1902, he relocated to Detroit to teach at the Polish seminary. He spoke eight languages and published *Szkaplerz Matki* [Mother Scapular], *Gramatyka Języka Polskiego* [A Polish Grammar] and *Katolicyzm i rozum sgadzają się* [Catholicism and Reason Agree].

8. Kazimierz Neuman (1843-1907), writer, editor, and publisher. A commissioned officer in the January Insurrection. He edited the following Polish-language newspapers in America: *Dziennik Chicagoski* (1896-1902); *Orzeł Biały* and *Opiekun*, Milwaukee, 1890; *Przyjaciel Młodzieży* [Friend of Youth]; Chicago, 1895-1897; and *Słowo* [The Word], Milwaukee, 1893-1895, a Catholic newspaper Neuman established locally in opposition to M. Kruszka's *Kuryer Polski*. In addition to the above-mentioned short stories, he also wrote *Trzech Pachiarzy* [Three Tenants], 1913.

9. Henryk Nagiel (1859-1900), lawyer, journalist, editor, writer. A graduate of Warsaw University Law School, he was affiliated variously from 1876 to 1888 with *Kuryer Warszawski* [Warsaw Courier], *Dziennik dla Wszystkich* [Everybody's Daily], *Kolce* [Thorns], *Wędrowiec* [The Pilgrim], and others before coming to the United States via Paris in 1889. In America, he edited or co-edited *Ognisko* and *Kuryer Nowojorski i Brooklynski* (New York), *Echo* and *Krytyka* (Buffalo), *Dziennik Chicagoski* (Chicago). Following his return to Poland in 1896, he edited *Słowo Polskie* [The Polish Word] in Lwów until his death. He authored *Sęp* [The Vulture], a detective story, and *Przewodnik Ilustrowany po Paryżu* [An Illustrated Guide to Paris]. While writing for *Kolce,* he used the pseudonym of Henio Żaba [Hank the Frog].

10. Hieronim [Jerome] Derdowski pseudonyms: Jarosz Derdowski; Herus Derda (1852-1902), editor, writer, Kashubian folk poet. In addition to *O Panu Czorlińscim*, he also wrote *Dla Śluby* [Two Weddings] and *Gdyby Mieć Tysiąc Talarów* [If I Had a Thousand Thalers], both issued in 1896. He also published "O Kaszubach" [The Kashubes] in *Przęglad Polski* [Polish Review], Volume 3, 1882-1883, prior to coming to the United States in 1884, where he edited/co-edited *Gazeta Narodowy* and *Pielgrzym Polski* in Detroit before becoming editor-in-chief of *Wiarus* in Winona.

11. Franciszek Jerome Roman Jabłoński (1863-1908), see chapter 12.

12. *Bencwał*, means "jerk" in Polish.

13. Rev. Kazimierz Słomiński, pastor and playwright. As assistant at St. Adalbert's in Chicago, he organized St. Anne's parish locally in 1903 and he was its first pastor until 1921. St. Anne's served as a focus for Polish amateur theatricals before and after World War I. Rev. Słomiński wrote numerous plays, including "Św. Dorota" ["Saint Dorothy"].

14. Szczęsny Zahajkiewicz (1861-1917), editor, journalist, poet, playwright. Educated in schools in Horodenka, Kołomyja, and Stanisławów. After graduating from the teacher's college with distinction, he obtained a position as teacher of Count Adalbert Dzieduszycki's children in Jezupol. He subsequently taught at Stanisławow and at the Piramowicz School in

Lwów. During this time, the *Towarzystwo Pedagogiczne i Wydawnictwo Dziełek Ludowych* [Pedagogical Society and Publishing House of Popular Minor Works] issued seventeen of his stories, seven of them in the Ruthenian language. After three years at the Piermowicz School, Bishop (later Cardinal) Puzyna chose Zahajkiewicz to teach at St. Stanislaus Kostka school in Chicago. There he helped to reestablish the dramatic circle, which performed many of the plays he wrote for the group, among them *Bright Mountain, or the Defense of Częstochowa* (a six-act drama), *Hedwig, Queen of Poland,* in which Helena Modjeska appeared in Chicago in 1892, and *Saint Hedwig,* written especially for Rev. Zieliński in St. Louis. He also directed plays for a number of other Polish societies in Chicago. His "Akademia Smorgońska" may be a pun on the name of Rev. Kazimierz Smogór (born 8171 Węgrów, Poland, died 1940 Steubenville, Ohio), who served as an assistant at Holy Trinity Parish in Chicago around the turn of the century and authored several books, including *Mądry Polak po szkodzie* [Wise after the Event]. Zahajkiewicz also published several humor magazines around the turn of the century: *Komar* [The Gnat] and *Kumoszka* [The Gossip]. See, Sister Mary Agnella Musiał, OSF, *American Literary Productions of Szczęsny Zahajkiewicz* (unpublished M.A. thesis, DePaul University, 1944).

15. *Śmigus-Dyngus,* or Easter Monday, on which women are surprised by males who douse them with water or sometimes more genteelly spray them with perfume.

16. Mary de Mańkowska (1873-1939), translator. The daughter of Andrew and Antoinette Kroll, she was educated in publish schools in Houston and later San José, California, from which she returned to marry Count Sigismund Mańkowski, who ran the Cotton Exchange Saloon in Houston. She was fond of Polish literature and was so moved by reading the Polish version of *Ten Years in Cossak Slavery* that she translated it into English "for the benefit of other nations, in order to make them acquainted with Polish literature." Its popular reception led her subsequently to translate Jasienczyk and Prus' *Faraon.*

17. Stefan Barszczewski (1863-1937), writer, editor, traveler. A member of the editorial staff of *Kuryer Warszawski,* he went abroad in 1886, spending four years in Paris, London, Vienna, and in South America to study the effects of the Polish immigration to Brazil. In 1891, he was a correspondent for *Kuryer Warszawski* from Buenos Aires, visiting Argentina, Uruguay, and Paraguay. The newspaper sent him in 1893 to cover the World Columbian Exhibition in Chicago. He remained in the United States for the next eight years, during which he actively participated in the political and social life of the Polish American community. In 1901 he returned to Warsaw, where he rejoined *Kuryer Warszawski.* He wrote several novels: *Czerwony Mesjasz* [Red Messiah] and *Ze wspomnień włóczęgi* [Reminiscences of a Rover]; short stories: "Eliksir prof. Bohusza" ["Professor Bohusz's Elixir"], "W osiem dni dookoła śiata" ["Around the World in Eight Days"], and "Parzygoda Kapitana St. Claira" ["Adventures of Captain St. Clair"]; sketches of the conquest of Central and South America: *Na szlaku sławy, krwi i złota* [On the Trail of Glory, Blood and Gold], Warsaw, 1928; a description of his travels to Paraguay: *Na ciemnych wodach Paragwaju* [On the Dark Waters of the Paraguay]; and two volumes on the United States: *Polacy w Ameryce* [The Poles in America], 1902; and *Obrazki Amerykańskie* [American Vignettes], 1905. Some of his works were translated into German, Czech, and Slovak. *Cuba Libre* is a five-act drama set against the Spanish-American War, with Polish Falcons as dramatis personae.

18. Rev. Mieczysław Barabasz, Ph.D. (1863-1914), professor, writer, poet, playwright, educator. Graduate of the Polish College in Rome, where he was ordained in 1887; pursued further studies at the Gregorian University in Rome, Catholic University in Louvain, and the medical school in Paris, France. He came to the United States in 1891. He was professor of Polish at the Polish seminary in Detroit, of which he later became vice-rector. From 1892 to 1914 he was pastor of Holy Mother of the Rosary in Baltimore, where he organized a local building and loan association. He wrote a drama, *Łupieży* ["Looters"], 1902, and published a Baltimore weekly, *Przyjaciel Domu* [Friend of Your Home], an independent Catholic newspaper. His collected verses, *Peozje i Wiersze* [Poetry and Verses], were published in 1911. He authored a "Memorial of the Poles to the Conference in the Hague" regarding the future

of Poland and contributed articles to the Polish press in America. He spoke six languages fluently.

19. Szymon Modrzewski, carpenter, poet, socialist. He published his poems in a number of Polish American newspapers around the turn of the century. After 1900 he frequently contributed to *Robotnik Polski* [The Polish Worker], the Polish socialist newspaper published variously in New York, Chicago, and Detroit. Some of the titles are: "Do sokołów i polskich żołnierzy" ["To the Falcons and the Polish Soldiers"], "Wzrost partyi socjalistycznej" ["Growth of the Socialist Party"], "Nie szczędźcie kul i bomb!" ["Don't Spare Bullets and Bombs!"} and "Bezsilność Polaków" ["The Helplessness of the Poles"].

20. Helena neé Sawicka Piotrowska, writer. After the turn of the century she began publishing correspondence, articles, vignettes, and short stories in *Ameryka-Echo* and later contributed articles in defense of Poland to the English-language press in America. During World War I she assisted Mme. Helena Paderewska in the Polish White Cross. Among her works is *Jak osiągnąć wykształcenie* [How to Obtain an Education], 1910.

21. Alphonse Chrostowski, writer, editor, publisher. Began his career with *Ognisko*, a radical newspaper in New York in the late 1880s, in which he published his *Rok Życia* [A Year of (My) Life] in column format. In 1891 he started the anarchistic newspaper *Reforma* [Reform], in the neighborhood of St. Adalbert's parish in Chicago. In 1892 he briefly headed *Ojczyzna* in Cleveland. The following year he started *Jutrzenka* [Morning Star] in Pittsburgh, which he subsequently relocated to Cleveland where it became the organ of the Polish Independent Church in America. Antoni Paryski of *Ameryka-Echo* in Toledo published two of Chrostowski's works, *Uwiedziona* and *Śmierć Ulianowa*.

22. Rev. Stefan Dąbkowski, CR. From 1901 to 1902 he was pastor of St. John Cantius, a Resurrectionist parish in Chicago.

23. Rev. Stanisław Siatka, CR (1869-1923), professor, author, clergyman. Educated in Zakliczyn, Myślenice, and Kraków; philosophical and theological studies in Rome, where he was ordained in 1896. Briefly served as vice-rector of the Polish College in Rome. Came to the United States in 1897. Assistant and pastor of several Resurrectionist parishes in Chicago, where he founded and edited *Sierota*, a monthly and later a weekly literary magazine whose proceeds supported the St. Vincent Ferrer Orphanage run by the Resurrectionists and the Franciscan Sisters of Blessed Kunegunda. For a time he served as director and president of the Chicago Publishing Company. In 1902 he was delegated to Brazil and Argentina in connection with the Polish immigration in those countries. The complete title of his pamphlet is: *Krótkie wspomnienie o życiu i działalności ks. Wincentego Barzyńskiego, CR* [A Brief Resume of the Life and Work of Rev. Vincent Barzyński, CR] (Chicago: The Polish Publishing Company, 1901).

24. Rev. Bernard Maria Skulik, Ph.D., (1867-?), publisher, writer, clergyman. Education in Myślowice and Kraków; philosophical and theological studies in Rome, where he was ordained in 1891. Came to the United States in the mid 1890s. Initially pastor of Immaculate Conception Parish in Brighton, Iowa, and from 1899 to 1910, of St. Hyacinth's Parish in LaSalle, Illinois, of which he wrote a parish history. He published and/or edited the following Polish-language newspapers in America: *Polska i Litwa* [Poland and Lithuania; Shamokin, Pennsylvania, 1894], *Przyjaciel* [The Friend; Shamokin, Pennsylvania, 1894-1895]; *Katolik* (Milwaukee, 1897), and *Rodzina* [The Family; LaSalle, Illinois, 1907-1911].

25. Dr. Franciszek Eustace Fronczak (1874-1955), physician, writer, clubman. In addition to the biographical information in the text, he became in 1896 the first assemblyman of Polish descent elected to the New York State legislature. Colonel in the U.S. Army; health commissioner of Buffalo for thirty-five years; columnist for the *Buffalo Express*. He received honorary degrees from the Jagiellonian University in Kraków in 1917 and from the University of Warsaw in 1918 and 1946. He belonged to the Polish National Alliance, Polish Roman Catholic Union, Polish Union of America, and Polish Physicians. He was decorated by many countries: U.S., Purple Heart; Poland, Polonia Restituta and Haller Swords; France, Chevalier, Legion of Honor, and Croix de Guerre; Belgium, Legion of Honor; Vatican City,

Knight of St. Gregory. During his lifetime, he wrote more than two dozen books and articles in English on medical subjects.

26. Jan Kuk, editor, writer. During his ten-your sojourn in America, he edited *Katolik* (Milwaukee, 1897), and *Żródło* [The Source; Milwaukee, 1898-1901], a Catholic magazine containing chiefly reprints of short stories and fiction. He likewise contributed to *Katolik* and *Kuryer Polski* in Milwaukee.

27. Bishop Franciszek Hodur (1863-1953), founder of the Polish National Catholic Church in America, publisher, editor, writer. Primary and secondary education at Chrzanow and St. Anne's (later Nowodworski) High School in Kraków; theological studies at the Roman Catholic seminary (affiliated with the Jagiellonian University) in Kraków, from which he was expelled before completing his final year, perhaps on account of his political activism. Came to the United States in 1893 and was brought to Pennsylvania by Rev. Benvenuto Gramlewicz and ordained in Scranton. While pastor of St. Stanislaus Parish in South Scranton in the late 1890s, he established the Polish National Catholic Church and *Straż* as its organ. Before and after the turn of the century he was sympathetic to the Polish socialist cause in the United States and contributed articles to *Robotnik Polski*. In 1904 he was elected bishop of the Polish National Catholic Church and three years later was consecrated in Utrecht, Holland, by Old Catholic Archbishop Gerard Gul. Hodur founded the Polish National Union, *Spójnia*, headquartered in Scranton. He published a number of booklets on the Polish National Catholic Church between 1901 and 1950.

28. A. Zdziebłowski, amateur playwright. A carpenter by trade in Chicago, he authored several plays for the Polish amateur theater in the United States around the turn of the century that continued to be performed into the 1930s. One of the most popular was *Bohaterka z Powstania* [Heroine of the Insurrection; a five-act drama, 1897]. Other works include: *Sybiracy* [Siberian Exiles; a five-act drama, 1898] and two four-act comedies, *Nieszczęśliwe Żony* [Unhappy Wives; 1905], and *Herod Baba* [A Virago; 1907].

29. Antoni Jax (Jaks), writer, playwright. Active in Chicago after the turn of the century, he authored some fifty dramas and comedies for the Polish amateur theater in America and also composed music for them. Among his most popular works are: *Z Pennsylvanii do Kalifornii* [From Pennsylvania to California], *Polish Uncle Sam*, *Legionista na polu chwały* [Legionnaire on the Field of Glory], and *Pod opieką anioła stroża* [Under the Protection of a Guardian Angel].

30. Stanisław Łempicki (1880-1935), editor, poet, writer. Came to Kansas City, Missouri, in 1901. Soon thereafter became an editor of the *Gazeta Polska Narodowa* [Polish National Gazette in Chicago; in 1909 an editor and after 1919 editor-in-chief of *Kuryer Polski* in Milwaukee. Chief organizer of the Federation of Poles in America. In addition to *Sonata Duchów* (1902), which earned him wide attention in the American Polonia, he also authored *Dzieci Słońca* [Children of the Sun; a four-act drama], *Historia Związku Młodzieży Polskiej w Ameryce* [History of the Young Men's Alliance of America, 1906], *Tragedia Morza czyli Zatopienie Tytanika* [Sea Tragedy or the Browning of a Little Titan], *Dzwon Zatopiony* [The Sunken Bell], *Świąt i Człowiek* [Man and the World], and *Surmy: Pieśń Patriotyczna* [Trumpets: A Patriotic Song].

31. Rev. Stanisław Nawrocki (1869-1918), clergyman, poet. Secondary education at Wągrowiec, Poland; theological studies in Rome and Baltimore; ordained in Chicago in 1887. Assistant and pastor at St. Joseph's, Chicago (1887-1891); pastor of St. Mary of Perpetual Help, Chicago (1892-1910), during which time he also organized St. Stanislaus B. & M. Parish in Posen, Illinois, in 1894, and St. Barbara's Parish in Chicago, of which he was appointed pastor. An excellent administrator, he oversaw the building of parish churches and schools during his various assignments. In March 1917, Cardinal Mundelein of Chicago invested him with the robes of a Roman prelate.

32. Tadzeus von Żukotyński (1855-1912), artist. Graduated from Riga (Latvia) Polytechnic in 1879; studied at the Fine Arts Academy in Munich, 1883-1885, where he received several silver medals; exhibited at the *Towarzystwo Przyjaciół Sztuk Pięknych* [Society of the

Friends of the Fine Arts] in Kraków from 1881 to 1886. Came to America in 1888, where he did a painting of St. Vaclav for the first Czech parish under his patronage in Milwaukee. In the same city he did ceiling frescos for St. John the Evangelist Cathedral (destroyed by fire in 1936); "Adoration" in the chapel of the School Sisters of Notre Dame (now demolished); and the "Martyrdom of St. Josaphat" in 1904 for the basilica of the same name. Rev. Wincenty Barzyński, CR, brought Żukotyński to Chicago in 1895 to do large frescos depicting St. Stanislaus Kostka and various Polish saints for St. Stanislaus Church. Thereafter Żukotyński did frescos and paintings for other Resurrectionist parishes in Chicago, including St. John Cantius, St. Hedwig's, and St. Hyacinth's. He likewise executed churches in Mishawaka, Terre Haute, and Saint Mary-of-the-Woods, Indiana. One of his last works was Stations of the Cross for Holy Cross Parish on the south side of Chicago in 1909-1910.

33. Ignacy Żabiński (c. 1845-1908), painter, amateur inventor. Veteran of the January 1863 Insurrection against czarist Russia. Executed paintings for various Milwaukee churches and public buildings which remain undocumented. Spoke several languages fluently; in 1908 demonstrated a wireless telegraph apparatus at the Pabst Theater in Milwaukee.

34. Teodor B. Modrakowski (1873-1930), artist. Prior to coming to the United States (c. 1897), he studied at the Colarossi Academy in Paris and with Groeber in Munich. Once in New York he studied with Robert Henri at the Art Students League and maintained an art establishment for a time at 106th Street and Lexington Avenue in Manhattan. Before World War I he kept a studio at 640 Madison Avenue. In 1923 he organized a salon of independent artists at the Bobcraft studios in Buffalo, New York, before relocating to the Los Angeles area, where he exhibited widely. Through his efforts, the Los Angeles County Fair received a permanent exhibition building at Pomona. He was a member of the National Arts Club, Mac-Dowell Club, California Art Club, Allied Artists Association, California Water Color Society, Los Angeles Painters and Sculptors Club, Artsland Club, and the Laguna Beach Art Association.

35. Bernard Kołpacki, a Milwaukee-based architect.

36. Helena Modjeska (Modrezejewska; 1840-1909), actress. Began her stage career in Kraków in 1861 and subsequently relocated to Warsaw where she performed. Came to the United States in 1876 with a small Polish utopian colony and settled in California, where she debuted in San Francisco in 1877. She toured widely throughout the United States over the next quarter century, winning acclaim as a Shakespearian tragedienne. See: Helena Modjeska, *Memories and Impressions: An Autobiography* (New York: The MacMillian Company, 1910), and Marion Moore Coleman, *Fair Rosalind: The American Career of Helena Modjeska* (Cheshire, Connecticut: Cherry Hill Books, 1969).

37. Antoni Małłek (1851-1917), organist, composer, teacher, publisher. Came to the United States in 1871 to his brother in Chicago. From 1872 to 1873, organist and teacher in Chicago; 1873-1874, in Milwaukee; 1875 to 1880, organist and justice of the peace in Northeim, Wisconsin; 1880 to 1916, organist and teacher at Holy Trinity parochial school in Chicago. In 1884 he bought a printing machine to publish Polish song books and issued seventeen of them containing many of his own compositions. In 1886 he founded *Ziarno* [The Seed], a monthly journal devoted to Polish music and songs, which he edited and published in Chicago until 1903. In 1889 he organized the Polish Singers Alliance which exists to the present day. The following year he was elected to the first of several terms as general secretary of the Polish National Alliance in Chicago.

38. Bolesław Józef Zalewski (1875-?), publisher, editor, conductor, composer. Came to the United States in 1892 with his father and settled in Chicago, where he conducted orchestras and choral groups. In 1910 he established a local music publishing enterprise. In 1924 he founded *Echo Muzyczne* [Musical Echo], a monthly and then a quarterly journal devoted to religious and secular music and its history, which he edited and published in Chicago until 1937. He served as president of the Polish Singers Alliance for a number of years and composed many pieces for orchestras and choirs.

39. Harriet (Hedwig) Smulska, singer. Daughter of Ignacy and Frances Mikityński; wife

of Jan Smulski, Chicago banker, civic leader, and publisher. Graduate of the Chicago Musical College. From 1894 to 1899 taught at the Kościuszko School in Chicago. Studied with Schiller and Jean De Reszke. Debuted in 1907 at Orchestra Hall in Chicago; concertized in various American cities.

CHAPTER 13: THE AMERICAN POLISH DIALECT

1. In 1922, Robert E. Park noted, "The language of the American Poles, though still etymologically Polish, contains an increasing number of American slangwords which are treated as roots and used with Polish inflections and prefixes, but their syntax and literary application (the latter more easily influenced than etymology by changes in the form thought) are growing more and more specifically local and neither Polish nor American." Examples of this can be seen throughout this chapter, including such words as *karą, biznesem,* and *salunie,* each of which contains English roots with Polish word endings. In commenting on the same phenomenon, Henry L. Mencken maintained that "the Polish-American journalists are rather more careful than most, but . . . their writings are full of Americanisms, in both word and idiom. Instead of writing *obchód* or *święcenie* they turn the English celebration (a term they have to use incessantly) into the facile *celebracja;* instead of *zderzenie* (collision) they write *kolizja,* and instead of *wypytywać* or *przesłuchiwać* (to question) they make it *kwestijonować.* In Polish the word for street (*ulica*) should precede the proper noun, e.g. *Ulica Kościuszkowska* or *Ulica Kościuszki,* but in American-Polish it is usually *Kościuszko ulica* (or *sztryta*), and that is what it promises to remain. The American-Polish housewife, on setting out for the grocery store, never says, ' *Idę do sklepu korzennego* (or *kolonialnego*),' which is standard Polish; she says, '*Idę do groserni,*' with *grosernia* correctly inflected for the case. Other nouns that have thus come into the language displacing Polish terms are *szapa* (shop), *sztor* (store), *buczernia* (butcher), *salun* (saloon), *sajwok* or *sajdwok* (sidewalk), *pajpa* (pipe), *kołt* (coat), *owerholce* (overalls), *pajnt* (paint), *strytkara* (street car), *wiska* (whiskey), *trok* (truck), and *piciesy* (peaches). In *skład-departmentowy* the first half is good Polish for a large store, but the second half is the English *department,* outfitted to work with a Polish tail." See: Robert E. Park, *The Immigrant Press and Its Control* (New York: Harper and Brothers, 1922), p. 432; Henry L. Mencken, *The American Language* (New York: Alfred A. Knopf, 1936), p. 623.

2. A *placki* [*placek*] refers to a small flat cake and *plastry* [*plaster*] generally connotes a honey-combed dessert or slice [*plastek*]. The best English translation is probably "tart."

3. *Morg* is the Polish word for *acre.*

4. As with many of the other polonized words, *Ajrysz* is the Polish phonetic equivalent of *Irish.*